To Cass!,
Thanks for all
you've done for
others and for
our (country)!

Col USAF, Ret

Apr.' 16, 2017

AN UNCAGED EAGLE

TRUE FREEDOM

An Inspirational Memoir

By
Colonel Richard "Dick" Toliver
USAF, Retired

SAGUARO PUBLISHING COMPANY
Goodyear, Arizona

SAGUARO PUBLISHING COMPANY
10914 S. San Ricardo Drive
Goodyear, Arizona 85338

First Edition: August 2009
First Edition, Second Impression: January 2010
First Edition, Third Impression: August 2010
First Edition, Fourth Impression: May 2011

Cover and book design by Jen Weber, courtesy of The Branding Habitat
Eagle illustration by John R. Doughty, Jr.
Author's photo courtesy of Beth Johnston

Library of Congress Cataloguing-in-Publication Data

ISBN-13 • 978-0-9840991-0-8
ISBN-10 • 0-9840991-0-7

Printed in the United States of America
11 12 RRD 9 8 7 6 5 4

DEDICATION

For my mother, Daisy,

who gave me life, inspiration, and

the passion to persevere despite adversity.

For my sister, Zella, and

brother-in-law Anthony Weaver Rye, Jr.,

for being my lifetime friends,

mentors, and exemplary role models.

For my precious wife, Peggy,

our beloved children, grandchildren,

and great grandchildren, including

those who became ours through love.

Contents

Dedication .... page III

Acknowledgements... page V

Foreword .... page IX

Introduction .... page XI

Prologue - Where Eagles Fly.. page XV

PART ONE   THE EARLY YEARS

Chapter One - The Odyssey Begins .... page 1

Chapter Two - Shattered Dreams .... page 15

Chapter Three - Beacons of Hope .... page 23

Chapter Four - The Tuskegee Experience .... page 39

PART TWO   VICTORY OVER ADVERSITY

Chapter Five - The Wild Blue Yonder .... page 87

Chapter Six - Pilot Training .... page 119

Chapter Seven – Making of a Fighter Pilot .... page 149

Chapter Eight - Baptism by Fire – First Combat Tour..................... page 161

Chapter Nine – Skies Over Europe .... page 185

Chapter Ten – Climbing Higher .... page 213

Chapter Eleven - Southeast Asia Revisited – Second Tour .... page 237

Chapter Twelve – Home of the Fighter Pilot .... page 273

Chapter Thirteen – F-15 Eagle Air Superiority Fighter .... page 285

Chapter Fourteen – Growing Spiritual Wings .... page 313

Chapter Fifteen - Misreading Road Signs .... page 335

Chapter Sixteen – The Door to Freedom .... page 359

Chapter Seventeen – Moving On .... page 367

Chapter Eighteen – On Eagle's Wings .... page 391

PART THREE   EXPERIENCING FREEDOM

Chapter Nineteen – New Horizons .... page 439

Epilogue – Coming Full Circle .... page 473

Index .... page 483

About the Author .... page 489

Tributes .... page 490

ACKNOWLEDGEMENTS

I can't say enough about my wife, Peggy, and our children, Gail, Renea, and Michael, who played a large part in getting this book started and completed. For years, they coaxed, encouraged, exhorted, and sometimes threatened me to write about the many stories they heard around the dinner table. When my Christmas and Father's Day gifts became materials and tools to get me started, I knew it was time to get going. Peggy's patience was superb in reviewing every word, line, and paragraph written during the eighteen months it took to complete the manuscript. Our children often participated in the process and provided excellent suggestions for clarity and improvement.

I owe a great debt to my friend, retired Colonel Donn Byrnes, who met with me one Saturday afternoon in Albuquerque to review and help finalize the first outline of the book. Donn later provided the initial editing that, at times, became terse and unsettling for me. However, his objectivity, courage, and eye for excellence kept me on point when I tended to get sidetracked by my emotions of the past. Donn persistently kept you, the ultimate reader, in mind, and I am deeply grateful for his efforts.

Mr. Ross Perot provided me a tremendous boost and encouragement when there was only an outline and draft introduction to the book. His faith in my ability to write and to tell a relevant story sustained me throughout the task. I am especially grateful for his kind words in the Foreword. Sharon Holman and Renee Jordan of the Perot Group, and Russ Verney, formerly of United We Stand America, provided crucial reviews and support in bringing the book to a conclusion.

I owe a special debt to those who sat down with me for interviews early on or conducted telephone discussions. These include Lowell and Patricia Bell, James and Shirley Stewart, Ray and Paula Willcox, Jack and Pricilla Murphy, and the late Willis A. Boyd. The list of others who gave unstintingly of their precious time and suggestions is extensive, but I want to express my appreciation to a few. Generals Ronald R. Fogleman, Charles A. Horner, John L. Piotrowski, and Lloyd W. "Fig" Newton; Lieutenant Generals Bruce Fister and Daniel James, III; Major Generals Richard W. Phillips and Gordon F. Blood; and Brigadier General J. Timothy Boddie provided invaluable corroboration and insights of the historical events that we shared during our careers. I am profoundly grateful and honored for their contributions.

Others include retired Colonels Bobby Black and Richard G. Rhyne; Lieutenant Colonel Calvin Jeffries; Lee Pritchard; Mr. Bill Hooten; Pastor James D. and Frances Porter; Lucimarian Roberts; Jane Drain; Doris Mitchell; Dr. Z. W. Dybczak; and my brother, David, Toliver, Sr. Still many friends, relatives, and associates were extremely generous in their encouragements, kind words, and prayers. To each person who spoke to me about the book, provided information, or often asked how it was coming along, I say a heart-felt thanks. You added the fuel that kept me going, and I trust you take pride in what you did to help make this book a success.

Acknowledgements

Jennifer and Mark Weber proved to be an outstanding team as the book neared completion. They carefully and expertly guided me through the maze of requirements and details necessary for self publishing. Jennifer's meticulous research and acquisition of the technical requirements, book layout, and illustration were outstanding. She deserves special recognition for hanging with me during the birth of their third son, Justin. John Doughty, Jr., did a masterful job in painting the eagle that appears on the cover.

Finally, I want to express my deep gratitude to my family and others who allowed me to share events and stories with the candor in which they happened in our lives. In so doing, I sincerely trust such openness will help those who may still be struggling to get free of a cage in their own lives.

Dick Toliver and Ross Perot
Plano, Texas, June 2009

FOREWORD

In the summer of 1993, Dick Toliver, a talented, intense, and accomplished man came to interview for a key position in United We Stand America. It didn't take long to see that he would be a vibrant member of our team as State Director of New Mexico. Dick was hired immediately and quickly proved my instincts to be correct. Within a few weeks, he organized the state of New Mexico into an effective political voice and later served as the Southwest Regional Director of twelve states for three years. When the Reform Party was created two years later, Dick served as National Spokesperson and Coordinator for Minority Community Outreach for the 1996 campaign. During this time, I had the opportunity to closely observe this outstanding man. Courage, perseverance, and faith were the attributes that characterized this patriot.

Dick spent his formative years overcoming incredible obstacles during some of the most challenging racial times of the Deep South. He dreamed of becoming a pilot in the United States military, and no one was going to prevent him from achieving that goal. "Nothing beats a failure but a try!" These words, deeply ingrained by his mother, fueled his determination. While still young, Dick was given many responsibilities, but they forged him into a man of great character and integrity.

Dick's exemplary record of military service speaks volumes about his courage and dedication. As a "Top Gun" fighter pilot, he flew 446 combat missions in Southeast Asia. Later he directed the testing and evaluation of several major weapon systems for the Department of Defense and allied military programs. He also held key roles in advanced research, development, and testing of tactical fighter aircraft. Dick served throughout the United States, Europe, North Africa, and the Persian Gulf, ultimately commanding a number of units and holding key staff positions in the Air Force. He retired as a full Colonel after twenty-six years of service and 4,000 hours of flying time. His military decorations include the Legion of Merit, Distinguished Flying Cross, Meritorious Service Medal with two Oak Leaf Clusters, and Air Medal with 27 Oak Leaf Clusters.

Dick's autobiography, AN UNCAGED EAGLE, is an inspiring saga of victory over adversity. His personal struggle and eventual freedom serve as a roadmap for anyone who feels trapped by life's circumstances. The lessons Dick learned have relevance for every generation, regardless of ethnic origin, gender, or religion. The pervasive thread throughout Dick's life is his faith in God, love of family, and compassion for those less fortunate than himself. For nearly forty-seven years, Dick and his wife, Peggy, embraced such faith to raise a dozen children by birth, adoption, and foster care. Of his many successes in life, I know he considers this his greatest accomplishment.

I have had the honor and pleasure of knowing Dick Toliver for over sixteen years. It is my privilege to present him to you as an outstanding husband, father, grandfather, great American patriot, and my friend.

Ross Perot
Founder and CEO
The Perot Group

INTRODUCTION

The overarching theme of this book is *victory* over *adversity*. The prevailing message is one of hope for anyone who has encountered adversity in his or her life. Such difficulties are caused by disappointments, death, illness, illiteracy, poverty, racial oppression, societal constraints, and other factors. Most people have faced these problems and found a way to overcome them in varying degrees. Others, however, remained trapped in a cage caused by the effects of adversity such as persistent anger, fear, frustration, hatred, and the inability to forgive. Escape from the latter depends first upon one's recognition of such imprisonment. Secondly, he or she must be willing to take the necessary steps that lead to freedom.

I submit that ultimate victory over adversity is only possible when freedom is gained from the deeper, inner emotional cage. Thus, some people can live a lifetime and never experience true freedom. Others achieve material or professional success while constrained by unresolved issues in their lives. In my case, that imprisonment lasted nearly thirty-three years. Like many, I was trapped in a cage of bitterness, despair, and hopelessness brought on by a broken home and poverty. I was a caged bird fluttering against unyielding bars of indifference, oppression, and the stifling effects of a blind, prejudiced society.

This autobiography tells the story of my life while highlighting some of the tremendous people who helped me overcome the adversities I faced and caused me to be who I am today. The odyssey begins with my family's escape from the Ku Klux Klan in the backwoods of northwest Louisiana in 1942. It continues with my boyhood days on dirt streets and outside privies in Shreveport to eventually dine with the future king of Saudi Arabia. It chronicles my Air Force career that included 446 combat missions in Southeast Asia, a lightening strike at 20,000 feet, a rocket-seat ejection over Germany, and a special assignment that had international ramifications. It is the story of the youngster who earned three dollars a week on his first job and ended up working for billionaire Ross Perot.

The inspiration for writing the book came from family, friends, and associates who believe my life was shaped by unique circumstances and special people all along the way. They believe my experiences can be an encouragement, inspiration, and motivation for others who may be discouraged by difficulties in their own lives. After considerable meditation, prayer, and soul-searching, I began this venture called *An Uncaged Eagle* in the summer of 2007.

Uncaged Eagles are those individuals who, through providential intervention, had a timely and significant impact on my life, upon the nation, and often the world. They are those who may have been born free or who were freed by overcoming many challenges in their own lives. These were courageous people who willingly paved the way for others with their blood, sweat, and tears. They were the "salt-of-the-earth" heroes and heroines who provided the moral and spiritual foundation for all generations. Some were uniquely created or predestined to help break down the barriers that imprisoned the down-trodden. Others struggled against deep dungeons of anger, fear, hate, and prejudice before discovering the freedom needed to help others less fortunate than themselves. Still some paid the ultimate sacrifice by giving their lives so that others could experience the freedom they would never know.

Throughout history, the quest for freedom has been described and documented in many ways; but these stories, songs, and movies often failed to enlighten us about the true path to freedom. As a veteran of war, I know freedom is not free nor does it come easy. America's history is replete with evidence of this fact. For instance, during the last 100 years, nearly forty million men and women served in the U. S. Armed Forces all over the globe. Over 1,155,000 have been wounded in action, and more than 625,000 made the ultimate sacrifice in wars since the early Twentieth Century, including Iraq and Afghanistan. Despite these astounding and noble sacrifices, universal or individual freedom has not been assured. The truth is, the sacrifices of mortals, however great, cannot liberate the souls of humanity. That kind of freedom must be sought from a higher power.

This book was written to inspire and motivate those who may still be trapped in an emotional cage of despair and frustration. Hopefully, they will be encouraged to seek the freedom I was blessed to find – the freedom to create, dream, forgive, love, and to pursue the life meant for us by our Creator.

Richard "Dick" Toliver
June 2009

PROLOGUE

WHERE EAGLES FLY

Summer, 1951

It was a hot, sweltering Sunday afternoon as I walked home from church on the oil-paved streets of my neighborhood. Many families had gathered on their porches to fan the stifling humid air while listening to the special Negro Spiritual Hour on the local radio station. The late Reverend C. L. Franklin, father of Aretha Franklin, was preaching a rousing sermon about an eagle that had been unwittingly caged by a chicken farmer. The story was told of a chicken farmer who discovered a strange-looking young bird in his flock. This particular bird did not associate with the other chickens and often seemed restless and agitated. As the bird grew, he begin to look, act, and strut about the yard differently than the other chickens. One day, the bird appeared to hear a sound high in the sky. He began to make strange noises, flapped his wings, and vainly struggled to get free of the cage. The farmer eventually called a friend over to witness the behavior of this peculiar bird. After observing the bird, the friend proclaimed,

> "My friend, this is not just a strange bird; what you have here is an eagle. Eagles are not meant to be caged in with chickens. You must set this eagle free so that he can go where eagles soar!"

After a bit of persuasion, the farmer reluctantly opened the cage. Slowly the eagle emerged, flew to the roof of the cage, and began to flap his wings. Next, he flew to a nearby tree and made sounds as if calling to the wind. Soon similar sounds were heard high above the farm, and the eagle flew to the top of the nearest mountain. With one last flap of his newly discovered wings, the eagle soared toward the sound above the distant clouds and beyond the sight of his earthly cage. Thus, after his prolonged and restless struggle, the eagle was set free to become what he was created to be. Reverend Franklin went on to conclude that the human spirit is like an eagle, and God created all humanity to be free. His sermon pierced my heart that day and inspired me to strive against the adversities I faced.

Summer, 1996

The night of August 11, 1996 was warm and festive in Long Beach, California. As the sun set over the Pacific Ocean, a gentle breeze blew in over a city charged with excitement. The legendary Queen Mary that had made its final voyage from Southampton, England thirty years earlier quietly graced the waters of Long Beach Harbor. Nearby, the Convention Center began to fill with several thousand members of the new Reform Party for its historical, First National Convention. Scores of international media teams assembled to cover Ross Perot's second bid to become President of the United States. His highly improbable garnering of nineteen percent of the popular vote in 1992 shocked the world and resulted in the formation of United We Stand America (UWSA). Not since Teddy Roosevelt ran on the progressive ticket in 1912 had such popularity been seen. The Reform Party went on to exceed the predictions of "expert" political pundits by gaining ballot access in all fifty states in just eleven months!

That night I, the great grandson of a slave, stood backstage waiting for my turn to speak. In a few minutes I would be called to a world stage before thousands of cheering supporters and a horde of glaring cameras. My task was to introduce billionaire patriot Ross Perot as the Party's choice to be the next President of the United States. While waiting, visions of the past flooded my mind. What a journey it had been. Fifty-four years earlier, my family barely avoided the deadly clutches of the Ku Klux Klan in a desperate escape from a small town in Louisiana. At that time, Ross Perot, the son of a successful cotton farmer, was growing up safely seventy miles away in Texarkana, Texas. Destiny brought us together in 1993, and a bond was forged by mutual admiration and respect for what each had achieved in his life. Our profound love for God, family, and country developed into a friendship that would last for the rest of our lives. That night in Long Beach, our spirits reached the boundless heights of those who dared dream beyond the cages that too often imprison the souls of humanity.

The crowd responded raucously to my speech that highlighted little known but powerful personal facts about Ross Perot. Dutifully, I stuck to the script prepared by the speech writers, but suddenly, my pent-up thoughts burst forth with an emotional rush. Although the speech writers had cautioned me to the contrary, I continued, "Thirty-eight years ago, I met another great man, Dr. Martin Luther King, Jr. I heard him speak; I shook his hand; and I felt the fire of his dream burning from his very soul."

Hearing these words, the auditorium burst into a deafening roar as I paused. "I have come to know Ross Perot, and testify tonight that he shares the same dream; he has the same fire; and he has the same hope for a greater America for all of its people! Please join me now in welcoming the man who truly has been called to lead this nation into the 21st century. Ladies and gentlemen, please welcome Ross Perot!"

PART ONE

THE EARLY YEARS

CHAPTER ONE

THE ODYSSEY BEGINS

My family's history in America dates back nearly 200 years and is anchored on a slave woman, Indiana Bell, born in Alabama about 1810. One of her three children, Minnie, married slave Harry Davis. In 1859, this couple gave birth to William Henry Davis, my great grandfather on my father's side. After the Emancipation of slaves, William Henry migrated from Alabama to northwest Louisiana and settled in the small town of Bellevue, Louisiana.

My great grandfather was a man of considerable means who purchased several hundred acres of land shortly after arriving in Louisiana. He was a powerfully built man who stood over six feet tall and weighed over 250 pounds. During his lifetime, William Henry had four wives and fathered approximately twenty-five children. One of these, Minnie, was named after his mother. This Minnie married my paternal grandfather, David Toliver. My father, Booker Taliaferro (named after the famous educator, Booker T. Washington) was born of this union.

At a young age, Booker traveled to the small village of De-berry, Texas where he met and married my mother, Daisy Lee, daughter of Bob and Zella Cole Anderson. Later, my father, mother, and their two young children moved back to Bellevue. With the help of relatives, my dad built a small home and settled among the Davis Clan. Booker's land was adjacent to a rising white farmer named Francis "Frank" Flournoy Vickers, a proximity that emerged into a serious problem in years that followed.

As told by my mother, my entry into this world was somewhat dramatic. It was a cool, autumn afternoon, October 30, 1938 when, alone and unassisted, she gave birth to me. In those days, most babies were born at home with an attending midwife. One would have been present, but it was the fourth Sunday, a big day at the church for food and fellowship. My mother encouraged the family and the midwife to attend church since she felt good and had no symptoms of my pending birth. Later, while she was in the kitchen cooking a pot of collard greens and baking sweet potatoes, Richard "Dick" Toliver decided to make his grand entrance into this world. It was a perfectly beautiful Sunday when all hell broke loose. At nearly nine pounds at birth, my mother had her hands full, but managed to get us both taken care of and put to bed. When the church-goers returned rejoicing over the food, fellowship, and worship service, the scene turned to utter bedlam with their exclamations: "Oh Lord have mercy!" "We shoulda stayed home!" "Help us Jesus!" "Oh my goodness!" I imagine there were also a few expletives directed at Mother Nature who visited rather suddenly on that fateful day. Nevertheless, I had experienced my first suckling, was sound asleep, and unperturbed by the delayed celebration of my birth. My mother gave birth to seven children; however, the circumstances of my birth fostered a special bond between my mother and me that prevailed for the rest of our lives.

The Great Escape

My first realization of life in this world occurred when I was about two years old. It was a simple, serene awareness of being among fruit trees, corn and cotton fields, and towering pines in the forest across the road from our house. These earliest memories were filled with the sounds of birds and crows as they soared above the fields and forest. Our dog, Silver, barked and jumped in hot pursuit of small creatures as they scurried to safety. Here, in a quiet world, I began to discern the beauty of nature and the cycle of life established by the Creator. I didn't understand any of it just yet. Nor were there any foreboding signs of the World War that raged across Europe and the Far East in the early 1940s. The rigid social barriers between Black and White folks in the small community of Bellevue precluded meaningful dialogue about world matters that affected everybody. In contrast, it was the occurrence of life, death, planting, harvesting, and natural disasters that precipitated immediate cooperation between the people of both races.

After the death of my great grandfather in 1921, a dispute over land boundaries evolved between the Davis descendants and Frank Vickers. By then, Vickers was a prominent White landowner in Bellevue. He and his wife, Beulah, had four sons and a daughter: Francis (Frank), William (Billy), John, Robert (Bobby), and Beulah. Vickers and his son Frank, Jr. were known for being very mean toward Black people. As they passed the Vickers' place on the way to school, my older brother and sister remembered Frank, Jr. hurling rocks and racial slurs while Frank Sr. looked on approvingly. Frank Sr. was five feet, seven inches tall and approximately 135 pounds. He appeared to hold a deep resentment against the descendants of my six feet plus, 250 pound great grandfather. Nevertheless, Vickers enjoyed the esteem of the Whites in the community, and he had a close relationship with the local sheriff, Steve Norris.

Frank Vickers persistently sought to usurp as many acres of the Davis' land as possible, and my father was the only Davis descendant to resist. Like Vickers, my father was also a small man in size; however, his quiet nature disguised a deep resentment for Vickers or anyone who willfully crossed him. When pressed beyond his limits, he would fight back with a ferocity that belied his size and demeanor. The feud escalated when Vickers kept several of the Davis' hogs that allegedly strayed onto his land. One day, it burst into a physical altercation between Vickers and my father in the A&P store near Shreveport. Vickers got the worst of it, and my dad had to make a rapid escape to save his life. Leaving my mother, Cousin Gilbert Jackson, and his wife, Jessie, he headed across the Red River hoping to reach relatives in Shreveport. My father was on the run when a Black man picked him up on the Texas Street Bridge and drove him to safety in Shreveport. That "angel in disguise" most probably saved his life.

The fact that a Black man struck a White man was intolerable in the White community of Bellevue. An example had to be made to "keep the Blacks in their places". In the early 1940s, the "appropriate" response to a crazy and "uppity nigger" was simple – lynching! Our family was repeatedly harassed by Sheriff Steve Norris, Frank Vickers, and known Ku Klux Klan members as they came daily looking for my father. This frightful experience was my first encounter with White men. Sometimes, a caravan of cars patrolled the Black community at night searching for my father or looking to expend their anger upon anyone who crossed their path. They searched the meager premises of our home in vain. They climbed onto the beds, looked into the loft, and ransacked the small barn outside. Their futile search left them in a greater fit of rage, spouting menacing words and expletives upon their departure. It was a frightening experience for my mother and her five young children - Wilbert ten, Zella eight, Arneater five, me four, and ten-month old David.

Several days later, my father took an extreme risk and returned home in the middle of the night to check on his family. Early the next morning, the tranquility of my world was ended abruptly by barking dogs and menacing voices outside our house. Frank Vickers, Sheriff Steve Norris, and the Klan had gathered outside the fence of our home intent on doing bodily harm to my father. They demanded he come outside to face what would have been a sure and instant death. My mother was barely able to restrain my father while sending my older brother to rouse the Davis clan for help.

With the aid of armed relatives, a standoff resulted and my dad escaped for the second time. The fact that the mob didn't rush the house can only be described as Divine Intervention. Not one of them was willing to be the first local White man to get killed by a crazy "nigger."

One night soon after, my sister, Zella, awakened me to the hustle and bustle taking place in our small home. She hurriedly dressed me amid the concerns of a house full of relatives who hastily assembled to ensure our family's safe getaway. Oblivious to this danger, my concern was for our dog, and I cried when told Silver couldn't go with us. I was not alone in my distress as my parents and relatives embraced and said their goodbyes amidst their own tears. We were loaded into a large, black panel truck and covered with bedding, clothing, and a few other household goods. My father's friend, Isom Cox of Shreveport, had been hired to get the family out of Bellevue in the middle of the night. The mission was treacherous, and it could have ended tragically if the family had been detected by Frank Vickers and his bunch. Thankfully, we arrived safely in Shreveport, but I lived a lifetime before the rest of this story could be written.

After taking refuge in Shreveport, my younger sister, Arneater, and I had one final sojourn to Bellevue. My great uncle, Luther Davis, was an itinerant preacher who traveled during the summer months.

His wife, Sara, wanted company and my sister and I were chosen to spend a few weeks with her. The excitement of going to the "country" filled our minds and, as only children can do, we had already forgotten the circumstances surrounding our departure from Bellevue.

Aunt Sara was a joy to be around, and she made the weeks with her the happiest of our young lives. We woke up each morning to the savory smells of home-made breakfast delights fit for a king. Later, we followed Aunt Sara on the morning chores of feeding chickens, collecting eggs, milking the cow, and gathering fruit from the orchards. At other times, my sister and I chased after pesky crows that raided the melon patches and seemed to laugh at the "scarecrows" meant to scare them away. At night, and usually completely exhausted, we fell asleep to the sounds of crickets, nightingales, and hoot owls. Soon it was time to go home, but the pleasant memories of this little bit of heaven tugged at my heart for many years. It was twenty-three years before I returned to reconnect with this place.

For the next two years, our family moved repeatedly due to my father's perpetual fear of being found by Frank Vickers and the "Law" of Bellevue and Shreveport. By then, many Davis descendants had left Bellevue to escape the continuous harassment by Frank Vickers. Many migrated to California to take advantage of the prosperity brought on by the mobilization of our nation during World War II.

Venturing ahead of us, my father joined other relatives in Oxnard, California to find a job and home for our family, which now included my younger brother, William Ray. The day of our departure arrived, and my grandfather, David Toliver, a railroad man, helped get my mother and her six children onboard the Southern Pacific train headed to California. Unlike the great escape from Bellevue, our departure for Oxnard was filled with excitement and promise of a new life in a state hailed as a virtual paradise. This time, the hustle and bustle was caused by hundreds of young men in uniform heading off to war. There were hugs, kisses, and tears, but now Blacks and Whites alike were caught up together in their support for those headed toward an uncertain future.

When we arrived in El Paso, Texas, the train was filled with hundreds of additional troops headed west. The "Colored" people were moved out of their original cars and squeezed together to make room for the White soldiers. Suddenly, the bad memories of Bellevue resurfaced and squashed the excitement. The journey turned into a stifling hot and uncomfortable train ride. Once again Providence intervened! Shortly after leaving El Paso, some of the White soldiers came to the Colored cars to offer space, food, and water in their section of the train. Their smiles and compassion dispelled any fears about their intentions. Some of the older children were allowed to go with these young men, and a much appreciated relief was provided to the Black families. Although I was only six years old, this act of kindness was etched in my mind and heart. I recalled the faces of those young "angels unaware" for many years and wondered if they made it back home safely. I didn't fully appreciate the profound events taking place about me, but I sensed a change taking place that would later be an unprecedented history-making transformation in America. My young mind would soon be awakened to the significance of WWII and the impact it had upon our nation.

Our family arrived at the Los Angeles Union Station in the summer of 1944 filled with anticipation and excitement for a new life. The cavernous passageways were filled with scores of uniformed men and families looking frantically for each other in a beehive of humanity. My father was finally spotted, and my mother and six children descended upon him with outstretched arms. We gathered our baggage and were soon on our way to our new home in Oxnard. To our surprise, my father had managed to purchase a 1941 Buick Special. This black, four-door sedan was huge, and it easily accommodated our family of eight. I soon staked out a spot in the car that looked over the shoulder of my father as he drove. Standing on the rear floor, I took in the incredible sights as we drove through the city.

My fascination with California began immediately and the trip to Oxnard was filled with awe and wonderment. The sights, sounds, and size of Los Angeles were greater than anything we had ever seen. The country was at war and gasoline was rationed, but the streets were filled with cars, trucks, buses, and olive-colored military vehicles with big white stars on the doors.

I got my first look at the vast Pacific Ocean as we drove along the coastal highway. The massive waves crashing against the rocky beaches were overwhelming in sight, smell, and sound. My father stopped the car along a stretch of beach to allow us a close-up view of this spectacular scene of earth, sea, and sky. All along the expansive beach, the water ebbed and flowed in a persistent, rhythmic pattern, sweeping the beach of footprints or small debris. I had no knowledge of what a symphony was, but I could hear and see the harmonious movement that lay before me. At once, I fell in love with the ocean and tried to take in all of its beauty. Too soon, we were loaded back into the car and on our way. I "rode shotgun" the rest of the way, not wanting to miss the unfolding scenes that awaited us at each turn of the road. I didn't know it then, but one day I would walk along beaches in other parts of the world and recall that beautiful portrait of the Pacific coast.

Our first apartment in California was crowded and meager, but having the family together again made up for it. Like many migrant families during WW II, we shared the duplex with a large Mexican family, and I soon learned to speak enough Spanish to make friends with our new neighbors. Shortly after our arrival, four of us Toliver kids enrolled in school just two blocks from home. All the teachers were White, but the classrooms were filled with multi-racial children; yet, there was no preferential treatment given to any child because of his or her race, skin color, or economic status. Within a very short time, our young minds adjusted to an integrated society, and we soon forgot the experiences of the South. We began an idyllic two years that left a lasting positive impact on our lives.

My mother found a job at the locally famous Colonial Steak House on Highway 1 heading toward Ventura and Santa Barbara. This restaurant and bar was frequented by the local elite, officers from the several military bases, and Hollywood movie stars. With both parents working, we were able to move into a larger apartment near Oxnard Naval Training Base. This complex had a large, beautiful playground covered by lush green grass and bordered by beautiful, fruit-bearing cherry trees. The recreational center was manned by a staff of kind, caring people who delighted in doing their part for WW II by taking care of the children of working parents.

The playground and recreational center became the center of my universe where lasting bonds and friendships were established. Children of all races played together, walked to school together, ate together, and often took naps together. Walking to school through the neighborhood was a wonderful adventure. Each bungalow was distinctively designed and surrounded by a manicured lawn with a swath of bougainvillea, hibiscus, pansies and roses. Sometimes we were late for school after dallying along, taking in the beauty and warmth of the mornings.

California was indeed a paradise, and our family enjoyed this precious time together. Terms of endearment were often spoken between my parents and their warm relationship was especially pleasing to us kids. My mother was called "Sugah" by my father, and he was called "Sweet Art" (Sugar and Sweetheart). They were called "Ma Deah" and "Daddy" by six happy kids. Some of my most pleasurable moments came each day as I waited in the apartment parking lot for my dad to come home from work. He smiled and warmly greeted me as "Jack the Bear." I would chin-up on his arm as we walked home. These moments reflected a deep and loving bond between my father and me.

Birth of a Dream

The thrill of living in our new home and surroundings was made even more exciting by some of the young naval pilot trainees who lived in the apartments. Seeing them in their flight suits was fascinating. The flight path to the base passed overhead of the playground, and sometimes the pilots would dip their wings or wave their hands as they flew by. My fascination with flying grew out of these experiences, and I wanted to be a pilot like the young men at Oxnard Airfield. Watching them fly, I would imagine myself climbing, rolling, and twirling around the beautiful, puffy clouds that filled the sky. I soon learned the difference between a C-47 and a P-38. I wanted to fly the latter, so I pestered my mother until she bought me my own toy P-38 model. Then I could fly! While other kids played cowboys, Indians, or soldiers, I could be found "flying" my P-38 around the playground. I had flown several thousand miles by the time the war ended! Years later, I recalled these experiences and noted my first pilot role models were young White men who trained to serve their country. My youthful dream of flying was impervious to race or color; all I wanted was to be like them when I grew up.

Life during WW II in Oxnard was filled with many memorable experiences. One was the "Blackouts" – when all the lights in the city would be extinguished at night to prevent suspected enemy detection and attack. Another was ration stamps and tokens issued to families based upon their size and circumstances to get scarce allotments of meat, oleomargarine, and sugar. In addition, the trains that passed through the nearby railroad crossings were loaded with troops, trucks, tanks, and artillery pieces. Sometimes we gathered and waved at the soldiers as they passed with arms outstretched through the windows. Some soldiers appeared to be waving through their tears; saddened by these sights, we waved back through ours.

It was a great time to grow up in America where the energy of patriotism and working together filled the air. Everybody seemed focused and committed to doing his or her part to win the war and to bringing our boys home safely. There were poignant reminders that some would not return home. One was the dreaded Western Union man who came too often into the neighborhood. His brown uniform and yellow bicycle meant sad news, and everyone would stop in their tracks to see where he was headed. I have vivid memories of neighbors rushing to assist at the sounds of wailing from those receiving news that a loved one had been lost.

On another day, I was intercepted by a neighbor weeping profusely as I walked home from school. Knowing this was not good, I immediately began to cry with her. It was April 12, 1945. Through her sobs she said, "Son, go tell your mother President Roosevelt just died." I didn't know who the President was or the great impact of that statement, but I rushed home in tears to tell my mother this news. It spread like wildfire, and soon the entire community went into mourning.

A short time later, another dramatic event occurred. A group of us kids were playing when we heard a sputtering noise from an airplane on final approach to the base. It appeared the pilot was trying desperately to make the field, but he was much lower than usual. The "Playground Mom" screamed for us to run to safety, but I was fixated on the airplane heading into the apartments about a mile away. Suddenly, my arm was nearly jerked out of its socket and I was hurled to the ground just as a deafening thud was heard. The pilot crashed into the last row of apartments in the complex. I took off toward the wreckage leaving a horrified caretaker behind. By now others were running toward the crash site, and I gave way to those trained to handle emergencies. I did get close enough to see several demolished apartments and the tail of the airplane sticking up out of the debris. As the emergency workers scoured the destroyed apartments looking for survivors, we were amazed there was no fire. Soon, a small girl was pulled from the wreckage and taken away. Next, the pilot who miraculously appeared to be alive was placed in the military ambulance and rushed away. To the astonishment of the crowd, no one else was found in the wreckage. This event left an indelible mark upon my young mind, and for many years, I wondered what happened to those two survivors. Fifty-five years passed before fate and circumstances provided the answer.

August 14, 1945 was just another great day in paradise for us kids playing in the playground. Suddenly, the city sirens shattered the peaceful calm, and the community broke into pandemonium. People ran out of their homes and into the streets shouting, "The war is over, the war is over, Japan has surrendered; the war is over!" The crowd took off running for the downtown square. My teenage cousins and older sister joined the horde. I joined the excited human wave headed to town. As we approached the square, soldiers and sailors rushed toward the outstretched arms of men, women, and children. The collision of humanity was incredible. The wild, spontaneous celebration nearly took my breath away, and I was caught up at waist level in the crushing sea of bodies. It was sheer madness as embracing and kissing abounded everywhere and with anybody. The revelry continued well into the night and lasted for several days. The unbridled intimacy of some revelers was apparent even to my young eyes, and couples sought privacy wherever it could be found. The outcome of these liaisons would be realized years later with the emergence of "Baby Boomers."

After the war ended, demobilization of the nation was hard for many families who had migrated west during the early 1940s. Black workers were especially hard hit. Many made plans to return to the

South and use their war-time savings to start anew. My mother was intent on being near her family in East Texas, so my father joined a group of relatives and headed back to Louisiana. We arrived in Shreveport, Louisiana on a cold night in November 1946. The first night back was a portent of things to come.

CHAPTER TWO

SHATTERED DREAMS

The home that awaited our return was too small for a family of six growing children, two of which were now teenagers. Nevertheless, we settled in to get some much needed rest. I awakened from a fitful sleep and attempted to find the bathroom. In Oxnard, all I had to do was get up, turn right, walk two feet to the bathroom, and take care of business. After bumping into luggage and furniture in the dark, I was confused, frustrated, and dangerously close to losing my eight-year old dignity. I sounded a loud, urgent alarm: "Ma Deah, I can't find the bathroom!" Hearing my distress, she yelled from the other bedroom, "Wilbert, Zella, get up and take that boy to the toilet." That should have been my first clue that California was long gone. Something was different. Not "Richard," but "that boy!" No "bathroom" but "the toilet!"

Since Wilbert was the oldest, he delegated this onerous task to the next oldest, my sister, Zella. My normally sweet sister was highly agitated by this middle-of-the-night summons, another clue that things were different. "Come on boy, let's go!" Zella grabbed me by the arm and propelled me through the kitchen and opened the back door of the house. The sudden blast of cold caused me to gasp for air, and I almost went potty right there! I shouted, "Where are you taking me? It's cold out there; I can't see!" Zella again grabbed me by the arm and struggled to get me out into the dark unknown. It was a battle between stark fear and the pressing call of nature. Fear was winning. We walked barefoot a short distance on the hard, cold ground before I discerned a building with a foul smell. I put on my brakes again and shouted, "Where is the bathroom?" Zella shouted back, "Right in front of you, boy. Hurry up. It's cold out here!"

To my recollection, I had never uttered a curse word, but I believe my first profane thoughts emerged that night: "There is no way in hell I'm going into that dark, smelly place." Before I could give voice to my rebellious thought, the cold night air and nature won the battle over fear. I took a hasty biological break right then and there. Greatly relieved, we bolted for the door, shuddering from cold. Zella was glad to be done with her burden for now, but I trembled from the prospects of the uncertainties that lay ahead. For a long while I lay in darkness pondering this woeful disruption in my life and the shattered dreams left behind in California.

The first major hurdle that faced the Tolivers upon returning to Shreveport was readjusting to an all-Black school environment. The politics of "separate but equal" in the South was a cruel lie. We immediately recognized the stark contrast between schools in Louisiana and those in California. The hostile negative attitudes of White Southerners toward the education of Black children were reflected in all the books, equipment, facilities, playgrounds, and services.

Unlike Haydock in Oxnard, West Shreveport Elementary School was nearly two miles away with no bus service for the surrounding area. Some students walked several miles to get there, and there were no paved streets, sidewalks, or beautiful green lawns. Gone also were the lovely flowers, trees, and beautiful bungalows. Because of the war, most homes in the neighborhood were badly in need of repairs, and the impending winter cast a gloomy pall over the community.

West Shreveport School had only one brick building that housed administration, restrooms, and a few classrooms. The hallway served as the school "auditorium." When students were required to assemble, we gathered in the hallway and sat on the floor. If a movie was shown, the hall lights would be extinguished and the exit doors would be closed to provide the theater effect. The rest of the classes were held in drab, wooden, ill-heated rooms with no shutters or shades to keep out the cold or heat. Books issued to Black students were hand-me-downs from White schools and often had missing pages or entire sections. Outside, the dirt playground was completely void of grass and filled with ditches caused by rain and perpetual erosion. Playing games on these abysmal grounds was a challenge, and getting an injury from stepping in potholes was a real likelihood. Even so, two basketball backboards stood with only the metal rims remaining to give the daring students a target for shooting hoops.

Despite these depressing conditions, the principal and teachers of West Shreveport were heroic in their efforts to instill in students the fundamentals of "reading, writing, and arithmetic." Mr. Edward. L. Greene, the principal, was a pinched-faced, balding man who wore bifocal glasses and was dedicated to maintaining a proper learning environment at the school. He had a zero-tolerance for poor behavior, and violators would immediately experience Mr. Greene's "corrective persuasion" on the spot. Given his kind of encouragement, I soon learned to settle any disputes I had as far from the school grounds as possible. In the meantime, the teachers were determined to impart as much knowledge as possible in spite of the political and financial constraints.

Our attempts to reintegrate into an all Black school were fraught with frustration and frequently resulted in altercations on the way home. Yet we tried hard to cope with the daunting issues at home, in school, and in the community. In addition, our emotions were constantly on edge due to the sudden turn of events beyond our control. Of all my siblings, I had the most volatile attitude and was prone to fight at the drop of a hat. Sometimes my mouth exceeded my ability and overloaded my behind, and my older brother, Wilbert, was called upon to bail me out. Notwithstanding these hurdles, the innate resiliency of children took hold, and we slowly re-identified with our peers and made lasting friends. One of these was Arthur Clover "AC" Washington. Although very young, a life-long friendship was forged upon mutual admiration, respect, and trust.

A Caged Eagle

The loss of jobs in the post-war era posed a severe challenge for those in search of meaningful work all across America. This was especially true in the South as persistent racism further constrained the prospects for Blacks in finding viable jobs. These circumstances caused my father to return to California to look for work while the family remained in Shreveport. I was extremely unhappy and wanted to go back to California with him. Of all the children, I took the separation the hardest. I hated Shreveport and wanted no part of the school, the community, or the city. Furthermore, I had become painfully aware of the blatant deprivation and oppression of Blacks in the South, and the crushing impact of these conditions was felt in my soul.

When Dad left, the world around me crumbled. My parents pretended their marriage was intact, but to a young precocious dreamer, the separation was devastating. Anger, bitterness, and resentment built up within me, and I withdrew into a dark, emotional dungeon of hopelessness. All the cajoling, threats, and other efforts of my mother and older siblings to shake me out of this funk failed. Worse yet, my anguish was compounded when I failed school that year. This was largely my fault, but it was still salt in my wounds. These circumstances made me feel trapped in a cage of despair with no hope of rescue.

The saving grace came later that summer when my mother took me to East Texas to meet her father, Bob Anderson, whom I had never met. This kind and gentle man seemed to sense my deep hurt as we strolled about his garden and nearby fields. The compassion and warmth that flowed through his twinkling eyes and kind smile eased the loneliness I felt by my dad's absence. A measure of peace fell over me, and before the visit was over, I had found a new friend. This was the beginning of a wonderful relationship of love and respect for the man we called Grandpa Bob. He never learned to read or write, but his wise counsel and sage advice were priceless.

The budding relationship between my grandfather and me provided a glimmer of hope. He was the balm that soothed my young, sick soul and gave me the inspiration needed to reignite my interest in school. My relationships with my mother and siblings also improved, and I began to take interest in the welfare of the family. For starters, I grew a small garden of vegetables like the one at Grandpa Bob's house. With the help of my mother, I soon became the proud producer of beans, potatoes, and other vegetables suitable enough to make a few meals for the family. This experience sparked my low self esteem back to life. When school started again, I was determined to do better and show the aptitude previously demonstrated in California.

My mother's hard work and persistence while in California paid off. The savings from her job there were used to build a new home in Shreveport. The house at 2907 Anna Street in Lakeside was partially completed by the summer of 1947, and we moved in despite work that needed to be completed before winter. Using my newly discovered "green thumb," I took it upon myself to gather flowering trees and shrubs from the nearby woods to decorate the yard. Ma Deah was particularly proud of the flower bed and beautiful rose bush that I planted near her window. Those roses grew for many years and brought much joy to her life.

Money from my father was slow in coming, and winter arrived before the house was finished. By then, my industrious mother started a drop-off laundry service for nearby White folks who paid a pittance for such service. The entire family was involved, and the four older children were assigned specific tasks in this endeavor. We were just below the economic rung of our customers, but their attitudes and demands for services were often demeaning and insulting.

Worse yet, I didn't take kindly to cleaning their terribly soiled clothing. Once again, I developed a deep-seated dislike for White folks and was prone to give them hate stares whenever I got the chance. To avoid confrontation and the loss of customers, my mother made sure I stayed in the backyard when they came to pick up their laundry. Thankfully, we earned enough money to complete the inner walls and room partitions of the house just before Christmas.

Christmas 1947 was particularly bleak as the family had very little in terms of material means. Despite our poverty, my sister, Zella, was determined to help Ma Deah bring a bit of cheer into our home. Zella led us younger siblings to the nearby woods to find a Christmas tree, courtesy of Mother Nature. We decorated the tree with home-made chains and cutouts made from scraps and crayons left over from school. There were no lights to put on the tree, but Zella would not be deterred. She took an extension cord from one room and a light bulb from another. Zella wrapped a piece of red tissue paper around the light bulb, and proudly hung it on the tree. A warm, soft glow filled the entire room. As we slept that night, my mother baked cakes and a hen. Wilbert and Zella filled little brown paper bags with nuts, candy, and fruit. The four younger siblings woke up the next morning filled with joy. Christmas had come to our home, and the solitary light still shone brightly from the corner of the room. Throughout my life, that light sustained my compassion and inspiration to help those less fortunate than me.

My father returned to Shreveport the summer of 1948. Unfortunately, job opportunities in California had not been good, and his contribution to our survival during that very tough year was minimal. This was a major factor in the deteriorating relationship between my parents, and the rift soon became obvious to us children. We endured many hardships during his absence and felt he failed in his responsibilities to the family. One night, an argument became extremely hostile, and we sided with our mother to protect her from physical abuse. We four older children armed ourselves with whatever we could find and took a defiant stand to protect Ma Deah. Angered and perplexed by this unexpected resistance, my father gathered his belongings and left the house in a huff. Later I found him living with a cousin and went to offer an apology for taking part in the rebellion. At ten years old, I didn't fully comprehend the disaster that had happened, so I begged him to return home and make things right. I sensed his hurt and frustration but couldn't understand the finality of my parent's breakup.

Witnessing my mother's suffering after my father left was very painful. I had never experienced such despair. Nor could I comprehend the heart-rending impact of a failed marriage after eighteen years. For many weeks, I awakened to my mother's early morning prayers and weeping. I knelt beside her, cried with her, and tried to understand the God from whom she sought help. Sometimes my two younger brothers woke up and joined us. We did our best to console Ma Deah, but the task was just too daunting for our young minds. Nevertheless, her profound faith in the midst of excruciating emotional pain gave us a small measure of hope.

My thirty-eight year old mother struggled with chronic fatigue, loneliness, and other emotions that I couldn't discern. She eventually gave in to the attentions of Hosea Dixon, a "male friend" who helped the family from time to time. This friendship led to a deeper relationship that resulted in the birth of my youngest brother,

Wendell. Dixon provided support for his son, but he was unwilling to step in as a father to the rest of us. The criticism of my mother from some neighbors, church members, and peers was also painful, and I engaged in numerous fights provoked by slurs against the Toliver name. This was my first bitter taste of hypocrisy from those who lived in "glass houses" yet were quick to throw stones. In the midst of this sad circumstance, I made youthful judgments against my mother and Hosea Dixon. Years later, the mistakes I made in my own life made me realize the folly of holding others to a higher standard than oneself.

Chapter Three

Beacons of Hope

Notwithstanding Ma Deah's personal struggles, she gathered strength and pushed us forward with everything she had. The personal challenges required reaching deep within to face harsh treatment, ridicule, and shame while striving to instill pride and perseverance within us. Having a baby out of wedlock was a significant hurdle to overcome, but by candidly dealing with the consequences, our mother taught us a powerful lesson: No matter how many times one falls down, he or she must have one more "get up" in them to keep pressing forward. She repeatedly said, "Keep your face toward the sun and the shadows will fall behind you." Another pearl of wisdom drummed into our heads was, "Nothing beats a failure but a 'try.'" Ma Deah used her circumstances to teach us to take personal responsibility for our actions and decisions regardless of the consequences. Most importantly, she taught us that God is the ultimate judge of our shortcomings, so we needed to seek forgiveness and reconciliation with Him rather than with man.

As I struggled with the shattered dreams of my early life, God faithfully provided help even though I couldn't discern His hand at work. Some of those I identify in this book as "*Uncaged Eagles*" were imprisoned themselves by circumstances or constraints of society. Yet, they possessed the freedom in their hearts, minds, and souls to reach out and help others along. This was the case with "Miz Rosie," the lady who gave me my first job.

Miz Rosie Chatman ran a one-room store a block from our house on Anna Street. She could have passed for "Aunt Jemima" with her ever-present long dress, apron, headdress, and demeanor. Her infectious laugh was more like a cackle, and her eyes sparkled when she spoke to children. Miz Rosie was amply sized with a heavily endowed bosom that literally suffocated kids during spontaneous hugs. She had very little formal education but possessed a sharp, entrepreneurial sense and was committed to helping those in her neighborhood. The store faced a small playground carved in the red clay on the remainder of the lot. The playground was built out of Miz Rosie's meager profits from selling bread, cold drinks, candy, cookies, a few canned goods, and ice. She equipped it piece by piece with a swing, see-saw, and merry-go- round. This generous gift was dearly appreciated since no parks or playgrounds existed elsewhere in the area. The playground was available on Sunday afternoons or other special days if children were in good standing with their parents. Miz Rosie sat on the porch of her little store and took pleasure in watching kids play and in seeing the joy derived from her gift to the community.

It was a hot, summer day when my sister, Zella, took me to Miz Rosie's store. Always questioning, I asked, "Why are we going to Miz Rosie's store? Do you have any money?" "No, but you need a job," Zella replied. I thought the better of too many questions. My mind began to envision candy, cookies, and pop at Miz Rosie's store, and I didn't care what I had to do to be thrown into that briar patch. Speaking as diplomatically as possible, I said, "Okay, let's hurry."

We arrived at the store and Zella asked Miz Rosie if she needed help for the summer. Miz Rosie sized up all ten years of me and said,

"Come here, sonny; give Miz Rosie a hug. What kind of work can you do?" Playing it safe, I stayed at arms length to avoid one of her patented expressions of kindness. Zella said, "Richard is a good worker and a fast learner. I am sure he can do just about anything you want him to." I chimed in, "Yes ma'am, I can count real good, clean house, and cook a little bit. I can also wash and iron." I should have stopped right there, but I really wanted to work in that store. Remembering that Miz Rosie had chickens, fruit trees, and a garden, I quickly added, "I can also take care of your garden, pick fruit, and gather eggs!" Miz Rosie cackled and her eyes twinkled even more. "Well, well, you just may be what I am looking for. When can he start?" Zella said, "I can leave him with you right now." "Mighty fine, mighty fine," Miz Rosie said. Zella continued, "How much will he be paid?" Miz Rosie's reply nearly took my breath away. "How about $3.00 a week?" I didn't give Zella a chance to answer. "Yes Ma'am, I am ready to start!" Zella smiled and said, "That's fine, I'll leave him with you for the rest of the day to learn what you want him to do."

With that exchange, my "working" career began. That first job gave me confidence in myself and instilled a deep sense of pride. More importantly, my contributions to the family's welfare did much to improve my self-esteem. I gave Ma Deah $2.50 per week, and she allowed me to keep fifty cents. I used some of that to stock up on school supplies for my younger siblings and me. Miz Rosie was a beacon of hope in my dark world. Her free-will attitude and spirit touched many lives in the community, and she made a difference in my life at a very crucial time. Years later, I identified Miz Rosie as the first *Uncaged Eagle* in my life.

The challenges to feed, clothe, and care for six children were formidable, but my mother's fierce determination and trust in the Lord eventually provided the foundation for my own faith in God. On one hand, I wanted to believe in the Jesus my mother prayed to daily, but the stark realities of our lives precluded my trust in a

White, blue-eyed Christ depicted on the posters I saw in church. If this Holy God really did care for people, why did He allow some to be so mean? Why were there so many hurdles to overcome? Why didn't honesty, integrity, and sheer hard work pay off more readily for those who held these values?

My mother recognized the need for her children to develop a strong foundational faith in God. Whether we believed as she did or not, Ma Deah insisted we attend a church revival to get "saved." That meant sitting on the "Mourning Bench" several nights to "mourn" until the Holy Spirit filled us with a penitent attitude. Then we had to ask the Lord's forgiveness, turn from our waywardness, and promise to walk righteously for the rest of our life. This was a very tall order for me, and I needed lots of prodding and threats to get me on that bench. There were no options, however, so eventually each of us complied with Ma Deah's wishes to avoid her own version of earthly retribution. We duly repented and accepted Jesus Christ as our Lord and Savior to avoid the hellish wrath she was capable of dispensing. Thus, all the Toliver children became members at Good-will Missionary Baptist Church and attended weekly Sunday school, morning worship services, and evening Baptist Youth Training. Despite persistent foot dragging, the seeds of my faith were established with the firm encouragement of my mother and the faithful men and women at Goodwill Missionary Baptist Church.

In 1950, Eliza Hawkins Long moved to our neighborhood with seven of her eight children. Like my mother, she was a single Black woman faced with the daunting task of raising her family under the difficult economic and racial constraints of the post WW II South. Like the Tolivers, the Long children pitched in to help their mother by working at whatever jobs they could find.

My mother met Eliza over a wash tub by the side of her house. Both desperately needed a soul mate with whom to share their innermost concerns. The Longs were devout Catholics, but it didn't stop these two women from sharing their faith, mutual hardships, and struggles. They soon became close friends and encouragers for each other. I met the four younger Longs - Wyonne, Delores, Calvin, and Barbara. Like our parents, we established a bond of friendship and trust that enabled us to share our youthful aspirations. Delores and I often sat on their steps, and I'd tell her about my hopes of leaving Shreveport one day to fly airplanes. Although only twelve, she had a mature sense and understanding of the depth of my aspiration and encouraged me to believe in myself.

Our friendship was interrupted when Delores was sent to a convent in New Orleans. I was deeply saddened by the loss of my dear childhood friend, but it was considered the family's duty to the Catholic Church. The consequence of that decision was revealed later in our lives.

With quiet determination, my brother, Wilbert, helped our mother keep us focused on school. Education was held in great esteem throughout the Black community, and graduation from high school was a "must" at all cost. In 1950, the inferior facilities for educating local Blacks took a monumental leap forward when Booker T. Washington (BTW) High School opened in our community. Named after the founder of Tuskegee Institute in Alabama, it was the first new high school in the area in thirty-three years. Built at an unprecedented cost of $2,000,000, it was a model school for Blacks as well as for Whites.

BTW offered a wide range of high school and college prep courses in science, math, and liberal arts. In addition, vocational training included typing, shorthand, bookkeeping, auto mechanics, carpentry, electricity, and other job-related courses. The principal of BTW was Mr. R. H. Brown, the former principal of Central Colored High School. He led an outstanding faculty who possessed a wealth of experience, and they were motivated to take the education of Blacks to the highest level possible. The educational advantages and environment at BTW ushered in a new era of hope for all Black people in Shreveport. These changes also resulted in benefits to the entire community by creating a larger pool of educated and skilled workers available to grow a greater Shreveport.

The first students graduated from Booker T. Washington High School in 1951. Wilbert graduated that year, and he was determined to go on to college. He had no money, so one of his teachers, a Tuskegee graduate, encouraged him to pursue a work scholarship program at Tuskegee Institute in Tuskegee, Alabama. This was above and beyond the aspirations of most of his peers, especially given the lack of resources. Nevertheless, he headed to Tuskegee Institute that summer with a few dollars and little more than the clothes on his back. Wilbert was the first among his siblings, cousins, and friends to attend college. It was a tremendous struggle, but he stayed focused and would not be deterred no matter the hardships he faced. He was determined to set a good example for the rest of us.

Shortly after Wilbert left for college, Zella married her childhood sweetheart, Anthony W. "AW" Rye, Jr., and started a family of her own. With the two older siblings gone, I became the "man of the house" and was immediately put to the test. Ma Deah became critically ill and was hospitalized for over a month the summer of 1951. It was especially difficult that year due to the scourge of polio that hit the entire nation. People of all races were stricken, and the hospitals were flooded with victims of every age. The dreaded iron lung was everywhere - in the wards, the hallways, emergency rooms, and anywhere space was available. Our daily visits to the hospital were very painful for my sister, Arneater. She left the hospital crying and worried that we had seen our mother for the last time. Arneater was eighteen months older than me, but I became the big brother who consoled her.

Miraculously, Ma Deah was not stricken with polio, but she nearly died from rheumatic fever and a terribly weakened heart. She fought back courageously, but it took many weeks to recover. I took over her Avon Cosmetics route to keep food on the table and to pay the utility bills. With the help of a $70-dollar monthly welfare check and my mother's management skill, we kept things together.

Renewed Inspiration

God works in mysterious ways and performs many wonders. He did so in my life when I was thirteen and barely hanging on. It was a hot, sweltering Sunday afternoon as I walked home from church on the oil-paved streets of my neighborhood. Many families had gathered on their porches to fan the stifling humid air while listening to the special Negro Spiritual Hour on the local radio station. The late Reverend C. L. Franklin, father of Aretha Franklin, was preaching a rousing sermon about an eagle that had been unwittingly caged by a chicken farmer. The story was told of a chicken farmer who discovered a strange-looking young bird in his flock. This particular bird did not associate with the other chickens and often seemed restless and agitated. As the bird grew, he begin to look, act, and strut about the yard differently than the other chickens. One day, the bird appeared to hear a sound high in the sky. He began to make strange noises, flapped his wings, and vainly struggled to get free of the cage. The farmer eventually called a friend over to witness the behavior of this peculiar bird. After observing the bird, the friend proclaimed, "My friend, this is not just a strange bird; what you have here is an eagle. Eagles are not meant to be caged in with chickens. You must set this eagle free so that he can go where eagles soar!"

After a bit of persuasion, the farmer reluctantly opened the cage. Slowly the eagle emerged, flew to the roof of the cage, and began to flap his wings. Next, he flew to a nearby tree and made sounds as if calling to the wind. Soon similar sounds were heard high above the farm, and the eagle flew to the top of the nearest mountain. With one last flap of his newly discovered wings, the eagle soared toward the sound above the distant clouds and beyond the sight of his earthly cage. Thus, after his prolonged and restless struggle, the eagle was set free to become what he was created to be. Reverend Franklin went on to conclude that the human spirit is like an eagle, and God created all humanity to be free.

Reverend Franklin's powerful message was a much needed ray of hope for me. Like that caged eagle, I was trapped by circumstances far beyond my control. But by the grace of God, I embraced the hope in his sermon and began to believe a better life was possible. Although only thirteen, I had a burning desire to experience that God-given freedom. It would take years of striving, struggling, and many life-shaping experiences before I would be liberated to soar like an eagle. I was not able to discern the hand of God in all this. Yet, He blessed me with special people at just the right place and time. These included family, friends, neighbors, school teachers, Sunday school teachers, and "angels unaware." When my needs seemed well beyond reach, my mother's assertion "the Lord will make a way" always proved true. I was slow to believe as she did, but I couldn't refute God's persistent and timely blessings in our lives.

Wilbert came home that Christmas sporting an Air Force ROTC uniform. It was the first time I saw a Black man up close in a blue uniform. I was immediately taken by his appearance and wanted to know more about the program at Tuskegee Institute. Right away, my thoughts turned toward Tuskegee Institute as a likely place for me to realize my dream of flying airplanes. Because he wore eyeglasses, Wilbert was disqualified for advanced ROTC by medical technicians at nearby Maxwell AFB. This decision later proved to be racially motivated, but by then, it was too late for him to re-enroll.

Wilbert graduated from Tuskegee Institute in 1956. This was a great day for Ma Deah as she saw her first born accomplish an enormous feat. The rest of us were also filled with admiration and pride in our older brother. Zella's husband, AW, drove Ma Deah and David to Wilbert's graduation. It was the greatest trip of her life. She returned raving about the beautiful campus and overall experience of a college graduation. These events reinforced my determination to finish high school. Wilbert forged a path that Zella, AW, David, and I followed later.

After graduation, Wilbert was drafted into the U. S. Army and served two years. Given his college degree, he entered as a Specialist and earned additional rank during his time in service. Wilbert settled in Detroit, Michigan after leaving the Army, and began a teaching career that spanned more than twenty-five years in the city's school system.

Over the years, AW and Zella proved to be a godsend to our family. They were the constant beacons of hope that kept me from falling deeper into a chasm of bitterness that, at times, threatened to consume me. Despite the challenges, they always found a way to bring some joy into our lives. They never let Easter or Christmas pass without providing gifts, clothing, food, or some other much needed support. In particular, AW's generosity, love, and patience often lifted me above the despair with which I struggled. To this day, I am very proud to say AW was my first role model and is still my dear friend.

Mr. Freddie Pineset was a WW II veteran who built a home next door to us on Anna Street. He sharpened his carpentry skills while serving overseas and building numerous camp support facilities. Mr. Freddie was a small, powerfully built, energetic man with an easy laugh and engaging personality. The latter earned him respect and trust by both White and Black clients, and he was paid well for his top-notch construction skills. We hit it off immediately when he hired me to pull nails out of lumber used to build his house. Later, he taught me basic carpentry skills, and I became his preferred helper for the next several years. Mr. Freddie also taught my younger brother, David, carpentry skills, and we worked as a team throughout Shreveport and the surrounding area. This relationship continued after high school and became the source of our employment in the summer during college years.

Mr. Mat and Mrs. Cora Sherman moved in later as our other next door neighbors with their grown son, Billy Ray. They were hard working people who soon became known for their kindness, generosity, and help to others in the neighborhood. Mrs. Sherman became "Mother Sherman" to us because of her sweet, nurturing attitude toward the children. Often, she called one or the other of us over and stuffed a gift of money into our hands. She just seemed to know when a few unexpected dollars could be used to meet a need. This was simply her "language of love."

Mother Sherman and Mr. Mat continued to be an inspiration in the neighborhood in the midst of a great personal tragedy. Billy Ray, their only son was killed in an automobile accident. The entire neighborhood was engulfed in an indescribable sadness. All of us did everything possible to console Mother Sherman and Mr. Mat, but it was she who consoled others over the loss of their son. Many months passed before Mother Sherman gathered strength enough to go on with her life. She began by taking in Billy's two children and their mother. Later, she added several foster children to her brood. For the next thirty years, and long after Mr. Mat passed away, Mother Sherman spent her life raising children nobody else wanted. She died early one morning at the age of seventy-eight while still trying to get the Child Social Services to let her have two more small children. Mother Sherman's generosity, kindness, and sweet spirit alleviated a lot of the negatives in our lives. Surely, this was *An Uncaged Eagle* who now soars in the presence of God.

Mr. Johnnie and Mrs. Dovie Price lived across the street. They showed me another kind of love. It was the love between a man and woman that exemplified a deep commitment and contentment with each other. The Prices were in their early fifties, but their behavior seemed like that of a younger couple. Mrs. Price saw her husband off to work every morning with a kiss and a wave. Every evening at the same time, Mr. Price turned the corner with a wide grin and wave to his Dovie who waited at the door. They had dinner together then sat outside in a swing behind a large hedge row. One could hear them talking and laughing until nightfall. Sometimes, I visited the Prices' and noticed a subtle smile or touch between them that was as natural as breathing. This reminded me of my family's time in Oxnard, California when such a connection existed between my parents. The warm, intimate relationship of the Prices made me aware of my own emerging manhood and sexuality. Their example gave me hope that I would one day meet a young woman who would make me feel like Dovie made Johnnie feel. The Price's unspoken intimacy was love in its purest form, and made me realize that such a relationship was possible. I treasured the thought in my heart and looked forward to experiencing one day the kind of love the Prices shared.

Dedicated Teachers

Not enough can be said for the teachers in Black schools prior to the advent of school integration. Severely hampered by racial constraints and regulations, they did a phenomenal job in educating the Black children, often surreptitiously. For instance, teachers were only allowed to teach or emphasize the accomplishments or contributions of Blacks during one week in February. Called "Negro History Week," this event was established in 1926 by a Black educator, Carter G. Woodson.

Teachers spent many extra hours preparing and presenting historical achievements of Black people in America dating back to the American Revolution. In addition, they gave extra credit to students for reading assignments from the limited books available in the library. Often, they used their own collection of papers to stimulate their students. Contests were held on the last day of the week to determine which student had the most unique story to tell from their newly discovered knowledge. For the first time, I learned about opera singer Marian Anderson, educator Booker T. Washington, scientist George Washington Carver, entertainer Lena Horne, singer Billie Holiday, and athletes Jesse Owens and Jackie Robinson. Thanks to radio, we knew about Joe Louis, the great boxer known as the "Brown Bomber."

I loved school and had an aptitude for math, science, history, geography, and art. My teachers and the librarian kept me challenged with extra books that allowed me to explore the world and dream of places I wanted to visit one day. Despite the lack of exposure to aviation, I still dreamed of flying. Historic Barksdale Air Force Base was less than ten miles away, and occasionally I was able to see airplanes take off and land. Since my dream was considered far-fetched in my school and community, I largely kept it to myself.

In the seventh grade, two of my teachers, Mrs. Pauline Young and Mrs. Odile Greene, decided I showed leadership potential and called me from the playground. Mrs. Young had been my third grade teacher and Mrs. Greene was the wife of Mr. Greene, the principal at West Shreveport Elementary School. These two ladies took a special interest in me and did a lot to help me become a young leader. With their mentoring and tutoring, I became a standout student and later was elected class president during my freshman and junior years in high school.

During my junior year, the rigors of working six nights per week took its toll, and my high class standing began to slip. Worse yet, I had to forego my passionate desire to participate in sports and other extra curricular activities. This was a great disappointment, but I simply had no choice. My mother needed help in supporting my three remaining siblings at home. By my senior year, my class standing slipped from first place to tenth out of 357 graduating students in 1957.

Ma Deah made a rare appearance the day students and families gathered in the school auditorium for the graduation awards. It was very disappointing when the program ended without my name being called. Several teachers attempted to soften my disappointment with gifts of shirts, neckties, handkerchiefs, and other useful items. We rushed out amid the laughter and excitement of those who had been awarded scholarships of $200, $500, and even a $1,000. Disappointment weighed heavily upon my heart as we got into our old car and headed home. I reached over to console Ma Deah and reiterated that I had been accepted at Tuskegee. Like my brother, Wilbert, I had been accepted on a work scholarship program. By then I knew that life was not fair, but at least I had a chance to get a college education. I swallowed hard and vowed to make Ma Deah proud of me one day.

A Helping Hand

Graduation was over, and we turned in the caps and gowns the following day. Mrs. Ruth Lincoln, the librarian and my distant cousin, had been one of my staunch supporters since fifth grade. She phoned me the day before and asked if I had heard from the principal, Mr. Brown, or the school counselor, Ms. Hazel Payne. When I said no, she made some remarks suggesting that I would, but gave no indication of why. I had no earthly idea why Mr. Brown wanted to see me, so I gave it no further thought. As I walked down the hall to return my cap and gown, several teachers came out to greet me in a most unusual and animated manner. Their normal reserved behavior was now totally unrestrained. Mrs. Pearl Lee, my freshman math teacher came out with a poster depicting the value of books and education I had drawn four years earlier. I still had no clue regarding their attention and the general excitement up and down the hall. As I approached the principal's office, I allowed myself to think maybe the teachers had collected a few dollars for me after all. At any rate, I didn't want to embrace any false hopes, so I entered the office with a bit of caution. The explosion of cheers and greetings nearly rocked me off my feet, and Mr. Brown and Ms. Payne hugged me with uncharacteristic exuberance. Several of my former teachers were present and followed suit with congratulatory words, warm embraces, and smiles. Finally, Mr. Brown blurted out, "Mr. Toliver, my office and the faculty have selected you to receive a scholarship offered by a rich White man in Shreveport. You are the recipient of $3,000 to help you through college!"

For the first time in my life, I nearly fainted and had to be helped to a couch. My head was spinning and uncontrollable tears blinded my vision. My brain simply couldn't comprehend what I had just heard. Someone gave me a glass of water and I tried to collect myself. With hands still shaking, I spoke in a quivering voice, "Is this really true?" "How did this happen? Who is this man? How did I get chosen?"

Mr. Brown spoke while Ms. Payne held out my high school transcript. He stated that a rich man in the oil industry, Mr. Austin E. Stewart, decided to help the Black community. He asked Mr. Brown to identify a worthy student with the aptitude and desire to go to college and succeed. Mr. Brown and the faculty at Booker T. Washington knew about my family situation, my work ethic, and my determination to make something of myself. After much deliberation, they concluded I was the most worthy for this tremendous opportunity. To complete the process, Mr. Brown and I had to pass an interview with Mr. Stewart within the next few weeks.

Following discussions with Mr. Brown, I rushed home to tell my mother, the rest of the family, the neighbors, the church, and anyone else I could think of. My Cousin Ruth Lincoln beat me to the punch, and called my mother before I got home. Ma Deah was waiting in disbelief until I told her the news was true. This time the tears that flowed were tears of pure joy. As the news spread through the community, our house filled with well wishers and jubilant neighbors. In fact, we had an impromptu church service with singing, praising, and a bit of old fashion shouting. It was a glorious day, and I didn't mind the spiritual releases. My reluctance to believe in God began to dissolve that day. He clearly revealed Himself without regards to color or race and became a reality for me in a way I had never experienced.

As scheduled, Mr. Brown and I met with Mr. Stewart in his office on the top floor the Commercial Bank building downtown. We arrived at the appointed hour and were very warmly greeted by his Executive Assistance, Mrs. Bebe Whitley. She was just over four feet tall with graying hair and a kind, smiling face. We were offered refreshments and seated in Mr. Stewart's outer office. The cordiality and respect shown us was an unusual experience in the Black community. I looked over at Mr. Brown and noted he was quite nervous and having a hard time keeping calm. I calmed myself by recalling the briefings and counseling for this visit over the past two weeks. My mother's advice had been simply to be polite, speak truthfully, don't forget to smile, and let the Lord do the rest.

Mr. Brown and I were finally ushered into Mr. Stewart's office. I was awe-struck by the size of the office and magnificent panoramic view of Shreveport and neighboring Bossier City from seventeen stories up. The massive Red River meandered between the twin cities that spread out for miles with fields, forests, and lakes that accentuated the landscape in a breathtaking view. I got my first look at Barksdale Air Force Base a short distance away and could see airplanes taking off and landing. Mr. Stewart smiled as he saw the expression on my face and asked if I liked the view. I told him it was the most beautiful view I had ever seen and imagined that it would be like this seen from an airplane. Mr. Stewart continued with questions about flying, and I told him about my dream of becoming an Air Force pilot one day. He then asked me about Tuskegee Institute and my intended course of study. Feeling more at ease, I stated my plan to get a degree in engineering and explained the reasons for it. After a few more questions and answers, Mr. Stewart spoke to Mr. Brown and expressed his thanks for helping him find the right student for the scholarship. He also congratulated Mr. Brown on the outstanding job he was doing at Booker T. Washington and for the contributions to the city and state as a whole.

Mr. Stewart concluded by telling me he was pleased with all he heard and was confident I would be successful at Tuskegee. He asked me to keep him informed about my progress once there. With that, the interview ended and we departed on an emotional high that matched the view we had just left. Mr. Brown patted me on the back and told me I had done a great job. Before parting, he also asked me to keep him abreast of my progress at Tuskegee Institute.

I silently vowed to comply with both requests and to make Mr. Stewart, Booker T. Washington High School, and everyone involved in Shreveport proud of me one day. Like that eagle in Reverend Franklin's sermon, my cage of despair had been opened, and I was eager to soar into a promising future. This was my moment of truth. Regardless of the difficulties ahead, no matter how long it took, I was determined to succeed in college. The scholarship was one of the greatest blessings of my life in many ways. Mr. Stewart planted a seed of truth about the goodness of White people as well as those of other races. Years later, memories of his kindness and generosity forced me to reject my own misguided prejudice. His rare courage and vision reflected a freedom unconstrained by racial and societal attitudes of our time. He clearly proved to be *An Uncaged Eagle* in my life.

Chapter Four

The Tuskegee Experience

On a late afternoon in early September 1957, I left for Tuskegee on a Trailways bus. I felt sadness as the sun set in the west and the bus traveled east along the winding, hilly, two-lane road called US Highway 80. The realization of leaving behind those I truly loved slowly emerged. The past ten years in Shreveport had been a difficult maturing process, and I allowed myself to feel a deep sense of relief. I pondered what lay ahead as the bus sped into the night and crossed the mighty Mississippi River. When we stopped in Vicksburg, the driver announced, "Folks, y'all got about forty-five minutes to get somethin' to eat in the restaurant. Y'all Colored Folks can get somethin' to go from the window around the back." This announcement shook me from my melancholy and brought me back to the harsh reality of traveling in the south. I wanted to give the bus driver a piece of my mind, but quickly remembered the stories of lynching in Mississippi for lesser offenses. My mother anticipated an event such as this and prepared a lunch for me, but I still had difficulty controlling my anger. When some of the Black passengers exited the bus and made their way to the back of the restaurant, I hissed under my breath, "I'll be damned if I spend a cent in this God-forsaken place!"

I stayed onboard and ate one of my sandwiches; however, my pride resulted in a thirst for a drink that lasted the rest of the night.

The denigration was not over. There was no toilet on board the bus, so the driver made frequent "pit stops" at gas stations along the way. Since the call of nature has no respect for race, the driver was obliged to make pit stops to accommodate everyone. The restrooms were posted with signs that read, "White Men, White Women, and Colored." To say the least, the condition of the latter at each stop left a lot to be desired. After the first stop, I refused to get off the bus for the subsequent breaks. My stubbornness caused a very uncomfortable night.

We arrived in Montgomery, Alabama early the next morning. By then, I was grateful to be able to take a biological break and get a drink of water in the "Colored" section of the bus station. At least there were separate restrooms for men and women, and a small food counter with stools. After switching to a Greyhound bus and continuing another forty miles, I arrived at Tuskegee on a Sunday morning just after sunrise. The sight of the small town was disheartening. The "Bus Station" was a two-room building with a small Greyhound sign on the edge of the highway. A "White Only" sign hung over a dinky little room that housed a few chairs, and the "Colored" waiting area was a bench outside. To make matters worse, one of my bags was missing, and the attendant became highly agitated when I insisted he fill out a loss report. After a considerable wait, I shared a taxi with two other students for the trip to the college campus.

I was still disenchanted until the taxi arrived at the college entrance where a sign proclaimed "Welcome to Tuskegee Institute, Founded 1881." My spirit was immediately lifted by the most majestic sights I had ever seen. The beautiful architecture of the turn-of-the century ante-bellum buildings were surrounded by old oak trees and evergreens of every hue and shape. Magnolias, crepe myrtles, and other flowering trees were interspersed as if to present a living canvas for artists of every persuasion. Each building was named after a renowned benefactor or personality of past generations such as Rockefeller, Carnegie, Huntington, and Washington. Each had a unique design that blended together to give the entire campus its rich, historic character. The statue of founder Booker T. Washington stood on a plaza near the center of the campus across from Dorothy Hall, the visitor's hotel. An inscription read,

> "He lifted the veil of ignorance from his people and
> pointed the way to progress through education and industry."

Nearby, a bronze bust of the great natural scientist, George Washington Carver, graced the entrance to the museum named in his honor. The rolling hills, beautiful landscape, and layout of the campus reminded me of the paradise left behind in Oxnard more than ten years earlier. I was overjoyed at seeing this unexpected "Black Paradise" located deep in the "Cradle of the Confederacy" as Alabama was called in those days.

The cab driver gave us his patented initial tour of the campus. Our collective responses apparently met the expectation of what must have been replayed countless times. We were completely overwhelmed by the first impression of our intended home for the next four to five years. Now I understood why my mother raved so much about her visit to Tuskegee Institute. I was equally inspired after just a few minutes on campus and very grateful to be at such a legendary place. I whispered thanks to my brother, Wilbert, for paving the way. He left some big shoes to fill, but with God's help, I vowed to follow in his footsteps.

Incoming male and female students reported to the offices of the Dean of Men or Dean of Women respectively. We were assigned dormitory rooms, provided initial meeting schedules, student information packages, and other rules and regulations for Tuskegee Institute. The matter-of-fact, impersonal manner of this process bothered some of the new students who apparently were on their own for the first time in their lives. Being an old hand at almost nineteen years old, I felt quite comfortable and was ready to get with the program.

A group of us fellows hired another cab to take us to the freshmen men's dormitories where we experienced an unexpected letdown. These WW II-type barracks were lined up like a military camp on the edge of the main campus. We noted the cab driver had carefully avoided this area during our initial campus tour. The barracks had served as "dormitories" for incoming male students since 1945. These two-story wooden buildings were covered with asbestos siding, were poorly insulated, and had no air conditioning. Two students were assigned per room, and a common shower and latrine were located at the end of the hall for about twenty-four students on each floor.

We were told the barracks had been the home of the legendary Tuskegee Airmen, thus it was an honor to live where their feet had trod. We were also told the monthly lodging fees were reduced, thereby making these "historical" facilities a significant bargain for the new students. Of course, none of this resonated with us, but as freshmen, we sucked in our guts and settled in the best we could. My roommate, John St. Clair, from Dunedin, Florida apparently had heard about the barracks and arrived with a huge box of goodies. His parents had included bed spreads, floor mats, wall pictures, and numerous other items intended to make John comfortable. He was a generous and likeable fellow, and we immediately struck up a lasting friendship.

All new students were required to attend mandatory orientation our first day on campus. This initial session introduced us to the amazing story of Tuskegee Institute that most had never heard. The history, legacy, and reputation for hard work made the college renowned for accommodating students who came from the many

Black communities across the South. The Institute, affectionately known as "Mother Tuskegee," was proudly touted as the "Pride of the Swift Growing South."

When we arrived in 1957, these hallowed grounds were deeply infused with the blood, sweat, and tears of great heroes and heroines who preceded us by seventy-six years. Founder Booker T. Washington was followed by Dr. Robert R. Moton and Dr. Frederick D. Patterson. In 1957, Dr. Luther H. Foster, the fourth president, led an outstanding faculty and staff who were dedicated to producing graduates that could compete anywhere in the world. Tuskegee Institute had progressed from humble and meager beginnings to an internationally known college, predominantly for Black students from around the world. It had developed premier Schools of Agriculture, Education, Home Economics & Food Administration, Mechanical Industries, Nursing, Veterinary Medicine, and Air & Military Sciences.

We soon realized Tuskegee Institute was a very special place. From the outset, new students were offered an opportunity to become a living part of its legacy. If we followed faithfully in the footsteps of those who preceded us, the weeks and months ahead would be the beginning of an exciting future. I was moved by this opportunity and made a serious commitment to do just that.

It didn't take new students long to settle into the routines of college life. Freshmen were placed on a short leash, and most of the student activities were scheduled for them. A great amount of personal discipline, however, was needed to keep up with the fast paced academics, extra curricular activities, and studying. I felt up to the challenge and was motivated by the history of Booker T. Washington, George Washington Carver, and other Black trailblazers of the past. Often, I stopped and read the inscriptions on Dr. Washington's monument or on the grave of Dr. Carver. At other times I visited the Carver Museum or read a book about the history of the people and development of the Institute. For the first time, all I had to do was go to class, study, attend the mandatory functions, eat, sleep, get up, and start all over again. The news from home also was good. My mother was adjusting to my departure and coping with my three younger brothers at home. Life was good, and I was enjoying my first year of college.

Legacy of Tuskegee Airmen

The introduction to the Tuskegee Airmen was one of the greatest experiences of my life. The tutelage, mentoring, teaching, and counseling provided by these great patriots benefited scores of those like me throughout our professional careers. Our personal lives were also enhanced by witnessing their outstanding example as officers, husbands, fathers, and combat aviators. Much has been written about these American heroes, but please allow me to share a brief synopsis here.

More than 15,000 men and women participated in what was called the "Tuskegee Experiment." Four hundred and fifty of the Tuskegee Airmen served overseas in either the 99th Pursuit Squadron (later the 99th Fighter Squadron) and the 332nd Fighter Group. These aviators flew over 15,000 sorties, destroyed or damaged over 400 enemy aircraft, destroyed over 1,000 military targets, and sank an enemy destroyer. Sixty-six pilots lost their lives, and thirty-two were prisoners of war.

The record of the Tuskegee Airmen is unequalled by any other unit in the history of American combat. Their success proved to the American public and the world that, when given an opportunity, Black people could indeed become effective military leaders, pilots, and major contributors to the nation's defense. The Tuskegee Experiment was recognized as the most prevalent factor in President Harry Truman's decision to integrate the military services in 1948. In addition, the Airmen's victory over extreme adversity was the benchmark that helped achieve equal rights by nonviolent direct action in the 1950s and 1960s. In my opinion, the Tuskegee Airmen were the greatest flock of *Uncaged Eagles* ever assembled.

The first two years of ROTC were mandatory at Tuskegee Institute. Courses were offered in both Military (Army) and Air Science (Air Force). I had chosen the Air Force years before when my brother came home sporting his Air Force uniform. I signed up as soon as possible during class registration. We were issued uniforms and given instructions for the first drill assembly jointly scheduled with the Army and Air Force departments on the football field.

I will never forget that exciting day. For the first time in most of our lives, we were introduced to original Tuskegee Airmen. Lieutenant Colonel William "Wild Bill" Campbell was the Professor of Air Science for AFROTC Detachment 15. He was a ram-rod straight, six feet plus officer with a demeanor that epitomized a military leader. Most of us didn't know about his great legacy, but everyone was overwhelmed by his presence on the field. He graduated in the third aviation training class in 1942 and deployed with then Colonel Benjamin O. Davis, Jr. to North Africa in 1943. As Lieutenant Campbell, he flew on the first combat mission of the famed 99th Pursuit Squadron on June 2, 1943. During eleven days of an assault against the heavily fortified island of Pantellaria, Lieutenant Campbell became the first Black man to drop a bomb on the enemy.

Colonel Campbell was also part of a distinguished family from Tuskegee who served in important roles during WWII. Thomas Campbell, Sr. was a field agent for the United States Department of Agriculture and Captain Noel Campbell was in the Women's Army Corps. Captain Thomas Campbell, Jr. was in the U. S. Army Medical Corps and later a prominent doctor at John A. Andrew Hospital on Tuskegee's campus.

Colonel Campbell was joined on the field by pilot, Captain Emmett Hatch, other officers, and Non-Commissioned Officers (NCOs). All were closely involved in training the cadets. The Army ROTC also had an impressive group of officers and NCOs, but this was the day to showcase the legendary Tuskegee Airmen. The event was an awesome gathering of Black officers and NCOs in both the Air Force and Army.

Weekly ROTC drills were held each Wednesday afternoon with a retreat ceremony on the main campus. This event reflected the patriotism held over from WW II and the Korean War. It was frequently attended by a large number of non-ROTC students, families of the officers and NCOs, and campus visitors.

The first year cadets were required to attend a 7:00 AM assembly each Friday morning. These sessions featured movies and film clips that documented the beginning of man's adventure in flight, the early development of airplanes, and aerial activities of WW II and the Korean War. Missing, however, were the stories and exploits of the Tuskegee Airmen.

This strange absence of history would later be attributed to "official orders" from higher ups at AFROTC headquarters. However, the reluctance of the Tuskegee Airmen to talk about themselves was equally bewildering. They seemed to adhere to an unwritten code of silence that emphasized exemplary character and performance rather than words. These heroes seemed content to let their actions and behavior speak for them. What a lesson in life. Most of us thoroughly enjoyed these early morning assemblies, and those previously ambivalent about mandatory ROTC quickly developed an interest in the Air Force. I found these sessions enlightening and stimulating and could hardly wait to get near an airplane. That day was nearer than I thought.

After a few weeks of school, I competed for the AFROTC Drill Team and won a spot with this prestigious marching group. The team was featured at halftime during football games and scheduled to participate in several major events in Alabama and Georgia throughout the year. Later, my progress earned a trip to nearby Maxwell Air Force Base (AFB) for an orientation flight. This was a dream I had held onto for over twelve years. Now it was coming true.

A few days later, Captain Hatch drove a group of us cadets to Maxwell AFB where we were assigned to fly with several White officers during their proficiency training flights. I was assigned to fly in a Beechcraft C-45 light transport. While airborne, I was invited to sit up front in the cockpit for a while. The pilot allowed me to handle the controls and showed me how to climb, bank, and turn. This was my first trip to heaven, and from that moment, I knew I was born to fly. On the way back to Tuskegee, Captain Hatch declared, "The Cadet of the Year next spring will earn a flight in a T-33 jet aircraft." I nearly blurted out, "Put my name on that list now!" Wisely, I kept silent and decided to work to be that cadet next spring.

Cultural and Social Exposure

Other activities at Tuskegee Institute and in the community were equally exciting and intellectually stimulating. Mandatory Sunday evening Vesper Services featured numerous cultural events and notable personalities. For the first time, I attended a live orchestra presentation when the Atlanta Symphony Ensemble performed at one of these services. I met and heard the great Negro poet Langston Hughes recite from one of his famous books, witnessed my first ballet, and was inspired by many famous personalities in art, music, and theater. Some students complained about the mandatory assembly, but I believe we all appreciated this "force-fed" cultural development.

The 1955 Bus Boycott in Montgomery, Alabama had a signifi-cant influence on Tuskegee Institute and the local community. This unprecedented twelve-month protest against segregated seating on public buses was successfully led by twenty-six year old Dr. Martin Luther King, Jr. The boycott ushered in the Civil Rights movement all across the nation, and it proved to be the foundation for non-vio-lent civil resistance. The White media attempted to confine the story of the boycott to local Alabama papers. But the peaceful nature of this social protest became world news and set the stage for similar actions as Black people throughout Alabama and the South began to use their economic power to bring about long overdue changes.

Tuskegee Institute, John A. Andrew Hospital on campus, and the nearby regional Veterans Administration Hospital brought a sig-nificant amount of revenue into the county each month. In fact, Ma-con County was considered one of the richest and most progressive counties in the state. The Black people in Macon County and in the town of Tuskegee began to boycott White businesses to force changes locally. Likewise, Tuskegee Institute's students were encouraged to avoid spending money in town and in the local areas. We were proud to be part of this social movement emerging "Deep in the Heart of Dixie." It was inspiring to see Black people come together and work effectively for the welfare of the entire community.

Greenwood Baptist Church was near the campus and frequent-ly invited motivating Black personalities to address the community and Tuskegee Institute students. The church was led by a dynamic leader and pastor, Dr. Raymond Francis "Chunky" Harvey. There I met the famous baseball player, Jackie Robinson, who was the fea-tured speaker one night in the fall of 1957. Everybody knew this su-perstar was the first Black man to play with the big league team, the Brooklyn Dodgers. The event was standing room only the night Jack-ie appeared at Greenwood. Ten years after breaking the color bar-rier in baseball, he still had a powerful aurora of dignity about him, and he was an impressive, articulate speaker. In a surprisingly soft voice, Jackie shared only a few of the challenges and obstacles he had faced. He spent most of the time encouraging us to stay focused on getting our college degrees and urged us to take a stake in America's future. He stressed the need to be prepared to counter racial prejudice with dedication and excellent performance when the opportunity came. One of the most impressive things I remembered about Jackie Robinson was his absence of anger. I left the church that evening wondering if I could ever be that calm in the face of adversity. I had a long way to go, but I desperately wanted to be like Mr. Robinson.

A short time later, students were invited to Greenwood Baptist Church to meet and hear the young, oratorically-gifted minister, Dr. Martin Luther King, Jr. That night, every space in the church was filled, and the crowd overflowed into the hallways and onto the outside steps. Dr. King was accompanied by Rev. Ralph Abernathy, who also was part of the Montgomery movement. Rev. Abernathy did a great job introducing Dr. King, and the applause was deafening when he came to the podium. Dr. King was a very handsome man not much older than many of the students. His presence filled the room and made him appear larger than life. His melodic tone, faint southern drawl, and measured cadence were mesmerizing. He began, "Thank you, Rev. Abernathy for that fine introduction. Good evening my brothers and sisters. Rev. Abernathy and I are very pleased to be with you this evening. And I want to thank my good friend, Rev. Harvey, for allowing us to come and share with you the great success story of the Montgomery Bus Boycott. I am pleased to say a mighty change is taking place in Alabama, and soon it will be taking place all across America."

At these opening words, the church erupted into a rousing, standing ovation and responded similarly to every recounted detail of the boycott. Dr. King concluded by calling those present to action in their respective towns and communities. He stressed the imperative of non-violence in whatever we did, and cautioned us of the difficulty ahead for such a strategy. Some of his statements were etched in my mind that night.

"No man can ride your back if you walk upright." "It is not so much what you are called, but what you answer to." "Never allow anyone to cause you to hate; let love be the redeeming quality as we face the challenges ahead."

All three ministers greeted virtually every one who attended, and I impatiently awaited my turn. Looking into Dr. King's face and shaking his hand for the first time that night changed my life! Although he had a calm, quiet demeanor, I felt his burning passion that emanated from a deep well of determination and strength. Here was a man, who at an early age had overcome many obstacles and mastered the anger and bitterness that plagued me constantly. I would remember this initial meeting with Dr. King for the rest of my life and tried to put his words into action. I met or saw him again, and each time I stood just a little bit straighter because of it.

The months at Tuskegee passed quickly, and I headed home for Christmas. College was all I'd hoped for, and I was blessed to have done well the first semester. I did my best to present a "college student" image in appearance, behavior, and speech. My vocabulary had improved and even "Ma Deah" became "Mother." Setting an example for my younger brothers now fell upon my shoulders, and I was determined to succeed as Wilbert and Zella had done. Like Wilbert six years earlier, I proudly wore my AFROTC uniform while visiting family, friends, and the church. The two-week Christmas break ended much too soon. Before leaving, I called Mr. Stewart and Mr. Brown to let them know about my progress.

I successfully completed the first half of the year and registered for the second semester. My progress and learning curve continued to improve under the tutelage of outstanding teachers and professors. Their dedication inspired us, and our thirst for knowledge grew immeasurably. My appreciation for aviation also grew, and I succeeded in being selected the freshman Cadet of the Year. The award, Chicago Tribune Silver Medal, was pinned on by legendary Tuskegee Airman retired Colonel George "Spanky" Roberts who graduated in the first class in 1942. I also earned that flight in the T-33 jet trainer at Maxwell AFB.

Captain Hatch and I drove to Maxwell for my thrill of a lifetime. Strapping into the cockpit, taxiing, and takeoff were breathtaking experiences. Once airborne, He demonstrated various maneuvers and then allowed me to attempt them. They weren't pretty, but he said I did just fine. The flight ended after one and one-half hours, and we returned to Maxwell to land. At last, I experienced rolling and twirling around clouds in a picture-perfect blue sky. Thanks to Emmett Hatch, my determination to become an Air Force pilot was greatly solidified that day.

It was soon time to pack up and head home for the summer. It had been a great first year at Tuskegee, and my optimism was sky high. I looked forward to the years ahead with great excitement and expectations. I was pleased to give a good report to Mrs. Whitley for Mr. Stewart and to Mrs. Payne, my former counselor at Booker T. Washington High School. Mr. Freddie Pinesett had a job waiting for me with his construction crew, and I was "off to the races."

The summer was uneventful except Mother had slowed down considerably. The summer break ended and it was time to return to Tuskegee. Another "homeboy" from Booker T. Washington High School, Ben Wilkerson, suggested we take the train back to Tuskegee to avoid the dreaded bus. He got no argument from me. As we departed, Mother tried to put on a good face, but she looked unusually sad and troubled. She stood there and waved as the train pulled away and we lost sight of each other. I felt something was bothering her, but she had chosen not to share it with me. An unsettled feeling fell over me, and it dampened the excitement of my return to Tuskegee.

Adversity and Perseverance

My mother did her best to teach me that the Lord never puts more on us than we can bear. I was slow in accepting that truth in my young life and suffered much because of it. Even though I didn't acknowledge God, it was He who sustained me through the next few years at Tuskegee.

My second year of college ushered in a number of adverse circumstances that severely challenged my ability to persevere. Increased fees and tuition greeted students at the start of the 1958-1959 semester, and I had to take a job to supplement my scholarship from Mr. Stewart. In addition, my academic load included core math and engineering courses. Within a few weeks, I received news from home that Mother was hospitalized with an undetermined illness. Unlike other times, she failed to recover after a few weeks of bed rest. The pressures mounted, and I struggled with the heavy load of classes, work, and worries about my mother's persistent illness.

As the year progressed, I tried hard to keep up with my peers by taking a full academic schedule while working. Unfortunately, the load proved to be too great and I failed some classes. The news from home continued to worsen. My brother Wilbert struggled to get his feet on the ground in Detroit while my sister, Zella, was hard at work trying to finish at Grambling State. Mother was obliged to rely on neighbors, friends, and a few relatives for her care. Distressed over these circumstances, I considered leaving school to help her. I also wanted relief from the overload at school.

I visited the Dean of Engineering, Mr. Jefferson Davis, expecting to be encouraged about my proposed solution. He was a kind, respectable southern gentleman who showed sincere compassion for my plight. But his firm response surprised and disappointed me. He said, "Mr. Toliver, you can't really help your mother, and the worse thing you can do is quit school and go back to Shreveport. I know it's hard, but if you quit now, you will never come back. I believe your mother wants you to stay here and do the best you can to finish what you started. Quitting now would be a very bad mistake, but the choice is up to you!" My distress was too great then to fully appreciate God's hand in the tough advice given by Mr. Davis. His words hurt, but I heard the truth and wisdom in them. Quitting simply was not an option. I had to reach deeper for the strength to persevere.

I made it to Christmas and went home to visit Mother. She was confined to bed and was at the mercy of the Confederate Memorial Hospital in Shreveport for limited medical assistance available to poor people. The "Spirit of the Confederacy" still reigned supreme throughout the hospital; thus very little was done to diagnose my mother's problems and treat her accordingly. Zella, AW, and I did all we could during the Christmas break, but we had to turn to our neighbors for their continued kind support. Despite Mother's poor condition, she was adamant that Zella and I return to college. The Prices, Pinesetts, Shermans, Ryes, and other friends stood in the gap for us as we reluctantly departed. Most of these people had their own problems with finances and health, yet they faithfully cared for Mother during the weeks and months that followed.

A bright spot for me at Tuskegee was the AFROTC, especially the Drill Team. I enjoyed the mentoring and training under the Tuskegee Airmen, and appreciated the growing exposure to many aspects of aviation. The leadership of the detachment changed during the summer when two more renowned Tuskegee Airmen were assigned - Lieutenant Colonel Hubert L. "Hooks" Jones and Captain (Major

Select) Lawrence E. "Larry" Roberts. They arrived at a crucial time in my life as well as others. Both had served in the 477th Medium Bombardment Group and flew B-25s in the famed 332nd Fighter Group. These men were outstanding role models in bearing, character, and presence. Their dedication and passion for excellence were infused in us, and our personal and professional development received their keen attention almost on a daily basis. They were committed to producing the finest military officers in the Air Force. In Lieutenant Colonel Jones' opening remarks to us, he firmly stated, "When you leave Tuskegee, you will leave as an Air Force Officer, period! You will not indulge yourselves as 'Black officers' in the Air Force!"

The other officers and NCOs were replaced during the summer of 1958. Like their predecessors, the individuals provided superior leadership not only in the classrooms and on the drill field, but also through their personal lives. Everyone was a mentor and teacher, and we cadets were privileged to be molded and shaped by them into future Air Force leaders. It was an honor to follow in their footsteps and to be encouraged to go forth as "Second Generation" Tuskegee Airmen.

The families of the officers and NCOs were equally impressive. The lovely wives and beautiful, well-mannered children displayed healthy, loving relationships. The wives were obvious assets in the careers of their husbands. They too had suffered racial discrimination, insults, slights, and exclusion from social functions of the units or bases where they were assigned. Yet their dedication to their husband's careers and to nurturing their children was evident by the successes of their families. Having come from a broken home, I admired these families and made it a personal goal to have one like them some day.

The Air Force Officer's Qualifying Test (AFOQT) was administered to determine potential candidates for commissioning and pilot training after graduation. It came at a particularly stressful time for me, but I took it rather than wait another semester. This proved to be another poor decision. I passed the overall test, but failed to qualify for flight training. Consequently, I didn't make the cut for local orientation flight training under the renowned C. Alfred "Chief" Anderson. Chief Anderson was a pioneer aviator who was called to Tuskegee Institute to develop and lead the training program for the Tuskegee Airmen in 1941.

Missing the opportunity to be trained by and fly with Chief Anderson was a serious blow to my aspiration of becoming a pilot, and it bruised my ego and pride. Nevertheless, I was given the opportunity to command the AFROTC Drill Team for the spring semester and inducted into the Arnold Air Society. Arnold Air Society was named after WW II General Henry "Hap" Arnold, the only five-star General of the Army Air Corps.

The summer of 1959 was a troubled summer for the Tolivers and the Ryes. Mother was in and out of the hospital as her health continued to decline. A young Japanese doctor was assigned to her case and finally diagnosed the multiple diseases of lupus, a degenerative heart condition, rheumatoid arthritis, and deteriorating bones. Despite this grave diagnosis, the doctor committed to trying to help my mother and promised to stay on her case.

As Zella and I left the hospital that day, my mind flashed back fifteen years to Oxnard, California when I was a kid pretending to attack "Japs" with my P-38. Now, a compassionate Japanese doctor gave us hope. That young doctor apparently survived WWII Japan to ultimately attend a poor Black woman in Louisiana. These paradoxical events left me ashamed of my youthful, blind prejudice. It was too much to deal with then, but these events figured prominently in overcoming the vestiges of prejudice in my life years later.

In mid August, Zella's father-in-law, Mr. Rye, (AW's Father) suffered a massive stroke and was hospitalized in critical condition. Miraculously, he rallied and began a slow recovery. Despite my doubts, God heard my prayers and those of countless others. My awe and humility caused me to make a serious attempt to get right with Him. My efforts were weak, but I hoped He heard the sincere thanks from the depth of my heart. It took a while, but Mr. Rye recovered and lived another ten years. The summer ended and Zella returned to Grambling. My younger brother David and I headed for Tuskegee. He graduated from BTW in May and was accepted in the Work Scholarship Program at Tuskegee Institute.

The year 1959 -1960 was especially demanding due to work and more difficult academic courses. My new employer was another Tuskegee Airman, retired Lieutenant Colonel Douglas Jones, manager of the canteen services at the nearby VA Hospital. I was pleased to learn he was a native of Shreveport, Louisiana. Later, I met Doug's beautiful wife, Wilhelmina, and the rest of their household. Of particular note to me was the fact that Doug, his wife, four children, and mother-in-law all lived together as one happy family. Vernon, the older son, and I had attended high school together in Shreveport.

AFROTC continued to be a bright spot in my college experience. My personal and professional development resulted in my promotion to Cadet Major and commander of the Drill Team and Arnold Air Society. As the semester ended, David went to New Jersey to work. I attended summer school and continued working at the VA canteen. Later, I visited Mother who was now completely bed-ridden. During the summer, Zella graduated from Grambling State with honors and a degree in Education after just three years. She was hired by the Caddo Parish School District and immediately took over the full responsibility of caring for Mother.

In September, David and I returned to Tuskegee. I began my

fourth year still very concerned about Mother's health but hoped she would survive until I could join Zella and AW in providing for her welfare.

The fall of 1960 ushered in increased sit-ins and demonstrations by Black students all across the South. This bold movement had begun the year before when four freshmen from North Carolina Agricultural and Technical College sat down at a F. W. Woolworth luncheon counter in Greensboro, North Carolina. They were refused service but returned the next day with twenty-five more students. Two weeks later, similar movements spread to several cities, and within one year, these peaceful demonstrations took place in hundreds of cities across the South. Locally, Tuskegee students already boycotted the town by not patronizing businesses. Given the lack of restaurants, there was little cause for lunch counter sit-ins; however, the fervor to participate in this historic change pervaded the entire student body, and several students traveled to other cities to participate.

My passion for ROTC activities continued. Lieutenant Colonel Jones approved the initial charter and formation of the Angel Flight, a sister unit associated with Arnold Air Society. The advisor for the Angels was Mrs. Mattye Dwiggins from the Institute's Office of Administration. She was a beautiful young widow who frequently supported the AFROTC program. With her assistance, we completed recruiting, training, and outfitting the Angels in time for the annual football rivalry between Tuskegee Institute and Morehouse College from Atlanta. Held every October in Columbus, Georgia, it was a festive holiday for Black people in Alabama and Georgia areas as well as for soldiers from nearby Fort Benning Army Post. Prior to the football game, a parade through the city was scheduled featuring bands from Morehouse and Tuskegee, the cadet Air Force and Army drill teams, scores of high school bands, and other participants. As Commander of the Angel Flight and AFROTC Drill Team, I was charged with preparing both organizations for the Columbus events.

On game day, excitement filled the air at Tuskegee as the teams, students, and supporters boarded the buses for the trip to Georgia. Lieutenant Colonel "Hooks" Jones and Major Larry Roberts met me before we departed and cautioned me to be careful and to keep the groups under control. Given the civil rights demonstrations being waged across the South, they warned me about the hostile racial atmosphere likely to be encountered in Columbus. I felt honored to be entrusted with such a responsibility and promised to heed their instructions and warning. Colonel Jones, however, still looked uneasy as we drove away.

The throngs from Tuskegee and Morehouse arrived in Columbus to thousands of cheering Black and White people who lined the parade route through town. Historically, this gathering was trouble free; but that year an unusual number of policemen and state troopers were poised for any trouble from such a large gathering of Black college students. The students, however, simply had football and its festivities on their minds. Hundreds of participants were soon marshaled and the parade began about mid afternoon. The Angel Flight and AFROTC Drill Team were given a position near the front of the parade, and we received a rousing reception all along the route. Our drill team performed marvelously and everyone's spirits were sky high by the time we finished.

Following dinner, we proceeded to the stadium for the scheduled pre-game activities. We arrived at the stadium and took our assigned places. Since this was an "Army" town, the Army Drill Team was seated across the stadium with the visiting soldiers. Again, the presence of policemen and state troopers was disconcerting as they moved menacingly through the crowds. During the pre-game activities, I led my drill teams in cadence calls across the field to our school counterparts. A very large, mean-looking policeman came up and said we were making too much noise and to knock off the yelling. I spoke without thinking and said, "Officer, this is a football game; what do you expect us to do!" He became very agitated at my reply and spoke angrily, "We ain't gonna tolerate no student demonstrations here tonight, so you better quiet down!" I said okay and he moved on.

Across the field, the Army drill team was surrounded by cheering soldiers and they apparently didn't get similar "orders." As the challenges continued from the Army side, I thought it would be okay to answer with a silent wave of our helmets which we did without further visitation from the "friendly cop."

Just before the kickoff, I headed to the men's room, but in haste, I stumbled near the top of the stairs. I immediately felt a vice-grip on my arm and whirled instinctively pulling my arm away from an unexpected adversary. To my shock, it was the same policeman who had confronted me earlier, and this time he had a partner with him. I was immediately grabbed by these two and literally dragged from the stadium. Outraged, I protested, "Officer, why are you arresting me? What have I done?" Neither said a word as I was deposited in a police van already filled with about two dozen other individuals in disbelief and distress. One of these was the Assistant Dean of Men from Tuskegee. Apparently he tried to intercede on behalf of several students and was promptly arrested.

At the police station, we were unceremoniously herded into the booking station like cattle. The desk sergeant had a smirk on his face when he asked the arresting officer, "What's the charge on these Nigras?" One replied, "Drunk and disorderly conduct and resisting a police officer!" All of us were herded off to the holding cell. These horrendous events occurred before the football game began when most of us were cold sober.

The Assistant Dean identified himself as a college staff member and was allowed to make a phone call. The rest of us paced the floor as our frustration turned to outrage. My concern heightened when I remembered Lieutenant Colonel Jones' admonitions back at Tuskegee. Although innocent of the charge, I had failed, and the sickness in the pit of my stomach almost caused me to throw up. I gripped the bars of the cell until my hands hurt. Never had I felt so completely helpless.

After an eternity, a group of officers from Fort Benning and a lawyer arrived to plead the case for those who had been arrested at the stadium. The officials from the military and both colleges convinced the Columbus Police Department that arresting students inside the stadium was a bad move. Furthermore, the action of a few overzealous police officers would seriously damage the relationship between the "good people of Columbus" and Fort Benning. In the end, all charges were dropped "in good faith" and everyone was released. The football game had long since been concluded, so we loaded the awaiting buses and headed back to our respective campuses.

The outcome of the arrest in Columbus did little to quiet my troubled state as we drove back to Tuskegee. The emotional stress caused a physical ramification that left me in pain on the back seat of the bus. I kept thinking of having to face Lieutenant Colonel Jones, and the prospect was as frightening as my ailment. Worse yet, a heavy anchor of shame plunged me into a bottomless pit of remorse.

We arrived at the campus about 2:00 AM. My attempt at sleeping was an exercise in frustration. I dozed off for what seemed like only a few minutes when a loud knock woke me up at 6:00 AM. The normally affable Captain Cave stood there staring like a hound from hell. He tersely stated Lieutenant Colonel Jones wanted to see me immediately. I hurried across campus to the ROTC building while my mind swirled in vain for a plausible answer for my abysmal breach of trust. I was overcome with nausea and tremors as I approached this dreaded confrontation.

Colonel Jones, Major Roberts, and Captain Cave were waiting for me as I reported in the best military manner possible under the circumstances. My pitiful effort did little to mitigate the highly charged air in Colonel Jones' office. He was livid, and his hawk nose seemed to snort flames as he struggled to control his anger. "Toliver, what in the hell happened in Columbus? Didn't you hear a damn thing I said before you left?" His explosive words and demeanor were worse than I had anticipated; however, there was unexpected anguish in his voice. I tried to recount the incident as best I could while explaining my innocence, but there was a disquieting guilt gnawing at my gut. Colonel Jones disregarded my explanation and nailed me to the cross with his next question. "Why didn't you just sit down and shut up like the cop ordered you to do?"

There it was! That was my crime, my guilt, and my sin. I stood speechless as Colonel Jones glared at me and said, "Give me one good reason why you should be allowed to continue in ROTC?" Words escaped me like proverbial rats leaving a sinking ship! The obvious answer engulfed me like the flames of purgatory, but it would have been self-incriminating. I had to face what I tried so hard to deny. My failure to do what that policeman demanded was deeply rooted in hatred and rebellion against everything he represented. When he came over and "ordered" me to obey a totally unwarranted command, the ugly, festering wound that dated back to my early childhood was ripped open. My resistance reflected the unhealed scars left by the escape from the Ku Klux Klan early in my life, the ten years of evading trouble with the law in Shreveport, and countless incidents of police brutality and oppression of Blacks on a daily basis. Instantly, I bristled at that policeman. He read the hatred in my face during that encounter, but I didn't care. Instead, I deliberately drew the drill team into my "silent" protest. Enough was enough!

Without realizing it at the time, I had unconsciously "sat down at the lunch counter." Earlier, I spiritually joined the protesting students across the South. It was safe and easy to do since there were no lunch counters available for demonstrations in Tuskegee. The opportunity to show real commitment was unexpectedly presented at the stadium in Columbus. Unfortunately, my reaction had been swift and woefully careless. I realized my arrest could have been avoided had I been more alert and willing to heed Colonel Jones' warning. The truth burned within me; I didn't want to obey that unreasonable cop. As my mind blazed through these thoughts, I couldn't disguise the deep-seated rage that boiled deep in my soul. Finally, my choked-up answer to Colonel Jones simply was, "Sir, I have no excuse for my failure."

The consequence of my indiscretion was unleashed in a very painful way. After an interminable time, Colonel Jones said emphatically, "As of now, you are busted to cadet Second Lieutenant. You are relieved of your command of the drill team and as commander of Arnold Air Society, and you are not to engage in any activities with the Angel Flight!"

Each statement was a cold dagger through my heart, and I trembled as he continued. "You will report directly to Captain Cave for all Drill and Ceremony activities, and continue to attend your ROTC classes." His final words were, "I made my mind up to expel you from the Corps, but a couple of good words spoken on your behalf saved you. But Toliver, if you so much as hiccup out loud you will be summarily dismissed from this Detachment. Have I made myself clear?" My reply was barely audible, "Yes sir."

With that, Colonel Jones stormed from the room. I stood rigidly at attention during this whole ordeal. Thankfully, Major Roberts knew I was about to pass out, so he told me to stand at ease. He and Captain Cave spent the next few minutes reiterating the disappointment they all felt and how close I had come to being put out of the Corps. Nevertheless, Major Robert's face was calm, and he showed a measure of compassion I deeply appreciated. After further instructions about my duties for the foreseeable future, I was dismissed.

The devastation I felt walking back to my room was nearly unbearable, and I couldn't hold back the tears. I desperately needed a friend but it was too early to seek solace on that Saturday morning. I sat down on a bench nearby and wept over the prospect of my uncertain future. My hopes of becoming an Air Force officer and a pilot hung on a very slender thread, and I was uncertain of my ability to endure the sentence just imposed. Worst of all, I had no one to blame but myself. After a while, I gathered myself together and vowed to persevere somehow.

I went by my brother David's room and awakened him to tell him the news. As Cadet Second Lieutenant Dick Toliver, Cadet First Lieutenant David Toliver now outranked me. The look on his face let me know he took no pleasure in this incredible turn of events. David always looked up to me as his big brother and leader in our family. The uncertainty in his eyes that morning compounded my sadness, but it helped me realize a lot of people still depended upon me to succeed. I had to dig deep to find the courage to face my friends and peers, the shame, and the monumental task ahead. I remembered my mother's saying, "Nothing beats a failure but a 'try'!" Somehow, I had to overcome yet another pitfall in my life.

The following weeks and months were torturous, but the Christmas break finally came. David and I went home to spend a couple of weeks with the family. Our vacation was overshadowed by Mother's continued deteriorating health. Despite the medical help she received, her days were filled with discomfort and pain. With considerable effort, she tried to entertain a few visitors on Christmas Day, but paid the price that night with excruciating pain. There were no hospices in those days; consequently, many patients endured their suffering at home. Nevertheless, my sister Zella, other family members, and I did our best to make Mother as comfortable as possible. Her plight was dismal, but we couldn't bear to give up hope. David and I returned to college and prayed for a miracle.

January 1961 at Tuskegee began with the usual hectic flurry of preparations for the semester's final exams. Given the circumstances in our lives, I had a very difficult time concentrating. Efforts to study Friday night and all day Saturday had been fruitless as an inexplicable gloom fell over me. On Sunday morning, January 15th, I lay across my bed tossing and turning when the telephone rang in the hall. The sound jolted me upright with a suddenness that startled my room mate who cried, "Roomie, what's the matter? Man, what's wrong?" Before I could answer, someone yelled, "Toliver, telephone!" I stood shaking at the door. In some supernatural way, I knew that phone call was for me even before my name was called. I said, "Oh my God, my mother is dead!"

My brother-in-law, AW, was on the other end of the phone. "Brother, we lost Mother this morning about 11:00. She was admitted to the hospital late Friday, but the doctors couldn't save her. They said she was just too worn out."

Never in my life, before or since, has such news been so devastating. Forty-seven years later, the recollection of Mother's death is still difficult for me, and I consciously avoided this portion of the story for a long time. No words can adequately describe the day my mother died or the events that followed.

By nightfall, I had borrowed enough money to get David and me home. My boss, retired Lieutenant Colonel Doug Jones was our gracious benefactor. In the meantime, we received word that my brother, Wilbert, would be driving from Detroit, Michigan to pick us up. We reluctantly waited, but those few days were filled with indescribable grief. Wilbert finally arrived with his fiancé, Dorothy, and Ray, my younger brother who had been living in Detroit. We drove home in virtual silence, each of us locked in our own thoughts and grief. Over and over I silently implored, "God, how could you be so cruel? Why did you take Mother before any of us could make her life better? Couldn't you have made her well just one more time? Why did you make her suffer so? You know she trusted you with all her heart. Why did you do this to her and to us? What kind of God are you?"

Of course, God does not respond to such impertinent questions. Nor does He allow Himself to be challenged about the ways in which He delivers one from suffering. Once again, I had a very hard time believing in the God Mother prayed to so faithfully.

We drove through the cold, wintry night and arrived at 2907 Anna Street early the next morning. As we stepped onto the porch, the wind stirred the dust and leaves that had collected. The stark reality of Mother's death shook us when we entered the frigid, quiet emptiness that filled every room. The reality of her loss was so overwhelming that we left after only a few minutes. We simply couldn't endure the finality of her absence from a home that meant so much to all of us. Henceforth, 2907 Anna Street would never be the same again. The floodgate of tears broke as we closed the door and went to find Zella and AW.

My sister and her husband handled all the funeral and burial arrangements while awaiting our arrival. Zella and my Aunt Rosie, Mother's sister, notified the remaining sisters and brothers, cousins, and a host of relatives and friends. Most arrived during the week. We gathered back at 2907 Anna Street Saturday to receive visitors before the funeral on Sunday, January 22, 1961. The presence of family and friends eased the loneliness some, but staying through the night was an incredibly painful experience. Some relatives spent the night with us while Wilbert, David, and I tried to get a few hours of sleep sitting up in the living room. Every time my eyes closed, I saw a horrible picture of Mother's last days of suffering. Morning didn't come any too soon.

The sky was dark and overcast with a bone-chilling freezing rain the day of Mother's funeral. We dressed and drove to the funeral home for the family's viewing. Seeing her in that casket was the most painful experience of my life. It was made worse by witnessing the grief of my sisters and brothers. My youngest brother, Wendell, was just two days from being ten years old. Someone put their arms around him and allowed him to hide his tears. This sorrowful day remained in all of our minds for a very long time.

The funeral procession traveled to Goodwill Missionary Baptist Church for the services. Along the way, cars and people stopped out of respect. We were surprised upon our arrival by the number of cars and people that lined the streets and filled the church to standing room only. Despite the bad weather, scores of people gathered to pay their condolences. Along with the multitude of relatives, the church was filled with neighbors, friends, schoolmates and teachers, and many we didn't know had known Mother. Every space in the church was filled, and some had to leave because there simply was no space for them. We learned later they braved the cold and remained in their cars during the entire funeral.

The family requested a short service, but the pastor allowed many people to speak of this remarkable woman who clearly impacted more lives than we had ever known. They gave testimonials, confessions, praises, and confirmations that an "Angel" had been in our midst. While Mother left a host of grieving loved ones behind, she also forged a legacy of love, compassion, hard work, and selfless service to her family, friends, and neighbors. At one point, the outburst of grief was so unbearable I excused myself and went outside. As I sat down in our car, my mother's close friend, Eliza Long, got in beside me. I trembled as much from grief as the cold. I loved

Mother more than life and was not prepared for the immeasurable loss of her untimely death. I had persevered against many obstacles so that I could help with her care. Now she was gone and so was my purpose for striving.

The precious lady beside me perceived my deep, inexpressible suffering. She gently pulled me to her bosom and said, "Richard, I know what you are going through, but you are my son now. I am going to love you like my very own because that's what your mother would want me to do. I am going to love all of her children like my own." "Mother Eliza's" words helped assuage my pain, and I was grateful for the love and friendship that had existed between her and my mother. She kept her word until her own death forty-six years later.

The church service finally ended, and I rejoined my siblings in the procession to the grave site. The freezing rain began to fall again, yet people continued lining up for the procession. My mother's funeral was the largest ever held at Goodwill, and the cortege was several miles long. It was comforting to see so many people express their compassion and love. No other event in my life has surpassed that dreadful day. As I walked from the grave, some of my high school friends hugged and escorted me to the car. I wanted to express my appreciation but was simply unable to do so. Many years passed before I could thank some of them for their tremendous outpouring of love during the saddest time of my life.

The family gathered once more after the funeral to embrace and say good-bye. Grandpa Bob, Mother's father, admonished us to follow her great example. She truly had been a loving mother, daughter, sister, and friend to so many. We encouraged one another to continue our pursuits for a better life through education, faith, and hard work. Wilbert, his fiancé, Dorothy, David, and I left a few days later and returned to Tuskegee and Detroit. My sister, Arneater, and brother, Ray, moved into the house on Anna Street. Zella and AW resumed teaching school and working to raise their family. As we departed, we realized that Mother sacrificed her life for her seven children. She died while still trapped in an earthly cage of disappointment, poverty, and physical suffering. But the Lord freed her soul from trials and tribulations. Death was not victorious here. Mother ascended into Heaven as *An Uncaged Eagle*!

The spring semester had begun when David and I arrived back at Tuskegee. David completed his final exams before we left, so he was able to register. My situation was very different. My performance in some of the engineering courses was less than satisfactory. Furthermore, the school had recently hired Dr. Z. W. Dybczak, the new Dean of Engineering, to improve both the quality of the program and the students. The immediate goal was to gain accreditation and to ensure Tuskegee's engineering graduates could compete successfully upon graduation. Dr. Dybczak insisted all students be reevaluated regarding their commitment and potential for continuing in the School of Engineering. Accordingly, I was called before him and his faculty committee. I hadn't met Dr. Dybczak, but he apparently knew of my misadventure in Columbus and the recent loss of my mother.

I was committed to graduating in engineering, but my academic performance was sporadic at best. When work and personal distractions were lessened, I demonstrated the ability to do well. After a critical assessment of the likelihood of my success, Dr. Dybczak made a momentous decision that allowed me to continue. If I rededicated myself to moving on with my life, he would permit me to receive "Incomplete" or "(I)" grades for the entire previous semester. However, I would have to structure my class load to include courses from both the current and previous semester. This required approximately two more years of dedication and hard work, and there would be no latitude for failure. I gratefully welcomed this opportunity and promised Dean Dybczak he would not be sorry. This man literally saved my life and gave me a chance to have a future. Years later I learned of his incredible journey to Tuskegee in 1960 to rescue others and me from academic failure or mediocrity.

The weeks ahead were indeed challenging, and I continued to struggle with the memory of Mother. Often, her face appeared in my mind, and many fitful nights were filled with visions of her suffering. We had exchanged letters in the past, and one day, I remembered the last letter she wrote me for my 22nd birthday, October 30, 1960. With trembling hands, I decided to read it again. It read:

"Hi There You Sweet Son,

How is everything? Fine I trust and hope. Yes, I received all your letters, and...Do forgive me for not answering sooner. I haven't been doing well...yet I've been trying to hold on somehow...I am overcoming by the help of God. I am not able to write much because of the conditions of my painful hands, but I want you to know that I am really and truly proud of you. I really appreciate the sweet consoling words from you. It means so much... Sure, I believe I can depend on you.

I hope you had a very happy birthday. I am saying it very late, but it's real. Happy Birthday, Dear Richard, and many, many more returns. May God forever surround you with His blessings...

I sit alone...praying tearfully for all of you daily... because you need Him while on the jobs, the school rooms, in your hearts and minds, and down life's highway...

...My time is running out, and thanks for yours. Do write soon and let me know the happenings... All the neighbors are well and extend best regards to you. Please remember that Mother still loves her sons...remember, when the sun pulls her curtains and pins them with the stars, I am your Mother"

I imagined hearing Mother's voice rising above her suffering. Slowly, I sensed her presence and could almost hear her say, "Richard, just keep facing the sun and the shadows will fall behind you. I know you did all you could for me, but now it's time to complete the race before you. Remember, it's not the one who runs the fastest in the race, but the one who holds out to the finish line. Also remember, nothing beats a failure but a 'try'." I had heard those words so many times. Now they came back with a resounding consolation to my heart. For the first time since Mother's death, I believed I could make it.

Following my mother's death, the Lord placed several people in my life to help me move forward. One of these was Mrs. Mattye Dwiggins who became a personal friend and a compassionate supporter. She hired me on occasions as a baby-sitter for her three young sons and to do chores around her home. I enjoyed these getaways from campus, plus Mattye paid me very handsomely.

In the early spring of 1961, I was given the task of leading the team that planned and executed the annual ROTC Ball. This festive event was an occasion for Detachment 15 officers and NCOs to teach cadets some of the social graces that future officers and their ladies needed to know. It was an opportunity for me to demonstrate my leadership ability despite my continued probationary status.

The cadets and their ladies made quite a splash the night of the Ball. The hard work of our team paid off. I had a lovely date but was not in the mood for revelry. I left her with friends and went outside to be alone for a while. As I sat reflecting on the past months, a hand grasped my shoulder and I looked up into the face of Lieutenant Colonel Jones. I rose quickly to attention, but he said, "Sit down, Toliver! Sit down." He had not spoken to me in over six months, and I felt uneasy about this unexpected encounter. His tone and expression, however, was surprisingly calm and soft. He said, "I guess you think I've been pretty hard on you these past months, don't you?" Before I could answer, he continued, "You and your brother have had things pretty rough, but I hope you've learned from this experience that life is not fair."

I relaxed a bit as he continued to speak, "Sometimes you have to tighten your belt and face very difficult situations, but if you want to succeed in life, you can't quit just because things get tough." I wanted to tell him I hadn't quit. Instead, I wisely said, "Yes, sir." His next words caught me totally by surprise. "Toliver, I am proud of the way you've handled your difficulties these past months, but now it's time you start preparing for summer camp. Why don't you come see me next week and let's talk about getting your class ready for summer camp?" I did jump up this time and almost hugged this man who, like Dean Dybczak, had just given me a second chance for my future. Barely able to contain myself, I blurted, "Yes sir! Yes, sir! Thank you, sir!"

Colonel Jones smiled warmly and walked back inside. For the first time in a long while, I felt overwhelming joy. Once again, I saw Mother's face, and this time she was smiling. I whispered softly, "Mother, I love you and miss you terribly, but I am going to make it. Thanks for your love, prayers, and confidence in me. You won't be sorry!" I lingered a while before rejoining the merrymaking inside. I felt like dancing and went to find my date and got out on the floor. It was a great night after all.

I went to see Colonel Jones the following week and received instructions for a rigorous program to get my peers and myself ready for summer camp. Our preparations included rigorous physical fitness training, drill and ceremonies, human relations, and adaptability to stress. The latter emphasized preparation for the prevailing racial climate in 1961 due to sit-ins and demonstrations of Black students nationwide. We had a dress rehearsal by late May and looked forward to the events ahead. The AFROTC summer camps were scheduled at Air Force bases all across the country. Tuskegee cadets would compete with cadets from universities and colleges nationwide.

The semester ended, and I took a summer course and worked until it was time for me to go to Reese AFB in Lubbock, Texas. Two other Tuskegee cadets, Jesse Averhart, Fred Grimes, and I arrived in the blistering heat of west Texas in mid July. As anticipated, we had our work cut out for us as racial bias and tension immediately met us head on. It was prevalent among the cadets from the South, on the base, and among some of the officers in the camp. Thankfully, Lieutenant Colonel Jones prepared us for this, so we were not overly deterred.

Only two other Black cadets were in our group of about 100 cadets, and each was assigned to a different unit. We rarely had a chance to talk with one another but used the "thumbs up" signal when passing to encourage each other. The weeks went quickly and included drill and ceremonies, base familiarization training, orientation flights, survival training, and group dynamics. As the weeks wound down, I was assigned to prepare a squad of cadets for drill competition and was selected to participate on the track team for our group. My drill team received very high marks during the unit competition, and I won the top award for the physical fitness obstacle course. Despite these accomplishments, I received an overall "Satisfactory" for the camp. Jesse and Fred were rated similarly, but the other Black cadet in our group was recommended for dismissal from the ROTC program.

Upon returning to Tuskegee, we discovered several of our peers faired far worse than the three of us at Lubbock. Several received recommendations for elimination from ROTC. These cadets were top performers at Tuskegee, yet they received these ratings regardless of the base to which they were assigned. These rating officers appeared to be predisposed to eliminate as many Black cadets as possible in 1961. Because of the widespread poor appraisals, Colonel Jones and Major Roberts went to Air Force ROTC Headquarters at Maxwell AFB, Alabama to petition our cases. Fortunately, they were successful. All the senior cadets at Tuskegee were allowed to continue in the program. They graduated and received their commissions as Second Lieutenants in the Air Force.

Colonel Jones and Major Roberts were reassigned later that summer, and a new cadre of officers and NCOs arrived to lead Detachment 15. Those two men were powerful role models for not only the cadets but for students and faculty alike. The impact of their mentoring and teaching persisted for many years. They helped me weather the personal storm of adversity I faced during their tenure at Tuskegee. In particular, the probationary status they imposed following my arrest in Columbus, Georgia prepared me for many encounters in my life and subsequent career. They drilled in me the reality that life is not fair and caused me to accept that early in my life. Most were likely to encounter injustices and roadblocks in their lives and careers. Quitting or whining, however, were not options for those who wanted to succeed. I thank God today for the late Hooks Jones and Larry Roberts. They were two remarkable *Uncaged Eagles* who had a tremendous and lasting impact on my life.

The new Professor of Air Science was Lieutenant Colonel George L. Knox, another original Tuskegee Airman and member of the third class to graduate in 1942. The new Commandant of Cadets was Captain James Timothy Boddie, Jr., a hotshot fighter pilot and graduate of Howard University. While I was home, he notified me of my promotion to Cadet Colonel and selection as Commander of the Cadet Corps for the fall semester of 1961-1962. I was elated over this honor and humbled by the responsibility as I began my fifth year at Tuskegee. Leading the Cadet Corps was the crowning glory of my ROTC experience and as a student at Tuskegee.

Free of family concerns back home or other personal commitments, I was very determined to make the most of the renewed opportunity. I kept my promise and let Mr. Stewart, my benefactor, know of my progress at Tuskegee. Mrs. Whitley responded with encouraging letters. Mr. Stewart went beyond his initial commitment and provided financial support through my fifth year of college. Thus, my excitement and anticipation of the final phase of college was sky high.

The Love of My life

The warm, respectful relationship between Captain Boddie and me began immediately and lasted for the rest of our lives. As Cadet Corps Commander, I was considered a "partner" with him in leading the cadets. Per his request, I reported two weeks early to prepare for the semester and to brief the freshmen class. We appeared together on the main campus gazebo to brief new students and potential cadets for the corps. Captain Boddie wore his flight suit, and I wore my summer uniform adorned with my cadet decorations. We were quite a dashing pair to the fifty to sixty students who gathered to hear our speeches.

A young lady near the back of the crowd caught my attention, and I observed her for the duration of the presentations. Somehow she looked familiar, so I made my way to her after the completion of the program. The allure of this young woman was even more startling up close. She was quite attractive, articulate, and surprisingly at ease in responding to my questions. Her easy smile accentuated the soft radiance of her face and twinkling brown eyes. I was impressed with her calmness and poise and thought, "This freshman really has her act together!" I asked her to join the group of students invited for refreshments at the nearby stores called the "Block." As we walked along, I learned Margaret Ann Hairston, called "Peggy," was from Baltimore, Maryland. Her father had read about Booker T. Washington and George Washington Carver and thought it would be a great experience for her to attend this famous college. Her mother traveled with her and was staying at Dorothy Hall, the campus hotel. "Wow! Some father!" I thought.

The time passed quickly, and Peggy graciously excused herself to have dinner with her mother. I felt the urge to ask her to stay longer but knew it would be inappropriate. Furthermore, how would it look for an "upperclassman" to appear to be moonstruck by a freshman student on her first day at Tuskegee? My mind spoke to me: "Whoa, boy! Get a grip on yourself. You don't have time to dally in activities that will take your mind off the task at hand. Keep your eye on the real target!"

My studies and job as Cadet Corps Commander kept me very busy for the next few weeks. My focus was interrupted one day when I met Peggy on campus. Again, I had the strange feeling we had met before Tuskegee, but it could not be so. Yet, just walking and talking with her aroused emotions that were unsettling. Peggy apparently had no similar feelings for me, but her friendliness drew me to her just the same. I trashed my pride and asked if I could call upon her sometime, and she said yes. My heart skipped as we parted, and I felt silly for being excited over this teenager who possessed the poise of a lady. Despite my busy schedule, I visited Peggy occasionally and did my best to impress her while trying to maintain the aloofness expected of an upperclassman.

Late one evening in October, my self-inflated ego was unceremoniously trounced. Leaving the main academic building at 10:00 PM, I saw Peggy coming down the hall. Thinking she had busted the 9:00 PM curfew for freshmen women, I blurted out, "What are doing here? You were supposed to be in your dorm an hour ago!" Looking somewhat amused, she said, "I am coming from class." Realizing the only possible answer, I felt foolish asking the next obvious question, "What class are you taking?" "Education 500," she said. I repeated,

"Education 500, that's a grad course!" With a bit of "Gotcha" in her voice she said, "Yes it is. I am a grad student!" With that she walked away leaving me with my mouth opened large enough to stuff in both feet as well as my crumbled self image. For nearly two months I had assumed Peggy to be a freshman student, and now I felt like an absolute horse's end.

Several weeks passed before I gathered enough courage to visit Peggy again. I had acted like an arrogant snob while this attractive, intelligent young woman was very much an adult. My feelings for her were unabashed, and I was determined to win her affections somehow. She surprised me again with her pleasure and warmth in seeing me. We continued seeing each other over the next several weeks, but she kept me at arms length.

Peggy had earned a Bachelor of Arts degree in English in 1960 at Morgan State University in Baltimore, Maryland. She expected to earn her Master's Degree in Education at Tuskegee Institute by mid-summer of 1962. Due to her adventurous spirit and thirst for knowledge, her father promised to send her to study in France after she finished at Tuskegee. When she spoke of this, I thought, "Wow! Who is this man?" I knew Black men who cared for their children, but I had never heard of one with such a vision for his child and who had the resources to commit to it. I looked forward to meeting Mr. Hairston one day.

Peggy and I had a lot in common, especially our aspirations to travel and to experience other cultures of the world. I was especially impressed by her depth and breadth of knowledge of many subjects. She was well versed in world history, art, music, and Greek mythology and often shared interesting vignettes with me. I felt our relationship was finally making progress when Peggy asked if she could give me the pet name "Dick" instead of Richard. I didn't care at all for Dick, but from that day on I became Dick Toliver.

One night, my "foot-in-mouth" disease flared up again. Peggy was sharing her excitement about the planned trip to Paris when I abruptly said, "Let me take you to Paris." She laughed and said, "How on earth are you going to do that?" I could hardly believe my own ears when I replied, "Marry me, and I'll take you to Paris, London, Rome, and anywhere else in the world you want to go!"

The seriousness of my reply caused Peggy to sit back for a few moments, and she looked at me in disbelief. I sincerely meant what I said. With a total loss of self control, I had blurted out what had been building in my heart for weeks. Despite the absence of even a kiss or an intimate embrace, I had fallen in love with Peggy and wanted to marry her. I had never said such a thing to any girl friend of my past, nor did I know then that true love required no physical confirmation.

Peggy laughed nervously and spoke haltingly, "Dick, you can't possibly mean that. You hardly know me, and you have so much planned for your life, and so do I." Undeterred, I said emphatically, "Then let's do it together!" Peggy seemed stunned by such an unromantic proposal, and she did her best to brush it off. Her response, however, lacked sufficient conviction to defuse the charged air between us. Neither of us spoke until the silence became painfully awkward. Since I had swept us into these deep emotional waters, I tried to get us back on solid ground. With a less convincing laugh, I said, "I surprised you, didn't I? Let's put the thought on the back burner for the time being. I realize you need to know me better, so please give me time to prove myself to you."

Peggy appeared relieved for the moment, and was ready to say good night. We did so with a bit of trepidation and uncertainty about our yet undefined relationship. On the way home, I replayed the scene in my mind and tried to deny the persistent conclusion. I was definitely in love with Peggy, but realized getting her to reciprocate would be another hill to climb. Preoccupied with showcasing my attributes, I failed to appreciate the source of Peggy's character and strength. She was a committed and devout Christian who took very seriously the Biblical caution about being unequally yoked. Unfortunately, my commitment to Christianity was weak. In addition, I had shown flashes of anger and hardness that made Peggy back away. Then I could only offer her a promise of a great future. Hopefully, she was impressed by my determination and perseverance in the face of adversity.

The Christmas season was soon upon us. As usual, the students' excitement of going home for the holidays filled the campus. This was my first Christmas since Mother died, so I elected to stay and work during the holidays. Peggy's father sent her a plane ticket, and she planned to fly out of Atlanta for Baltimore. We said goodbye without an embrace, kiss, or any words to suggest we were in a serious relationship. I desperately wanted to hold her close and tell her how much I loved her and would miss her. We did, however, agree to write each other during the break.

The campus was a dreary, lonely place for the few students who stayed on as caretakers. To make matters worse, we ate our meals in the basement cafeteria at the hospital. The loss of Mother earlier in the year and Peggy's absence made Christmas 1961 the most miserable I have ever experienced before or since. Just when my feelings couldn't get any worse, a letter arrived from Peggy. I was excited but decided to wait until work was over for the day before reading the much anticipated mail. When I did open the letter, Peggy's words were like a cold knife through my heart. In short, she wanted to retreat from our budding relationship and just be "friends." She thought I was a wonderful guy, but the plans for her life didn't include a permanent relationship at this time. She hoped we could still be friends upon her return. I cannot describe the emotional hell I descended into for the remainder of the holidays. I was a zombie without awareness or responses to anything around me. My emotions were a canker of anger, bitterness, despair, and loneliness. Self-pity played havoc with my psyche, but somehow I managed to gather myself together for the New Year. Peggy's rejection brought me to my knees, but I was responsible for putting my heart at risk. I resolved to concentrate on my studies, finish school, join the Air Force, and never, ever fall in love again!

January passed like a blur. I successfully completed my exams and passed the baton to my friend and new Cadet Corps Commander. I didn't visit Peggy and fully intended to squash my feelings for her. But who can control hearts when lives are predestined to be joined? Yielding to fate, I showed up at Peggy's dormitory one evening in late January 1962. It proved to be the turning point of our lives.

Peggy had one more surprise for me. She bounded into the lounge smiling and acting like I was a long-lost friend. Her joy at seeing me was as real as my confusion. I strained to keep myself under control as she grabbed my hands and smiled at me with a fire in her eyes I had not seen before. Cautiously, I brought up the infamous letter, and she just waved it off and said, "Oh Dick, please forget about that!" Remembering what that letter put me through, I protested. Peggy suddenly embraced me and kissed me in mid sentence. Forty-seven years have passed since that moment. Still I cannot find words to fully describe the emotional explosion and powerful awakening of all my senses. Nor can I describe the sweetness of Peggy's love expressed in that first embrace and tender kiss.

For a long time, we sat looking at each other. We embraced, held hands, kissed, and savored every moment. Without knowing it, our hearts were inextricably united by a power not yet realized by either of us. We tried to express ourselves, but words were no longer necessary. It became apparent why Peggy seemed so familiar to me the first day I met her. She was the one that often escaped in my dreams. Many years later, we came to understand that when God made each of us, He had the other in mind. Then, we were about to act out the most extraordinary, improbable, and intense year of our young lives.

After our "reunion" in January, the relationship between Peggy and me became stronger than anything we had ever experienced. We wanted to get married right away and begin our lives together despite a serious lack of resources to do so. I sought advice from Captain Tim Boddie and Staff Sergeant Frank Cyrus of the ROTC detachment who by then were my very close friends and confidants. Tim had been smitten by the beautiful Mattye Dwiggins, and both were sympathetic to our state of minds. Frank's sage counsel guided me through evaluating the "assets" versus "liabilities" of a decision to get married before graduation. I recalled the teaching of Mother: "Where there is a will, there's a way!" With that in mind, I put my skills and ingenuity to work, secured a place to live, revised my academic schedule, and negotiated a work contract with Tuskegee Institute for the coming summer. My adrenalin and motivation were running on all cylinders. Twelve months later, Peggy and I were married, earned our respective degrees, and had our first child!

Peggy and I were married in the parsonage of Greenwood Baptist Church by Reverend Harvey, the pastor who earlier had invited Dr. Martin Luther King, Jr. to Tuskegee. It was a small wedding attended by a few of our friends, but it didn't lack the intensity and excitement of a royal wedding. Peggy's father refused to come to what he called the "damned South," but he did send his wife, Elsie. At first sight, she embraced me, called me son, and kissed me. That day, another relationship with lasting ramifications was born.

Couples who have stood the test of time may tell you the consummation of marriage between two young lovers can never be adequately described. Perhaps no attempt should be made to do so. Yet, given the humble circumstances of our marriage, I attest to the fulfillment on our wedding night that far surpassed our expectations. No king or queen, rich or poor, famous or lowly couple could have experienced more exquisite pleasure than we did. Our small apartment might as well have been the Taj Mahal, New York's Waldorf Astoria, or a castle by the sea. Our marriage truly had been made in heaven, and the joy on our wedding night was etched in our hearts and minds forever. On that night, we surrendered to each other parts of us that had never before been touched. Those precious memories sustained us as we traveled through the event-filled years that followed.

As Peggy and I began our lives together, we were called to lend a helping hand to Delores Long, my childhood friend. She had left the Catholic Convent a year earlier after dedicating eight years of service to the church. As time passed, Delores realized the decision to enter the Convent was more for the family and church than for her. Still a devout Catholic, she wanted to rejoin her family and eventually teach young children. I had met with the Long family after finishing AFROTC Summer Camp a year earlier and encouraged them to let Delores apply for admission to Tuskegee Institute. The family didn't have the money to do so, but the work scholarship program still existed. They managed to gather enough funds to allow Delores to test the waters the summer of 1962. Still recovering from life in the convent, she faced an uphill battle, academically and emotionally. My dear wife took Delores under her wing and became a friend, sister, and tutor. With a determined effort, Delores successfully completed summer school. She secured a federal loan for fall tuition but needed a place to stay. Peggy and I rose to the occasion and invited her to move into our small apartment for the fall semester. We truly became a family of three.

Our daughter, Gail Denise, was born at John A. Andrew Hospital a few days before I graduated. Becoming parents of a beautiful, precious little girl was the crowning glory of the love between Peggy and me. Gail was the exclamation point of God's grace and mercy in our lives. Dr. Joseph R. Mitchell, the first Black obstetrician in the state of Alabama, was our doctor. He was a God-send to Tuskegee and touched the lives of many during his twenty-four years of dedicated service. Through the common thread of life, Dr. Mitchell was linked to scores of families who passed through or lived in Tuskegee. He delivered the babies of Lieutenant Colonel and Mrs. Bill Campbell, Major and Mrs. Larry Roberts, and Captain and Mrs. Tim Boddie. Others included singer Lionel Richie; Robin Roberts, co-anchor of Good Morning America; and Patti Grace Jones-Smith, formerly the highest ranking Black woman in the Federal Aviation Administration and the daughter of the late Lieutenant Colonel Douglas and Wilhelmina Jones.

One week after Gail's birth, I was commissioned a Second Lieutenant in the United States Air Force. My good friend, Captain Boddie did the honors of pinning on my bars and swearing me in before the entire cadet corps. Nearly sixteen years had passed since I left my idyllic life in California. Five and one-half of those years were spent at Tuskegee. At last, the first major race in my life had been completed, but I didn't reach this goal on my own. Many people entered my life, opened doors, and helped me achieve this major milestone. Their impact in shaping me can never be measured. Some were in my life ever so fleetingly; others remained throughout; several made a difference unknowingly; a few touched me intimately; but all affected me forever. Peggy and I were about to embark upon the road of our lives with anticipation and excitement. There was just one more thing I needed to do before departing for my first Air Force assignment – visit Shreveport to see Mr. Stewart and my family.

The day after becoming a Second Lieutenant, I boarded the bus for Shreveport. I wore my new uniform out of pride but also to provide a safeguard against racial discrimination. Thanks to the influence of the U.S. Supreme Court, civil rights activists, and the Freedom Riders, the Interstate Commerce Commission in 1962 banned racial discrimination on buses and in bus stations. This was my first bus trip since the ban, and I intended to exercise my rights during the trip home. That was one of the most ill-advised decisions of my life.

The first major stop was Jackson, Mississippi. The "White" and "Colored" signs were still posted at the entrances of the waiting rooms, so the Black and White passengers entered as they normally did. I entered the White section of the bus station and went to the restroom. I immediately encountered a sea of hate stares, but the shock of my action enabled me to finish my business and return to the coffee counter. I ordered a cup of coffee with as firm a voice as possible and sat down to drink it. A huge, red-faced cop entered the waiting room and glared at me with utter contempt. I tried to appear calm but lost the battle. My hands began to shake so hard the cup rattled in the saucer, and I wasted a few drops on my uniform. I remembered Emmet Till, a 14-year old Black teenager from Chicago, had been murdered in Mississippi in 1955 and the perpetrators got off scoot-free. Suddenly, exercising my civil rights was not so important, and I prayed to get back safely on the bus and depart unscathed. God takes care of the poor folks, children, and fools. That night, He took care of me, and I escaped what could have been the consequences of a grave mistake. The bus driver and passengers finally reloaded the bus while giving me incredulous stares. As the bus drove away, I kept hoping the witnesses to this "bold assertion of my civil rights" remained in shock long enough for us to cross the Mississippi River. To this day, I thank God for allowing the bus safe passage across the Stateline.

My visit home was greeted by congratulations and celebrations in my old neighborhood, the church, and high school. The visit to Mr. Stewart's office was especially enjoyable and gratifying. I had my uniform freshly pressed, my shoes spit-shined, and entered his office with my best military bearing. Mrs. Bebe Whitley, Mr. Stewart's executive assistant, met me at the door and struggled to keep from hugging me. The entire office gathered around to congratulate me, and their pride was real. I sincerely thanked Mr. Stewart, Mrs. Whitley, and everybody for their encouragement and support over the past five years. It was an emotional and heart-warming visit that I never forgot. When I departed, Mr. Stewart asked me to keep in touch and stated he was confident of my future. The desire to make him continually proud was deeply rooted in my heart.

I returned to Tuskegee to complete the task of securing continued room and board for Delores. God provided the answer and underscored His persistent intervention in our lives at crucial times. My other childhood friend, AC Washington, and his wife, Almeta, now lived in Tuskegee while he pursued a Master's Degree in Science. After a brief discussion, AC and "Meta" moved into our apartment so that Delores could complete her first year of college. Their gracious effort helped Delores go on to graduate with a degree in Education. She returned to Shreveport and taught middle-school students for twenty-five years. AC completed his Master's degree and later earned a Doctor of Philosophy Degree in Biochemistry at the Illinois Institute of Technology, Chicago, Illinois.

As I prepared to leave for Eglin AFB, I reflected on my life at Tuskegee Institute. It would always be a special place for me, and leaving was bitter-sweet. The transformation in me was beyond my expectations. It was here I looked into the mirror and found the courage to accept who I was. Many great hurdles and pitfalls were overcome. Lifetime friendships began. At Tuskegee Institute, my true manhood emerged through the love of my wife and the birth of our first child. Here the foundation of knowledge was established from which to launch the boundless pursuit of wisdom. I had waited over eighteen years to become a "soldier" in the U.S. armed forces. Now I was ready to serve and vowed to do everything possible for the betterment of my family and my country.

PART TWO

VICTORY OVER ADVERSITY

CHAPTER FIVE

THE WILD BLUE YONDER

I received an initial duty assignment to the Air Force Flight Test Center, Edwards AFB, California and was ecstatic for a number of reasons. Edwards AFB was my first assignment choice; I would be returning to California, my long lost "paradise"; the Flight Test Center was an ideal assignment for a young engineering graduate; and I could introduce Peggy and Gail to many of my relatives residing throughout California. It was too good to be true. A month before I graduated, my orders were changed to Eglin AFB, Florida, with a reporting date of February 13, 1963. Eglin was my second choice and was located in northwest Florida. Given its location, we decided to keep Peggy and the baby at Tuskegee while I went ahead to find a place for us to stay.

I boarded the Greyhound bus at Tuskegee the evening before my official reporting date. The road to Eglin was a winding two-lane highway through the forest and small towns of southern Alabama and Florida. As usual, the small bus depots or gas stations had no decent facilities for "Colored" passengers, so the trip was very uncomfortable. There was some consolation, however. The trip was short, and it most probably would be my last bus trip through the south. I arrived at midnight in the small town of Niceville, Florida near Eglin AFB and took a taxi to the base.

I checked in, got a room in the Bachelor Officer's Quarters (BOQ), and breathed a sigh of relief for an uneventful trip. My sleep was shattered early the next morning by the roaring sounds of jet fighters taking off seemingly from just outside my room. I dressed and went outside and discovered the runway was less than two miles away. The ramp was filled with jets being serviced by maintenance troops. The nearby buildings, hangars, and ramp were part of Eglin's Flight Test Center, the major activity of the main base. I didn't mind the noise and was thrilled to be on an Air Force base with jet fighters flying overhead. Highly energized, I walked to the Officer's Club (O'Club) for my first breakfast as an officer on active duty. Eglin was crucial to our nation's defense, and I felt good to be here on the first day of the rest of my life!

My orders required me to report to the Directorate of Armament Division, Detachment 4 (Det 4), Aeronautical Systems Division. Det 4 was subordinate to Headquarters Air Force Systems Command, Wright-Patterson AFB, Ohio and was located at Eglin. Before departing for the O'Club, I took a final look at myself in the mirror to be sure I would make the best possible first impression. Confident I could pass for a "poster boy", I arrived at my duty station shortly after 9:00 AM. The first person I met was a large, friendly captain named Roger Flocken. He heard Det 4 was getting a new officer, but appeared quite surprised to see who it was. The redhead secretary in the outer office was equally surprised. Both of them stumbled through greeting me while trying to collect themselves. Amused by this initial encounter, I wondered what the rest of the day would be like.

Roger was my assigned sponsor and orientation officer. He inquired about my billeting arrangements, housing and transportation requirements, and other needs. He seemed genuinely sincere in helping me get settled as soon as possible. Roger told me about Det 4 and its people until it was time to meet the boss. Nearly 100 people were assigned to Det 4, of which about two dozen were military. All others were civilians with multidisciplinary experience in weapons development, and most had served in either WW II or the Korean War.

The news of my arrival and ethnicity spread quickly throughout the office, and each person I met seemed curious and surprised. Without meaning to do so, I set the commander back in his chair with a sharp, heeling-clicking salute as I reported for duty. Lieutenant Colonel Nobel E. Brown, a soft-spoken man, smiled appreciatively, returned my salute, and welcomed me. He introduced me to his deputy, a civilian named Ed Witkowski and Miss Flo Donaldson, the executive secretary of the office.

Colonel Brown asked me about Tuskegee and my college experience. I proudly gave him a verbal resume and threw in my tutelage under the Tuskegee Airmen for good measure. Later I learned he flew bombers in WW II and probably knew about the Airmen. Colonel Brown told me about the mission of the office and about some of the work being done. He advised me I would be the understudy of civilian project leaders in the Gun Development section until I got up to speed. I would then be assigned my own project. He then asked Captain Flocken to introduce me to the rest of the office and take me next door to meet the Detachment Commander.

As we walked to the other offices, Roger commented that my military bearing and salute was the sharpest he had ever seen. He told me he was also a ROTC grad from the University of Illinois, but he couldn't ever remember being that sharp. I appreciated the immediate feedback and decided to relax my "drill field" image a bit. Roger added I was also the first and only Black person assigned to the detachment. I gathered that much from the initial reception thus far. Being the first Black among White people didn't bother me.

What mattered most was equal treatment and recognition for the top performance I intended to render.

The next office was comprised of four middle-age, distinguished looking civilians who were gun experts. The walls and desks were covered with pictures or models of various guns installed in the latest jet fighters or bombers. During the introductions, each shared a bit about themselves and briefly told me about their current projects. Bill Aumen and Joe Fagerstrom were from the North and worked on the AR-15 (forerunner to the M-16 rifle) and 7.62mm guns. Earl Wilson and Joe McKimmey were Southerners and were experts on the larger guns including the Caliber-50 machine gun, 20mm cannon, and M-61 Gattling Gun. I immediately appreciated their friendly attitudes, expertise, and offer to help get me up to speed. They made me feel very welcome, and I looked forward to learning more about their projects.

Colonel Ben F. Hardaway, the Det 4 commander, was an impressive "Steve Canyon" type with command pilot wings and a ram-rod straight, six-foot stature. He stood up to return my salute and seemed pleased I reported in a military manner. He was also a veteran of WW II and the Korean War. I later learned he was a West Point graduate who insisted his officers maintain their military bearing and behavior despite the predominance of civilians in the detachment. Score one for my Tuskegee training. The rest of the people gave me a warm and sincere reception, but most seemed surprised by my appearance, bearing, and speech. Others appeared surprise by my positive attitude.

After the introductions, Roger and I went to lunch. Later, he drove me to the housing office where I was able to sign up for a duplex apartment on base that would be available in three weeks. This was truly a God-send since the availability of off-base housing for Black military families was limited to non-existent in the nearby towns. The good news continued when I was told base housing was getting new furniture and appliances, and I could sign up for the items needed. Getting my housing needs resolved on the first day on base was an incredible blessing, and I could hardly wait to tell Peggy about it. Our indefinite separation had been reduced to just three weeks.

Roger and I returned to the office that we shared with Joann. My desk was piled high with history books on gun development dating all the way back to WWI. These were courtesy of Joe McKimmey who I had met earlier. Joe came over to tell me about the books. "I thought you'd like to learn a little bit about guns, so I brought over a few books. There's a lot of history here, but it's good background for you. I got some more when you get done with these." Joe spoke in the deepest drawl I had ever heard, but he was so genuine. I liked him immediately. I loved history, so reading about gun development was right down my alley. Joe seemed pleased that I appreciated his effort, and a respectful friendship between us began that very day.

My first day on the job was a wonderful experience. Eglin was not California, but I felt it was where Peggy and I were supposed to be. Roger dropped me off at the BOQ, and I changed and went to dinner at the Officer's Club. Afterwards, I called Peggy to tell her about my first day and the good news about housing. She was ecstatic and literally jumped for joy. She missed me as much as I missed her and Gail, and we could hardly wait to be together again as a family. Motivated to hurry things along, I dove into the books that night determined to be a great understudy to Joe McKimmey.

I arrived the next day to find my desk equipped with supplies and utensils that Joann provided. Later Flo Donaldson came by to see if I needed anything else. She was still curious and asked me to tell her more about myself (wife, children, family, college, etc.). Apparently, I was atypical to their preconceived notions of Black people, so I tried to be as modest as possible while Roger listened in.

Afterwards, Roger showed me around the base and arranged a trip to Hulburt Field, the base for counterinsurgency developments.

On the way, we stopped by the office of Captain John L. Piotrowski, a project officer for counterinsurgency weapons development. Captain Piotrowski was a tall, friendly officer who greeted me like a long-lost brother. He seemed unusually pleased to meet a young Black officer and almost said as much. He eagerly showed me around his office that was cluttered with cutaway fuses, bomblets, and weapon components. These munitions were being developed for the counterinsurgency aircraft we were going to see at Hulburt. Captain Piotrowski was very animated about his projects and invited me to come back anytime. Since I eventually would be involved with guns, he felt sure we would have an opportunity to work together. I left his office feeling as if a lasting friend had been discovered. Fate and years proved me right.

The trip across the base and through Fort Walton Beach was a beautiful drive. Being close to the water, Eglin and the city were lush with palms, oaks, pines, and other foliage that gave a tropical appearance. Fort Walton Beach was a tourist town with beautiful white beaches dotted by hotels, seafood restaurants, and sea life museums. Despite its attractions and beauty, Roger felt obliged to warn me that Blacks were not allowed to patronize these establishments. He also took me by the Eglin Officer's Beach Club on a beautiful strip of land just east of Ft. Walton. I appreciated his candor, and tried not to let the racism of the South dampen my excitement of being stationed at Eglin.

Hulburt Field was a throwback to WW II and Korea with the ramps filled with vintage propeller aircraft such as the T-28, C-47, B-26, and A-1E. These aircraft were modified or retrofitted to carry munitions and guns in pods on pylons. The emerging crisis of Southeast Asia was brought home by the intensive efforts both at Eglin and Hulburt Field. A sense of urgency existed to restore a conventional weapons capability in the Air Force that had been deemphasized in favor of space technology. My trip to Hulburt Field would be one of many over the next several months as I became an avid student of weapons development.

On our return trip to Eglin, we stopped by to see the quarters I had been assigned. Our new home was located near the beach in a quaint neighborhood of duplex units on a tree-lined street called Boatner Drive. As we drove up to 14B, my assigned unit, the workmen were putting finishing touches to interior and exterior paint. I was able to walk through to get a feel for what we would need for furniture and appliances. The unit consisted of two bedrooms, a bath, combined living room and dining room, kitchen, laundry room, and small storage room for yard tools. This outstanding apartment was in lieu of my $100 per month housing allowance. As we departed, several young wives were out sunning their babies or strolling along the sidewalks. I envisioned Peggy and Gail in this environment and got another warm feeling about being assigned to Eglin. We would indeed be happy here.

The next three weeks went by quickly. My good fortune continued when I was allowed to select household goods the week before I left to get Peggy and Gail. Staff Sergeant Donald Malone, from Birmingham, Alabama, was in charge of issuing the items at the warehouse. He made sure we got the best of everything authorized and promised to change out older items as newer ones came in. Sergeant Malone not only ensured a timely delivery but also spent a few evenings assisting me in getting the house ready for my family.

I took off for Tuskegee the first Friday in March to get Peggy and Gail. While there, I went to Montgomery to purchase our first automobile, a 1959, four-door, Chevy Impala with air conditioning. The Chevy was large enough to hold most of our personal belongings. We loaded up on Sunday morning and said good-bye to our friends knowing that an event-filled chapter of our lives was closing. Peggy softly whispered, "Thank you Lord for all you have done for us, and please give us a safe trip to Florida." I had no trouble saying, "Amen!"

We drove straight through and arrived at our new home before nightfall. I picked Peggy up and carried her across the threshold of our new home. The apartment was modestly furnished, the kitchen stocked with food, and beds were made in each room. Peggy's delight was more than enough thanks for my efforts as I brought Gail in and deposited her in a new crib. A few minutes after our arrival, our next door neighbors came over with cold drinks and snacks to welcome us. The kids from the other apartment came over to see their new playmate who was not quite ready to go outside to play. During the visit with our neighbors, we learned Boatner Drive was a collection of doctors, lawyers, dentists, or other professionals. All offered their help in getting us settled or for any future needs we might have. All in all, it was a wonderful beginning in our new home. Not lost on us was the fact all of our neighbors were White, yet the color of our skin didn't seem to matter one bit. I had not experienced such a refreshing occasion since my days in Oxnard, California. Peggy and I agreed that Boatner Drive would be a great place to start raising our family.

I spent the next two months learning much about the history of guns, the research and development process, and projects in the office. Joe McKimmey was especially helpful and ensured the right focus and priority of my orientation. By early May, my progress was rewarded by being assigned to monitor the Det 4 Comparative Evaluation of two 20mm Gun Pods. One pod, the SUU-16/A, was configured with the M-61A1 Gatling Gun developed for the Air Force by General Electric (GE) Corporation. The other, the MK-4, was configured with the MK-11, twin-barrel cannon developed for the Navy by the Hughes Corporation. The fire power of these guns were 6,000 and 4000 rounds per minute, respectively.

This project provided my first experience with inter-service competition and rivalry. Earlier, the Air Force awarded a contract to GE to design and develop a gun pod driven by residual propellant gas. The Navy, however, made a case at the Pentagon that its off-the-shelf MK-4 gun pod could meet the requirements of the Department of Defense. As a result, the Air Force directed a modification to GE's original design and prepared for an unscheduled comparative evaluation. The SUU-16/A gun pod was the interim configuration for the test.

Extensive planning and coordination were completed prior to the arrival of the gun pods in early May. As Project Monitor, I worked closely with the Air Proving Grounds Center (APGC) project officers, civilian contractors, and military maintenance technicians. The team consisted of individuals with impressive credentials and positive attitudes. They included Captains Charles McIver, John F. Harvell from APGC and Captain John H. Reddock from the Eglin Flight Test Center. Captain McIver was project lead, and Captains Reddock and Harvell were the primary Air Force test pilots. An additional pilot, Navy Lieutenant Commander Daune L. Varner, was assigned from Patuxant River Test Center in Virginia. The armament technicians were led by Staff Sergeants Lawrence A. Butler and John H. Epperson. By June, everything was in place. Despite higher politics, we had become a solid, seamless team determined to conduct a comprehensive and objective test program.

The assimilation into the Air Force community for Peggy and me went equally well during the first months at Eglin. Joe McKimmey was the only one in my office who socialized with us after duty hours, and we soon reciprocated visits in our homes. We quickly made friends with our neighbors and met two other Black families on base, Major Bob and Izzie Mason and Major Jim and Jean Williams. Also, one of my classmates from Tuskegee, Emma Jean Gregory, had completed Officer's Training School and had been assigned to Eglin in March. She found another classmate of ours, Meredith McCleary, living and teaching school in Fort Walton Beach. Meredith, a fiercely dedicated teacher, invited us to participate in motivating students at the newly opened Combs High School, the first for Blacks in Fort Walton Beach and the surrounding communities. Emma Jean and I were also invited to speak to the Black parents about opportunities in the Air Force upon graduation from high school and college. Our presence in Combs High School and at local gatherings were small steps for us, but they were greatly appreciated by the principal, teachers, and parents.

The summer months continued to be eventful and exciting with regards to my job. The initial fit and compatibility checks were completed on an F-100 jet fighter for each set of gun pods. Next, we conducted live firings on Eglin's static range. I received a special treat one day when asked to be the "trigger man" on a live ground firing. It was my first time in the cockpit of a front-line fighter jet, and I thoroughly enjoyed the experience. In comparison to the T-33 I flew five years earlier, the cockpit of the F-100 was awesome.

The flight test phase proceeded as scheduled; however, an occasional test event provided unexpected drama. For example, the MK-4 lost an entire forward section of the gun pod during a firing event. This massive component impacted the wing of the aircraft and the pilot had to take immediate evasive action to preclude a critical mishap and possible ejection. Other problems required the utmost in creativity and ingenuity to keep the program on track. Sometimes engineers worked through the night to solve a particular problem. In addition, scheduling of ranges, test support, and other resources were often challenging. Despite these problems, I managed to capture, record, and report the test results to my bosses in a timely manner. The latter was easy because I enjoyed being on the flight line, observing live firings on the ranges, and the debriefings after each test sortie.

The pilots who flew the test missions were particularly impressive. All of them wore the orange flight suit of test pilots and g-suits on each mission. Each seem to have an exaggerated swagger when he came out to fly, and all of them smiled a lot. They enjoyed what they were doing, and I wanted to do what they did. My childhood dream returned in force, and I wanted to be a pilot right then and there. The dream had to wait, but I stopped by the personnel office a short time later and signed up for the Air Force Qualification Test for flight training.

The summer of 1963 was also filled with intense civil rights struggles all across America. Pro-segregation attitudes persisted and often resulted in indiscriminate and violent acts on innocent people. I drove Peggy and our baby to Shreveport to visit my family and to pick up my younger brother, Wendell, who was going to spend the summer with us. On the way back to Florida, we encountered a very unpleasant incident. There were no hotels to accommodate us, so I parked behind a shopping area in a small town in Mississippi to get a few hours of sleep. We were abruptly and loudly awakened by a police officer beating on my car shouting, "Boy what are doing here?" I replied, "Officer, I am just trying to get a few hours of rest before driving on to Florida." Unrelenting, he continued, "Well this here ain't no rest stop; move on!"

The policeman's actions were insulting to Peggy and me and frightened Wendell. I drove on into the night, thankful that I had sense enough to keep silent. The anger in me was choking, but it served to keep me awake until we arrived home early the next morning. There were many negatives associated with the demands for social change in America, but I was determined to be happy in my assignment at Eglin.

Our spirits were uplifted by a visit from my mother-in-law, Elsie. Peggy's father wanted to get a first-hand account of the welfare of his daughter and new grandbaby. Mom, as I now called Elsie, was sent to report on this Toliver fellow who stole the apple of Harvey Hairston's eye. She brought along two of Peggy's young nephews, Little Harvey and Terry; who had a ball with "Uncle" Wendell. Mom's attitude, kindness, love, and thoughtfulness were those of a saint, and we thoroughly enjoyed her visit. She left a month later confident that I was a good husband and father. Furthermore, Peggy and I shared the news that we were expecting our second child. We thought this would be a surprise to Mom, but she was ecstatic. I discovered something I had not known before. Mom and her husband were married seventeen years before they had the first of their four children, and they had only three grandchildren at this point. At sixty-four years old, the news of a fourth grandchild was a welcomed event, and she was certain her husband also would be delighted.

The flight testing was completed in August, and we began drafting the final test report. Thanks to the advice of Joe McKimmey, I kept a comprehensive test journal, collection of movies and photos, and documentation of relevant events. Joe reviewed these items as the test progressed and was comfortable with the accuracy and thoroughness of my efforts. I spent the next few weeks editing movie strips, preparing slides, and writing the associated script for a presentation to the Office of Assistant Secretary of the Air Force. Colonel Hardaway asked me to accompany him to the Pentagon to assist with the presentation. This was a huge opportunity for a Second Lieutenant, and again I was thankful for those back at Tuskegee who prepared me for such a time as this. The trip also allowed me to visit Baltimore and meet Peggy's father for the first time. The good news continued. I was notified that my test scores qualified me for pilot training. All things considered, it was a great summer.

Our trip to the Pentagon was delayed until September due to the "March on Washington for Jobs and Freedom" led by union leaders A. Phillip Randolph and Bayard Rustin. Approximately 200,000 multiracial supporters gathered at the Lincoln Memorial for Dr. Martin Luther King, Jr.'s "I Have a Dream" speech on August 28, 1963. The crowd included clergy of every faith, students, blue-collar and white-collar workers, politicians, and a huge slate of celebrities. The event was called " the largest political assembly in America's history," and it ignited non-violent protests in unprecedented numbers throughout the nation.

Colonel Hardaway, the APGC Project Officers, and I arrived at the Pentagon for an early morning appointment. We were met and escorted by staff members who assisted in setting up our presentation. I was overwhelmed by all the visual history and mock-ups as we walked through the halls. The size, maze, and hurried steps of scores of people in uniforms of every service was truly an education for me. While we waited for the Assistant Secretary of the Air Force, I carefully reviewed my part of the briefing. Surprisingly, I was very calm and reassured myself we had done the best job possible. In addition, the contractors and military technicians had taught me the ins and outs of both gunpods.

The room was called to attention as several general officers, senior civilians, and attendant staff members entered the room. The group was an impressive array of rank, and I quickly counted about ten one- and two-star general officers. The test results we were about to present took on significant importance. Until then, I had not fully realized the importance of the test results. Col. Hardaway made the preliminary remarks regarding the test objectives, methodology, environment, number of sorties, and related facts. After responding to a few questions, he called me forward to make the slide and film presentation. My briefing covered a detailed description of each gun pod, target and impact patterns, accuracy results, comparative performance, and lastly, film of live firings. The latter was the most dramatic as I showed the in-flight separation of the forward section of the MK-4 gun pod during firing and the pilot's escape maneuver. Some of the general officers were pilots so they got a charge out of such a graphic event.

The test results clearly proved the SUU-16/A gun pod was superior to the MK-4 gun pod, and my briefing corroborated this.

At the conclusion of the presentation, Det 4 received high marks for the results of the evaluation. My enthusiasm and knowledge of the gun pods were cited by the senior officer present, and he personally congratulated me on my briefing. The general advised our team that we would get a decision within the next few weeks regarding the next phase in the gun pod development. My first trip to the Pentagon ended on a very high note. I left the building feeling great and looked forward to my weekend in Baltimore.

My Father-in-Law

Despite my swearing off bus trips earlier in the year, I took the most convenient and cheaper way to travel from Washington, DC to Baltimore, Maryland. I wore my full dress blue uniform to make a good first impression on my father-in-law. Mom had given a good report upon her return from Florida, but he was still thought to be upset over losing Peggy. I felt a bit uneasy as the bus approached Baltimore. Mom was out of town, so a member of the family, Eddie Mason, his wife, Roberta, and two little girls met me at the bus station. They greeted me very warmly and took me to Peggy's Aunt Carrie's house to await Mom's return. I received a cordial welcome from Aunt Carrie and her husband, Raymond, but their nervousness left me uneasy. The evening wore on, and it was time for Eddie to take his family home. Apparently reading my thoughts, he said, "Dick, I know you've heard horror stories about Uncle Harvey, but he is not that bad. He and I get along just great, and from what I see of you, you'll do just fine." I appreciated Eddie's words but they did little to quell my rising doubt about coming to Baltimore without Peggy and Gail. Eddie agreed to drop me off at the Hairston house on his way home.

We arrived at 2267 Reisterstown Road where I met a small, terribly bow-legged, elderly woman about four feet tall. Eddie introduced me to Aunt Irene who was in an absolute tizzy over the prospect of Harvey coming home before Mom arrived. Eddie tried to reassure me, but I noted a worried frown on Roberta's face as they left. Aunt Irene and I sat and tried to make light conversation about Peggy, Gail, and our new home in Florida. I soon exhausted my stories, so we sat uncomfortably in silence for a long while. About two hours later, we heard a loud commotion coming through the kitchen door. Aunt Irene jumped off the chair and hurried toward the noise that sounded like someone breaking in. She spoke apologetically, "Harvey, Peggy's husband Dick is here. Elsie is not here, and I haven't heard from her!"

There was no reply from Harvey, but the loud noise continued as he brought in groceries from the car out back. I stood in the dining room waiting to speak whenever he appeared. After several minutes Harvey passed where I stood, totally ignoring me as he went to his bedroom. I was speechless, not because he ignored me, but by the size of this "giant" of a man I had heard so much about. The great Harvey Hairston was a little over five feet tall, about four feet across, balding, and woefully impolite. I was still standing when Harvey returned to the dining room to eat the dinner Aunt Irene had hurriedly prepared for him. She said, "Harvey, if you don't need anything else, I am going up to bed."

Aunt Irene took his unintelligible grunt as a "no" and beat a hasty retreat from the room. The resultant silence in the room was only broken by Harvey noisily devouring the food on his plate. He seemed to deliberately exaggerate everything as if this was his way of throwing "gorilla dust" to mark his domain. Despite my irritation and growing impatience, I kept quiet and didn't interrupt his dinner. Harvey finally finished and sat back in his chair. Seeing this, I spoke cautiously, "Mr. Hairston, I had to make a trip to Washington, DC this week and thought it would be a good time for me to come over and meet you." Still no reply. I continued, "Peggy and I have a beautiful little girl named Gail; they both are doing just fine." Still ignoring me, Harvey got up, turned on the TV, and sat down without a word. That did it! I stood up abruptly, while trying to control my anger.

"Listen, I came here to see you because I thought it was the right thing to do. I know you were upset when Peggy and I got married, but we loved each other and wanted to begin our lives together. That was eighteen months ago. We are happily married, and I am taking good care of your daughter and grandbaby. Whether you like it or not, we have a baby with your blood and my blood running in her veins. We are going to have another child in January, and it too will be a Toliver-Hairston. If you don't want to have a relationship with us, that's just fine with me. I will not trouble you again!"

I turned to leave and was halfway through the door when Harvey said, "Boy, come back here and sit your black a-- down!" Stunned by his crude words, I whirled ready to engage in a physical brawl. Harvey was still sitting in his chair grinning at my anger and obvious confusion. Looking at me for the first time, he began to laugh and spoke in a more conciliatory tone, "Sit down, boy!" I was boiling mad, but something within urged me to do as this man requested. Reluctantly, I returned to the room and sat down across from him. His next words almost made me laugh, "Got a temper, haven't you?"

I started to retort but stopped myself in mid sentence as Harvey laughed even harder. I was slow to realize he intentionally tried to intimidate me as if to see what I was made of. He provoked me to extreme anger, but seemed pleased I stood up to him instead of cowering under his deliberate rudeness. We looked at each other for a long while, each sizing the other up and deciding what our next words would be. Harvey spoke first, "So tell me about yourself, Mr. Lieutenant."

Again, he spoke in a congenial manner, and I tried to respond accordingly. I told him about my past, including a few of the tough hurdles. When I got to Tuskegee and meeting Peggy, I told him how impressed I was with how he provided for his family. I thanked him for sending Mom down to the wedding and for sending her to see us the past summer. I spoke these last words from my heart while looking directly into Harvey's eyes. The upper hand shifted to me because apparently he was not used to someone saying nice things to him. As we continued, the tension in the room began to dissolve, and a mutually respectful attitude emerged. The more we talked, the impressions I formed about Mr. Harvey Hairston early on reappeared. I really liked this man because we had a lot in common, and I looked forward to having him as my father-in-law. We were still talking when Mom arrived about 5:00 AM the next morning. She witnessed something very special when she entered the room. The two men she dearly loved were acting like friends for life after just one overnight meeting. She proclaimed, "Praise the Lord!"

The bus trip back to Washington, DC and flight back to Eglin were filled with a lot of reflection. It had been a whale of a weekend, both for my career and personal life. I had much to share with Peggy. I still considered God in a detached manner but felt the need to thank Him about how great things were going for me. From the depth of my heart, I uttered a sincere prayer of thanks to Him.

Shortly after our trip to the Pentagon, Det 4 received the go-ahead to proceed with the development of the SUU-23 gun pod. This was the original version where propellant gas was tapped to drive the gun pod instead of an external Ram Air Turbine. At the same time, we learned the Navy had been given permission to pursue a contract with Hughes Tool Company to build over 1000 MK-4 gun pods. The MK-4 gun pods were to be used in Vietnam by the Navy and Marine Corps while the Air Force would be equipped with the SUU-23 gun pods. So much for using the results of the Comparative Gun Pod Test results to facilitate a DoD acquisition decision! This Pentagon action eliminated any illusions I had about decisions made in the best interest of the services or taxpayers. Nevertheless, I immersed myself in my work determined to do the best job possible.

Confronting Racism

Racial unrest across the South intensified following the violence that erupted in Birmingham, Alabama September 15, 1963. On that peaceful Sunday morning, four little girls were killed when the Ku Klux Klan bombed the Sixteenth Street Baptist Church. The murder of these innocent young girls shocked the nation and re-energized the civil rights movement nationwide. Until then, the racial climate on Eglin AFB festered under a false sense of well being. Institutionalized racism existed in the assignment of dormitories, promotions, and lack of job opportunities for Blacks. I was aware of these conditions but was content to let the "dead dog lie." I had applied for pilot training and looked forward to getting out of Florida as soon as an assignment came through. This was not to be.

I received a call a short time later from Staff Sergeant Kennis Hankerson, an NCO at Eglin who had been on my drill team at Tuskegee Institute. Kennis pleaded with me to join Eglin's Black NCOs and Airmen to develop a strategy to counter racism at Eglin AFB. Dr. King's speech in Washington, DC and the bombing of the church in Birmingham galvanized a civil rights movement on base. I reluctantly agreed to attend provided support could be obtained from the other Black officers on base. The two Black majors I knew refused to get involved. Like me, they had created a comfortable existence in their lives and didn't want to rock the boat. I wanted to follow suit, but the experiences in my life and the legacy I had embraced at Tuskegee would not let me be content.

I contacted three other Black second lieutenants, Emma J. Gregory, Aaron Cobb, and Alfred McGee, and persuaded them to join me. We attended a gathering of the Black airmen one Sunday night on the main base and found overwhelming discontent. The situation for other Blacks at Eglin was worse than I had known. There was a rigid pattern of segregation on base in barrack assignments, living quarters for NCOs, job assignments, opportunities, and career progression. In addition, the commanders at APGC and the base appeared unwilling to enforce a DoD directive to ensure equal opportunity on or off base. My cohorts and I left the meeting very disturbed by the magnitude of discrimination on the base, and we dreaded the risks of taking on such an enormous challenge so early in our careers. I certainly didn't want to jeopardize my pending assignment to flight school, nor did I want to spoil the cordial relationship with those in my office. I suggested we think about any possible actions and gather at my house in a few days.

When I discussed the meeting with Peggy, she agreed that getting involved could be a serious problem for us. Yet, she didn't see how I could avoid providing whatever leadership and support possible to the Black men and women on base. We decided more information was needed about DoD directives regarding commanders' responsibilities to ensure equal treatment for those under their commands.

Lieutenants Cobb, Gregory, and I visited the legal office during our lunch hour on Monday and met a very helpful and sympathetic captain. He reviewed with us the Secretary of Defense (SECDEF) Directive 5120.36, July 26, 1963, to help combat inequality on military installations and the surrounding communities. The SECDEF's directive followed up President Harry Truman's Executive Order 9981, July 26, 1948 that established "Equality of Treatment and Opportunity in the Armed Forces."

President Truman's Executive Order formally ended segregation in the military; however, fifteen years later, many military commanders failed to carry out the intent and spirit of the 1948 order. To combat widespread inaction of military commanders, Secretary McNamara published Directive 5120.36. The directive obligated commanding officers to use the economic power of the military to influence local businesses in their treatment of minorities and women. In addition, commanders were granted approval to declare areas or establishments off-limits to military personnel for discriminatory practices.

Directive 5120.36 was a tremendous encouragement to us and served as the basis for petitioning the commanders at Eglin to eliminate flagrant discrimination against Black personnel. The legal officer agreed with our premise and cautioned us to thoroughly document all alleged acts of discrimination with facts, dates, and times. He also agreed to meet with us to review information and advise the best course of action. Armed with this information and support, we felt better about advising the Black military personnel on base.

I presented the information obtained from the legal office at our next meeting with the airmen. We requested they document and record actual events and places where the APGC and Base Commander could clearly be held accountable for implementing SECDEF's directive. Once sufficient evidence was gathered, we planned to present the case to the commanders for resolution. The group formed several committees to gather information in various locations on and off base. We all agreed to be very careful and circumspect in our pursuits. Recognizing the volatile attitude of some, we cautioned everyone to avoid any premature confrontation with those likely to be opposed to our efforts.

The next two months were spent gathering information and canvassing the local communities to determine which businesses would serve or accommodate Black people. Virtually none of the restaurants, hotels, recreational areas, or entertainment facilities served Blacks. In most cases, there was clear evidence of patronage by military personnel. In one case, Lieutenants Cobb, Gregory, and I attempted to attend an Air Force Association (AFA) meeting at a premier hotel in Fort Walton Beach. We entered the hotel and proceeded to the meeting room where we were asked to leave. We advised the person that we were members of AFA stationed at Eglin, but he still insisted we leave. We recognized a few people from Eglin and circulated in the room. The proprietor shut down the service at the bar to keep from serving us. The atmosphere in the room quickly turned sour so we left. Clearly, this was a case for the petition.

We held several meetings to determine the progress and validity of the data gathered in our campaign. Some members of the group grew impatient and wanted to push the issue of getting served at restaurants in the local areas. Despite our caution, Lieutenant McGee and a few airmen stopped at a McDonald's fast food restaurant one evening and attempted to get served. A physical altercation ensued with some of the customers, and McGee and the airmen were roughed up pretty badly. To make matters worse, McGee and the others were arrested for disorderly conduct. The incident was all over the front page of the local papers the next day, and I had been identified as a one of the ringleaders.

Everyone in my office was shocked because there was no indication of my activities after duty hours. Some members of Det 4 felt I had betrayed their kindness and immediately treated me like the plague. Lieutenant Colonel Brown called me in to tell me Col. Hardaway was very upset. I, along with the others, were summoned to appear before Major General James E. Roberts to explain our disorderly conduct.

We had a weekend to prepare for our meeting with General Roberts, so we hurriedly met with the enlisted people to gather additional evidence. With the help of our friend from the Legal Office, we worked through the weekend putting together a representative list of grievances and a convincing presentation. Hoping appearance would help, we pressed our uniforms, spit-shined our shoes, and prepared to look our best for a meeting that God only knew what.

We reported to APGC headquarters and were ushered into the general's conference room. General Roberts was seated at the head of a huge table with mostly full colonels on either side of him. All of them looked as if they had been tormented by demons from Hades, and their expressions told us we were about to go there. We faced unadulterated hate stares but lined up smartly and saluted, "Sir, Lieutenants Cobb, Gregory, McGee, and Toliver reporting as ordered."

His red face became apoplectic as he yelled, "What the hell have you guys been doing on my base?" Before I could respond, General Roberts began a loud tirade that foretold our immediate doom. He told us how he was going to end our careers and how unpleasant our lives would be in the process. We dutifully stood at attention during the several minutes of "butt chewing" that put a simple rebuke to shame. When he finally stopped to catch his breath, I hurriedly said, "Sir, may I speak?" He retorted, "Say what you damn well please, but nothing is going to change my mind. We don't need troublemakers like y'all in the Air Force!"

Swallowing hard, I hastened to cite SECDEF's Directive as the rationale for our trying to gain the same fair and equal treatment that White personnel at Eglin enjoyed. I quickly presented our list of grievances and reiterated several flagrant acts of discrimination on and off the base. I highlighted specific examples of the exclusion of Blacks in jobs and base-wide activities on base. Before I could finish, Gen. Roberts turned to his staff and shouted, "Is this bull s--- true? Why haven't I heard of this before?" The staff members began to stutter and stammer because they couldn't refute the hard evidence we presented. Sensing the validity of our grievance, the veins in the general's neck bulged even more. I had never seen anyone that mad, and we thought he was about to have a heart attack. He yelled at us, "Get the hell out of here!" We fell over each other as we fled on spaghetti-like legs through the doors. We marched in smartly, but we stumbled out.

We remained outside the closed doors, but could hear General Roberts chewing on his staff. Apparently he had been led to believe the racial climate at Eglin was just fine. I remembered that Major Mason, one of the Black officers on base, had told me he often played golf with General Roberts. After a while, the captain from the Legal Office came out and told us we were free to leave. He didn't know what action General Roberts was going to take against us, but promised to let us know as soon as possible. We went to our offices with much foreboding.

The infamous Black lieutenants on Eglin AFB were kept in limbo for several weeks. I continued to do my job and was even sent on temporary duty to monitor gun development tests at contractor facilities. My status in Det 4 was reflected in the endorsement block of my next performance report. My first two reports were written by Lieutenant Colonel Brown and favorably endorsed by Colonel Hardaway. The latest report was written by the senior civilian, Ed Witkowski, and endorsed by Lieutenant Colonel Brown. However, I was actually rated two notches higher in the rating blocks. Despite the lack of an endorsement from Colonel Hardaway, my rating improved from "Effective and Competent" to "Very Fine."

None of us lieutenants received any official feedback on the meeting before General Roberts, but there were noticeable changes throughout the base. Black clerks soon appeared on the counters in the Base Exchange; Black teenagers were hired as "bag boys" at the commissary; another Black barber joined the single Black barber at the base barber shop, and a Black beautician was hired at the base beauty shop. There was a competition to identify the most courteous person interacting with customers at all the stores, movies, snack bars, cafeterias, and other outlets base-wide. In addition, several businesses in the nearby towns began to openly advertise for the patronage of all personnel assigned at Eglin's nine bases. These events, coupled with our lack of expulsion from the Air Force, were a clear indication that we had successfully made our case. The other evidence was the greatly improved morale of Black personnel and their families at Eglin. My faith in God and prayer life also improved.

The Death of Camelot

I was returning from lunch with Peggy on a beautiful fall day at Eglin when the nation suffered one of the greatest tragedies in history. President Kennedy was assassinated Friday, November 22, 1963 in Dallas, Texas. I was listening to the radio when the program was abruptly interrupted with the horrific message: "Ladies and gentlemen, the President has been shot in Dallas. President Kennedy has been shot and is being rushed to a hospital. Others in his motorcade have been wounded. Standby for further information!"

I immediately stopped my car along with several people to confirm what had just been announced. Others had heard the news, and we gathered around cars with engines running and radios on, listening for additional information. All of us were in a state of disbelief, and a few men and women began to cry. After about fifteen minutes we re-entered our cars and continued on toward our destinations.

When I arrived at my office, the most incredible news greeted me: "The President has been assassinated in Dallas!" Everyone was in a state of shock, and many were weeping unashamedly. I was so choked up I couldn't speak. This was not supposed to happen in America. We had been in the throes of racial violence in many cities across the South. Now President Kennedy, who had shown compassion and concern for Black people, had been killed in a Southern city. At that time, the entire office and detachment were released to go home for the weekend. America was in a state of mourning unlike any other time in our lives.

We spent Saturday, November 23rd, engrossed in the continuous coverage of the preparation for the President's state funeral. Leaders and dignitaries arrived from all around the world. Now and then, viewers got a glimpse of Mrs. Jacquelyn Kennedy and the entire Kennedy family enduring their profound grief in the most dignified and regal manner ever witnessed. On Sunday, November 24th President Kennedy's body was transported from the White House to lie in state under the rotunda of the nation's Capital. Approximately 250,000 people braved near-freezing weather to grieve and pay their respects to our fallen Commander-in-Chief.

As tens of thousands passed President Kennedy's flag-draped coffin, news from Dallas plunged our nation into even greater confusion. Lee Harvey Oswald, the alleged assassin, was being transferred to a more secure facility when he was gunned down by Jack Ruby, a bar-owner with alleged ties to the mafia. This incredible event took place during live TV coverage. The pandemonium that followed cannot be adequately described even today.

The funeral mass and burial of the President took place on Monday, November 25th. The sadness that Americans, the world, and my family suffered with the Kennedys has never been equaled. I believe, as many who love our country do, America has never been quite the same. President John F. Kennedy, the 35th president, represented the hope, potential, and promise for a greater America. Thus, his tragic loss was said to be the "Death of Camelot."

A New Year

The New Year, 1964, began with an unexpected gift from my father-in-law, Harvey Hairston. He found out Peggy and I had deferred buying our first television in order to help my sister, Arneater, and her children for Christmas. A registered letter arrived at our door on January 1, 1964. Realizing the letter was from Peggy's mom, we nervously opened it. To our delight a note said "Merry Christmas." Attached was one hundred fifty dollars in cash! Considering my take home pay was one hundred fifteen dollars every two weeks, we jumped and shouted for joy. This was an incredible act of kindness that we least expected, and it truly made our day. However, the purchase of the television had to wait.

David, who was visiting from Tuskegee, Peggy, and I were playing scrabble about 10:00 PM that night when Peggy went into labor and I rushed her to the hospital. It was a full house in the old wood-framed hospital that housed the maternity ward. The four delivery rooms were also full. I joined the anxious dads in the waiting room to see who would get the prize for being the first baby born on New Year's Day. Our second daughter, Renea, was the third birth at about 1:15 AM on January 2, but we were very happy to have another beautiful, healthy baby. Our neighbors and family joined in the celebration of this joyful addition to our young family.

The months that followed passed swiftly, and I continued to do my job and other assigned tasks in weapon development. I received my assignment to pilot training in February. My excitement was beyond anything I ever experienced, and we could hardly wait to leave. Air Training Command had eight bases where I could be assigned; six of these were located in Texas, Oklahoma, and Arizona. I requested Williams AFB, Arizona because most Blacks who had been assigned there successfully graduated. Others had been successful to a lesser degree at the bases in Texas and Oklahoma.

When my orders were received, I just about dropped to my knees. The assignment was to the worst base of all - Craig, AFB near Selma, Alabama. I had no proof, but felt my political activities at Eglin somehow figured in this assignment. I believed my reputation as a troublemaker while stationed at Eglin may have been forwarded to

Craig AFB. My dream of becoming a fighter pilot would face a real challenge in a reputedly hostile environment.

All things considered, the fifteen months at Eglin AFB were eventful and exciting. By the time we loaded up our car in May and headed to Baltimore, we were a family of four- Peggy, Gail, and our three-month old daughter, Renea. We said good-bye to our friends and departed May 12, 1964. Notwithstanding my assigned base, we looked forward to the next phase of our lives.

GRANDPARENTS OF DICK TOLIVER

Circa Late 1880s

Minnie Bell Davis
Mother of William Henry

William Henry Davis
Paternal Great Grandfather

Circa Mid 1900s

David Toliver
Paternal
Grandfather

Bob Anderson
Maternal Grandfather

Minnie Davis Toliver
Paternal Grandmother

MOTHER AND FATHER

Booker T. and Daisy Anderson Toliver
Circa 1940s

**High School
Graduate**

**Dick at 13 Years Old
Jr. High School**
Lost my shirt but
can't say how.

**First Year
AFROTC Cadet**
Tuskegee Institute

BROTHERS AND SISTERS

Zella
Early 1950s

AW
Early 1950s

Arneater
Circa Mid 1950s

Wilbert
Circa Mid 1950s

David
Circa Mid 1950s

DICK AND PEGGY AT TUSKEGEE INSTITUTE
Circa 1962

Dr. Zbigniew
"Paul" W. Dybczak

Wedding Day

2/Lts Class of '62-'63

Dick's
Swearing-In
Ceremony
2/Lt USAF

Peggy Receiving Her
Master's Degree

Lieutenant
Colonel Hubert L.
"Hook" Jones

Eglin AFB, FL 1963-1964

Gail
Eglin AFB, FL 1963-1964

First Dinning In
Eglin 1964

Peggy
Eglin 1964

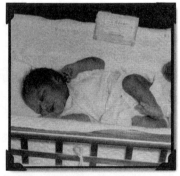

Renea
Eglin AFB, FL 1963-1964

Renea, Michael, and Gail
1965

CHAPTER SIX

PILOT TRAINING

Base housing at Craig AFB was very limited, and students were not normally assigned quarters during their one year of training. Given this, I left Peggy and the children with her parents in Baltimore and reported to Craig AFB the first week of June, 1964. I checked into billeting and was assigned a room in the student's temporary quarters. These were WW II vintage single-story buildings with a screened-in porch the length of the building. A central latrine and showers were located in the middle of the building. The small rooms were sparsely furnished and equipped with individual sinks to accommodate two students per room. There was no air conditioning, but each room had two windows to help circulate the hot, muggy air typical of Alabama in the summer. I was glad to be at Craig for pilot training, so I didn't mind the austere living conditions.

I unpacked my bags, selected a portion of the room, and lay down in my skivvies to cool off and take a nap. I was abruptly awakened by a second lieutenant who entered the room and shouted, "Hey, what the hell are you doing in my room?" The young man standing in the door was obviously upset, and I knew immediately what his problem was. I stared back at him without answering but smiled derisively. He dropped his bags outside the door and ran down the corridor speaking to whomever was within earshot. "Hey, you guys see who they got me rooming with? I'll be damned if I am going to stand for this!"

Within minutes, a small crowd gathered outside my opened door to see this strange sight. The scene was comical until an older guy entered my room uninvited and began looking around. I asked tersely, "Have you lost something?"

He stopped and said, "I'm Jim Rousey, and I am here for Class 65 H. Who are you?" I said, "Well what do you know? My name is Dick Toliver and I'm also here for 65 H. I guess that makes us classmates!" Rousey seemed surprised and said, "You here for pilot training?" I stared at Rousey with growing irritation. Apparently he sensed this and decided to leave my room. On the way out he picked up a large new bath towel I had draped across the chair and asked, "May I borrow this towel?" Chagrined by his brazen request, I said yes just to get him out of my room. He jauntily strutted out of my room as if to impress the onlookers. I never saw my towel again.

The irate lieutenant returned to the billeting office and got his room assignment changed. I thought if this little encounter was an indication of things to come, my self-control and tolerance would be sorely tested during the year.

Approximately thee hundred student pilots were assigned to Craig AFB in Classes A through H. Dozens of other officers were assigned as flight instructors, staff, and support. Class 65H was the last of the current training year. Approximately one-third of the thirty-seven students were officers with prior service in varied career fields. The remaining were recent graduates of colleges from across the South, the Air National Guard, and foreign countries of Afghanistan, Norway, and Ecuador. When I arrived, only one other Black student pilot was stationed at Craig, but he graduated within a month.

We gathered for our first assembly and were introduced to Colonel Richard Ault, the 3615th Pilot Training Wing Commander. He was followed by other wing staff including Major Richard Good, Commander of the Student Squadron, and Captain Russell C. Roberts, Commander of the T-37 Training Flight. Captain Robert L. Pritchard, the senior ranking officer in our class, was designated class leader. Following the initial introduction to the wing leaders, we were given the opportunity to introduce ourselves to each other.

I spotted the second lieutenant who had briefly stepped into my room the day before. His name was Franklin Mitchell. A few officers huddled around Rousey and Mitchell and made no bones about letting me know I was the topic of their discussion. This little grandstanding apparently was meant to intimidate me, but they didn't know my deep resolve and history of overcoming obstacles. I didn't let this keep me from mixing with the class. In fact, some of students were quite cordial. The foreign students greeted me and seemed happy to see another face of color. Later, Lieutenant Akram Shenwar of Afghanistan and Lieutenant Jamie Varela of Ecuador became my close friends. Others who seemed impervious to my race and became my friends included Bob Pritchard, Steve Hinman, Bud Reed, John Troyer, Jim Taylor, and Jim Williams. All except Steve Hinman were from the South.

The three-week academic phase of Preflight Training got off to a great start, and my grades ranked in the top quarter of the class. This surprised some, but the courses were a breeze compared to the grueling engineering courses back at Tuskegee. Furthermore, I thoroughly enjoyed learning everything about the Cessna T-37, the jet in which we would begin our initial training. I also enjoyed the introduction to aviation physiology and ejection seat training. I got a charge out of the latter because some of the students dreaded being rocketed up a fifty foot rail to simulate an ejection. We had a few cases of nausea before and after the ride, and at least one case of a wet flight suit.

The real challenge was finding housing for my family in Selma. A decent place to rent was virtually non-existent. I thoroughly searched the area to no avail. Finally, I resorted to knocking on doors where professional Blacks lived to ask if they had a room or two for rent in their homes. By the grace of God, I found an eighty-four year old retired school teacher, Mrs. Lindsey, who lived alone and needed assistance in day-to-day living. The home appeared to have been cared for in the past, but it was sorely in need of maintenance and pest control. Out of desperation, I agreed to move in and began cleaning and fixing up the two rooms offered by Mrs. Lindsey. She also agreed to let us use the kitchen, dining room, and living room provided I hired someone to clean the place. I hired a person to clean and scheduled the Orkin man once per week for the next few months. Despite the forty-minute drive to Craig, I looked forward to having my family together again.

Class 65 H completed academics and reported for flight training the first week in July. This was a tremendous day for everybody as we finally were about to get our hands on a jet. We were excited about meeting our assigned instructors, receiving initial briefings, and getting a flight line tour. My instructor was First Lieutenant David R. Fairburn, a Georgia boy who had been flying since he was fifteen and was also an avid motorcyclist. Dave was very friendly and showed no signs of racial prejudice. The fact that I was as old as Dave, had a family, and was pending promotion to First Lieutenant gave us a lot in common. A mutually respectful relationship began from the start.

I had my first flight a few days later and was allowed to take the controls after Dave demonstrated a few handling qualities of the jet. He was surprised when I asked permission to attempt a few loops and rolls I had practiced in my flight in the T-33 six years earlier. He agreed, and I attempted the maneuvers while talking my way through each using the textbook parameters. They were not pretty, but Dave was impressed by my eagerness and lack of fear. During our return to base, Dave flew over several bike trails he and his friend had blazed. I received a "Good" on my first ride and looked forward to the next five flights before the first scheduled progress check.

I spent every night studying the Emergency Procedures that had to be recited or written verbatim before each flight. These procedures covered potential critical mishaps that could occur during startup, taxiing, takeoff, or in flight. With Peggy's help, I was well prepared each day. I prepared for the prescribed events in the subsequent flights; however, I became a bit concerned when Dave seemed more interested in checking out new bike trails than meeting the syllabus requirements.

My first progress check was scheduled with a different instructor who was not friendly and seemed perturbed he had to fly with me. My recollection of him is very clear today; however, I choose to call him Lieutenant D. I was totally challenged from the outset of the flight. I knew all the preflight procedures, but the drama began during the air work. I was handling the jet all right until the instructor told me to give him a "sight picture" turn and to hold my altitude in the process. Puzzled, I said, "Sight picture turn? What's that?" Lieutenant D. yelled, "You mean you don't know what a sight picture turn is?" Determined to do well, I said, "If you tell me what it is, I'll try to do it." Clearly irritated, he said, "Can you locate the intersection of the canopy and glare shield over the instrument panel?" That seemed easy enough, so I said, "Yes." He shouted, "Well, make a turn while keeping that point on the horizon!" I attempted to keep the aircraft level but lost altitude on each turn. By then, Lieutenant D. was clearly agitated and said, "What the heck have you been doing the past five flights?" I tried to salvage something by saying, "Dave let me practice a few rolls and loops. Would you like to see some of those?" Lieutenant D. was not impressed, and he terminated the flight. It was very quiet on the way back to the base.

Perturbed about how the air work had gone, I didn't do well in the landing either. Not surprising my first check flight was a "Bust." Captain Roberts, the Flight Commander, Lieutenant Fairburn, and Lieutenant D. participated in the debriefing of my flight. I had not mastered the techniques desired at this point, but I was unwilling to take all the blame for my lack of progress. I liked Dave, but felt obliged to cite the time lost looking for potential bike trails. I was eager to learn and felt my deficiencies could be overcome if given another flight or two. My confidence apparently swayed Captain Roberts, and he allowed two additional flights. The bad news was I had to fly them with Lieutenant D. I sucked in my gut, and thought, "When the going gets tough, the tough get going!"

During the two flights, I learned how to do a "sight picture" turn and a lot more. Lieutenant D. was tough but good, and my positive attitude and fearlessness won his tolerance. I was reassigned to Dave Fairburn and continued training for my solo flight without any further difficulty.

Initial solo flights began the third week of July. The class engaged in competition to see who would be first to get thrown in the traditional "Solo Dunking Tub." Jim Rousey and a few others led the class, but I was confident of being in the top third. Dave agreed that I was ready to solo; however, I was not scheduled to fly for almost two weeks. After watching my classmates solo, I inquired about the unexplained delay. I was assured of being scheduled in "due time," but nearly one half of the class soloed, and I still had not been scheduled. My opportunity finally came late one Friday afternoon following a thunderstorm. I was scheduled about the time most of the class was dismissed for the weekend.

The weather in the area was still a problem, but I navigated around it to the auxiliary field. I successfully completed the three pre-solo traffic patterns and landings, and stopped to let Dave exit the aircraft. Excited and confident, I took off to perform three more mandatory traffic patterns and landings to be declared "Solo Qualified."

The first two patterns and landings went without incident. I was told to expedite the last pattern due to the pending sunset. On my third turn to final approach for landing, one of the instructors in the mobile control unit called out a "bogey" at the far end of the field. This caused me to divert my attention at the most critical phase of the landing. A second call told me to beware of a crop duster in the vicinity of the field. While searching for the traffic, I failed to slow the aircraft down on final approach. I touched down very fast and nose first. This resulted in a classic "Porpoise" or a bounce back into the air. Recognizing my error, I immediately executed the proper procedure, a go around. However, contradicting calls from the mobile control unit were confusing and frightening. I heard an instructor yell, "Abort, abort!" Then I heard Dave who had joined the others yell, "No! Take it around, take it around!" The other voice yelled again, "You've got traffic at the end of the airfield!"

I had just lifted off when the instructor yelled again, "Abort, abort!" Confused and uncertain, I pulled the power back and tried to land again. I touched down very hard simultaneously on all three wheels and started to brake with only a limited amount of runway remaining. I was about to breathe a sigh of relief when the nose gear gave way, and I struggled to keep the aircraft on the runway by using maximum braking. The nose gear collapsed, scrapping metal and shooting off sparks in the process. The aircraft finally stopped at the end of the runway, and I hastily exited the cockpit. By then, Dave and two others from the mobile unit were racing down the runway in a vehicle toward me.

I was sick over the failure on my part, but very angry over the conflicting and confusing instruction I had received from the mobile unit. When they reached me, I shouted, "Why did you guys tell me to abort? I recognized the porpoise and initiated the proper procedure to recover from it. Why didn't you let me continue?" One of the instructors said, "Did you see the crop duster at the end of the field?" I shot back, "No! Was he a factor?" I turned to Dave and asked, "Dave, why did you tell me to continue?" Dave admitted he didn't think the crop duster was a factor, and confirmed my proper go around procedure. I was getting sicker by the minute. I had broken an aircraft and most likely flunked my solo flight. It was of little consolation to me that the three instructors looked about as sick as I felt.

Dave called wing headquarters to report the incident, and the Director of Operations (DO) was dispatched to the auxiliary field. I stood apart from the three instructors as they got their story together in the dark beside the broken jet. Colonel Williams, the DO, arrived about an hour later with maintenance personnel who inspected the damaged jet with flash lights. Fortunately, the damage was not too severe.

The instructors started explaining what happened. I immediately spoke up and reiterated I had made five satisfactory landings prior to the mishap. I also stressed the conflicting instructions from the mobile unit that ultimately caused me to abort my go around. Had I been allowed to continue, I was certain the next landing would have been successful. Dave agreed with my statements and went on to say I did a great job keeping the aircraft on the runway. His willingness to take part of the blame for this incident probably preserved my tenure in pilot training, and he gained my respect forever.

The DO pulled the three instructors aside for further discussion. Afterwards, I rode back to the base with the mobile controllers to pick up my car. Before we parted, Dave informed me I was to report to the flight line at 8:00 AM Saturday morning! I shouted, "What?" Incredulously, I asked, "Dave what's going on here?" A bit timid, he said, "The DO thinks you need to repeat this ride as soon as possible. I'll meet you here tomorrow morning and we'll go do it."

It was 9:30 PM when I headed home, and Peggy had not heard from me since early Friday morning. Understandably, she had been very concerned and became even more alarmed when I told her what happened. Like me, she could hardly believe I was scheduled to repeat the flight the very next morning. Nevertheless, she insisted we do what we always did in a crisis, pray. So we prayed and finally had dinner. I checked on my little girls and we went to bed. Before I fell asleep, I continued to thank God for giving me a wife who put her total trust in Him. Peggy's faith in the Lord gave me the strength to deal with the difficult circumstances the next day.

Morning came quickly. I didn't mind because I wanted another opportunity to complete my solo. On the way to the base, I played back the whole saga of the flight the day before and mentally flew the traffic patterns needed to succeed. I knew I could fly the aircraft well enough to make safe traffic patterns, but the stress of yesterday's events lingered. I had to reach down deep to find the courage and determination to press on. Surprisingly, Dave provided the spark I needed. As we walked across the quiet flight line, he said,

"Dick, you've got to pretend you are Billy Mitchell,
Hap Arnold, or some other hero. These guys faced a
hardship or two, but they went on to become our greatest
leaders in the Air Force. I believe you can do the same."

Slowly, the faces of my heroes filled my mind. The quiet confidence of Colonel Bill Campbell, the stern gaze of Colonel Hooks Jones, and the assuring smile of Major Larry Roberts appeared before me. It was as if they stood on the ramp along with Captains Emmett Hatch and Tim Boddie as Dave and I taxied out. I recalled the hard lesson learned from Colonel Hooks Jones that life isn't fair, but victory comes to those who don't quit. Those timely reflections filled me with the fortitude needed at one of the most challenging moments of my fledgling flying career.

The sky was clear and the winds light as we flew to the auxiliary air field. There were no crop dusters or other distractions to be seen. I successfully flew the required three pre-solo traffic patterns without any problems and prepared to land and let Dave out. He surprised me by saying, "Good job, Dick. Let's head back to Craig." I exclaimed, "What? Why aren't we continuing with my solo flight?" Dave looked away and said, "I can't clear you to solo this morning." Angrily, I said, "Then what the heck was this whole exercise for? What more do you guys want?" Dave was speechless and continued to look away.

We flew back in total silence. I landed and parked the aircraft. Still angry, I said,"What grade do I get for this ride?" Dave answered, "Dick you did a great job. I'm giving you an "Excellent" for the flight. As far as I am concerned, you are cleared to go solo, but it's going to be up to the flight commander and DO. They'll let you know Monday."

At that point, I realized Dave had been put in the position of proving he had been wrong in clearing me in the first place. Apparently the DO and the others believed I would fail under the pressure of the task imposed upon me. But they could not foresee the power of the prayers of my precious, faithful wife. Nor did they understand the fire that blazed in my belly, the dream that would not die, or the destiny I had to achieve. By the grace of God, I was determined to get my wings, or they had better be prepared to close this blankety-blank schoolhouse down!

I reported to the flight line each day for another week without being scheduled to fly. I made use of the time by "chair flying" every night and going over every procedure I could. My solo flight was finally scheduled for August 8th after most of the class soloed. Once again, Dave and I headed for the auxiliary field to do the deed. The weather was great and my determination was sky high. Anticlimatically, the flight went without a hitch. I flew the required pre-solo patterns and landings and let Dave out. I completed three more successful patterns, landed to pick up Dave, and headed home. This time, the trip back to Craig was a happy one for both of us. Our instructor-student-friendship relationship had been sorely tested, yet we prevailed. The look on Dave's face showed relief and admiration for me. I am certain he saw the same on mine. There would be a few more months of flying the T-37, but on this day we looked forward to a successful conclusion. The schoolhouse was safe!

A few days after my solo, I received word that John "Poncho" Anderson had been killed in an aircraft accident at an Air Force base in Texas. Poncho was my classmate at Tuskegee and finished as a distinguished graduate in Mechanical Engineering and AFROTC. He was a proud, happy Texan, and one of the smartest guys in our class. Everybody loved Poncho, especially the girls. I was devastated by this tragic loss and realized how easily it could have been me. Poncho was killed during his solo flight and his death highlighted the inherent risks in flying, particularly for students. I dedicated myself to pressing on in memory of my friend whose life was cut so short. Whatever success I achieved, a part of it would always be for Poncho.

The second tragedy struck very close to home. Lieutenant Dave Fairburn and his friend, Lieutenant Edgar "Ed" Harper, also a young instructor, were riding their motor bikes one Sunday afternoon. Both were traveling at high speed when Lieutenant Harper collided with a vehicle at the crest of a hill. He was killed instantly, and Class 65 H experienced its first loss. Most of us attended the memorial service at the mortuary downtown where we met Ed's parents. He was a graduate of the Air Force Academy and had been their pride and joy. It was very sad to see their hopes for an illustrious life end so tragically. I never forgot the pain and sorrow in Dave's face as he stood beside his friend's casket. What was done could not be undone by any amount of remorse, regardless of how deeply felt. There was a lesson in this for us, but we didn't fully appreciate it then.

The pilot training program included concurrent physical fitness training (PT) throughout the year. We spent two sessions a week playing baseball, flag football, or water sports in the base pool. I enjoyed these sports because of my athletic ability and excellent physical condition. Unknown to me, I provoked the ire of one of my classmates who was filled with racial hatred. His name was John, and surprisingly, he was from the state of Maine. My first physical encounter with John happened one day during flag football. After catching a pass and heading for a touchdown, I was nearly knocked unconscious by a blind-sided block. I struggled groggily to my feet with a severely sprained wrist caused by the fall. Several class members came to my aid while John stood by glaring menacingly at me. Some admonished him for his deliberate and unnecessary roughness. I wanted to retaliate immediately, but Bob Pritchard, the class leader, calmed me down and took me to the dispensary. To preclude a recurrence of this incident, Pritchard promised to warn John to stay away from me. No one understood the cause of John's obvious hatred for me or Black people in general.

A few weeks later, John proved he was not the brightest lamp on the pole. This time we were engaged in water polo at the base pool. Being a poor swimmer, I stayed in the shallow end. Without warning, I felt myself being dragged to the deep end of the pool. As I went under, I recognized the crazed face of John holding onto my legs. Poor John did not know two things about me: First, I had been quite a street fighter back in Shreveport and could put up a tough struggle. Secondly, I was the neighborhood champion for "hold-your-breath-under-the-water-in-Ma Deah's washtub!" I immediately applied these skills in a leg lock and a bear hug. I intended to hold my breath to the bitter end. John apparently realized this too late and his eyes became as big as saucers. His frightened look turned to stark fear. We were face-to-face to the point of almost kissing as we sunk to the bottom of the pool with him in a death grip. Moments later, several classmates jumped in and dragged both of us to safety. We held onto the side of the pool gasping for air and glaring at each other. It was a comical sight, except for the fact John's unwise prank could have had grave consequences for both of us.

In light of John's venomous attitude, I requested a meeting with Major Good, the Student Squadron Commander. I strongly insisted John be given an order to cease any physical contact with me for the remainder of the year. Major Good understood the urgency of the request and made it happen. From that day forward, the worst I suffered were John's hate stares from a distance. I never found out the reason for his deep hatred, nor did I care. My regret was that other Black people would probably be blind-sided as I was. But that was a matter for the Lord to handle.

My flying continued to improve, and I thoroughly enjoyed that part of being at Craig. Conversely, the deteriorating racial climate throughout the South, especially in Selma was another matter. The Civil Rights Act of 1964 outlawed discrimination and segregation in public places and established the Equal Opportunity Commission to enforce these new laws. However, Selma and other cities in Alabama continued to be rigidly segregated. When local Black citizens or Black military personnel at Craig tried to exercise their rights in Selma, they encountered violent resistance. In addition, a hastily enacted Selma ordinance was particularly egregious. Selma's officials passed a law that prohibited more than two Blacks on the streets at any one time! This outrageous ordinance applied to families, relatives, and military personnel. Furthermore, it was subjectively applied to Blacks and strictly enforced by the notoriously racist Sheriff, Jim Clark.

The voting rights campaign for the Black citizens of Selma intensified in the fall of 1964. Only a few hundred of the 30,000 Black citizens were registered voters. Our landlady, Mrs. Lindsay, and her next door neighbor, a school principal were two of these, and they were targets for racial violence. This threat became very real one night when a cross was burned on the lawn between the two houses. I was gravely concerned for the safety of my family, especially since Peggy was pregnant with our third child. I was determined to get my family out of Selma as soon as possible, and made plans to send Peggy and the children back to Baltimore. I also requested a transfer to a pilot training base out of the Deep South.

In the meantime, as the only Black officer at Craig, I was again drawn into a local situation I desperately wanted to avoid. I felt obliged to meet several times with the Black NCOs and airmen at Craig to determine an acceptable strategy to counter the racism on and off base. Help came unexpectedly.

Jamie Varela, a classmate from Ecuador, was arrested, held for several days, and roughed up allegedly for dating a young White girl in Selma. When released, he contacted the Ecuadorian Consul in Washington, DC. The fat hit the fire, and the Pentagon dispatched a general officer to investigate the matter. Brigadier General Robert Dixon received an earful during his visit. He discovered that foreign students of color and Black personnel faced flagrant discrimination on Craig, in Selma, and in the surrounding community. These conditions persisted despite the SECDEF Directive regarding Equal Opportunity in the Armed Forces. In 1964, there was little evidence the wing commander at Craig complied with the directive.

General Dixon met with the commanders at Craig and visited officials in Selma. While he could influence changes on base, the entrenched segregation and propensity for violence against Blacks in Selma were not about to be resolved. Nevertheless, he summoned all the Black personnel to the base theater for a meeting. General Dixon promised the discriminatory practices on base had been addressed with the wing commander and that we would see immediate results. He reiterated what we knew about the deplorable racial environment in Selma and cautioned us to avoid going to town unless it was absolutely necessary. The only concession obtained from city officials and law enforcement was "safe passage" for military personnel dressed in their uniform. Black military personnel would still be restricted to two persons maximum in Selma, and they had to abandon any attempts to integrate public facilities.

Totally displeased, I protested these unacceptable conditions and requested an immediate transfer from Craig AFB. I cited the recent experience of the cross burning, the real threat to my family, and the detriment to my successful completion of flight training. Other NCOs who lived in town raised similar concerns about the safety of just traveling through Selma enroute to the base. General Dixon was sympathetic to our predicaments and agreed to meet with base officials to arrange for base housing for as many as possible. Black airmen and foreign officers of color were literally restricted to the base to ensure their safety. General Dixon stated he would take back to Washington an accurate assessment of the conditions at Craig and work to secure transfers for those who sought them.

I met the same day with Major Good and accepted an apartment offered on base, and arrangements were made to move me on base immediately. When we moved into our apartment, I was surprised to find at least a half dozen of my classmates and other students living on base. Yet, I had been denied an opportunity to sign up for housing when I arrived. Peggy and I decided to just grin and bear this injustice and be grateful for being out from under the shadow of the Ku Klux Klan.

Moving on base minimized the threat to our safety, but the ugly tentacles of Selma's prejudice soon reached us again. Peggy agreed to take one of our White classmate's pregnant wife to see the local town OB/GYN doctor on contract with the base. When entering the doctor's office with her friend, she was told the "Colored" waiting room was around back. Peggy maintained her composure but chose to wait in the car. She wondered how the White doctor handled providing care to Black and White women in the same facility. How did White women accept being attended by a doctor who handled a Black women just on the other side of a partition? We agreed this was another very foolish paradox of segregation.

We were told earlier about the availability of a doctor for Peggy, but not that she would have to enter the back door to be seen. Major Good had another visit from me. There was little argument over our refusal to accept the provision made for us. He arranged for Peggy to be taken by a military vehicle to Maxwell AFB Hospital in Montgomery for all her appointments. We accepted, and that was the end of the subject. Our baby would be born in the Air Force hospital at Maxwell.

Class 65 H completed primary flying in the Cessna T-37 in mid December 1964 and prepared for basic training in the Lockheed T-33 in January 1965. I was very happy to finish in the upper third of the class. We had three weeks to spend with our families and to enjoy Christmas after a strenuous six months. Peggy and I were grateful for this time and attempted to get involved in a base Christmas party planned for orphans from Selma.

Earlier, each student in all eight flying classes was asked to give a minimum of five dollars to help cover the cost of the party. Others were asked to volunteer to assist Santa Claus who would land in the base helicopter and deliver gifts to the children. Peggy and I volunteered to help but were advised our help was not needed since the party was for White orphans only.

It was clear the Wing and Base Commander ignored the previously mentioned SECDEF directive. The White only tradition was long-standing and had not been challenged. My conscience would not allow me to keep still because of the gross inequality of this program for Black people on and off base. Nor could I disregard the needy Black children we knew existed in Selma.

Major Good appeared to be expecting me when I arrived in his office. Before I could speak, he said, "Toliver, you know we can't have Black and White children from Selma together out here; so what do you think we should do?" Having given considerable thought to the situation, I said, "Sir, I would like half the money collected, and I'll hold a Christmas Party for the Black youngsters in town." He looked at me in astonishment and struggled to find words for a reply. I took advantage of the moment and added, "Sir I also request permission to shop at the Base Exchange and Commissary after hours to gather things needed for the party." Major Good could only stare at me for this bold request. Shaking his head in disbelief, he said, "Toliver, how are you going to accomplish this with just two people?" I explained that a few friends in my class and on base would help. I also planned to solicit help from the people in town and ask the local churches to help get the word out. Major Good finally agreed with me. He also promised the necessary security and transportation when the time came to hold the party in town.

The task of gathering the needed support in town proved to be more difficult than expected, but I called upon my former landlady,

Mrs. Lindsey for help. Eventually we were able to obtain help from the YMCA, school teachers, church members, and former neighbors. Peggy and I were pleased with the support from our classmates, Jim and Brenda Williams and Bud and Sandy Reed. We also had help from our immediate neighbors Don and Libby Good and Harry and Pat Harrup. Our base team assisted with shopping and preparing gift packages. We purchased nearly every item of school supplies, clothing, toiletries, and toys from the Base Exchange. Similarly, we emptied the bins in the Commissary of canned goods, frozen turkeys, and everything needed to cook one heck of a meal in the cafeteria of the school that had been appropriated.

The party was held a few days before Christmas. Such an event had never been conducted before. We were glad for the military policemen who escorted my team from the base. A highway patrolman was parked a half block away with several cars parked behind him. Despite this ominous sight, we proceeded to have a great party for over one hundred children. Peggy planned and conducted the program that allowed the children to showcase their talents in a heartwarming way. The smiles on the faces of the youngsters were worth every difficulty and risk. At the conclusion of the party, the children left excited and happy, each with their own bag of goodies. Afterwards, we went door-to-door to dispense the leftover gift packages. We headed back home, and everyone let out a sigh of relief when we turned safely into the base. Major Good was relieved to hear the party went well and that we encountered no reaction from potential detractors. He later commended me in my final training report.

Christmas 1964 was very special for Peggy and me because of the joy we provided to a few of the Black children in Selma. We were grateful for overcoming the obstacles placed in our path and for my flying success. It was also a blessing to have gained new friends over the past months. One was a complete surprise. Frank Mitchell, the lieutenant who refused to be my roommate, had quietly watched my attitude and performance over the months. He had a change of heart and wanted to get to know me better. He also came to me for academic help. I assisted Frank, and we became friends and study partners in my home. Frank stopped by before going home for Christmas and wished us well. He said he wanted his father to meet me one day and would tell him about Peggy and me while at home. We had a wonderful Christmas with our two little girls while awaiting the arrival of our third child.

Our class began advance training in the T-33 at Craig AFB in January 1965. My initial instructor was Captain William "Bill" Simon, a likeable, easy-going fellow, and we hit it off immediately. On our very first flight, he allowed me to demonstrate the acrobatic maneuvers I had learned in the T-37. Flying had really become fun, and I looked forward to each flight.

On the morning of February 3, 1965, Peggy called me from the flight line to say it was time to go to the hospital. I rushed home, gathered up the girls, deposited them in the base nursery, and sped down the highway to Montgomery. I had packed the car with blankets, towels, a plastic sheet, and an assortment of tools and first aid items. Fortunately, none of these were needed, and our son, Michael, was born later that evening at the Maxwell AFB hospital. The Lord continued to bless my family as mother and baby were healthy and well. The entire Toliver clan was especially delighted since Michael was the first male born in the family in twenty-three years. A few days later, Peggy's mother came from Baltimore to be with us for a few weeks. As usual, she was a tremendous blessing for all of us.

I completed the Transition Phase of T-33 training and was assigned to Captain John P. Stroud for the Instrument Phase. He spoke constantly about how tough the weather was in Germany and how he was going to make me the "best damn instrument pilot in the class!" I wanted to be the best, but his verbal antics stretched my tolerance. In addition, Captain Stroud was extremely nit-picking, and graded me down for the least deviation from his standard of perfection. After several weeks, I successfully completed my instrument check ride but was still assigned to Captain Stroud. God had a reason for this, but it was a while before I fully appreciated it.

Bloody Sunday

On Sunday, March 7, 1965, our baby had a cold and needed medication. The small dispensary on base was closed, so I headed for a drugstore in town. Because of my focus on flying and my family, I was unaware of the increased racial tensions in Selma. Consequently, I didn't know about the march planned that day by the National Student Nonviolent Coordinating Committee and the Southern Christian Leadership Conference. I became concerned when numerous cars and trucks sped by me waving rebel flags with boisterous White men carrying clubs and yelling obscenities at every Black they passed.

I was tempted to turn back, but our baby needed the medicine. When I reached the Edmund Pettis Bridge on the main highway through town, it was blocked by some of the vehicles that passed me. The occupants rushed toward the crest of the bridge where mounted policemen were viciously swinging clubs at the marchers. I couldn't see the fallen bodies but heard the screams of people being beaten and trampled. Puffs of tear gas rose in the air, and the violence I witnessed defied human comprehension. The "posse" rushing from the east side of the bridge was so intent on joining the free-for-all that I was able to turn around and speed back to the base.

My rage left me speechless and in tears. The frustration of not being able to retaliate was even greater. I felt like going back to inflict pain on those who attacked the marchers. Seeking revenge would have been just as wrong and could not be justified under any circumstances. Peggy did all she could to calm me down while guarding our babies from the horror that followed me home.

The outrage was exacerbated that evening when ABC TV showed actual footage of the carnage I witnessed at the bridge. The network appropriately called it "Bloody Sunday." Many Americans and people around the world witnessed the vicious and unwarranted attack against the marchers. The Black military personnel on base and in Selma were especially upset. We had sworn "to defend our nation against all enemies, foreign and domestic," yet we were helpless to stem the tide of evil that swirled around us. The outrage, repudiation, and overwhelming support of America's White population helped us through those dark days that followed.

Over the next few days, Dr. Martin Luther King, Jr. and thousands of supporters from all across America descended upon Selma. The voting campaign was helped when Federal Judge Frank M. Johnson overturned Governor Wallace's ban on black citizens' right to assemble and peacefully protest. As a result, on Sunday, March 21, 1965, Dr. King and key civil rights leaders from across the nation led over 3,000 marchers toward Alabama's state capital Montgomery. Many at Craig lined up against the fence and shouted encouragement as the marchers passed, now escorted by National Guardsmen federalized by President Johnson. By the time the marchers reached Montgomery on March 25, their numbers had swelled to 25,000; but the price of success was high. The Selma-to-Montgomery march was marred by inhuman brutality and stained by the blood of martyrs. Three months later, President Lyndon Johnson signed the Voting Rights Act of 1965. It was very difficult for Peggy and me during those turbulent times in Selma, but I never lost sight of the goal of getting my wings.

Death Storm

Class 65H entered the last and most anticipated phase of flight training – formation flying. Some of us secretly envisioned ourselves as future members of the Air Force Aerial Demonstration Team, the Thunderbirds. I recalled seeing the Thunderbirds in Shreveport when I was just a kid. We gathered on a distant hillside and watched the breathtaking and colorful maneuvers above the horizon and treetops. So I was very eager to learn the techniques of flying in harmony with other aircraft.

My progress continued, and I was confident of graduating in June. However, the adverse spring weather in Alabama put a crimp in the flying schedule. Low clouds and frequent rain caused numerous cancellations and resulted in flying several formation flights in marginal weather. One day, I was scheduled as solo lead of a two-ship flight with Captain Stroud and another student in the second aircraft. The weather was particularly ominous that morning, and I knew Captain Stroud would be critical of every aspect of my flight lead abilities.

I navigated to the assigned area in northern Alabama only to find limited clearance in which to practice flight maneuvers. We were sandwiched between cloud layers about 2,000 feet above the ground with four to five miles of lateral clearance. My ability and ingenuity were overtaxed after several minutes of leading the flight in such a restricted area. With the weather deteriorating, I signaled to Capt Stroud to take the lead of the flight. He refused to do so. After leading the flight for a few more minutes, I was completely out of ideas about what to do next. Again, I signaled Captain Stroud to take the lead and looked straight ahead.

I could almost hear Captain Stroud cursing as he aggressively flew by me signaling a join-up at a higher airspeed and bank angle than that prescribed for students. I attempted to join up but we entered the clouds and I lost sight of Captain Stroud's aircraft. I immediately rolled down and away to avoid a possible collision but abruptly pulled up to avoid ground impact. In the process, I stalled the aircraft and became disoriented in the clouds. I reached for the ejection handle but was unable to get a proper grip on it. At that moment, I felt the cold tentacles of death gripping me and almost resigned myself to dying. But it was not my time.

God truly works in amazing and mysterious ways. On that fateful morning, He chose to work through Captain John Stroud's habitual yelling. In my mind, I heard Stroud shouting: "Toliver, fly the damned instruments! Fly the damned instruments!" I immediately trained my eyes on the instruments and determined a nose-high, inverted position with rapidly decreasing airspeed. I executed a wing-over maneuver on the attitude indicator to allow the nose to fall through the artificial horizon and to regain flying airspeed. While descending through the bottom of the clouds, I saw the tree tops just outside my canopy and rolled wings level to avoid a collision with them. Still lacking enough airspeed to climb, I held the throttle full forward and prayed to avoid the trees just below the aircraft. An eternity passed before I gained sufficient airspeed to gradually climb back into the clouds.

I checked my Radio Magnetic Indicator to determine a heading home. The continuous spinning of the needle confirmed my altitude was too low to lock onto a radio signal, so I continued climbing unsure of where I was headed. Still in the clouds, I reached 3,000 feet above the ground and finally locked on to the Birmingham tacan station. I turned to the estimated direction that enabled me to lock on to the Selma tacan station. While flying toward Craig, I heard the weather recall on the emergency radio frequency for all flights from Craig. A repeated call was made for my flight which had not been heard from in over fifteen minutes. Captain Stroud radioed that I had disappeared in the clouds and was missing. I attempted to respond but my voice was so choked up that my transmission was unintelligible, but at least they knew I was not dead.

The ensuing radio communications were fast and furious. A senior officer came up on my operating frequency and used in-flight direction finding procedures to locate my approximate position from Craig. Although I was still in the clouds, he gave me a heading and told me to descend to 1,500 feet. Following his instructions, I broke out of the clouds over the town of Selma and immediately recognized the Edmond Pettis Bridge, the site of Bloody Sunday! The violent scene of a few weeks earlier flashed through my mind, but now that same bridge was a landmark that guided me to safety. I located the base, contacted the tower, and headed toward the airfield at minimum altitude to stay below the clouds. I was low on fuel and decided against making a normal traffic pattern entry. I flew across the runway at a 90 degree angle and about 800 feet for a circling approach to land. Moments later, I was safely on the ground and a floodgate of fear, rage, and tears erupted uncontrollably. I taxied to the parking area and saw Captain Stroud rushing toward my aircraft.

When we boarded the crew truck, I lost control and cursed Stroud for his irresponsible actions that almost cost me my life. Still upset when we reached the flight building, I left for home. At that point, the debriefing didn't matter. I had enough, and decided to quit the struggle right then and there. Peggy met me at the door and knew something awful had happened. She had become increasingly concerned about my propensity to strike back at my adversary, real or perceived. It was a long time before I could relate the events of the morning, but she didn't disagree when I told her I had enough. I said through clinched teeth, "Those SOB's tried to kill me today! I can't take it anymore! I don't want to leave you a widow and the children without a father. Nothing is worth that!" Peggy tried to calm me down, but she didn't disagree with my decision. The phone began to ring a short while later, but I refused to answer it. I was too upset to deal with anyone from the flight line, nor did I trust myself to maintain self-control.

About two hours later, Don Good, my neighbor came over to tell me two students and an instructor from Class 65 H were missing. This news sent me spiraling into an abyss of hell. Given my earlier near-death experience, I decided all the more to quit the fight. Our doorbell rang while I was still in this state of mind. An accident investigation officer from the wing was at our door, and the bad day got worse.

The investigation officer confirmed that the wreckage of two aircraft had been located and there were no survivors. Frank Mitchell, my friend from Birmingham; Houshang from Afghanistan; and Dave Small, an instructor, had been killed! The officer wanted to interview me regarding the weather and flight conditions earlier that day. I related the flight conditions in my assigned area and discovered the two airplanes had crashed less than 20 miles away and within minutes of my incident! I later learned the flight apparently was led by Houshang with Mitchell and Dave in the second aircraft. The decision to launch the flying operation in such poor weather was a bad one. But the decision to schedule students as solo flight leads proved fatal. I was very critical of Captain Stroud's behavior and actions that almost proved fatal. My survival that day was only by the grace of God.

The tragic loss of three lives was excruciating to our class and many others on base. I was especially grieved over the loss of Frank Mitchell. Our friendship was real, and it was a beautiful testimony of two young changed hearts. We both looked forward to a future where race would no longer matter. Collectively and individually, our class dealt with these losses and decided to continue or not. I was given about two weeks to consider my decision to withdraw from pilot training. My life had been spared, but I could not decide what to do next.

Peggy and I meditated and prayed long and hard. I also called my friends and mentors at Tuskegee for advice and encouragement. In the end, Peggy agreed we had come too far to quit. Both of us were still confident of my flying ability but felt the circumstances that morning had been stacked against me. However, having survived the experience, I felt stronger and more determined than ever. Also gone was the fear of whatever the instructors could throw at me in the remaining two months. I was assigned another instructor and successfully completed the Formation Phase with a strong grade. My success was another example of God's amazing grace. It also reflected the outstanding support of a young faithful wife who persistently encouraged me even when I doubted myself.

Survival

On May 31st, our family returned to Tuskegee Institute for David's commencement. He received a Bachelor of Science Degree, was a Distinguished Military Graduate in AFROTC, and commissioned a second lieutenant in the Air Force. This was a tremendous accomplishment and would have made our mother proud. Zella, AW, and our younger brother Wendell came for the event and to deliver Wendell to us for the part of the summer. Dr. Martin Luther King, Jr was the commencement speaker. His comments against America's increasing involvement in Vietnam disturbed me considerably. I went to shake Dr. King's hand after his speech and asked him why he was against America's intervention in Southeast Asia. His escorts pulled him away before he could answer; however, for a fleeting moment, Dr. King looked at me with a sadness in his eyes. That was the last time I saw him alive, and history would prove him prophetic about the war in Vietnam.

A few weeks before completing pilot training, I began a search for a station wagon to accommodate my family of five. The racial climate in Selma and the surrounding communities was still at full boil. For example, Black shoppers were generally ignored when entering businesses such as an automobile show room. Even though I dressed in my military uniform, I was ignored in about a dozen auto dealerships visited in Selma, Montgomery, and Birmingham.

Someone suggested I try the Reliable Oldsmobile Company in Selma, and I did so one Friday afternoon. A very nice gentleman greeted me when I walked in and said, "Good afternoon, Lieutenant. What can I do for you today?" Mr. Rufus Porter, the owner, introduced himself and welcomed me to his dealership. I was surprised by his courtesy and friendliness but told him I was looking to trade my car in for a station wagon. He told me about a new 1965 Vista Cruiser that might satisfy our needs. I let out a whistle when I saw the wagon and said that was probably more than I could afford. Mr. Porter smiled kindly and said, "Well, let's see if you like it; maybe we can work something out. Why don't you take it home and let your wife see it. Keep it for the weekend and let's talk Monday." This unexpected offer and kind treatment set me back on my heels. I could hardly believe this White businessman in Selma was going to allow me to drive an expensive automobile off his lot and keep it for the weekend. Mr. Porter observed my shock and smiled even broader and said, "Lieutenant, if you've been out there flying those jets at Craig Field, I am sure I can trust you. I know you have insurance that will cover you. So go give it a whirl!"

I left my car and drove back to the base in an ecstatic mood. I parked in front of our apartment and brought Peggy outside to see the Vista Cruiser. When I explained what had happened, she was equally dumbstruck. Later we drove around the countryside and let the unprecedented kindness of Mr. Porter sink in. We made up our minds to buy the car because it was a beauty, but Mr. Porter's attitude played an important part in our decision. After a long year of darkness in Selma, his act of kindness stood out like a bright beacon of hope for that community and the South.

We didn't know at that time that "Captain" Rufus Porter was a veteran of WW II who served in the Philippines. He grew up in the small town of Georgiana, the site of country western singer Hank Williams, Sr's home and museum, near Greenville, Alabama. He graduated from Auburn University, but had to delay starting his business until after the war and until he was able to save enough money to do so. Reliable Oldsmobile opened in 1946, and Rufus married Ann from Hayesville, Alabama in 1953. Despite their roots and upbringing in small-town Alabama, they shared the common values of fairness, kindness, and respect for all people, regardless of color or social standing.

Peggy and I experienced this kindness in 1965. Forty-three years later, the late Mr. Porter's light still shines brightly today through his wife, Ann Farrior Porter, their son William, and their two daughters. Recently, it was my privilege to personally thank Ann and William Porter for their husband and father, who was *An Uncaged Eagle*.

Late June finally came, and my class standing was high enough to qualify for fighters. The list included the F-100, F-101, F-105, and the new F-4. One week before graduation, an F-4 was flown in for us to get a first hand look at the newest fighter in the Air Force inventory. That did it for me! I chose the F-4 and the Tactical Air Command. The assignment called for a few months flying in the backseat with an experienced pilot then upgrading to the front seat. Those of us eager to get into the new aircraft thought this was a small price to pay to get what we wanted.

On June 25, 1965 the dream born in Oxnard, California during WW II was finally realized in Selma, Alabama. My silver wings were awarded, and I was assigned to fly the latest fighter jet in the Air Force. What a journey it had been, and Peggy had a huge role in my success. Her daily prayers, unshakeable faith in God, and belief in me were the source of my resolve. My wings were silver, but the light of Christ in her life shone much brighter. Our future looked even greater. Later that day, we loaded up our new station wagon, made the babies comfortable in the back, and took off for Davis-Monthan AFB in Tucson, Arizona. I was assigned to the 4453rd Combat Crew Training Wing where the next phase of our lives awaited us.

CHAPTER SEVEN

MAKING OF A FIGHTER PILOT

After visiting my relatives in Louisiana, we began the long trek across Texas enroute to Davis Monthan (DM) AFB in Tucson, Arizona. We spent the first night at Dyess AFB in Abilene then drove to El Paso where we spent the second night. Peggy had never traveled west of Louisiana, so it was a pleasure to recall what I remembered about the vast and exciting land of the West. The expansive prairies and rolling hills of west Texas were richly populated with cattle ranches, oil fields, and cow towns. This largest state in the union was still impressive to see. I was finally returning to the West where my dream of flying airplanes was born.

We arrived in Tucson the first of July 1965 and found a nice furnished apartment ten minutes from the base. While moving in, we discovered the complex was largely occupied with young pilots or other military personnel newly assigned to DM. The assimilation with our neighbors was immediate and trouble free, and Peggy and I enjoyed the beginning of our new life as a fighter pilot family.

We got another very pleasant surprise the Fourth of July. My good friends Captain Tim and Mattye Boddie and their five boys arrived from Tuskegee Institute and initially settled in the same apartment complex! Tim's prior fighter experience enabled him to be assigned as an instructor pilot, and he would be joining our class for some of the systems training. This was a very special time for our families, and our lifetime friendship was further solidified by these happy circumstances.

Meeting "Chappie" James

The first gathering of new pilots assigned to fly the F-4 Phantom II was a momentous occasion. Approximately forty of us gathered in a large classroom for introductions and initial briefings. The group was mostly comprised of captains, first lieutenants, and a few second lieutenants. One of these, second lieutenant Jim Whitehurst, and I were the only Black pilots in the group; however, this fact soon became less noteworthy. All of us had recently earned our pilot wings and shared the excitement of checking out in the newest jet fighter in the Air Force.

The briefer suddenly called the room to attention as the door was literally darkened by a six feet four Black man. I had heard of "Chappie" James before, but had never even seen a photograph of him. Apparently, the others in the room had never seen a Black full colonel either, so we stared in total awe at this powerful and imposing giant of a man. Chappie's thundering voice shook the room and made him even more impressive. "Sit down, gentlemen. I am Colonel Daniel James, the Director of Operations of the 4453rd Combat Crew Training Wing, the finest damn fighter wing in the Air Force. You will do well to remember that and to help keep it that way!"

Colonel James held our full attention as he outlined the projected future of the F-4 cadre and how we would fit in as emerging fighter pilots. As expected, we were to spend the initial five months at DM paired with experienced pilots who had flown earlier fighters such as the F-84, F-86, F-100, and F-101. We would spend the time at DM getting familiar with the handling characteristics of the F-4 and gaining knowledge of its multiple weapon systems capability. Afterwards, we could expect assignments to operational units that were being equipped with F-4s and anticipate a front-seat conversion during that assignment. We were particularly encouraged to learn that some initial follow-on assignments had already been identified and could be selected while we were at DM. Thus was the introduction to this legendary Tuskegee Airmen whose reputation as a fighter pilot would soon be etched deeply in our minds. This initial meeting with him left us in great spirits and heightened anticipation about our future. The buzz after he left the room continued for some time as many questions were answered about him.

Colonel James' history dated back to Tuskegee Institute in 1942 where he completed the Civilian Pilot Training Program and became an instructor in the Army Air Corps. Later, he entered as a cadet and received his commission as a second lieutenant in 1943. He began his fighter career and was assigned to various units in the United States until the outbreak of the Korean War in 1950. There he flew 101 combat missions in the F-51 and F-80. After Korea, Colonel James became an all-weather fighter pilot at numerous Air Defense Command bases and held commands at the squadron and wing level. Later, he served at the Pentagon and in Europe until 1964 when he was assigned to Davis Monthan as the Director of Operations for the wing.

The next briefer outlined the academic and flight schedule for the duration of our time at DM. Having recently completed the rigors of pilot training, we were thrilled to be presented a "gentlemen's" schedule. We looked forward to having time to really learn the aircraft, Tactical Air Command, and the world of fighter pilots. We were also delighted to be able to spend more time with our families and visit the many interesting sights in the area. Since no formal name had yet been specified for pilots assigned to fly in the rear seat of the F-4, we were simply called "guys in back" or GIBs. It really did not matter what we were called so long as our role was significant and we were allowed to fly the jet. Thus so, we became GIBs for the foreseeable future.

The briefer continued with a detailed description of the F-4 as an all-purpose fighter with the capabilities of an air-to-air interceptor, conventional weapon platform, and a nuclear delivery system. The primary air-to-air weapons consisted of the AIM-7 Sparrow, long range missile and the AIM-9 Sidewinder, close-in heat seeking missile. The conventional ordnance included an impressive array of conventional bombs, rockets, and a 20 mm gun pod (the one I worked on at Eglin AFB two years earlier). The nuclear weapons capability featured the existing arsenal of weapons carried on the F-100 and F-105 fighters. The overall capability of the F-4 was linked by state-of-the-art Pulse Doppler radar, integrated avionics, and dual jet engines that collectively produced approximately 34,000 pounds of thrust.

The weeks that followed went smoothly, and we eagerly immersed ourselves in the task at hand. We spent many hours in the simulator learning and perfecting techniques for radar intercepts, air-to-ground radar bombing, and instrument flying. The novel capabilities of the F-4 kept us inspired and motivated to become an integral and reliable member of the combat crew concept. Our positive attitudes and performance facilitated the acceptance by older pilots who heretofore had not shared their cockpits with an additional pilot. As the team concept developed, the front seat pilots relinquished "stick time" to the GIBs. On one occasion, I had the opportunity to fly formation with my friend, Captain Tim Boddie. As two of the five Black pilots at DM, this was thought to be a first in the F-4. The three other Black pilots were Major Chuck Funderburg, Captain Clark Price, and Second Lieutenant Jim Whitehurst.

In addition to a modest training schedule, lasting bonds of friendship were established with neighbors and classmates alike.

The Friday night happy hours were especially noteworthy as Colonel James frequently "held court" at his favorite place at the bar. On occasions I sought to get close enough to be noticed by him, but it was impossible without literally fighting my way to the bar. As a first lieutenant, I hardly qualified as a "bar thumper" and had no stories to compare with those who surrounded Colonel James. I waited for a better time to speak to this man who had become my idol.

From weekly briefings, we knew about the United States military involvement in Vietnam as "advisors" and "pacification teams." However, few knew or understood the political ramifications of our nation's commitment to the government of South Vietnam. Most accepted the government's explanation that the North Vietnamese made two attacks against U. S. warships in the Tonkin Gulf in August 1964. As a result of this "The Gulf of Tonkin Incident," Congress gave President Johnson approval to conduct military operations in Southeast Asia without declaring war. In January 1965, the Vietnam War escalated and military men, aircraft, and equipment were deployed to several bases in Vietnam. By the summer of 1965, over 100,000 personnel were assigned. Still, most Americans, the military included, considered Southeast Asia in abstract terms. It was too far removed to cause personal concern.

The weekly intelligence reports during the summer of 1965 indicated a deteriorating political situation in Vietnam while the military build up in the North intensified. Despite these events, we were uncertain of our national objectives in the region and the potential impact it would soon have for us at DM. We watched the situation with a detached attitude, yet wondered why the military was not allowed to destroy or neutralize developing airfields and air defenses in North Vietnam. The national security objectives in Southeast Asia were well above our pay grade. Accordingly, we stayed focused on becoming the best fighter pilots in the world and on being ready to defend our nation when called upon.

Finding My Father

None of my siblings nor I had seen or spoken to our father in seventeen years until David and his new wife, Rachel, located him. They were enroute to their first duty station in northern California and used an old address to find him. After a few uncomfortable minutes, David and Rachel drove on but wrote our father after arriving at his duty station, the Satellite Test Center in Sunnyvale, CA. Peggy, the children, and I had an unexpected opportunity to visit my father on Labor Day weekend in 1965. The class was released for several days to celebrate the holiday or to visit the sights in and around Arizona. We were allowed to travel as far as New Mexico, Nevada, and California. The chance to visit California was exciting, so I rushed home to gather Peggy and the children for a quick trip to "My Paradise." Also, my younger sister, Arneater, and family had moved to California two years earlier and lived in Watts, a community south of Los Angeles. Recent racial riots left the area smoldering and we wanted to make sure they were okay.

The last known address of my father was in Redlands, California but we didn't have a telephone number. The route to Los Angeles went through Redlands so we decided to make an effort to locate my father during the trip. We headed west with considerable excitement mixed with uncertainty. The drive across Arizona and eastern California was a beautiful experience, and the sunset on the western horizon brought back many wonderful childhood memories. Our children slept peacefully in the back while Peggy and I enjoyed being a young Air Force family with very few cares in the world. It was one of those great moments in our lives.

My thoughts changed as we arrived in Redlands near midnight. I was only nine years old when my father left Shreveport. At twenty-six, married, and with three children, I pondered the possible outcome of an unexpected visit. Mother had been dead for over four years, but the memory of her suffering and death were still painful in my mind. What would my reaction be when I faced the man charged with so much suffering in our lives?

We located the house where my father was thought to reside. After carefully identifying myself, a lady there gave me directions to another address across town. We finally located that house, and I knocked on the door while Peggy stayed in the car. Given the late hour, we were concerned about our reception as total strangers. Fortunately, I was able to identify myself as a relative of my father, Booker, and the people invited me into their home. I called for Peggy while my father was awakened and brought in to meet us.

I was not prepared for the sight of the man who entered the living room. He seemed much smaller than I remembered. He was frail, grey-haired, and his face was lined with age and the marks of a hard life. He squinted at me as I spoke bluntly, "Do you know who I am?" He responded, "I guess you are one of my children." Somewhat disappointed, I said, "I am Richard, the one who begged you to come home seventeen years ago! Do you remember that?" He answered, "I don't reckon so." It was difficult for me to continue without showing my rising anger. "Do you know you have a daughter and five grandchildren living in Los Angeles?" He seemed surprised but showed no emotion. "How long have they been in California?" I spoke through clenched teeth, "Two years!"

I could only stare at the sad-looking man standing before me. For a long while, we faced each other without speaking. I thought, "How could this man be so apathetic about meeting one of his children he had not seen for so many years? Did we still mean so little to him? How could he seem to be so impervious to all the pain and suffering he caused my mother and the six children he left behind?" I decided to leave before losing my self control. I gave my father the address and phone number of my sister and left for the car. I hadn't known what to expect, but my sorrow of so many wasted years was overwhelming. In retrospect, I was too angry, emotional, and young to contribute to a more fruitful visit. The late hour and my unexpected visit certainly did not help the matter. It was after one o'clock in the morning, but I stayed wide awake as we drove on to Los Angeles.

We arrived a little before three o'clock A. M. and got an incredible shock of our lives. The riot three weeks earlier left Watts looking like a war zone. Scores of businesses were destroyed by fire and left as charred hulks of bent frames and tangled pipes. The missing doors and windows of many buildings were boarded up, and piles of debris littered the curbs and parking lots. The streets were patrolled by city and state police vehicles, and we were warily observed while looking for my sister's apartment. Apparently the out-of-town license plate precluded us from being pulled over.

We found my sister's place and were relieved to find her and the children safe. The quality of the relationship between Arneater and her husband, James, was evidenced by his absence. After visiting for a short while, we went to bed. All of us were surprised when my father showed up the next day. My sister was pleased to see him and welcomed him with open arms. Despite her hardships, she still had an incredibly soft and sweet spirit toward our dad. Later, Peggy drove Arneater outside of Watts to shop while I attempted to have a meaningful dialogue with our father. In the end, there were just too many questions and years to overcome. We parted with very little reconciliation, and many years would pass before another attempt was made. Peggy and I completed the three-day visit with Arneater and her family and headed back to Tucson. My emotions were a jangled mess of confusion and unresolved anger with my father. I also left displeased with my brother-in-law over the poor conditions of Arneater and the children. Nevertheless, I was grateful for having made the trip. We arrived home without incident, and I quickly put my attention back on finishing up at DM within the next few weeks.

Chappie's Parting Words

I completed my preliminary F-4 combat crew training on November 8, 1965. My follow-on assignment was MacDill AFB, Florida for advanced training. My end assignment was to be Naha Air Base in Okinawa, Japan. Shortly before leaving DM, I worked my way through the crowd at the bar and spoke to Colonel Chappie James. The man was even more intimidating as I stood before him. At 150 pounds soaking wet, it was a sight to see. I resisted the temptation to turn and fade back into the crowd. In as firm a voice as possible, I said, "Sir, I will be leaving next week, but would like to talk to you before I go." Glaring down at me, Colonel James said, "Toliver, what do you want to talk about?" Surprised that he called me by name, I spoke haltingly, "Sir, I want to be a colonel like you one day, and I want to know how to make that happen." There was a trace of amusement on Chappie's face as he continued to stare down at me. Before turning back to resume his conversation with the group gathered around, he said, "Be at my house at two o'clock Sunday afternoon."

Elated, I departed. On the way home, it occurred to me that I didn't know where Colonel James lived, but that would be a small matter to correct. Peggy shared my excitement about the appointment with Colonel James, and we spent the good part of Saturday getting my Class A uniform and shoes ready for the visit. I wanted to look impressive with my wings and five months of training as the down payment on becoming a colonel fighter pilot.

Peggy beamed her approval of my appearance as I left for my appointment Sunday afternoon. I rang Colonel James' doorbell at two o'clock sharp and was standing at attention when he opened the door. I smothered a smile when the hulk of an unshaven man in his house robe and slippers stood stifling his own smile. Colonel James said, "Come on in Toliver. You're interrupting my football game!" I followed him to his study noting the beautifully decorated home with furniture and items from around the world. The walls and bookshelves in his study were filled with awards, plaques, and memorabilia that reflected over twenty years of service. I could not hide my admiration and appreciation for this man who allowed me into the privacy of his home. He broke my reverie when he asked, "So what do you want to talk about?" I began, "Sir, I know you had to overcome a lot to get where you are. I want to know how you did it. As you know, I am just getting started and would like for you to share a bit of your wisdom with me."

Colonel James began by asking me what I thought was needed to succeed in getting ahead in life and in the Air Force. I related some of the obstacles in my life and how I had worked to overcome them the past twenty years. Colonel James said, "Toliver, you're on the right track. Now just go out there and continue to do the best damn job possible. Don't ask for favors and don't expect any. For God's sake, don't whine about how tough life is. The world doesn't owe you anything but a living; but you've got to go out and earn it. And always love America. I know it seems like she doesn't love you at times, but you have to treat her like a wife and stay with her through thick and thin. You've got to make her love you by what you do for her. And one more thing, if you go out there and **** ** my Air Force, I will personally track you down and plant my size thirteen shoes in places you don't even want to know about!"

I had a clear vision of an undesired appendage extending from a certain part of my anatomy, so I committed to heeding Colonel James' warning. Above all, I wanted to make this man proud of me.

It had been a great five months at DM, and Peggy and I thoroughly enjoyed our short stay. We had grown together as a young couple, and our time together had been like a delayed honeymoon with our precious little ones. We were anxious to get on with the next phase of our lives as I sought to become the world's greatest fighter pilot.

We left Tucson a few days later and headed for Baltimore, Maryland. We stopped at Holloman AFB, New Mexico to visit our former neighbors from Craig AFB, Don and Libby Good. Don was also an F-4 GIB. Later, we stopped in Talladega, Alabama to visit AC and Almeta Washington, our friends from Tuskegee. AC was now a science professor at Talladega College. Things were good for our friends, and we felt blessed to have them in our lives.

Upon arriving in Baltimore, we got Peggy and the children temporarily settled in with her parents. After three weeks of leave, I headed for Florida in good spirits and anticipated having my family together again by Christmas.

Chapter Eight

Baptism By Fire - First Combat Tour

America had made considerable progress in racial desegregation by 1965, but many hotels and motels from Florida to Maryland still refused to accommodate Black travelers. As a result, I drove straight through and reached MacDill AFB at one o'clock the morning of December 6, 1965. The entire base was a maze of activity, many buildings were open, and lights were on everywhere. People hurried about as if to put out a fire. The scene was more startling when I arrived at the billeting office and found it littered with stacks of luggage and equipment. While I was checking in, First Lieutenant Joe Butler, one of my classmates from DM, entered the lounge and shouted, "Dick Toliver, where the hell have you been? We are shipping out in three weeks!" Surprised, I said, "Shipping out to where? What's going on? We are scheduled to be here for six months. What happened to our follow-on assignments?" Joe shouted, "Man, that was just so much B--- S---; we're going to Southeast Asia. Most of us have been here about two weeks getting our stuff together, but you have about three weeks left. We are on our way, baby! We are going to war!"

I tried to digest what Joe said. He was a bachelor, so his exuberance was understandable. This was shocking news for those of us with families. The deployment was classified, so no one notified me while I was on leave. My first thoughts were about the welfare of Peggy and the children. We were not the least bit prepared for a long separation, let alone my going to war. The practical and emotional requirements for such an event were overwhelming and had to be dealt with in an incredibly short time.

I was also concerned about my lack of aircraft experience in the face of combat. Like most new GIBs, I had only thirty hours in the F-4. This was in stark contrast to what we were led to believe as far back as assignment selections in pilot training. Furthermore, none of us had completed the prescribed basic survival school or jungle and water survival training. The thought of going to war was incredulous, but the activities on the base reflected a massive wing-wide effort around the clock. I signed in and was given a package with my name on it. The enclosed information was even more alarming when I realized appointments for weapons training, immunizations, and refresher training flights had already been missed. Exhausted, overwhelmed, and brain dead, I finally went to bed about 3:00 AM.

I signed into the 15th Tactical Fighter Wing (TFW) early the next morning and received official orders and departure instructions. The orders confirmed a large part of the wing was being deployed. The destination was left blank, and many spaces were stamped "Waived." The orders required hundreds of others and me to be in place for deployment not later than December 24, for a December 26 departure. This gave me just seventeen days to complete my belated preparations, get back to Baltimore, resettle my family, and return to MacDill by Christmas Eve. This daunting task tied my stomach in knots, and I wanted to scream in protest. Colonel Chappie James warned me about whining when things got tough, but these were the most challenging circumstances Peggy and I faced in our young marriage. Gritting my teeth, I began eating the elephant a little bit at a time.

I completed the application for my passport and dog tags, received the first of several required shots, and was scheduled for makeup briefings and small arms training. In addition, late arriving pilots had to shop at local military surplus stores because the base had exhausted its supply of jungle gear and related accessories. I was also directed to report to one of the fighter squadrons for a couple of refresher flights.

The reality of my pending deployment slowly sank in, but I deeply regretted the awesome load about to be dumped on Peggy. I called her that night and tried to break the news as gently as possible. There was no easy way to tell her she was about to be left alone with three young children while I went off to war. Worse yet, we had only a week to find an apartment, buy furniture, and get her settled before I returned to MacDill. The frustration and uncertainty left us in an emotional quagmire. Only by the grace of God, were we able to cope with the hand suddenly dealt us. The one consolation was that Peggy and the children would be with family and friends while I was gone.

The next ten days went by at a hectic pace, but I managed to get everything done except the flying. I was granted permission to depart for home on the evening of December 17th. Once more I took to the highways and drove through the dark, cold night. I managed to find a few places to stop for coffee, food and gas but finally had to get some sleep at a rest stop in Virginia. I woke to the freezing cold and drove on to Baltimore, arriving at daybreak.

We immediately began the search for an apartment, shopped for furniture, and completed arrangements for Peggy and the children. The hardest part was facing the fact I might not come home. Peggy did her best to stay strong, but I felt the deep concern in her heart. The dark cloud of the unknown that hung over us nearly snuffed out hope for our future. The sadness of the pending separation was aggravated by unexpected racism encountered while searching for a decent place to live. We called ahead for an appointment only to be turned away once the proprietor discovered we were Black. Angry and frustrated, I dressed in my Class A uniform and barged into a corporate office downtown and explained my situation. The owner relented and agreed to rent an apartment to me provided I paid three months rent in advance as a security deposit! I had no choice but to agree.

Thanks to Sears' credit program, we purchased furniture and appliances needed, but could not get a delivery date until early January 1966. With the help of Peggy's family and friends, we assembled a team to help her get settled after I departed. We were also fortunate to get Peggy's bachelor brother, Jimmy, to move in with her and the children. With things settled as best as possible, we spent our last night together in an emotional wasteland. Families that have experienced such devastation know that of which I speak. Those who have been spared will never know the depth of despair to which the human heart can descend. For their sake, I am thankful they haven't had to endure such an experience.

I caught a flight out of Andrews AFB, Maryland December 23 that was headed for Patrick AFB, Florida. After spending the night there, I took a bus to MacDill on Christmas Eve and arrived to face two of the loneliest days of my life. Christmas Day was spent with Eric Boykins, one of my Tuskegee classmates also stationed at MacDill. By midnight, I was back in my room, bags packed, and ready to go.

The flight line at MacDill on December 26, 1965 was a sad day in the lives of hundreds of families. Approximately two dozen C-130 Turbo Prop transports were lined up for a mass departure. The last goodbyes were tearfully spoken to husbands, fathers, sweethearts, sons, and friends. I located my assigned aircraft and boarded to escape more emotional farewells. Having just left Peggy and the children, I was unable to bear the scene on the ramp. The sooner we got underway the better.

The transports were packed from floor to ceiling. The nylon webbed canvas "seats" were spaced just wide enough to allow shoulder to shoulder occupancy. Once loaded, we could not see or communicate with the persons on the opposite side of the aircraft. Considering the investment in the training and careers of fighter pilots, the Air Force showed little regard for our comfort for a 9,000 mile trip. There would be grumbling.

All personnel were finally loaded, the doors closed, and a slow procession of transports taxied for takeoff. Even with earplugs, the massive drone of turbo props sounded like a funeral dirge. We were soon airborne, and the journey to the "unknown" was underway. The prospect of what lay ahead seemed to hit all of us at once, and the sudden silence could be "heard" over the hum of the engines. Each face reflected a myriad of private thoughts, but the deep sadness was visible for all to see. I closed my eyes to hide the emptiness in my soul and tried to think of the many good times Peggy and I had experienced. Several hours passed before any attempts to communicate with another person were made.

About seven hours later, the air caravan landed at Forbes AFB near Topeka, Kansas to refuel and to allow us to stretch our legs. We resumed our journey west, and I got my first glimpse of the Colorado Rockies at sunset from about 18,000 feet. The breath-taking sight gave a little respite to the somber mood that still persisted among the passengers. We arrived at Travis AFB near Sacramento, California after midnight and were provided quarters for a few hours of sleep. The next scheduled stop was Hickam AFB, Hawaii but the leg was cancelled early the next day due to excessive headwinds at the planned altitude for the heavily laden C-130s.

A two-day delay was expected, so we were released to visit San Franciso and other nearby cities. My brother, David, and his wife, Rachel, were stationed at the Air Force Satellite Test Facility in Mountain View, and they came to get me. The visit was a god-send that allowed me to share openly my pent-up emotions about the events of the past three weeks. I also told David about my visit with our dad and sister, and encouraged him to follow-up with both. Feeling some better, I rejoined the group, and we took off for the scheduled nine-hour flight to Hawaii.

We arrived at Hickam the evening of December 30 and stayed overnight. Few bothered to check into the BOQ. Within minutes, the entire contingent rented cars, thumbed rides, or otherwise found their way to Waikiki Beach. The city was inundated with hundreds of excited, fatigue-clad men bent on making the most of one night in Honolulu. I had wanted to visit Hawaii since my childhood and was thrilled to join in the revelry. Everywhere the city was festive for the holiday season. The local people as well as tourists were exceptionally nice to us "troops bound for war." They shook our hands, bought us drinks, and kissed some goodbye. The downside to this welcomed diversion was the early show time the next day, New Year's Eve. Most of us made it, but the temptation for some was too much. It took considerable effort to round up the strays, and get everybody reloaded and airborne again.

Fate smiled upon us again during takeoff. We had to abort due to a mechanical problem. Our aircraft was seriously broken, and at least several hours were required to fix the problem. The jubilation on board was louder than the engine noise. Sensing a rapid exit, the loadmaster aided our cause by lowering the ramp the moment we reached the parking area. We didn't know how many aircraft aborted sympathetically, but our group was first to the auto rental place and first to reach Waikiki beach one more time. Later, word somehow reached us that we could spend New Year's Eve in Hawaii and depart on New Years Day, 1966. As the news circulated around the beach, the partying reached a fever pitch. The previous handshakes turned to warm embraces, Mai Tais and Hawaiian food flowed freely, many "practiced" good-bye kisses, and some disappeared altogether. The second roundup of strays was not as successful as the first one, and a few delinquents followed later. The pervasive comeback for those carefree sojourners was, "What they gonna do, send us to Vietnam?"

The next leg of our journey took us across the vast Pacific, flying over many islands and atolls steeped in the history of WW II. Our refueling stop was an atoll called Kwajalein located in the chain of the Marshall Islands. While stretching our legs, we surveyed the rusted relics of the major battle that took place there. Historical markers stated approximately 8,000 Japanese soldiers died while Americans lost 372 killed and nearly 1,600 wounded. America's success on the atoll ultimately help lead to victory in the Pacific. Though brief, it was a poignant stopover.

We reloaded and headed next to the Philippines. January 1, 1966 only lasted about six hours as we crossed the International Date Line into January 2nd. The caravan landed mid afternoon at Clark Air Base near Angeles City, the Philippines. We were ushered into a large room in the terminal and briefed on our final destination – Cam Ranh Bay, South Vietnam! The reality of our journey set in as we had only about three hours to go. With arrival instructions, we took off on the final leg of our seven-day odyssey to South Vietnam.

Cam Ranh Bay was located on a peninsula of the South China Sea midway between the border of South and North Vietnam. The U. S. Army operated a deep sea port on the southern tip. The airfield, located on the northern end, was built by the United States Army Corps of Engineers and turned over to the Air Force on November 1, 1965. A single major road existed on the entire peninsula to link the

U. S. Army and Air Force bases.

The 12th TFW was established at Cam Ranh on November 8, 1965. Colonel Levi R. Chase was the new Wing Commander and Colonel James Allen was the Director of Operations (DO). Colonel Chase was a highly decorated fighter pilot of WW II and the Korean War and one of the leading aces of North Africa with ten victories. Colonel Allen was a 1948 West Point graduate and also a combat veteran of the Korean War. Initial combat operations at Cam Ranh Bay began November 8, 1965 with aircrews drawn from stateside units. The 558th Tactical Fighter Squadron (TFS) and 43rd TFS were deployed temporarily from the 15th TFW at MacDill AFB, Florida. The 557th TFS was activated December 1, 1965 and the 559th on January 1, 1966 with the arrival of new aircrews. The 391st TFS joined the wing January 26th.

Our air convoy arrived at Cam Ranh Bay Air Base about 5:00 PM on January 2, 1966. The stark scene looked like something from a bad Hollywood movie. The ramp was made of large coated aluminum planking. The Wing Headquarters and Flight Operations were Quonset huts connected by wooden passageways. The noise of the nearby mobile generators competed with the verbal instructions of the reception team that greeted us. Further down the ramp, F-4s previously flown in were parked in the open. A few were painted camouflage while the others retained the original gray paint scheme. At a glance, the base was a lucrative target for a rocket attack from across the inlet. We were issued side arms, but this did little to dispel our immediate concerns for safety.

The arrival team assigned the incoming pilots to their respective squadrons - the 557th, 558th, and 559th. I was assigned to the 559th and realized most of the squadron had been on the same aircraft since leaving MacDill. We collected our duffel bags and were directed through ankle deep sand to our "quarters." This complex of four Quonset huts was enclosed by multiple layers of concertina wire with a security guard at a single opening. The insides of the huts were open with about 40 WW II-vintage cots lined against the walls. Boxes of C-rations were stacked at the entry way, and a canvas water bag was placed at the midpoint of the hut. Cot selection depended on friendships established during the trip. Joe Butler, Mike Trent, and I got along well since leaving MacDill so we became bunkmates right away.

Our evening meal was selected from the crate of C-rations. Most of us had never eaten C-rations so this experience was the first of many in the coming months. Afterwards, we sat around trying to adjust to the austere conditions and wondered how the days ahead would unfold. Surviving the first night, however, was a memorable event. Imagine the scene of forty tired, sweaty, flatulent bodies trying to sleep in an open facility. The horrendous snoring was bad enough, but the toxic air reached an explosive level. More than a few restless souls got up in the middle of the night for a cigarette break or just to get a breath of fresh air. So began the combat tour at Cam Ranh Bay.

Into the Fray

The first few days were filled with briefings about the base, our mission, and preparations for flying. The 12th TFW was tasked to conduct air superiority, armed reconnaissance, close air support, interdiction, combat air patrol, escort, and other missions assigned by Headquarters 7th Air Force in Saigon. The area of operations included Vietnam, Laos, and Cambodia. The wing was heavily tasked to interdict North Vietnam's supplies and equipment on the Ho Chi Minh Trail that ran through Laos and Cambodia. Missions flown in Laos and North Vietnam were called "Counters" that reduced the twelve-month tour one month for every twenty-five flown.

With the initial briefings completed, combat maps prepared, and life support and survival gear issued, the 559th was ready for combat. Nicknamed the "Billy Goats" after our mascot, the squadron was comprised of four flights - A, B, C, and D. We quickly adopted more creative names, and D flight became "Tom Rowdies" to reflect the personality of our Flight Commander, Captain Tom Roberts. Captain Ken Holcombe was the Assistant Flight Commander, and Captain Al Leveret, "Andy" Anderson, and Dale Young were the other aircraft commanders. The five GIBs were Captain Bob McConnell, Joe Butler, Mike Trent, Gary Bennett, and me. We were crewed respectively with Al, Tom, Ken, Dale, and Andy. Tom and Ken had previously seen action in Southeast Asia during a temporary deployment to Thailand in 1964. During that time, Ken scored an aerial victory over a North Vietnamese MIG 17.

I flew my first combat sortie January 7, 1966. By February 11, I had logged twenty-five combat missions, was awarded my first Air Medal, and declared "Combat Ready" for surviving sustained combat operations. I was the only Black pilot in the wing of about 180 pilots, but this small footnote no longer mattered. My acceptance as just one of the guys was based upon my performance and willingness to take on any additional duty assigned. It was also due to a reciprocal attitude toward my fellow comrades in arms. We became more than brothers, and the sincere caring and respect for each other prevailed throughout the 559th as well as the other squadrons. I formed lifetime friendships with Captains Lee Plotnitzky, Al Stipe, Dave Jacobsen, Jack Gagen, Jim Thornton, and others. One day, I was jokingly called "Der Baron" by someone who had been to Germany. Another suggested the Germans had their Red Baron, but the 559th boasted its very own "Black Baron!" Because of the rapport we shared, I accepted that title which persisted for several years.

The early part of the tour was relatively free of enemy ground fire, but that changed in early March with our increased operations in Laos. The intensity of anti-aircraft artillery (Triple A) and the threat from surface-to-air missiles (SAMs) also increased. Enemy small arms fire was routinely encountered during close air support missions in South Vietnam, but we encountered significant ground fire Valentines Day, 1966. Our flight was diverted to conduct armed reconnaissance along the Ho Chi Minh Trail to detect and destroy a mobile Triple A unit that had downed two aircraft. With the help of a Forward Air Controller (FAC), a suspected target area was located and we began a search along the route. Shortly thereafter, someone yelled, "Triple A, Triple A, left seven o'clock!" Everyone executed a high speed jink maneuver to reposition for the attack. The flight of four unloaded twelve tons of bombs on the area and the guns went silent. Scratch one for the good guys!

Later in the month, I was the GIB for Colonel Allen, the DO. The mission was a close air support sortie flown in the highlands of South Vietnam across from the Ho Chi Minh Trail in Laos. Again, with the aid of a FAC, we identified a suspected assembly of trucks and equipment and began our attack. During the third pass, our F-4 was hit with a volley of machine gun fire that entered the left intake. The jarring impact and noise sounded like we had been hit by a freight train. While climbing to a safe ejection altitude, I gave Colonel Allen a heading toward Plekiu Air Base, the nearest available emergency divert runway. We shut down the left engine to extinguish the resultant engine fire and completed other emergency procedures. Our wingman confirmed the fire was reduced to a huge contrail of heavy smoke so we continued to Plekiu and made a safe landing. Colonel Allen and I set a record exiting the aircraft while the emergency response team quickly foamed the smoldering engine, thus saving the jet. Later, we were cited for expert airmanship and professionalism under enemy fire. I took care of my own laundry bill, and my reputation as a GIB was given an appreciable boost.

For the first three months, the officer's kitchen and dining room consisted of three garbage cans with smoke stacks, a propane grill, and tables covered by partial tents. The food included C-rations, powdered eggs and milk, packaged oatmeal, and occasionally stale bacon. Vegetables and fresh food were non-existent. The austere conditions motivated everyone to improve dining facilities and living quarters. When not flying, the wing pilots joined in building an officer's club that featured a kitchen, bar, and dining area. In addition, I was designated the Squadron Housing Officer and Fire Marshal. That meant locating, acquiring, confiscating, or gaining possession by any means possible items that could be used to improve our Quonset hut. Once an item was installed, I made sure safeguards were in place to preclude accidental fires. With the help of a few squadron buddies, we successfully "acquired" plywood, mattresses, discarded furniture, and any other item considered useful. Our aggressive and creative forays extended to the nearby U. S. Army's deep sea port, Saigon, and other in-country bases. The C-47 Gooney Bird assigned to the base extended our pillages as far away as Clark Air Base in the Philippines and Tachikawa Air Base, Japan. Our modus operandi was simply, "If it ain't nailed down, it must be free for the taking!" By early spring, our creature comforts were greatly improved.

The passing months ushered in increased missions flown against the flow of North Vietnamese Army (NVA) personnel, equipment, and arms into South Vietnam. Taking advantage of poor weather, the NVA launched a major assualt against the Special Forces base in A Shau Valley. The valley was near the Laotian border and a key part of the Ho Chi Minh Trail. The base was manned by American Special Forces, South Vietnamese irregular soldiers, and Chinese mercenaries. On March 9-10, 1966, the base came under a fierce attack and was overrun. I was flying in one of about fifty aircraft diverted to provide close air support.

We orbited overhead a heavy cloud layer that obscured the area below. Over the radio, we could hear the raging battle beneath and made repeated attempts to penetrate the weather using F-4's onboard radar. Unfortunately, our efforts were in vain. In the meantime, a flight of two A1E propeller-driven Skyraiders managed to get beneath the clouds and provided support to the besieged camp. Two more A-1s soon joined the battle but one of them was shot down and crashed landed on the heavily damaged landing strip. The other one took a severe hit and diverted to Da Nang Air Base.

Two more A-1s successfully penetrated the 800 foot cloud ceiling and provided cover during a daring rescue of the downed pilot while encountering heavy enemy ground fire. The downed pilot was picked up and thrown into the aircraft head first. That incredible feat was led by USAF Major Bernie Fisher , Captains Francisco Vasquez, Jon T. Lucas and Dennis Hague. The rescued pilot, Major Dafford W. "Jump" Myers was a long-time friend of Major Fisher. Major Fisher later received the Medal of Honor for his heroics that day. Captain Lucas received the Silver Star, and Captains Vasquez and Hague received the Distinguish Flying Cross. The extraordinary heroism of these individuals clearly identify them as "*Uncaged Eagles*" under fire. I crossed paths with Major Fisher and Captain Lucas later in our careers.

It was small consolation, but some of us were later tasked to fly a number of missions against the NVA in A Shau Valley. The ground fire was intense and we received numerous hits but no aircrafts were lost. In turn, we inflicted heavy damage upon the enemy, but the battle for that strategic piece of land continued for several years.

Beyond the Fear of Death

Despite my success in combat, there was a persistent tug at my heart. Like tens of thousands before me and the hundreds around me, I faced the reality of death almost on a daily basis. In solitude, I reflected over my twenty-seven years and hoped there was enough good to receive favorable consideration before God. I missed my wife and children terribly and worried I would never see them again. Peggy reflected the same fear in letters she dutifully wrote me every day. She tried to stay upbeat and rarely wrote anything that might upset me. Her letters, however, indicated the tremendous struggle she had dealing with the uncertainty of my welfare for days or weeks at a time. Like all wives and loved ones back home, Peggy heard about the losses of so many aircraft on a given day. Yet, it sometimes took days for our letters to arrive confirming we were okay. I didn't discuss these concerns with anyone for fear it would belie the tough image expected of a combat fighter pilot.

Reaching a very low point, I poured my heart out in a letter to my brother, Wilbert, in Detroit, Michigan. I expressed my deep admiration and thanks for his great example and asked him to look after Peggy and the children if I failed to return home. I also wrote Mr. Austin E. Stewart, my benefactor in college, and others who had made a difference in my life. Deep down, I needed to reconcile as many personal accounts in my life as possible.

My brother was so moved by my letter that he drove down to visit Peggy and the children and vowed to honor my request in every way possible. Mr. Stewart was similarly touched by my letter and had it published anonymously in the local newspaper. My sister, Zella, read the letter and recognized it came from me. Shortly thereafter, scores of friends and relatives throughout Shreveport and around the country began a special prayer chain for my family and me. I recalled my mother's fervent faith in prayers and believed in those offered up for me.

Later, I visited Major Gene Hofstead, the Senior Chaplain at Cam Ranh Bay. He sensed my dilemma and provided words of encouragement. In addition, he invited me to attend a special Sunday night, low-key worship service. It included singing, personal sharing, and the chaplain's candid words about a variety of personal needs. Surprisingly, several pilots from the fighter squadrons attended this service, yet no one seemed ashamed about being there. Chaplain Hofstead's sermons spoke to the doubts, fears, and uncertainties that many of us had. He encouraged us to have faith in our country and to believe we were engaged in the noble cause of freedom for the people of South Vietnam.

The turning point for my fears came on April 10, Easter Sunday Morning. Chaplain Hofstead and a cadre of helpers constructed a giant cross at the Hawk Missile site on a hill overlooking Cam Ranh Bay. I was walking to breakfast at daybreak, when the brilliant sun rose over the South China Sea. It cast a long shadow of the cross across the base below. My faith and Christian walk left much to be desired, but I was deeply struck by this startling image. Foregoing breakfast, I headed for the cross on the hill and Chaplain Hofstead's Easter Sunrise service. As he preached about the sacrifice of Jesus Christ on the cross, a long-sought peace came over me. When I walked away from that experience, my lingering fear of death slowly ebbed away. I also left with a renewed sense of purpose and confidence that I would see my wife and children again. I continued to attend Chaplain Hofstead's Sunday night service and was grateful for his encouragement at such a crucial time in my life. Twenty-five years passed before fate allowed our paths to cross again. This time, it was a privilege to properly thank retired Colonel Gene Hofstead for being "*An Uncaged Eagle*" in my life.

On April 26, I was on a mission against a heavily fortified hostile headquarters near A Shau Valley now occupied by the NVA. Andy Anderson and I were leading the flight when both engines flamed out due to smoke and heat over the target area. I assisted Andy with the emergency procedures and directed him toward a nearby ridge line. We barely crested the hill and glided toward the valley floor as Andy got one, then both engines restarted. While climbing to altitude, I realized the ejection handle was in my grip and had been pulled within a fraction of firing. Incredibly, Andy had done the same thing and we had to reinsert the handles to preclude ejection. With both engines running and bombs remaining, we made one pass on the target and later were credited for destroying a major hostile complex. Andy and I considered it just another day in the combat zone, but we earned an Air Medal for the mission.

The 12th TFW conducted combat operations over an extended period without suffering the loss of aircraft or aircrews. That changed in May. The 559th lost its first aircraft to Triple A during a close air support mission in the highlands of South Vietnam. The aircrew, Captain Jack Gagen, a Marine exchange pilot, and GIB First Lieutenant Frank Malaguerie were successfully rescued several hours later. A short time later, the 558th lost an aircraft and its aircrew to hostile ground fire. Numerous other aircraft were seriously damaged by ground fire, but the aircrews managed to return safely. These sobering reminders highlighted the consequence of daily combat. Nevertheless, we pressed on, confident of our experience and skills in executing the missions assigned. We were reinforced by the superlative leadership of Captains Tom Roberts, Ken Holcombe, and others in the wing and squadrons. I was especially proud to be part of such an outstanding group of fighter pilots.

The GIBs in the wing got a special lift when Colonel Chase approved a plan to upgrade us at the local level. Tom, Ken, and the other flight commanders were identified as our instructors, and the training would be scheduled whenever time and available jets permitted. Since most of the GIBs were considered equally qualified, the line up was simply in alphabetical order. Accordingly, Gary Bennett was first up. Unfortunately, he had to abort his first training sortie due to an aircraft problem and subsequently ran off the runway. That ended the upgrade program as quickly as it began. Poor Gary took severe heat from all of us for the remainder of the tour.

In late May, I was summoned to the Squadron Commander's office. Having no clue for such a call, I did a quick audit of my recent behavior and performance and came up blank. Upon entering the commander's office, I was greeted by menacing stares from Lieutenant Colonel Ellis, the Commander, Major Lane, the Ops Officer, and all four Flight Commanders, including Tom Roberts. Tom was the first to speak. "Toliver, you have gone and ****** up now! What the hell were you thinking about!" I considered Tom a great guy and friend, but was dumbstruck and stared at him in disbelief. Racking my brain, I thought what the heck is he talking about? The group continued to stare at me as if I had just kissed their favorite lady or kicked their pet dog. Since I had done neither, my inherent combative nature became agitated, and I prepared to fight my way out of this hornet's nest if necessary. Sensing this, Major Lane said sarcastically, "Toliver, go pack your bags, you're going home!" Tom chimed in, "That's right, Dick. You're out of here!"

My mouth was wide open but no words came forth. I couldn't believe my ears. I had only flown enough counters to merit one month reduction in my tour. It would have been great to see my wife and babies, but it would be wrong to leave before earning the right to do so. Furthermore, I loathed the thought of someone taking up the slack for my premature departure. None of this made sense so I bristled and blurted out, "Tom, what the hell is going on? You know I haven't done anything to get kicked out of the squadron. What's this all about?" I was on the verge of exploding even further, so everybody in the room decided this charade had gone far enough. Major Lane handed me a piece of paper that said something about delivering a broken aircraft to Hill AFB, Utah. Still confused, I asked what this had to do with me. Someone said, "Damn Dick, do we have spell it out? You and Jack Gagen have been picked to fly that hunk of junk to the States if it will make it."

Everybody had a good laugh at my expense while the opportunity of a lifetime slowly sank in. Sure enough, an F-4 jet had been damaged beyond repair at the base. It was scheduled to be flown to Clark Air Base in the Philippines for interim repairs, then flown to Hill AFB for more extensive repairs. The pilots chosen for this unexpected gift were selected from a hat with all the names of the 559th. Captain Jack Gagen, the Marine exchange pilot, and I were the lucky ones pulled from the hat! If the jet made it to Hill AFB, we would be granted ten days delay enroute back to Cam Ranh Bay. No further discussion was needed. Within an hour, Jack and I were packed and ready to go. We departed for Clark Air Base before the day was over.

Getting the F-4 repaired enough to make the journey across the Pacific proved to be a very tough task. A week later, Jack and I were still unable to complete a successful test flight of the jet. After ten days, we were notified another aircrew would be sent to replace us. With the help of the Transient Maintenance Crew at Clark, we "borrowed" a part from a transiting F-4 on base and successfully completed the test flight. The same crew "found" the needed part in base supply, and two hours later, Jack and I were enroute to Guam. An escort aerial tanker was waiting for us the next day, and we continued on to Hickam Air Force Base, Hawaii. We said goodbye to the tanker about a hundred miles out of San Francisco and streaked into Hill AFB twelve days after leaving Cam Ranh Bay. Getting that broken F-4 to the States was nothing short of a miracle. The statute of limitations have long since expired, so I can say several limits were pressed in the effort to get home. But what could they do? Send us back to Vietnam? We split up at the Salt Lake City airport and headed home to enjoy those precious days for getting the aircraft to the States in one piece, but just barely.

Peggy was waiting for me with open arms, and we spent a few glorious days together with our children. The trip home was truly a blessing. We were encouraged by family and friends, and Wilbert flew down from Detroit to be with us for a couple of days. The visit was marred by the shocking news we received from our friend and former neighbor at Craig, Don Good. His wife, Libby, had suffered a sudden diabetic coma and died. Don had been released from his tour in Vietnam to take care of their baby girl, Jamie. I left a few days later for Cam Ranh Bay hoping the unexpected visit and news about the Goods were not an omen of our own future.

The ribbing Jack and I received upon our return was brutal but expected. We were considered real "dirt bags" for accepting the trip and chided for not giving it to someone else. Being ostracized by our jealous buddies was an acceptable price for the time spent at home. The extra missions piled on for the next several weeks were also easy penance for our "desertion." Thus, it happened I was flying on June 29, 1966. That day, 7th Air Force Headquarters scheduled the first simultaneous attacks against key military targets in Hanoi and Haiphong Harbor in North Vietnam. It was an exceptionally clear day, and smoke from both target areas rose thousands of feet into the sky. My flight was tasked to provide close escort for the RC-121 Electronic Surveillance aircraft that supported the mission. With multiple air refuelings, we stayed on station five hours to cover the primary attacks and post-strike reconnaissance. I climbed down from the jet that night terribly exhausted but proud of having taken part in my first of many missions to the infamous Red River Valley of North Vietnam.

The attack on Hanoi and Haiphong Harbor raised the war over North Vietnam to a higher level. The 12th TFW was tasked to fly escort for electronic surveillance missions in the vicinity of Haiphong Harbor and Hinan Island. I was happy to get back in the groove of flying, and in a thirty-day period logged ninety hours of combat over Laos and North Vietnam. On several occasions, I was involved in thwarting would be attackers against the surveillance aircraft, and one day we chased a suspected MIG all the way to the Chinese border. Our fangs were hanging out, but we could not get close enough to make a visual identification. It was close, but no cigar!

The Nightingales

In July, the pending arrival of the first nurses assigned to Cam Ranh Bay caused an unbridled uproar. The flight surgeon who lived in our compound received a lot of attention and was elevated to a place of esteem among the pilots. Allegedly, he had the real word on the nurses' arrival date and promised to put in a good word for those he thought worthy. Consequently, the bachelors did everything possible to win the flight surgeon's favor and sought to secure a place at the head of the planned receiving line. I was flying the day the nurses finally arrived, and the other married pilots were relegated to being spectators. Though not an eyewitness to the grand arrival, my subsequent observations of the nurses and their contributions to the war effort deserve comment.

The first six nurses assigned to Cam Ranh Bay apparently had been hand picked for their appearance, commitment, fortitude, and willingness to step into a raw war zone. With all due respect, none of them would have successfully competed in a beauty contest based upon age, size, shape, or hair style. Furthermore, the very senior Lieutenant Colonel who led the nurses was said to have deliberately chosen the least attractive in the Air Force. Her intent was to miti-gate the expected "hardship" they would face in the den of ravenous wolves under the duress of war.

First of all, the Lieutenant Colonel underestimated the atti-tudes and state of lonely men. Secondly, it only took about a week for the nurses to be transformed into the most beautiful females ever to hit the beach. Thirdly, to the great credit of the nurses, they man-aged to hold the most voracious suitors at bay. Lastly, they gave un-stintingly of their time to those in real need of their medical services.

When Cam Ranh Bay became the medical processing center for war casualties, these nurses demonstrated the greatest personal com-mitment I have ever seen. Many of the wounded troops were broken, blind, maimed, or suffered from a plethora of critical injuries. Most had to be stabilized before being air-evacuated to the States. Often, the nurses worked furiously alongside the doctors to save the criti-cally wounded. Many times their efforts went for naught.

The Nightingales spent twelve to eighteen hours per shift pro-viding medical attention under the most difficult circumstances. Of-ten, I witnessed their tears after a futile attempt to save a young life or felt their grief and frustration after holding the hand of a soldier who died. I observed the impact of this in their faces. Some gave beyond the call of duty and in ways that cannot be described or understood apart from the crucible of men and women at war. Not enough can ever be said for those ladies who came to Cam Ranh Bay in 1966. I believe they embodied the character, essence, and soul of all military nurses who serve our nation in times of peace and war. Their personal sacrifices are manifold, profound, selfless, and too often, unheralded. No monuments will ever be sufficient enough to honor them properly. No words can truly tell their stories, nor can the gratitude they so richly deserve ever be adequately expressed. I am proud to call these "Nightingales" a very special breed of *Uncaged Eagles*.

Wrap Up

The first replacement pilots and new GIBS began to arrive at Cam Ranh Bay in July. One of the GIBs was Guion Bluford, the second Black aviator assigned to the wing and the future first Black astronaut to fly in space. The experienced GIBs were called upon to help carry the load during the transition in the wing. This was an emotional challenge for us because the new pilots were former GIBs who were the first to upgrade to the front seat of the F-4. We made the best of a poor situation caused by the Air Froce Personnel Office. We were highly proficient in every phase of combat operations except putting the piper on the target. Our flying skills included combat lead support, tactical formation, armed reconnaissance, aerial refueling, and air-to-air intercepts. The new pilots willingly accepted and utilized our experience, thus contributing to the success of their transition. In addition, a few experienced pilots were transferred to the 559th from the other three squadrons, and the wing continued to operate with minimum combat losses.

My new front seat pilot and bunkmate was Kenneth W. Cordier, a very likeable and compatible fellow. Ken was married, and he and his wife, Judy, had two young children. Like me, during the earlier part of his tour, Ken missed his family very much and was nervous about speaking of them. I let him know we could speak openly about our families, doubts, and fears. As a result, our relationship became very special. This friendship spread to other new pilots, and I was sought out for advice and experience as a trusted GIB in the squadron. Some of the others who joined the 559th were Captain Jerry Shilt, Captain Lawrence Faison, and Lieutenants Robert Biss and Herbert Ringsdorf. Before long, the squadron was a tight-knit group again that relied heavily upon each other as the missions to North Vietnam increased.

October was one of the most intense periods of flying, but I could see the light at the end of the tunnel. I earned a two-month curtailment to my tour and was scheduled to go home at the end of the month. On October 3, I volunteered for a mission to a heavily defended area just north of the Demilitarized Zone called Finger Lakes. This was a depot facility of the NVA, and the defenses had knocked down several aircrafts. Captain Jerry Shilt and I were paired and were successfully attacking the target when one of our hydraulic systems failed. We released the remainder of our weapons on the next pass and diverted to nearby Da Nang Air Base. Da Nang was in the midst of recovering several combat damaged aircraft, so we continued on to Cam Ranh Bay.

We used the emergency gear extension system in preparation for landing. Our situation immediately deteriorated when only one main gear and the nose gear extended. The Supervisor of Flying at Cam Ranh Bay advised us the base had never conducted an approach-end barrier engagement on a foamed aluminum runway. We were given the option of attempting an engagement or to consider ejecting along the beach. Before we could decide, the daily beach patrol told us sharks were sighted earlier in the day. Our options shrank to one.

Jerry and I completed all possible emergency landing procedures and decided how best to touch down with a main gear up. We made a successful engagement with the barrier but it failed immediately. The aircraft slid off the side of the runway and nearly flipped over. Fortunately, one wing burrowed into nearby sand dunes and helped absorb the momentum of the jet. We were banged up a bit, but neither was seriously injured. Later we were cited for "saving a valuable weapons system" and awarded the Pacific Air Forces Order of the Able Aeronaut. Again, the laundry bill was our responsibility.

I flew my last combat mission on October 27. By then, I had logged 231 missions. Twenty-eight of these were over North Vietnam, seventy-nine over South Vietnam, one hundred and eight over Laos, and sixteen were support sorties. In addition, I had flown 485 hours of combat time. These were considered "outstanding accomplishments" and resulted in a recommendation for the Distinguished Flying Cross and the 12th Oak Leaf cluster to the Air Medal. Also, I had been promoted to captain and received an assignment to Hahn Air Base Germany. My last two days were spent clearing the base, visiting friends, and offering last minute encouragement to Ken Cordier, Bob Biss, Herb Ringsdorf, and my other closest buddies. Ken and I shook hands and had a solemn farewell. My last words were, "Ken, check six," the expression every fighter pilot understood to mean "watch your rear." Having survived my baptism by fire, I departed on October 30, 1966, my 28th birthday.

I spent November getting reacquainted with Peggy and the children, and visiting family. The separation had been tough for all of us, and we tried desperately to resume the wonderful life we had back at DM. It was not to be. Gail, Renea, and Michael were nearing four, three, and two years old, respectively. Peggy did her best to keep me alive in their young minds, but it was hard for them to make the transition from my photograph to "daddy" in the flesh. It would take more time than we could imagine. In the meantime, I tried to keep my troubled emotions under wrap, but an inner turmoil wouldn't subside. Inexplicably, I felt guilty for being safely at home while my buddies were still flying combat in Vietnam. The foreboding I felt became a sad reality the day we departed for Germany.

Many of the pilots from Cam Ranh Bay that were reassigned to Germany had the same departure day of December 5, 1966. We met at McGuire AFB, New Jersey with our wives, children, and relatives who came to say goodbye. Some we had met before at DM and Craig AFBs. Initially, the gathering was happy and festive. I learned my friend, Captain Tim Boddie, departed from Davis Monthan for Cam Ranh the same day I left Vietnam. He moved in with my former bunkmate, Ken Cordier, and was given my combat map, Tech Manual, and related items.

Later, a few more pilots arrived with the latest news from Cam Ranh Bay that immediately cast a dark cloud over those who had been assigned there. The news about my former squadron, the 559th, was especially troubling for me. On November 11, pilot Captains Bob Biss and Herb Ringsdorf and GIBs First Lieutenants Harry Monlux and Dick Butts were lost on the same mission. They were shot down in North Vietnam by Triple A on a mission led by Captain Ken Cordier. On December 2, Ken and First Lieutenant Mike Lane were shot down by a surface-to-air missile near Yen Bai Airfield northwest of Hanoi. All of them were listed as MIAs.

This horrendous news left all who heard it greatly distressed. The mood of those scheduled on our flight turned very somber. Some wept openly; others tried to find solace with their families. Those of us from Cam Ranh Bay felt this was a very sad close to that chapter in our lives. We hoped the new assignment would be a salve to the pain caused by the loss of our brothers in arms.

CHAPTER NINE

SKIES OVER EUROPE

On the evening of December 5, 1966, over 200 men, women, and children were loaded on board a huge four-engine jet for the flight to Frankfurt, Germany. Final destinations included U.S. bases in England, Germany, Italy, and other locations in Europe. My family and I were headed to the 50th TFW at Hahn AB in the Eiffel Mountains in central West Germany near the Mosel River Valley. Apart from the noise of babies and small children, the eight hour flight across the Atlantic was relatively quiet. Many of us were still lost in our thoughts about those missing or killed in Vietnam. Yet, we were very grateful to have survived and to be back with our families.

My thoughts eventually turned to Germany and my youthful desire to see this beautiful country someday. I also looked forward to the expected transition to the front seat of the F-4. My past four years in the Air Force had been swift and productive. They included a short tour as an engineer, pilot training, a combat tour, and over 500 hours of fighter time. In addition, I was scheduled to pin on the rank of captain in February. After waiting eighteen months, the dream of upgrading to the front seat of the F-4 appeared within reach. My optimism rose as we winged our way to Europe.

Peggy and I had gathered information about Germany and purchased a beginner's book on the language. During the flight over, I memorized a few suggested words and phrases thought to be useful. We arrived mid-morning December 6 and completed the initial process for entering the European Theater. We were met by two sponsors with vehicles from Hahn Air Base, Lieutenants Joe Bianco and Bill Wilson. Joe loaded my family into his vehicle and Lieutenant Harry Harrup who served with me at Craig, Davis Monthan, and Cam Ranh Bay loaded up with Bill. On the way to Hahn, I attempted to use my limited knowledge of the German language. We stopped at a roadside facility that was labeled "Damen" and "Herren." Harry and I decided "Damen" meant "The Men," and "Herren" was plural for "Her." We promptly entered the room labeled "Damen." The surprise on the faces of women and our embarrassment were clear evidence we both needed more schooling.

Peggy and I were very excited to be realizing our dream of traveling in Europe. The two-hour trip to Hahn presented spectacular, picturesque scenes along the way. We crossed the mighty Rhine River and passed through numerous villages with ancient castles straight out of the story books. We also saw remnants of WW II that still existed in some towns and villages. When we entered the Eiffel Mountains, the countryside turned to postal cards of snow-covered fields and cottages nestled in endless hills and valleys. Peggy took this opportunity to recall for the children some of the pictures she had shown to them earlier. Even though they were young, their young minds appreciated the beauty of the German countryside. All of our spirits were lifted by this positive first impression of the country we would call home for the next few years.

Upon arrival and checking into guest quarters, Harry Harrup and I received notice of assignments to the 10th TFS. We spent a couple of days getting our families temporarily settled and then reported to the squadron. The Commander, Lieutenant Colonel John S. Finlay,

III and Major Willis A. Boyd, our assigned Flight Commander, gave us a warm welcome. We were introduced to others in the squadron and given initial briefings on the mission of the 50th TFW and the part the 10th TFS played in it.

The mission of the 50th TFW was similar to that of our previous assignment – air superiority, armed reconnaissance, close air support, and interdiction. The added task was the nuclear strike mission and the continuous 24-hour alert commitment. The wing consisted of three squadrons, the 10th, 81st, and 496th. The first two were recently equipped with F-4s and primarily assigned nuclear strike roles. The 496th was the Air Defense squadron and flew the F-102. The 50th TFW wing was one of about a dozen U.S. fighter units assigned in Europe to support the North Atlantic Treaty Organization (NATO), the main deterrent to the threat posed by the Soviet Union and the Warsaw Pact.

There was much to learn; however, I was pleased to be told the first priority was to get our family settled. This task was crucial due to the lack of base housing caused by the wing's transition from F-100s to F-4s. The demand for base housing doubled due to the F-4's crew requirement of two versus one for the F-100. In addition, furniture and appliances, normally available in overseas housing supply, were extremely limited. Thus, locating adequate housing and furnishings was a considerable challenge for newly arriving personnel.

We found accommodations in the apartments where Major Boyd lived in the small village of Kastellaun about thirty minutes from the base. Two other squadron members, Lieutenants Dick Strunk and Bob Thompson, and their families also lived there. Major Lee Plotnitsky of the 81st TFS and formerly my squadron mate in Vietnam was also a tenant. Being neighbors facilitated the mandatory recall roster for the wing and car pool while we waited for our Vista Cruiser to arrive from the States.

Jan Boyd, Bill's wife, organized a support group for the younger wives in our apartment complex that included Carol Strunk, Rita Thompson, Phyllis Plotnitsky, and Peggy. We especially appreciated Mrs. Carol Finley, the commander's wife, for making a trip to Kastellaun to visit the wives whose husbands were in the 10th TFS. As our families settled in, our wives planned family gatherings and outings to many nearby towns and villages. They also made friends with our German neighbors and their children. Soon, the children were exchanging words and phrases in both German and English. These experiences made life pleasant and fostered lasting friendships.

Settling in Kastellaun required immersion with the German people and their culture. Peggy's adventuresome spirit and affinity toward the Germans made this a delightful experience for everybody. Before long, we were friends with several families such as Herr and Frau Krautkremer and their teenage daughters, Ria and Annette. Ria was our baby sitter and our very patient "lehrerin" or teacher of the German language.

During the first few weeks in the squadron, I learned the upgrade plan for experienced GIBs was delayed indefinitely. Contrary to what we were told upon leaving Vietnam, the Air Force was still embroiled in a disjointed, inconsistent policy of filling the cockpits in the F-4 units. By late 1966, the luck of the draw largely determined when new pilots were assigned to the front seat or when GIBs upgraded. Consequently, a large number of First Lieutenant Aircraft Commanders arrived in Europe with little more than 100 hours in the jet. Others like me had approximately 500 hours in the jet and would soon out-rank many pilots in the front cockpits. This caused a huge morale problem for F-4 units throughout Europe. The challenge to resolve the problem was left to Wing or Squadron Commanders by establishing local upgrade programs when the mission and resources allowed it.

The situation was especially difficult for me because I had more time in the F-4 than any of the pilots or GIBs in the squadron. I was also the first scheduled to pin on captain. This was a difficult pill to swallow, but the squadron's mission priorities precluded an upgrade program for the foreseeable future. Nothing could be done except pairing me with Major Bill Boyd and petitioning the Air Force for resolution of the wide-spread problem in Europe.

I received another disappointment a few weeks later when several awards from Cam Ranh Bay arrived. My recommendation for a Distinguished Flying Cross had been downgraded to an Air Medal, and the recommendation for the Air Force Commendation Medal apparently was never considered. This was my first realization that the awarding of medals did not always match the performance of the recipient, in the air and on the ground. I paid no attention to this matter while in Vietnam and expected to be recognized for my performance in due time. Such was not the case then or later. When compared to others who served at Cam Ranh Bay, I came up short. I had done my best and decided to let this slight pass.

These disappointments were not the only ones I faced in early 1967. My family had successfully settled in Kastellaun, but Peggy and I struggled to reestablish the great relationship we had prior to my departure for Vietnam. We were not alone in this predicament. Several other young couples experienced the same frustrations. Unknowingly or unwittingly, most of us guys came home expecting our wives to be the sweet, dependent, devoted young wives we left behind. We still expected to be "lord and master" of our households. Conversely, most of us failed to appreciate the profound impact of prolonged stress, uncertainties, and loneliness of the wives and families during our absence. Nor did we understand that the precious innocence of our youth had been ripped from our lives by war and destroyed forever. While we were away, the wives, of necessity, became independent. They cared for the families, managed the finances, kept the car in good order, and performed all the daily chores. These courageous young women were no longer the helpless and submissive spouses that our inflated egos expected.

As pilots, we escaped to our cockpits and to the many Happy Hours at the Officer's Club. Meanwhile, the wives were left alone, especially during TDYs, to care for the children and home front, often while unable to assimilate in the foreign community. These unrealistic demands and expectations often left our wives in tears, and more than a few gave up and returned to the States. Thankfully, I was one of the fortunate few.

I discussed my problem with a friend and his nurse girlfriend while on TDY. During the discourse, she helped me understand the tribulations Peggy endured during my year in Vietnam. She also helped me see the situation through the eyes of a woman. The light came on for me that day, and I began to "find my way home." After many months, I felt the desire to truly embrace my wife and children. I told Peggy about my revelation before returning home. She was excited and met me on the steps of our apartment the day I returned home. Our three young children also were caught up in the celebration. After missing for a very long time, it was great to be home. The real heroine in this near disaster was Peggy, and I can't praise her enough. Our marriage was saved by her deep, abiding faith in God, gentle spirit, and willingness to endure my callous attitude and behavior during those trying times. I didn't know how blessed I was then, but Peggy was *An Uncaged Eagle* in my own home!

Aircraft Commander

The prospect of my upgrading to the front cockpit of the F-4 received a jump start in the spring of 1967. The Air Force Military Personnel Center (AFMPC) apparently heard the pleas of the GIBs in Europe and sent Major General Robert J. Dixon, AFMPC Commander, to address the situation. The pilots were summoned to the Officer's Club on a Friday afternoon for a briefing on personnel issues regarding the rated force. General Dixon's presentation did not address my situation of high time in the F-4, combat experience, and rank. Nor did he recognize that some GIBs were approaching two years in the back seat! At the conclusion of his briefing, I rose to plead my case. Everybody in the room, especially the commanders, was shocked and expected me to be chewed up and spat on the floor. General Dixon stared at me for a long moment with his renowned hawk-like scowl, but to my surprise he said, "Have we met before, Captain? What's your name?" "Sir, I am Captain Dick Toliver. We met when you came to Craig AFB in 1965." There appeared to be a flash of recognition, and with a slight smile, he turned to his aide and said, "Get that man's particulars. I want to know why it has taken so long for him to upgrade." Turning back to me he said, "Captain Toliver, your problem should be an easy one to fix. Next question!"

I retreated back into the crowd, but it was like the Red Sea parting! No one joined me at the bar where I stood alone wondering if General Dixon really did remember me from Craig AFB. Most thought I had committed a fatal error by speaking without the consent of my commanders. I soon left for home to share the encounter with Peggy. We spent the weekend pondering my immediate future.

On Monday morning, I was called in for a meeting with Lieutenant Colonel Finlay, Major Taylor, and Major Boyd. The gamble had paid off. My upgrade program began immediately, and Major Boyd was my assigned instructor pilot. Fate had allowed me to come face-to-face with General Dixon at just the right moment and place. He made a difference in my attitude, career, and my life.

In June 1967, I deployed to Wheelus Air Base, Libya for my first-front seat gunnery training. On June 6, a war exploded between

Israel and its Arab neighbors, Egypt, Syria, Lebanon, and Jordan. U. S. fighters were recalled immediately to their home bases in Europe and prepared to respond as directed by higher authority. We landed at Hahn and received briefings on possible deployment scenarios while the aircraft were reconfigured with air-to-air missiles and the 20 mm gun pod. We were sequestered in the BOQ and directed not to contact our families. Before authorities in Washington, D. C. could make up their minds, Israel won the war in just six days! The Israeli Air Force (IAF) accomplished an unprecedented and decisive victory over their adversaries. The world would forever recognize Israel and the IAF as a premier force with which to be reckoned.

Later that summer, an apartment became available in Hahn Air Base housing, and I moved my family on base. We left many friends in the German community, but it was time to make things easier for Peggy and the children. Our German friends made a difference in our lives with their ready acceptance of us and their warmth, generosity, and kindness. The relationships and visits to Kastellaun continued for the remainder of the tour.

My experience and time in the F-4 facilitated the transition to the front cockpit. Flight procedures and routine maneuvers went like clockwork. Developing as a top gunner proved to be more challenging. I was fortunate in getting help from Captain Jim Thornton to improve my gunnery scores. Jim came from Cam Ranh Bay and was a recent graduate of the Tactical Fighter Weapons School at Nellis AFB, Nevada. Others who took a personal interest in my career were Major Bill Boyd and Colonel Aaron J. Bowman, 50th TFW Director of Operations. The friendship and encouragement from these officers were invaluable in my development as an aircraft commander and seasoned fighter pilot.

Tough Losses

Peggy and I were planning our second Christmas in Germany when we received the sad news that her father, Harvey Hairston, had suffered a heart attacked and died. We departed with the children for Baltimore to attend the funeral. Peggy's father's passing was a terrible shock to all of us, and I regretted not being able to have more time with him. My father-in-law was a rock for us while I was in Vietnam, and I had grown to love him deeply. Likewise, many at his service voiced great love, respect, and appreciation for his generosity in their time of need. He was a self-made man who prevailed over the many hurdles throughout his life. He loved his family dearly and was one of the greatest providers I knew. None in his immediate and extended family ever suffered from the lack of food, clothing, or shelter at any time in their lives. Given my experiences early in life, this was especially important to me. All who knew this man would sorely miss him. We returned to Germany in early January and celebrated a delayed Christmas with the children.

I resumed flying in mid January and completed upgrading to Aircraft Commander in March 1968. I was sitting on Nuclear Alert the morning of April 4, 1968. Someone approached me and put The Stars and Stripe newspaper in my hand. Huge headlines covered the front page: "MARTIN LUTHER KING, JR. ASSASSINATED IN MEMPHIS, TENNESSEE!

My eyes clouded over in disbelief, and my hands shook so badly I could hardly read the print. I bolted from the room overwhelmed by grief and gasping for air. This terrible tragedy was incomprehensible. I sat in my room and cried openly while my thoughts were: "I am sitting on alert with a nuclear bomb with more destructive power than all the bombs dropped in all the wars on earth. Yet, I am completely powerless to do anything about this horrendous evil just unleashed in my beloved country." My mind reflected back to when I first met Dr. King. I recalled his "I Have a Dream" speech in Washington, DC and remembered seeing him marching from Selma to Montgomery. I heard him speak for the last time in May 1965 at my brother's graduation. No longer able to perform my duties, I requested to be relieved for a few days.

When I arrived home, Peggy and some of the neighbors had heard the news and gathered to offer consolation. We appreciated their sympathy but nothing could ease the grief we felt. We met that night with a few other Black officers and their families to gather strength from one another. Later, when Peggy and I prepared for bed, I challenged God for His reason for this despicable murder. What possible good could come from such a tragedy? How could an omnipotent and caring God allow this travesty to happen when our nation needed the likes of Dr. King? I loved America as Colonel Chappie James and other Tuskegee Airmen taught me. But what on earth could I possibly do to help her at a time like this? For a lowly captain in the Air Force, there were no immediate answers.

The violence that erupted in the cities back home compounded the loss of Dr. King, now grieved around the world. This great American was an icon of peace and non-violent change against injustice and racism. Our nation and the world lost an irreplaceable treasure. While I grappled with Dr. King's death, the answers to my questions that slowly emerged in my mind were simple: "Keep on doing your job. Maintain a positive attitude. Pursue excellence in all you are assigned, and be prepared to make whatever contribution you can when the opportunity comes."

With those thoughts in mind, I returned to work determined to keep Dr. King's memory alive in my heart and honor him by continuing to offer my very best as an Air Force officer and fighter pilot. Peggy and I committed to doing whatever we could whenever there was an opportunity to make a positive difference in the lives of others.

Those That Made a Difference

The person most responsible for the enjoyment of our tour in Germany was Peggy. Her persistent positive attitude about every experience affected the children and me, whether during day-to-day activities, traveling, or dealing with challenges in life. She never complained about the inconveniences of living overseas such as the lack of supermarkets, shopping malls, or American goods and services. Our children particularly benefited from Peggy's attitude as life for them was a constant adventure and lots of fun. This included walks through the nearby woods or trips to German villages for shopping and sightseeing.

Major Bill Boyd continued to be a champion supporter of my career. He offered me an opportunity to participate in the 1968 North Atlantic Treaty Organization (NATO) Allied Air Forces Central European (AFCENT) Meet. This event was an annual gunnery competition between the Second and Fourth Allied Tactical Air Forces (ATAFs) of AFCENT. The host base was Jever, a German Air Base near Bremerhaven in northern Germany. Participants for the 50th TFW were selected from the 10th TFS and 81st TFS with an alternate crew from the 81st. Maintenance technicians were selected from both squadrons. Major Boyd was the designated team leader for the wing, and he wanted me to be his GIB for the competition. This was the first year for the F-4s in the competition, and our teams made a respectable showing.

The closing festivities were held in the Officer's Club at Jever and attended by the top Generals in AFCENT. The club was a beautiful facility that featured numerous large murals of WWI and WWII German fighters shooting down Allied aircraft. General Maurice A. Preston, Commander of HQ USAFE and 4ATAF, was hosted by Lieutenant General Johannes Steinhoff. General Steinhoff was the Inspector General of the German Air Force and a former Luftwaffe fighter pilot in WW II. His remarkable facial scars allegedly were caused by a fiery crash in a German ME-262 jet.

I was particularly pleased to meet and hear stories from these legends and was standing near Steinhoff when he spoke to me: "Captain, how do you like flying the Phantom?" All eyes, including General Preston's focused on me when I answered, "Sir, I enjoy it very much. It's a great aircraft!" General Steinhoff continued to question me about the F-4's capabilities and asked if I knew the Germans were considering replacing their F-104s with F-4s. I knew about the consideration currently being made by the German Ministry of Defense and answered in the affirmative. General Steinhoff's next question totally surprised me. "Well, Captain, how would you like to come to Memmingen Air Base in October to demonstrate the Phantom to the German people?" Attempting to remain composed, I answered, "Sir, if our headquarters grants approval, I would be honored to come." Turning to General Preston, General Steinhoff said, "What do you say, General Preston. Can this be arranged?" Without delay, General Preston said, "Yes, I believe so. I'll have my staff get with yours to work out the details." General Steinhoff smiled broadly at me and said, "Well, Captain, I look forward to seeing you in Memmingen!"

With that discourse, one of the most fantastic experiences of my career was put into motion. I thought how much Major Bill Boyd played in this by his confidence in my ability. He witnessed the conversation and smiled his approval. I was truly grateful for his friendship and leadership. We were greeted by our families and squadron members upon our arrival back at Hahn. The news of the offer from General Steinhoff had already reached the base, and Lieutenant Colonel Gast and Major Taylor personally met us at the aircraft. After the meeting on the flight line, we departed for home to spend the weekend with our families.

The official tasking from Headquarters USAFE arrived the next week. Colonel Robert Lyles, the Wing Commander, called my commanders and me to his office for a review of the events and to give us his specific instructions. This was a significant event with huge implications, and Colonel Lyles wanted to make sure it was carried out in a superior manner. Lieutenant Colonel Gast assured him that would be the case and was tasked to put together a detailed plan for the visit to Memmingen.

Captain Mick Larkin, another highly experienced F-4 pilot was appointed as the second pilot for this visit. Two top-notch crew chiefs were authorized to fly in our back seats on the trip to ensure technical assistance on the spot. Mick was the designated demo pilot while I was scheduled to conduct interviews and explain the F-4 capabilities to the visitors. We completed the plan, obtained Colonel Lyles' approval, and he sent it to Headquarters USAFE for final approval. General Preston approved the plan and reiterated the potential ramifications of the visit. With the plan successfully completed, I was granted a few weeks of leave.

My mother-in-law, Elsie, and Peggy's sister-in-law, Yvonne, came over for a month's visit. Losing her husband of forty-nine years six months earlier had not deterred Mom from looking after her children and grandchildren. Her presence in our home was a tremendous blessing, and she always made a spiritual difference whenever she came. This was the first trip outside the U.S. for Mom and Yvonne, and we wanted to share the wonderful experience of traveling through Europe. Our travels included Holland, Belgium, Luxembourg, Bavaria, Switzerland, Austria, and Italy. These trips allowed us to see much of the beauty of Europe and to experience the different cultures in each country. These were very special times for our children to enjoy the attention of their doting grandmother and aunt.

I returned to work after three weeks, highly energized and ready to fly. October came quickly, and we deployed to Memmingen as scheduled. The annual German October Fest was in full swing in

Bavaria, and the blue skies were as clear as the colors in the Bavarian flag. We were met by the Wing Commander and a host of base support people. Other NATO participants included several German Air Force units, the Canadians, French, and Italians.

The Open House began the next day at 8:00 AM as thousands flooded the base and flight line. The F-4 was the center of attention, and General Steinhoff came by with an entourage of German officials to get a first-hand report. Shortly afterward, Mick Larkin made a spectacular maximum afterburner takeoff and flawlessly performed the planned demonstration. General Steinhoff and the crowd were thrilled with the performance of both Mick and the "Phantom" as they called the F-4. The response of General Steinhoff, the dignitaries, and the public suggested the Phantom was the winner of the day. I led the team home that evening and reported to Lieutenant Colonel Gast who met us on the flight line.

Word of our successful trip reached Headquarters USAFE and was passed on to Colonel Lyles. He expressed his appreciation for a "job well done," and Mick and I received a lot of "Atta Boys" from our peers. A few weeks later, we received news the Germans decided to purchase F-4s to replace their aging F-104s. It felt good to have been a small footnote in Germany's decision.

My performance as a pilot and my additional duties were recognized by my commanders and senior wing leaders. I received a career-broadening opportunity late October by an assignment to the USAFE Air to Ground Operational School (AGOS). I qualified as a Ground Forward Air Controller (FAC) and was subsequently deployed to Nuremburg, Germany to serve as FAC during training with both U. S. and NATO units.

In November, Peggy and I were given an opportunity to reach out to the German community. The base chapel needed someone to take charge of the annual "Dank Tag Fest," or sharing Thanksgiving with German children at a nearby orphanage. American homes were opened to busloads of orphans to celebrate our traditional Thanksgiving Day. In 1968, the former Wolfgang Kinderheim Orphanage honored Dr. King by changing its name to the Martin Luther King, Jr. Kinderheim. Peggy took over the program that year and continued each year we were in Germany. She recruited participants, prepared the list of homes, coordinated the transportation, and briefed the families on the rules for involvement. Our family, along with scores of others, was truly blessed by these experiences. The children were excited and overjoyed with each visit. This one-day outing was the highlight each year, and everyone looked forward to the next year.

Several other individuals and families entered our lives providentially. Their example, friendship, influence, love, or support came at just the right time, and they helped us become who we are today. These included Bill and Jan Boyd, Jim Thornton, Roger Wells, Charles and Fran McGee, Art and Ann Peterson, and Bernie and Realla Fisher. These people contributed much to the success Peggy and I enjoyed in the Air Force, and we forever thank God for allowing them to cross our paths.

From the beginning of our relationship, Major Bill Boyd did everything possible to promote my goals in the Air Force. Besides upgrading, this included a recommendation for Regular Officer status and selection for Squadron Officer School. Bill was one of the finest persons I encountered during my career. He was a highly experienced fighter pilot but eschewed the typical bravado exhibited by most others. Instead, he had a quiet, confident nature that made those around him feel at ease. Most importantly, Bill was totally void of prejudice toward people because of their color, social status, or rank.

I learned that Bill's character and core values reflected the environment and circumstances of his life growing up in upstate New

York during the 1930s. Bill worked hard to get through high school and college and was commissioned through the Aviation Cadet Program. In 1956, he married Janet, his high school sweetheart. When we met at Hahn, he had flown several different fighters over a twelve-year period. Bill had an identical twin brother in the Air Force who was killed earlier in an aircraft accident. This, more than any other experience, affected him for the rest of his life and influenced him to be the kind, wonderful man I came to know. Many years later, he told me, "The two of us still get together in my nightly dreams." Bill died just two months after he shared this story with me.

Captain Jim Thornton's persistent friendship and encouragement were two constants that provided a great amount of pleasure in my life. His attitude, personal flight instructions, and professional advice contributed much to my development as an aviator. His gunnery expertise was especially helpful to me when I encountered trouble with dive and skip bombing. Jim's patience and encouragement caused me to cherish him as a friend forever. We also enjoyed a special trust from our Commander, Lieutenant Colonel Phillip Gast. Jim was assigned the additional duty of Squadron Maintenance Officer to resolve some serious deficiencies on the flight line. As Squadron Equipment and Supply Officer, I worked closely with him to acquire the critical resources needed to get our jobs done. Regardless of the magnitude of the task, Jim always kept a sense of humor that minimized the difficulties we faced.

Captain Roger Wells, another person in the squadron, had a significant impact on me by my observation of him. He was a prior enlisted man who worked his way to Officer Training School and subsequently completed Undergraduate Pilot Training. Later, he successfully completed the Fighter Weapons Instructor Course at Nellis and was now a "Top Gun" fighter pilot. Roger was regarded as the ultimate fighter pilot. His imposing persona, outstanding skills, swagger, and crushing handshake impressed all who met him.

Most pilots in the squadron openly tried to emulate Roger in every way, but I was one of his silent admirers. He was my standard of excellence. I wanted to achieve his level of performance as an aviator and that was my personal challenge for the immediate future.

Colonel Charles E. McGee, his wife Fran, and teenage daughter, Yvonne, arrived the summer of 1968. Colonel McGee was the new Chief of Maintenance, and I soon got the chance to meet him through my additional duties and time on the flight line. He was a highly decorated fighter pilot whose handsome appearance and demeanor exuded character, integrity, and leadership. Peggy and I also were privileged to become friends with his family during chapel services and other social events. Colonel McGee was one of the finest persons I ever met and a role model for young Black officers as well as those of other races. Often he and his wife Fran met with or visited young officers in their homes. If the family served hot dogs, the McGees ate them as if they were scrumptiously prepared meals. They had the exceptional ability to make young couples feel at ease while being great examples by their actions rather than words.

I was especially thankful for Colonel McGee's presence in our lives, and tried to emulate his many attributes. For the first time in my adult life, I found a man whom I wanted to call father. Unashamedly, Peggy and I admired and loved him and his family. Colonel McGee was an original Tuskegee Airman who downed a German fighter in WW II. Because of his tremendous humility, I didn't learn this until eleven years later. I realized then it would take me a lifetime to follow in the footsteps of this great, unpretentious *Uncaged Eagle*.

Our new neighbors across the parking lot were Major Bernard "Bernie" Fisher, his wife, Realla, and their six sons. Bernie earned the Medal of Honor for rescuing his buddy "Jump" Myers who was shot down in A Shau Valley in 1966. As one of the pilots overhead that day, I was honored to be his neighbor two years later. Bernie was assigned to the 496 TFS, but he was accessible to many who sought to meet him and hear his story. He was the first Mormon I knew and who demonstrated a lifestyle contrary to that of a "typical" fighter pilot. He didn't smoke, drink, curse, or exhibit a pompous attitude. I remember most his humility, serenity, and obvious love for his family. The Fishers were a model family in every sense of the word. Sometimes their home would be overrun by the neighborhood kids, especially when Bernie served homemade ice cream to whomever was visiting. The Fisher's presence had a positive impact on all the families in the neighborhood, and Peggy and I were proud to be part of this Air Force family.

Art Peterson, his wife Anne, and their five children moved in downstairs from us. Art was a WW II veteran who saw action in the Pacific. He was a career civil servant and served as Chief Civilian Personnel Officer in the 50th TFW. One of the most notable attributes of both Art and Anne was their genuine acceptance of all people without regard to their race, color, or religion. Their upbringing in the heart of a rural Pennsylvania community fostered their love of God, love of country, and respect for one's fellowmen. Art and Anne lived this creed every day and faithfully taught their children to do the same. Peggy and I appreciated the Petersons even more as racial prejudice still persisted at home and overseas. Without making an issue of it, the Petersons did much to promote acceptance, fairness, and mutual respect in our community. Our families spent a lot of time together, and the Petersons became life-long friends.

Another Personal Loss

In January 1969, I was notified of another family tragedy in the states. My thirty-two year old sister, Arneater, died suddenly from a ruptured vein in her head. I left immediately for Los Angeles where I found her five children, ages four to twelve, in dire straits. The neglect suffered by my sister and the children exacerbated the grief caused by her death. Following the funeral, my siblings and I were forced to make difficult decisions for the welfare of Arneater's children. We prevailed with the help of some of her in-laws and the Los Angeles County's Child Services.

Our families agreed to provide care and homes for all five children. When I called Peggy to explain the situation, she simply said, "Dick, do whatever you have to do. I'll support you." It was very comforting to hear those words that confirmed the tremendous character of the woman I married. I love her dearly to this day for her support then.

Zella and AW took the youngest child, four-year old Shirlevia. Earl and Nancy Brown, Arneater's in-laws accepted eight-year old James, Jr. Wilbert and Dorothy took nine-year old Tharpsky. David and Rachel took ten-year old Daryl. Peggy and I agreed to take the older child, Glenette, but faced completing official adoption procedures in less than thirty days. This process normally required six months to a year in the best of circumstances.

Again with the aid of county personnel, I was introduced to Mrs. Dorothy K. Davis, a renowned lawyer whose clientele were largely Hollywood movie stars. I visited her office in Beverly Hills and was very impressed by the obvious affluence. I concluded the cost of her services was well beyond my reach. After discussing my situation, I asked the fateful question. Her answer was even more astonishing: "Captain Toliver, I sympathize with your loss, and appreciate what you and your family have decided to do. If you will pay for the associated court costs, I will consider that payment enough." Words cannot adequately express my gratitude for the help of this great humanitarian. Mrs. Davis, Glenette, and I met with a Child Court judge and he approved the adoption. I received a bill a few weeks later for less than $300.

My cousin, Annie, her brother Louis, and Earl and Nancy Brown were outstanding in their support. They provided transportation, lodging, food, and tremendous moral support on a daily basis. I would never have been able to accomplish what I did without their generosity and love. They were there for me from the moment I arrived to well after my departure.

Glenette and I arrived back in Germany to the waiting arms of Peggy and the children. They did everything possible to make Glenette feel welcome and an important part of the family. In addition, Peggy spent many hours helping Glenette with her school work and in combating depression. Assimilating her into our family, school, and the neighborhood was a tremendous challenge, but we were determined to go forward as a happy family. Our wonderful friends and neighbors welcomed Glenette into their hearts and played a major part in her adjustment to the Air Force community.

Finishing Well

A large turnover occurred in the squadron during the summer of 1969, and we tried to make the transition as seamless as possible. Lieutenant Colonel Gast, the Commander, was promoted to full Colonel and reassigned to the Pentagon. Lieutenant Colonel Taylor moved up to Squadron Commander and Lieutenant Colonel Jack C. Trabucco was the new Squadron Operations Officer. Bill Boyd was promoted to Lieutenant Colonel and moved up to Assistant Operations Officer. Newly assigned Major Vance Cribb was my Flight Commander, and I was appointed Assistant Flight Commander.

As new personnel assimilated into the squadron, I was uneasy about Major Cribb's occasional negative comments directed toward me. Furthermore, he privately displayed a racist attitude I had not encountered for quite a while. Later, he downgraded my Effectiveness Report in the very areas that were the hallmark of my performance.

My greatest disappointment was in Lieutenant Colonel Taylor, now the Squadron Commander. Previously, he indorsed every one of my reports since his arrival, yet he failed to question Major Cribb's sharp departure in my rating.

I requested a meeting with Lieutenant Colonels Taylor, Trabucco, Boyd and Major Cribb to identify actions needed from me to regain a top rating. Neither Lieutenant Colonels Taylor and Trabucco nor Major Cribb was specific, so Lieutenant Colonel Boyd spoke up. He reiterated I was one of the finest officers he'd ever met and offered to help chart a course for me. Lieutenant Colonel Taylor seemed pleased with this response and turned the matter over to Bill.

Bill encouraged me to take the high road and to continue performing in my usual superior manner. As Assistant Operations Officer, he promised to ensure Major Cribb's future ratings were commensurate with my performance. My passion for the Air Force was deeply rooted in an unshakeable commitment to my country, my family, and my people. Racial prejudice, setbacks, pitfalls, or whatever else would not hinder me so long as I had breath.

Another arrival that summer was Major Jack Murphy, his wife, Pricilla, and two young children. Jack was an outstanding professional who brought to the squadron experience from the Strategic Air Command (SAC). He was assigned as my primary GIB, now appropriately called the Weapon System Operator (WSO). Jack quickly became an expert F-4 WSO and perfected a number of existing navigation and radar bombing procedures.

The months went by swiftly as TDYs, base modification, and new aircraft avionics posed numerous challenges for the squadron and wing. My relationship with Jack Murphy continued to be a pleasure in the squadron and at home. We had a lot in common, and our families frequently visited each other. Jack's maturity and expert airmanship enhanced our crew performance during all phases of mission training and on the gunnery range. We enjoyed flying together and closed out 1969 on a low level mission along the scenic Rhine River. My optimism began to rise as we entered the New Year, 1970.

On other operational fronts, 1970 ushered in many changes for U. S. fighter squadrons throughout Europe. Libya's President Kadafy expelled the U. S. forces in late 1969 and the loss of Wheelus Air Base and nearby gunnery range was significant. Colonel Daniel "Chappie" James was the Wing Commander there and reportedly prevented a disastrous loss of critical resources to Kadafy's forces. The closure of the historical Weapons Training Detachment at Wheelus posed an immediate problem in locating comparable gunnery ranges in other countries. During the first few months of 1970, we scrounged range time in Belgium, Holland, Spain, and Deccimomanu Island in the Mediterranean.

In addition to the preceding problems, Hahn Air Base was scheduled for temporary closure in April for runway repaving. The nuclear strike commitment did not change, so aircrews traveled to Bitburg and Spangdahlem Air Bases to sit alert. These requirements caused considerable disruption to our daily operation as well as in our families. The resilience of aircrews, maintenance personnel, base support personnel, and our families was admirable, and the mission of the 50th TFW continued uninterrupted. Colonel McGee, as Chief of Maintenance, did a Herculean job of keeping our aircraft flying.

Lieutenant Colonel Bill Boyd continued to be my faithful mentor and friend. Once again, he was selected to be the 50th TFW team leader for the 1970 AFCENT Meet. Bill recommended to the Wing Commander the teams from Hahn Air Base for the AFCENT Meet. He selected Jack Murphy and me as one of the four U. S. Teams. For whatever reason, Bill tasked Major Cribb to be the back up pilot for the team. Using the improved avionics of the F-4D, Jack developed techniques to improve the accuracy of the avionics navigation system. These techniques would be crucial to our success during the low level navigation competition.

That year, the Second and Fourth Allied Tactical Air Forces (ATAFs) competed for the best overall mission capability and gunnery. General Joseph R. Holzapple was the Commander of USAFE and Four 4ATAF. The competition was held at Spangdahlem Air Base in the Eiffel region of West Germany. The AFCENT teams arrived at Spangdahlem on June 3rd for the 10-day competition. The eight participating countries were Great Britain, Belgium, Denmark, France, Germany, Holland, Italy, and the United States. Following careful briefings on the rules of engagement, flight procedures, and safety, the competition got underway.

The outcome of competition was very close up to the last event of night navigation and radar bombing. Each country was allowed one aircrew for this last sortie, and Jack and I were selected for the U.S. team. Eight aircraft taxied to the marshalling area while being advised of threatening weather. We were cleared for takeoff but shortly encountered severe lightning and thunderstorms all across France. It was the worst weather I had seen in my three and one-half years in Europe. Consequently, Jack and I had to make numerous detours along the route. We then worked hard to get back on course and make up lost time. Jack did an incredible job providing me continuous airspeed and course corrections. We finally reached the range entry point from a different direction than previously practiced. We made course and time corrections until the last few seconds when Jack signaled me to initiate timed release of the bomb. While I executed a climbing turn, Jack yelled "Splash," indicating we had successfully released our bomb within the qualifying time. We would not know the results, however, until we landed.

Totally exhausted, we headed for Spangdahlem while encountering low clouds about 1,000 feet above ground. Neither of us spoke as we mentally reviewed the mission and hoped we had been successful. On the flight home, I experienced a mild case of the "leans," a type of vertigo caused when the pilot's actual aircraft attitude gets confused with the base of the clouds. I quickly resorted to my instruments but my corrections were erratic. This continued for a couple of minutes before Jack turned on the intercom and said in a concerned voice, "Dick are you okay?" My delayed response was somewhat garbled. Using my personal call sign and speaking more urgently, Jack said, "Talk to me, Baron!" I realized Jack felt something was wrong up front, so I told him I was flying on instruments, but could not shake the momentary distraction. Jack confirmed our level attitude and used the aircraft's radar to ensure a safe separation from a ridgeline about fifteen miles ahead. He asked me to allow him to take control of the aircraft while I got my head in synch with the visual references below the clouds. Since I taught Jack how to fly the F-4, I was confident of his ability to fly the airplane. After a short time, I regained my visual equilibrium and took control of the aircraft. We chuckled about another vignette to add to our event-filled flight that night.

About fifteen minutes from the base, the cockpit suddenly went dark from complete electrical failure. This critical emergency was heightened at night, and I immediately extended the Ram Air Turbine (RAT), the emergency generator. The RAT restored electrical power to essentials such as the radios. With the radios and intercom back on the line, I declared, "Mayday! Mayday! Zweibrucken Center, this is AFCENT 14 with a critical emergency. Request clearance direct to Spangdahlem Air Base." Hearing this, Jack was temporarily relieved and, I later learned, released his ejection handle. The sudden loss of electrical power at low altitude, at night, and with a pilot who momentarily suffered vertigo was just too much. Jack was within seconds from ejecting and who could blame him?

The air traffic controller cleared us direct to Spangdahlem tower's frequency, and I visually sighted the base while descending. I made contact with the tower and was cleared to land. As I slowed to lower the landing gear and flaps, we lost electrical power again. Once configured for landing, I increased power to regain partial electrical power and radioed the tower of my increasing difficulty. I could see the flashing lights of the emergency vehicles along the runway when we lost electrical power for good and continued the approach in complete silence and blacked out cockpits.

I made a successful landing but failed to react immediately to the loss of the antiskid protection along with electrical failure. The main landing gear tires locked immediately and exploded within seconds of each other. The resultant grinding of the magnesium alloy wheels caused plumes of fiery sparks that reflected against our canopies as I struggled to keep the aircraft on the runway. We had no intercom, but I could hear Jack yell over the screeching wheels, "We are on fire!"

I managed to get the aircraft stopped on the runway. My adrenalin was sky high and I was over the side in a flash. Then I realized Jack was not behind me. The sparks and red-hot remnants of the wheels ignited the ruptured hydraulic lines and flames began to spread under the wings. I shouted, "Come on, Jack! The aircraft is on fire!" For some unfathomable reason, Jack had one leg over the side of the aircraft with the other still in the cockpit. He seemed intent on gathering his flight gear. I yelled even louder, "Jack, what the hell are you doing? Leave that stuff and get out of there!" Seeing the flames, Jack scurried down the wing and joined me in our dash to safety. When at a safe distance, I yelled again at Jack, "What the hell were you doing? You never stay with a crashed aircraft!"

The arriving emergency crews drowned out Jack's mumbled reply and hid his embarrassment. We watched anxiously as they extinguished the flames before any serious damage was done to the aircraft. The wing commander arrived to appraise the situation. Satisfied that the emergency had been taken care of, he offered to take Jack and me to our operations hangar.

When we entered the door, the thunderous applause from our aircrews and maintenance troops shook the building. Jack and I had been the only aircraft to make it to the range on time and deliver a qualifying bomb. Thus, the Americans won the Broadhurst Trophy for 4ATAF team. Another member of 4ATAF took top honors for the Canberra Trophy. The maintenance crew chief came up and presented me a dummy practice bomb freshly painted black. Before speaking, I looked over at Jack and Bill Boyd and acknowledged their simultaneous nod. A few minutes ago, these men had stood outside the hangar eagerly waiting to welcome Jack and me back. Their anticipation turned to horror when they witnessed our dramatic landing. Now Jack and I were safe, and we could celebrate the conclusion of our fantastic journey together. I graciously accepted the trophy and thanked everyone for making this success a real team effort. Jack and I simply had the privilege of making the last pass across the goal line.

Concluding ceremonies were held the next day with dignitaries of participating AFCENT nations in attendance. General Horace M. Wade, Chief of Staff of Supreme Headquarters Allied Powers Europe, in a surprising political gesture, presented the winning trophies to German Lieutenant Colonel G. Lutz, 4ATAF team captain. Our team was disappointed but accepted General Wade's decision, but the NATO pilots knew who the real winners were in 1970. The personal satisfaction for Jack and me would last a very long time, and I was eternally grateful for Bill Boyd's faithful support of my career. He was a steadfast friend and mentor who helped open the doors of opportunities for me when others refused to do so. Bill Boyd was a quiet, fair-minded *Uncaged Eagle* at a crucial time in my life.

Earlier, I had tentatively agreed to an assignment at the Air Force Academy as an Air Officer Commanding (AOC). However, Jack's and my success at AFCENT '70 changed my mind about leaving the cockpit. With only five years of flying, my gut sense told me it was too soon to leave. Furthermore, the war in Vietnam was still raging, and I felt my contribution there was incomplete. Peggy and I discussed this dilemma, and she advised me to do what I thought was best for my career as long as our family could be together. Two of our four children, Glenette and Gail, were in school, so a location out West was our first choice for the next assignment location.

Trusting my gut feelings, I requested a meeting with Wing Commander, Colonel Smith, to advise him of my decision to withdraw from consideration for Air Force Academy. He was disappointed but understood my desire to stay in the cockpit. Despite my late decision, I secured an assignment as an instructor pilot at George AFB, California. We were thrilled about this since I would be returning to Davis Monthan AFB, Arizona for the Instructor's Course. Also, this assignment put us close to many relatives in the state I dearly loved.

We spent the last few weeks wrapping up our tour in Europe and saying good bye to scores of American and European friends. It had been a tremendous tour that we would cherish for many years to come. By then, Glenette had made new friends and was still adjusting to being a teenager free of the trauma of her earlier years. Peggy did her usual preparing of our young ones for new experiences at our next assignment. Our last night in Germany was spent with the Krautkremers and Herr Gunter Kronlein, a German artist who painted portraits of our children. We departed Frankfurt on July 7, 1970 for the United States and new adventures that awaited us.

Chapter Ten

Climbing Higher

We arrived in Baltimore and planned to spend a few days before leisurely traveling to visit other relatives in Louisiana and Texas. Mom's health caused us to change our plans. Her condition had seriously deteriorated without our knowledge, but we were compelled to take responsibility for her care and welfare. After consulting with Mom's doctors, Peggy's three siblings, and other relatives, it was decided Mom would come with us to California. I had the five-year old Vista Cruiser repainted, mechanically overhauled, and refurbished to accommodate my family of seven for the trip across country.

We enjoyed the positive changes that had taken place in America during our three and one-half years in Germany. Our children especially enjoyed flashing or receiving the two-fingered "Peace Sign" to travelers along the highway. For the first time in our lives, we were able to stop and eat in restaurants and check into motels all across the south. We also experienced the social changes such as the Peace Movement, anti-war attitudes towards Vietnam, economic and cultural changes, and the predominant use of the term "African American" versus "Black" people. Of note, I had long since heeded Dr. King's words of, "It's not so much what you are called, but what you answer to." Thus, I was not offended by either term. Furthermore, we taught our children, "Black is beautiful, but everything beautiful isn't necessarily Black!"

The visits with family and relatives were happy reunions. We stopped in Shreveport to visit Zella, AW, and their family at their new home. AW had earned a degree in Education in 1966 at Wiley College in Marshall, Texas. Their older daughter, Linda, had completed two years of college. Their son, Anthony had finished high school and joined the army, and Deborah, their youngest was a junior in high school. Mr. Rye, Sr. was doing well surviving ten years beyond the stroke he suffered in 1960. While in Shreveport, I called Mr. Stewart, my benefactor, and Mr. Brown, my high school principal, to give them a report on my career and my life.

Our children had never met my eighty-six year old Grandpa Bob, Mother's father, so the visit to his little country house in East Texas was a special treat. I explained how much Grandpa meant to me growing up and what a positive impact he had on my life. The children also got a first-hand look at his water well, vegetable garden, chickens, yard dog, and outside privy. The latter was a real eye-opener. No one was interested in going "potty" while there. Grandpa Bob had waited over a year to ask me if man had really gone to the moon. He believed I flew fighter jets that went faster than the speed of sound. So if I said man had gone to the moon, he would believe it. It was a privilege to explain it to him, but he accepted it as truth simply because I said so. Our relationship of over twenty years was still a great blessing for me. After a few days, we resumed our travel.

During the next three days, we drove across Texas and southern Arizona to Yuma, and then turned northwest toward California. The scenery and tourist attractions were great experiences for the children and especially Mom. She had never been west of Alabama so it was a special thrill for her. Without ceasing, she praised God for his handiworks in the mountains, deserts, the people and every aspect of His creation. Before long, everybody in the station wagon was proclaiming, "Praise the Lord!" I did not dare protest.

The trip across country took ten days, and we arrived in Victorville in mid July. The same day, I was able to get my family settled in temporary quarters in Victorville and prepared to check in at George AFB. We got a surprise visit the next day from my favorite first cousin, Annie Felder. Annie was one of eight children of my mother's sister, Lonnie, and we had a close relationship since childhood. Annie heard we were due to arrive in California and used her ingenuity to track and locate us. She spent a couple of days with us and caught us up on many relatives residing in California.

I reported for duty at the 479th TFW, later changed to the 35th TFW, commanded by Colonel Fred A. Treyz, a WW II veteran fighter pilot. I was attached to the wing for two weeks for refresher flying and wing orientation. It was great to be back in the jet and meeting pilots I served with at other bases. I also met Lieutenant Colonel William E. Brown, a Tuskegee Airman and Chief of Standardization and Evaluation (Stan Eval). His deputy was Major Art Longmire, one of two other African American fighter pilots at George AFB.

Flying over the Sierra Nevada Mountains and the Mojave Desert of California was breathtaking and I thoroughly enjoyed doing so. On a single sortie, I flew over Sequoia National Park and 14,494 foot Mt. Whitney; a few minutes later I flew just above the floor of Death Valley, 282 feet below sea level. It took just two weeks to confirm the validity of my earlier decision to stay in the cockpit, and I was excited every day going to work. I smiled a lot those days.

In the meantime, Peggy, Mom, and the children settled in quickly. The elementary school for Gail, and now Renea, was just one block and within sight of our base house. Glenette, now in high school, took a bus to nearby Victorville. We were fortunate to find a doctor for Mom in Apple Valley, about ten miles away. He catered to numerous movie stars who lived there, including western stars Roy Rogers and Dale Evans. The doctor took a special interest in Mom and promised to have her restored to good health in a few months. To round things out, we purchased our first family dog, Pixie, a wire-hair dachshund. Our family was now complete, and everyone was happy.

An Awakening

Following wing orientation and refresher flying, I was sent TDY for several weeks to Davis Monthan AFB for Instructor School. I was one of two captains in a group of six majors who had considerable fighter time. Despite their rank and experience, I was determined to do well in academics and in the air. My advantage was the fire in my belly and the thrill of being at the instructor school. Everybody got along swell, and my motivation was sky high. The prolonged time spent in the rear cockpit of the F-4 finally paid dividends. The experience and de facto instructor role at Hahn gave me an edge in becoming a formal instructor. Demonstrating basic flight maneuvers, performing aerial refueling, and landings from the rear cockpit was old hat for me.

The air-to air phase came at the end of the course, and I was particularly eager to improve my skills in this area. The light bulb came on for me one day during academics. The instructor explained the pursuit of an adversary in terms that were familiar to me. These included aerodynamics, vectors (magnitude and direction), force of gravity, nose position of the aircraft, and a line connecting the three and nine positions on a clock. He explained the optimum maneuvering environment as an egg-shaped envelope. One needed to envision instantly positions or planes where the nose of the aircraft, airspeed, vectors, and gravitational force could be used to gain or preserve energy. The whole pursuit of an adversary had to be imagined inside the egg-shaped envelope. Whoever mastered the concept in the air would likely win an engagement. Hallelujah! The engineering courses I had in aerodynamics, vector analysis, and related disciplines at Tuskegee came back with a resounding application. I could actually visualize flying the aircraft with a vector perpendicular to my cockpit protruding through the top of my head and through the top of the canopy. I could hardly wait to put this concept into practice.

The proof of this knowledge came on my final check ride on an air-to-air sortie. The mission consisted of a series of one-on-one engagements with the student instructor pilots in the rear cockpits and the instructors in the front cockpits. I successfully maneuvered the aircraft into the pursuit envelope of the other student on several events. We set up for the final event, a head-on engagement. The instructor warned me the other instructor would likely be flying this engagement. My fangs extended and the determination in me burned like fire. We passed abeam each other with the call, "Fight's on!"

Several pictures flashed in my head, and I saw a position of advantage in a fleeting second. That was all I needed. After about forty-five seconds of aggressive maneuvering, my instructor shouted, "Hot damn, Dick, you are about to get him! You got your nose behind his Three-Nine line. Holy ****, you got him! You got him!" He yelled, "Fox II! Fox II!" In real life, the latter indicated a heat seeking missile could have been fired successfully. We both let out a series of loud whoops and howls, and laughed all the way back to the base.

During the debriefing, the other instructor and student looked sheepish and conceded I won every engagement. The exhilaration I felt was indescribable; I had found my niche as a fighter pilot. From that day on, air-to-air was my forte'. It was a great note upon which to return to George and begin my duties as an instructor pilot.

Shortly after I returned from DM, a military house became available and I moved my family on base. The house was very small, but the advantages of living on base were worth the inconvenience of limited space. The safety and warmth of an Air Force community played a large part in our decision.

In September 1970, I was assigned to the 4535th Combat Crew Training Squadron where Major Clark Price was the Assistant Ops Officer. Clark and I served with Colonel Chappie James at DM. Major Kermit "Kerm" L. Traster was my Flight Commander. In his own words, he was "a good ole boy from Georgia," but we hit it off from the start. Major Al Stipe, formerly from Cam Ranh Bay and Major Dave Jaquish, who we met at the base chapel, were neighbors and instructors in the squadron. Most everyone else in the squadron was a major or lieutenant colonel with extensive fighter experience in numerous aircraft. As one of three captains, it was great to fly with and rub shoulders with so much experience. My performance report from the Instructor School circulated around the squadron, so I was quickly accepted as an instructor and ready for students.

My first assigned students began training in July. They included pilots cross training from other aircraft, recent graduates from pilot training, and navigators fresh out of Navigator School. I was also assigned Colonel Charles A. Grabiel, a Korean War Veteran, who downed two MIG-15s in air-to-air combat. As an officer, student, and person, Colonel Gabriel was one of the most outstanding gentlemen I have ever met. His attitude, infectious smile, and warm personality earned the greatest respect from all who came in his presence. He was on an abbreviated syllabus, and scheduled to be a Wing Commander of the 432nd Tactical Reconnaissance Wing at Udorn Royal Thai Air Force Base, Thailand. I had the privilege of flying with him on several gunnery and air-to-air sorties and was humbled by being considered his "instructor!" It was also a blessing to begin a relationship with Colonel Gabriel that lasted many years.

The recent graduates from pilot training were the easiest and most fun to train. One crew was particularly enjoyable, First Lieutenants Clem Burt Meyers, pilot, and Francis "Frank" Sutscheck, a navigator. These two had a tremendous attitude and excellent grasp of the F-4 as a total weapon system. Burt was a terrific pilot, and Frank readily absorbed the procedures and techniques needed to be a great WSO. On the other hand, pilots transitioning from cargo or bomber aircraft presented greater challenges. Some made the switch against their will, but this was the only way they could stay in a cockpit. The cause of this anomaly was the protracted war in Vietnam that depleted the number of fighter pilots available to fill F-4 and other fighter cockpits. Assigning navigators to WSOs duties in the rear seat of the F-4 without fighter orientation was another challenge for instructors.

To overcome these problems, I gained approval from the Squadron DO to conduct additional training and orientation flights. The special training focused on making both the pilots and navigators experts on the F-4. The premise was the more they knew about the aircraft, the less intimidating it was. I solicited help from Captain John Madden, an instructor in the Academics Squadron and attached to the 4535th for flying. John was a tremendous instructor in the classroom as well as in the air. Next, I scrounged additional flying hours and scheduled extra simulator time at night. The extra flying hours were spent on basic handling qualities and confidence maneuvers for pilots experiencing the most difficulty in the F-4. Additional hours in the simulator were used to better prepare the navigators for WSO duties and procedures.

My program was notably successful, and other instructors soon adopted it for their students. The extra training and involvement with my students took considerable time, but I thoroughly enjoyed being an instructor. Despite the long hours, living on base enabled me to get home quickly and spend as much time as possible with my family. Peggy continued to be a supporting wife. She and Mom did an excellent job nurturing the children.

The practice of spending extra time training combat crews paid off for a young first lieutenant in the squadron. Gene Jackson, a young African American pilot, had been in the 4535th since July. We spoke to each other and chatted in the pilot's lounge a few times, but because of my students, I took no further interest in him. Passing in the hallway one day, Gene appeared downcast and deeply worried. I asked what the problem was, and he told me about an upcoming flight evaluation due to problems in the gunnery pattern. Gene was assigned to another flight and my friend, Major Al Stipe, was his instructor. I asked Gene to come by my house to talk about his problem and to see if I could help.

That night, I learned Gene was a native of Lufkin, Texas and a graduate of North Texas State. He was commissioned in 1967, and finished near the top of his pilot training class at Reese AFB, Texas in October 1968. Gene completed one tour in Vietnam as a GIB and was slated to return after his upgrade at George. We discussed techniques in gunnery patterns, and I asked him to "chair fly" a few patterns for me. Gene was a highly intelligent and dedicated young pilot who was passionate about being a fighter pilot. I concluded my help could be useful, but it was risky getting involved with another instructor's student from a different flight. Remembering those who helped me, I decided Gene was worth the risk.

I approached Al Stipe the next morning and told him about my visit with Gene. I asked if he would object to me flying a couple of flights with Gene. Al agreed, and I talked it over with Major Traster, my Flight Commander. Kerm was bit nervous about how my request would be perceived by the other Flight Commander and Operations Officer, but he gave me his blessing to proceed. I visited Lieutenant Colonel Sprague and Majors Whitten and Price. Although surprised, they approved my request after checking with Gene's Flight Commander and instructor. Major Whitten called me in to tell me I was cleared to fly two range sorties with Gene but added, "Don't cut Jackson any slack. Bust him if he can't handle the jet on the range. And Dick, from now on, we are going to assign all the students who are having problems to you!" I replied, "Sir, I will grade Gene like any other student, and I will be happy to help wherever possible."

Gene was ecstatic when I told him we were going to fly together. We were scheduled in a flight of four to the gunnery range and prepared for live passes. I discovered Gene's problem on his very first pass. During the set up for the final turn to the target, he was attempting to fly to the target without completing the path across the ground ninety degrees to the target. The correction was to project an imaginary line from the target and a vertical position where the aircraft should be for final tracking and piper placement. After a couple of dry passes, Gene got the picture and I cleared him hot on the next pass. "Voila," Gene dropped a qualifying bomb on that and each subsequent pass. My next challenge was quelling his exuberance at having discovered the "sight picture" for an effective bombing pass. The debriefing went great. Other students witnessed Gene's recovery from the brink of an evaluation that may have ended his budding fighter career. For good measure, I flew the other allotted sortie with Gene and recommended he be continued in training.

Majors Al Stipe and Kerm Traster congratulated me for having the courage to get involved in a situation that could have had negative repercussions for me. Instead, I helped save a future fighter pilot and earned a lot of respect in the process. Gene thanked me profusely, and a lifetime relationship began. At eight years my junior, he considered me a caring big brother and an example to emulate. Gene graduated with his class and returned to Southeast Asia to set an enviable combat record. My students, Burt Meyers and Frank Sutscheck, finished first as a combat crew.

Our Air Force Community

The excitement and pleasure of living and growing in the Air Force community at George AFB was a great time for the Toliver family. We were blessed to have terrific neighbors, new friends, and professional associates in the local community. Major Al Stipe, his wife, Sue, and their three children became immediate neighbors when Sue alerted us to a larger, vacant house next to theirs. Given my family of seven, this was a God-send. We moved in with the help of the Stipes, students, and friends. We continued our friendship with Captain Joe and Sue Merrick, formerly at Hahn Air Base, who lived across the street. Also joining us at George were our great friends from Hahn, Lieutenant Colonel Bill and Jan Boyd and their two boys. Joe was an instructor in the wing, and Bill was the chief of the 2nd Aircraft Delivery Group at George.

The Air Force environment was especially great for our children as the community was one of togetherness, respect, and absence of overt racism. Most of us taught our children to get along and accept others in the neighborhood and at school, based on merit, good behavior, and mutual interests. This harmonious atmosphere did much to discourage any latent prejudice that may have been harbored by a few. We also worked to ensure top quality schools on base and in the community where our children attended. By then, all four of our children were in school and doing very well, thanks to the constant tutoring of Peggy. Notwithstanding my professional duties, I served as President of the Parent Teacher Association, and Peggy took academic courses for certification to teach in California schools.

We were blessed at George AFB to be able to share our Air Force experience with many family members. Zella, AW, and their two daughters, Linda and Debra, came for a visit in the summer. Our gatherings at Thanksgiving and Christmas were festive occasions as dozens, led by my cousins Annie and Louis, came for visits. It was especially exciting for some to actually visit the flight line, get a first-hand look into the cockpit of the F-4, or witness a maximum take-off during a Functional Test Flight. These were happy times for everyone.

Until Major Dave Jaquish, I never met an openly Christian fighter pilot. I didn't even know such a person was possible. I totally embraced the image of the aggressive, confident, fearless, and swaggering fighter pilot who sometimes raised hell just for the fun of it. Also, I did my fair share of bar talk at Happy Hours and threw down a few. My regular attendance at the base chapel services was due mostly to "doing the right thing" with my family. Dave, however, displayed none of this. He faithfully attended chapel and participated in the Officers' Christian Fellowship (OCF) Bible study. The OCF, a fellowship of military Christians, dated back to WW II. Active in all branches of the military, it focuses on small Bible study groups at bases, on board ships, and at stations around the world. Its purpose is to unite Christian officers for biblical fellowship and outreach and to equip and encourage them to minister effectively in the military society. Dave's everyday life was a great example of OCF.

Dave took a personal interest in me, but he never attempted to proselytize or try to change my outward persona or frequent salty vocabulary. Instead, he invited my family to lunch after Sunday service. In full view of others, he joined hands and blessed the food before we ate. I also keenly noted the warm attitudes of Jane, Dave's wife, and his three children toward him. They laughed a lot with each other, and the children loved to hang onto Dave whenever possible. I truly loved Peggy and our children, but we didn't have that outward, loving relationship. Deep down, I wanted what Dave had, but was too vain to ask him about it. He was a top-notch pilot, great instructor, and respected by all who knew him. He didn't curse, boast, or swagger. To the contrary, he possessed a quiet confidence and a strong faith in God. Perplexed by my opposing desires, I decided to concentrate just on being a great fighter pilot and instructor.

I wasn't ready to be completely like Dave quite yet. Perhaps some day I would try to emulate his spiritual attributes.

Man Plans, God Executes

A year passed at George, and I successfully graduated two classes. Life was good and we were experiencing a great time in our lives and career. My performance report identified me as "one of the finest instructor pilots in the squadron" and "one of the most capable, conscientious, and reliable officers in the wing." I was considered the "Last Word" on procedures, techniques, and technical data on the F-4 and recommended for promotion well ahead of my peers. Without warning, one man sought to alter the course of my career.

Lieutenant Colonel James M. Hines became the Commander of the 4535th the summer of 1971. Apparently he did not appreciate my performance and reputation in the squadron. I noticed his cool attitude toward me but felt it would improve with time. While passing him in the hall one morning he said, "By the way, Toliver, you're going to the Command Post." His announcement was like a bullet through my heart. Colonel Hines never broke stride as I stared after him in disbelief. He gave no explanation for this shocking news and obviously did not care about the impact such a move would have on my career. The Command Post was a crucial job in the wing, but it was considered a dead-end job for fighter pilots, especially the younger ones. I'd worked extremely hard to become a top instructor and sought to be selected for the Tactical Fighter Weapons Instructor Course, or the "Top Gun School" at Nellis AFB, Nevada. All those bright hopes for my immediate future were callously dashed against the rocks in that passing encounter in the hall.

I immediately went to see Major Traster, my Flight Commander, to find out if he had been consulted in this decision. Kerm was just as shocked and upset as I was. He couldn't believe the manner

in which Colonel Hines broke the news to me. We both decided to go
see newly promoted Lieutenant Colonel Bill Whitten, the Operations
Officer. He told us a requirement was levied against the squadron
and that Colonel Hines made a unilateral decision to send me. Bill
tried to ease my disappointment by telling me I would still be attached to the squadron as an instructor. As new Operations Officer,
he didn't argue my case any further. Major Clark Price had been
recently promoted and reassigned to Washington, DC. Thus, I had
no support in the squadron above Kerm Traster.

The sickness in my stomach left me unable to perform that day
so I requested leave and went home. When I broke the news to Peggy,
she was hurt and speechless. She believed as I did, that we were on
course to a great fighter pilot career with no doubts about our future.
My outstanding performance was well documented in the squadron
as well as the wing, so there was only one conclusion left for us. It
was very difficult to accept, but in our minds, Jim Hines raised the
ugly specter of race in his decision. This reality caused a resurgence
of anger and bitterness I fought so hard to overcome. It seemed every
time I made a positive step forward, someone came along to knock
me backwards a few paces. At such times, I recalled the words of
Booker T. Washington years before at Tuskegee Institute: "I will allow
no man to drag me down so low as to make me hate him."

Had it not been for my loving wife and mother-in-law, I would
have given in to hatred, not only for Jim Hines but also for a long list
of others who had caused me pain. These precious women shared
my pain and prayed fervently for me to be able to persevere in spite
of man's efforts to push me backwards. I was also blessed to be encouraged by my friends Bill Boyd and Dave Jaquish. They agreed I
had been dealt with unfairly, but neither allowed me to wallow in
self-pity. Both still voiced their confidence in my ability to succeed
in the Air Force. Armed with prayers and moral support, I reported
for duty at the Command Post.

The Wing Operations Center (WOC) was commanded by Lieutenant Colonel William H. McMurray, a former U-2 pilot. His deputy was Major Charles Fridley with whom I served with at Cam Ranh Bay, Vietnam. Both these officers appreciated my background and experience, and they welcomed me to the Command Post. Both were highly experienced aviators and still motivated to do the best job possible in their positions. Lieutenant Colonel McMurray had served with U-2 pilot, Francis Gary Powers when he was shot down by the Russians in 1960.

Upon reporting to the WOC, I learned the 35th TFW was due a repeat inspection from HQ Tactical Air Command. An earlier evaluation resulted in a "Marginal" overall rating, and a number of key personnel had been fired. Colonel Treyz, formerly the Vice Commander, was now Commander, and Colonel Frank R. Fischl, Jr. was the new Director of Operations. Lieutenant Colonel McMurray had been assigned as the WOC Chief. Thus, the wing was in transition, and I faced a considerable challenge in getting up to speed in my Command Post job while the wing prepared for reevaluation. I promised Colonel McMurray my complete dedication in preparing for a successful inspection, but I let him know of my desire to move on as soon as possible. He understood and agreed with my personal goal. With that understanding, I rolled my sleeves up and dove into the task at hand the only way I knew how, focused and at full throttle.

I worked day and night to learn everything possible about the operation of the WOC- how, who, what, when, and where. My first objective was to understand fully the scope and depth of the WOC's mission. This included its function as the key information center for wing; message traffic control during emergency and rescue operations; and coordinator of daily flying and maintenance operations. The WOC was also responsible for implementing the Emergency War Plan as directed by higher headquarters. Next, I identified the "make/break" issues of operation. I studied the latest evaluation report to determine what went wrong during the last inspection. With a clear understanding of the role of duty officers, I submitted several recommendations pertaining to both officers and non-commissioned officers. Finally, I asked Lieutenant Colonel McMurray to put me on the duty schedule as some of my suggested changes were implemented.

I was barely settled in my job as Duty Officer when an emergency call came in one night in early October. Our next door neighbor, Al Stipe, had been critically injured in an automobile accident and had to be air lifted to Travis AFB for emergency surgery and protracted care. We had grown to love the Stipes dearly, and our children got along beautifully. Our entire family got involved in supporting the Stipes during the long, difficult weeks that followed. Rather than a duty, it was a privilege to assist the family in whatever way we could. Al eventually recovered but was not able to fly again.

We did not have to wait long before the Tactical Air Command (TAC) Inspector General (IG) and his team arrived unannounced. The exercise began early one morning before shift change. Consequently, my shift was extended several hours into the evaluation. The flying operation involved the entire wing with multiple simulated emergencies for both operations and maintenance. In addition, the TAC IG directed me to implement the Emergency War Plan. Lieutenant Colonel McMurray and Major Fridley were called in, but I remained on duty until late afternoon of the first of the three-day evaluation.

The WOC was the hub of activities for the duration of the TAC IG visit, so we were in a fish bowl the whole time. Fortunately, we met the challenge, and the 35th Wing received an overall "Excellent" during the TAC IG's out briefing. In particular, the WOC received an "Excellent" with several events rated "Outstanding." Everyone in the wing was jubilant, and the celebration at the O'Club went well into the night. I had the privilege of being the Duty Officer that evening.

Colonel Treyz was still happy the next morning during the wing staff meeting and personally congratulated me by saying, "Dick, you and the entire Command Post did an outstanding job during IG inspection. I appreciate your efforts, but Mac tells me you want to leave us. Where do you want to go?" Without hesitation, I answered, "Sir, I would like to go to the Fighter Weapons Instructor School at Nellis." Colonel Treyz turned to Colonel Fischl, the DO, and said, "Frank, why don't you see if you can get Dick into the next class at Nellis?" Barely able to contain myself, I said, "Thank you, sir! Thank you!"

Several officers around the table clapped spontaneously as Colonel Treyz smiled and winked at me. Later, Bill McMurray and the other WOC staff were as happy as I was and heartily congratulated me. Bill told me to go home and pack my bag because I was as good as gone. Two weeks later Colonel Fischl called me in to tell me I had a January 1972 class date at Nellis. In addition, I was notified of a follow-on assignment to Thailand for my second tour in Southeast Asia. This incredible turn of events from start to finish took place in just six months. Regardless of the intent and motivation of Lieutenant Colonel Hines, God clearly executed a different plan for me. That night, my friends and family celebrated the good fortune of my next assignment.

In the fall of 1971, Peggy was hired to teach English at Victorville High School, so she and the family would remain at George AFB during my four-month TDY. Mom was also a great asset to have in our home during these times. Her constant presence and influence in the lives of all four children were immeasurable in their growth into adolescence and teenage years.

I first heard about the USAF Fighter Weapons Instructors Course, or "Top Gun School," from my friend, Captain Jim Thornton, while stationed at Hahn Air Base. He graduated from the school in 1968 and advised me to set my sights on attending as soon as I could.

Jim, and later Captain Roger Wells, were great examples as graduates of the school, and I decided to follow in their footsteps. The Fighter Weapons School had its beginning as the Aircraft Gunnery School at Las Vegas Air Force Base in 1949. It became Nellis Air Force Base in 1950. The initial school involved a group of World War II combat veterans dedicated to teaching the next generation of fighter pilots. The mission of the school was to teach graduate-level training in weapons and tactics employment to fighter pilots.

The first "Top Gun" gunnery competition took place in May 1949 with most of the pilots flying the F-80 Shooting Star and F-84 Thunderjet. A little known fact is the winners of that first competition were four Tuskegee Airmen competing in their P-47N Thunderbolts. The team was comprised of Captain Alva Temple and First Lieutenants Harry Stewart, James H. Harvey, III, and Halbert Alexander of the 332nd Fighter Group, Godman Field, Kentucky. The maintenance crew was led by Staff Sergeant Buford Johnson who did a fantastic job in keeping the P-47s in top shape for the competition. Their winner's trophy was inadvertently "lost" for over fifteen years before appropriate credit was given to the Tuskegee Airmen for this outstanding achievement.

In 1954, the school was renamed the "USAF Fighter Weapons School." Students trained in the primary fighters of that day and progressed to the F-100 and F-105 by 1960. In 1965, the F-4 was added to its courses. I reported to the 414th Fighter Weapons Squadron at Nellis AFB a few days after New Year's 1972. The squadron was commanded by Lieutenant Colonel Donald Armstrong and the Operations Officer was Lieutenant Colonel William "Bill" Wilson. Two of the instructors I knew earlier were Major Dave Jacobsen, formerly of Cam Ranh Bay and Captain Roger Wells, my example of excellence back at Hahn Air Base, Germany. Others included a cross section of instructors from the USAF and exchange pilots from the Navy, Canada, and Australia.

My class of twenty-one was loaded with outstanding talent from Tactical Air Command, Pacific Air Command, and US Air Force Europe. Six in the class were WSOs, one was Hawaiian, one Japanese American, and I was the sixth African American pilot to attend the school in its twenty-one year history. All of us were singularly focused on becoming the best of the best in tactical fighters. The prize at the end of the four-month course was a coveted little grey patch with the bull's-eye and bullet. Individual competition was expected to be extremely tough, but we got off to a great start and melded together as a class.

The Fighter Weapons School was designed to be the most intense, rigorous training in the Air Force, period. The school was matchless in academics, preparation, and flying. The ultimate application of the knowledge and techniques were stressed to ensure success in the air battle. As students, we were expected to master every technical aspect of the aircraft, its handling qualities, weapons, and support systems. We had to become experts in air combat theory and practice, air-to-ground weapon delivery, electronic countermeasures, and survival. In addition, all students selected for the school were expected to leave their pride, thin skin, and vanity at the gate. There were three posted placards which caught the attention of new students as they walked through the door:

> "Rule 1.   You'll never get a second chance to
>   make a first good impression!"
>
> "Rule 2.   Never fail to take the opportunity
>   to keep your mouth shut!"
>
> "Rule 3.   Don't worry about the piss ants
>   when the elephants are storming the wall!"

Some learned these lessons the hard way.

Prior to our class, the school changed the syllabus to begin with air-to-air training. The intention was to place the most difficult phase up front. If the student passed, he would be cleared to continue the course. If he was unable to make the grade in air-to-air, he would be discontinued and the school would save considerable time and resources.

I flew my first sortie, an aircraft handling exercise, with Major Dave Jacobsen whom I liked and respected from our prior relationship. We had fun exploring the maneuvering envelope of the F-4E that now had an internal gun in the nose and more powerful engines. The time spent in the rear cockpit of the F-4 as a WSO and while instructing students paid off. Dave was impressed with my performance and expressed confidence I would do well in the school. Next, we entered the air-to-air phase. The instructors assessed our performance and analyzed every aspect of the flight during the debriefings. This process took about two and one-half hours before the flight and about the same afterwards. The flights normally lasted forty to forty-five minutes. Thus, a single mission required about five hours, not counting the preparation prior to the preflight briefing.

I was scheduled for my air-to-air flight evaluation with Lieutenant Colonel Armstrong, the Squadron Commander. Another instructor and two students made up the flight of four in a two versus two scenario. My task involved preflight preparation, flight briefing, prescribed maneuvers, formation, and a detailed debriefing and assessment of all participants. I was graded on every facet of the mission which lasted about six hours from beginning to end. I gave it my absolute best and hoped it was enough to earn a good grade. At the conclusion of the debriefing, Lieutenant Colonel Armstrong stated, "This was the strongest student mission I have ever witnessed. Dick, you did an outstanding job. Keep up the good work!"

The news of my flight spread quickly throughout the squadron, and was a blessing and a curse. It was great to have my ability recognized, but my vanity was a great detriment for me. I passed Rule 1 through 3, but there should have been Rule 4 on the entrance wall of the squadron: "Be ever so humble in your success!" Regardless, I flunked it miserably, thereby incurring the resentment and wrath of several instructors and a few of my peers. To make matters worse, I had a few words one night at the O'Club bar with Lieutenant Colonel Bill Wilson, the 414th Ops Officer. He approached me and made some unflattering comments which I thought were inappropriate. Very unwisely, I responded in kind. That was a kiss of death.

The next three months were some of the toughest in my career. Virtually every mission, exam, or event I participated in was critically evaluated and critiqued. Whether or not a few of the instructors went overboard, I had no one to blame but myself. When the pressure reached a critical point, a few unexpected friends appeared. Major Dawson R. "Randy" O'Neil was one of them. He came up to me at the Ops Counter one day, placed his hand on my shoulder, smiled broadly and said, "Sir Toliver, I hear things are going a bit rough for you. Well, hang in there. My fellow aviators tell me you are doing a great job. So keep on keeping on!"

Another one was my classmate, Captain Edward Mangis, and only the second Christian fighter pilot I met. Ed insisted I accompany him to an early breakfast at the Officer's Club. He and several Christian officers stationed at Nellis prayed for me and others in the class. Ed continued to be a close friend and encourager during the course and years after we graduated.

Another classmate and former Thunderbird pilot, Captain Thomas Gibbs, invited me to his house one weekend to relax and chill out for a few hours. Tom later took me to see Lieutenant Colonel Roger Parrish, the Commander of the Thunderbirds. During the meeting, I learned the Thunderbirds were considering the first African American candidate for the team, Captain Lloyd W. "Fig" Newton stationed in the Philippines. Later, I was asked to visit Fig and offer encouragement to him and his family.

The actions and words of the foregoing individuals were sorely needed. Their friendship and confidence in me reinforced my determination to stay the course. Furthermore, they enabled me to refocus on why I was at Nellis. Despite the unwanted special attention I received, it was still great to be in the school. Each training phase provided an enormous opportunity to hone skills and instructor techniques. The flying was challenging but exciting. With a few weeks to go, I was confident of making it through.

My final flight check and last sortie was scheduled with Captain Roger Wells, the fighter pilot's fighter pilot. I had not spoken to Roger much during the past four months, and he acted as if we never knew each other. Nevertheless, he was absolutely spectacular during the preflight briefing and instruction. The mission was a Dart sortie that allowed live firing on a small target towed 1500 feet behind an aircraft. As wingman, my role was to maintain a fighting wing position in close proximity to Roger who was the lead shooter. My performance would be graded by the ability to stay on Roger's wing throughout the maneuver and be prepared to roll in and fire after his hot pass. The event was a high-g maneuver flown at approximately 400 knots. High-g meant that four to six times the weight of the pilot's body would be forced against the seat of the aircraft during the event.

We took off as scheduled and proceeded to the air-to-air range. My adrenalin was pumped up, and I was fiercely determined to be welded to Roger's wing at every turn. Visual and radio contact was made with the tow aircraft and the maneuvering began the moment we passed abeam of the tow aircraft. In one breath, Roger performed a six-g break, and I was about a quarter second behind him. We completed a 180 degree turn in a matter of seconds and I acquired the tow aircraft and Dart about the same time he did. The tow pilot cleared us in for a hot pass, and Roger closed within the prescribed position and fired. He shot the dart off and had to pull up abruptly to avoid the debris. He yelled, "The dart's gone, the dart's gone! Where are you Dick?" I yelled, "On your right wing!" He responded, "Sierra Hotel. Let's go home!"

The air in the room during the debriefing was totally euphoric. Roger was elated for having scored a direct hit on the Dart, and he gave me an outstanding grade for maintaining wing position throughout the maneuver. He stated since I stayed on his wing during the event, he was confident of my ability to roll off on a real adversary and shoot him down. The mission was complete, and I successfully finished the course.

The graduation exercise took place a few days later. All twenty-one of us graduated and headed back to our respective bases in PACAF, TAC, and USAFE. Our careers were significantly enhanced by numerous doors of opportunity in fighter operations, weapons testing and development, and work in the aerospace industry. I had the privilege of serving with or repeatedly crossing paths with several of my classmates and instructors over the years. Dick Myers and Ron Keys would eventually become four-star generals. Dick became the Chairman of the Joint Chiefs of Staff, and Ron Keys commanded Air Combat Command (Formerly Tactical Air Command). Tad Oelstrom rose to Lieutenant General and retired as the Commander of the Air Force Academy. Most others in my class reached the rank of Colonel. Thus, the Fighter Weapons School Class of May 1972 set an enviable record of service as top fighter pilots and leaders in the Air Force.

I returned to George AFB in mid May 1972. Having missed the opportunity to attend the Air Force Basic Survival School back in 1965, I was scheduled to attend the thirteen-day school at Fairchild

AFB, Washington. The reports of harsh treatment of U. S. prisoners of war in North Vietnam resulted in significant changes focusing on counter propaganda and survival tactics. The training environment and props had also been modified to replicate known prison camps in North Vietnam and Laos. Of necessity, the training was very difficult and unpleasant, but I took it in stride. It gave me confidence in my ability to survive should I suffer the misfortune of getting shot down and falling into the hands of the enemy.

Our neighbor, Al Stipe's parents, Miller and Eve Stipe, lived in Spokane, Washington. Since Fairchild was nearby, they invited me to spend the weekend with them after survival training. Following Al's near fatal automobile accident, our families became very close, and they wanted to reciprocate in some way. We were joined by Al's brother, John, wife Kay, and two young children for a beautiful two days at the Stipe's cottage on Lake Coeur d'Alene, Idaho. Miller took us on a long cruise on his boat through many nooks and coves along the lake. Knowing that I would be leaving for Southeast Asia in a few days, the Stipes showered me with compassion, kindness, and lots of love. Eve embraced and encouraged me as only a mother could do for a son who was about to go off to war. That weekend with the Stipes confirmed my belief in the goodness of people and the beauty of America. Along with my family and relatives, they represented the America I loved and motivated a willingness to lay my life on the line again.

One final task awaited me upon my return to George AFB. A by name request from HQ TAC identified Peggy and me to participate in the June 1972 USAF-Wide Career Motivation Conference at Maxwell AFB, Alabama. The purpose of the conference was to identify critical career considerations and recommend specific actions to encourage top people to stay in the Air Force. Representatives were selected from a wide spectrum of career field and duty stations worldwide. An exciting aspect of the conference was the addition of wives to the TDY orders, a first for Peggy and me. Again, Mom's presence in our home permitted us to take advantage of this unique opportunity.

The conference lasted one week, and I participated on the Aviation Panel for issues concerning pilots and navigators. It was intense and everyone worked hard to identify personnel issues that could be resolved with a firm commitment and reasonable resources. A total of 236 recommendations were submitted for Air Staff evaluation. By February 1973, eighty- six were approved, and fifty-nine were still being considered. I was especially pleased to learn one of my recommendations was approved: preliminary fighter training for navigators selected to be WSOs in the F-4 or other fighter aircraft. The conference was a wonderful experience, and it allowed Peggy and me to have a few evenings to ourselves just prior to my departure. We later received several letters of commendation for our participation.

The conclusion of each assignment caused me to reflect and to be grateful for the blessings in my career and for the family. During the two years at George AFB, a lot happened. My decision to remain in the cockpit proved to be one of the most crucial in my life. But it was the faith, love, and prayers of my wife, mother-in-law, and children that provided the wind beneath my wings. I faced the uncertainty of war again, but they reinforced my resolve to survive. The Air Force's policy of allowing families to remain in place during the sponsor's Southeast Asian tour was an added blessing. I had much for which to live.

Chapter Eleven

Southeast Asia - Second Tour

Duty, Honor, Country

I was scheduled to leave from Travis AFB, California mid-June 1972. My brother, Captain David Toliver, flew down to Ontario from Grand Forks AFB, North Dakota to travel with us and to assist getting my family back to George AFB. On the way to Travis, we planned a trip through Los Angeles and along the coastal highway to Oxnard. We wanted to retrace the path our father drove twenty-eight years earlier when we first arrived in California. It was also an opportunity for my family to meet other relatives and show the children where my dream of flying was born.

We were about to begin the trip to Travis when the postman delivered the mail. The letter on top was from Becky Rose, the wife of Alan, our friends from Hahn Air Base. As Peggy read the letter out loud, her face clouded over and she stopped in mid-sentence. Alan had been shot down over North Vietnam and his status was Missing in Action (MIA). Everybody in the station wagon was listening and wanted to know what happened. Peggy could not disguise the truth of the bad news that came at such an inappropriate time for us.

Our hearts sank low, and we tried desperately to not let this be a bad omen for us. Peggy led us in prayer before we continued. We prayed for Alan and others who were shot down and known to be POWs, those listed as MIAs.

The mood in the car was quiet and somber until we reached Santa Monica. We headed north on Highway One with the Pacific Ocean to our left and the Santa Monica Mountains on our right. Along the way, we paused for sight-seeing, stopped in Oxnard to visit relatives, and located sites where we lived during WW II. This was the first visit for David and me in over twenty-six years. The house and projects no longer existed, but the elementary school I first attended and the small church on the street where I lived were still there. We also found the Colonial Steak House where our mother worked and where two individuals still worked since WW II. One of them, John Carruthers, remembered our mother, Daisy and her friend, Maggie. He also had a son who was married to one of our cousins. What a small world.

We had a great visit with some relatives who were part of my great grandfather's lineage. Like him, one family of eight siblings had produced fifty-seven offsprings. It took several hours to explain that to our children. Before driving on, I stopped on the side of the road across from Oxnard Air Field and watched a few small aircraft fly overhead for landing. Memories of my childhood rushed back like an avalanche and left me speechless. What a journey it had been for me. God willing, I would return again one day and fly myself off that airstrip.

We drove on through Ventura and Santa Barbara and spent the night at Vandenberg AFB in Lompoc. The next day's journey took us through San Luis Obispo, Monterey, San Jose, and finally into San Francisco where we spent the last two days. Though many changes had taken place in California over the past years, it was still an expansive and beautiful state. We enjoyed its beauty and the people we met during the trip. I held the memories close as my departure time approached.

That moment of truth came on June 20, 1972 when we arrived at Travis AFB. We joined scores of other families in the departure terminal to check in and say our good-byes. Our final moments together were spent hugging and kissing through tears. It was very difficult to let go. Standing there, I remembered the words of the farewell speech of the great, late General Douglas McArthur regarding "Duty, Honor, Country." For the first time, I truly understood those words. Answering their clarion call required the utmost of human courage. It dictated leaving behind the most cherished treasure – my family. Like the scores around me that day and like thousands had done before, I had to answer the call of Duty, Honor, Country.

I looked into Peggy's eyes and saw the mirror of my own soul. I read the agony of our pending separation. The gnawing concern for the uncertainty of our future burned through her attempted façade of courage. I heard the quiet cry of her heart and felt the pain of letting go of my life, lover, and soul mate. I finally turned and walked toward the door that led to the awaiting jet. I didn't look back for fear I wouldn't have the strength to continue the journey. Only God heard my mournful, silent prayer.

I arrived at Clark Air Base in the Philippines for the four-day Jungle Survival School. The course included accelerated instructions, two days and nights in the jungle, lots of rain, various jungle creatures, and escape and evasion from the Philippino Negrito Tribesmen. Although of short duration, the course exposed us to a jungle similar to that in Vietnam. More than anything else, it gave me the confidence I needed to survive if faced with that situation in combat.

As previously requested by my classmate and former Thunderbird pilot, Tom Gibbs, I located Captain Lloyd W. "Fig" Newton who was being considered for the USAF Aerial Demonstration Team. Fig was assigned to the 523rd TFS and flew F-4Ds and was on rotation to Da Nang Air Base, South Vietnam. After about a day and a half with Fig, I was convinced he was a tremendous choice to become the first Black member of the Thunderbirds. He had an outstanding attitude, charisma, intellect, and poise. In addition, he was a handsome young officer with a fine military bearing. We talked a lot about how great it would be for him to make the Team, and I encouraged Fig to continue his pursuit of this great opportunity. My visit with Fig was the beginning of a great and lasting friendship.

Operation Linebacker

I arrived at the 388th TFW, Korat Air Base, Thailand June 27, 1972. The Wing Commander was Colonel Richard E. Merkling, Colonel Mele Vojvodich, Jr. was Director of Operations (DO), and Major John E. Jaquish was the Wing Weapons Officer. John welcomed me to the wing and briefed me on its role in Operation Linebacker One and the duties I could expect as a squadron Weapons Officer. Linebacker I began in early May and the 388th, along with the other wings in Thailand, were heavily involved. The operation was President Nixon's response to failed political negotiations with the leaders of the Democratic Republic of Vietnam (North Vietnam). Restrictions were lifted on targets in North Vietnam above the 20th parallel for the first time since 1968. Strikes were permitted against vehicle targets, lines of communication, roads, waterways, bridges, railroad bridges, railroad tracks, supply targets, air defense targets, and industrial/power targets. The targets were located in some of the most heavily defended cities and areas of the world, including Hanoi, Hai Phong, Than Hoa, Thai Nguyen, and Vinh. The targeted airfields included Gia Lam, Hoa Lac, Kep, Phuc Yen, and Yen Bai. It had been seven years since my first tour, but my recollection of these places was vividly clear.

I was assigned to the 469th TFS commanded by Lieutenant Colonel Edward M. McHale and Major Frederic H. Smith, III as the Operations Officer. That same day, the squadron lost an aircraft and the aircrew was listed as missing in action. When I arrived at my assigned hooch, several squadron members were grieving the sixth loss in the wing since the beginning of Linebacker. Others were packing the personal belongings of First Lieutenant Kevin Chaney, whose bunk I inherited. Though not superstitious, this circumstance, coupled with the news of Al Rose getting shot down the day I left home, was an ominous beginning to my second tour.

I reported to the squadron the next day and received the briefing on the squadron's operation by Major Smith. He expressed concern about the low experience of some aircrews and asked me to prepare briefings on tactical formation, evasive tactics, and the optimum use of the F-4's weapons and electronic counter-measure capabilities. Later, I revisited Major Jaquish at wing headquarters for a briefing on the line-up of organizations, aircrews, and weapons systems in the wing. The 388th was a composite wing of multiple units with various aircraft and missions. Most aircraft were equipped with Electronic Counter-Measures (ECM) Pods and Tactical Electronic Warning Systems (TEWS). The units included the following:

- 17th Wild Weasel Squadron (F-105G)

- 34th Tactical Fighter (F-4E)

- 469th Tactical Fighter Squadron (F-4E)

- 35th Tactical Fighter Squadron (F-4D, Deployed from Korea)

- 67th Tactical Fighter Squadron (F-4C, Deployed from Kadena)

- 42nd Tactical Electronic Warfare Squadron (EB-66)

- 7th Airborne Command and Control Squadron (EC-130E)

The gathering at the Officer's Club that night was "old home week" for me. Lieutenant Colonel Lyle Beckers, Captain George Lippemeier, and Captain Joe Lee Burns from Korea were previously stationed with me at Hahn Air Base. Captains Charlie Cox, Jim Beatty, and Joe Moran were formerly in the 414th at Nellis AFB, and Captain Dick Myers was in my Fighter Weapons School Class at Nellis AFB.

The daily launches of the 388th task forces were an impressive operation. The sights and sounds of early morning departures were an awesome demonstration of aircrews and their machines taking off with purpose, dedication, and focus on the mission for the day. Being part of the Linebacker Operation was professionally fulfilling, but most of us had our personal motivation. We were deeply passionate about doing our part to help end the war, win the release of our POWs, and get a full account of the MIAs. Like me, many had a list that fueled our resolve each day. My personal list consisted of Fred Cherry, Dayton Ragland, Lorenza Conner, Ken Cordier, Herb Ringsdorf, Dick Butt, Alan Rose, Rudy Zuberbuhler, and Keith Lewis among others captured or missing since 1965. All of us were painfully aware that more than 50,000 young Americans had already paid the ultimate sacrifice for freedom at home and abroad.

The 469th was tasked to conduct interdiction, escort, and combat air patrol missions. I flew the first combat sortie of my second tour on July 16, 1972. It was a strike mission against supply lines in the southern part of North Vietnam. I still recognized the countryside, mountains, and major landmarks. We flew over one of these, Bat Lake, north of the DMZ. At 20,000 feet, the Flight Leader did not expect Triple A or surface-to-air missile (SAM) threats. He was wrong! As Number Four in the formation, I was a bit wide and checking the Bat Lake area. As if on cue, a string of Triple A rose from an undetected gun site toward the opposite wingman. I yelled, "Triple A! Triple A, left seven o'clock low! Break left, Two!"

The flight leader did the same and visually acquired the last of the volley. Number Three broke into my direction, and we all accelerated away from the threat. Once safely out of the threat area, the flight leader called for a rejoin to a tactical (spread) formation from that point on. Incredibly, my first sortie was almost a repeat of the last mission I had flown seven years before. I noted the lackadaisical attitude toward potential threats while over enemy territory and used this event as an object lesson in my next aircrew briefing.

On another mission to North Vietnam a week later, an emergency call came from the Airborne Command and Control Center (ABCCC). A group of South Vietnamese troops had been ambushed near the Cambodian border and needed immediate close air support. The Mission Force Commander called my flight out and tasked me to respond. I contacted ABCCC and advised them that each of my flight of four F-4s was armed with twelve 500 pound bombs with fuse extenders. ABCCC told me that was the perfect ordnance needed for the mission. The target was a group of entrenched hillside bunkers that housed enemy troops firing on trapped friendly troops in the valley below.

My WSO assisted in navigating the flight to the area, and we picked up an airborne FAC upon arrival. The specific targets were difficult to acquire so the FAC marked the general area for us. I directed the flight to set up an attack using different headings and rolled in for a spotter bomb. It set off several secondary explosions below so the FAC requested multiple passes in that vicinity. We struck a main complex of troops and ammunition, and the entire area erupted into a spectacular series of secondary explosions and fires. I made the decision to stay on the target a bit longer and planned to divert my flight to Ben Hoa Air Base about twenty minutes away.

As we departed the target area, I requested ABCCC to alert Ben Hoa Air Base that we were inbound for a priority landing. In the meantime, the FAC contacted ABCCC and reported the bomb damage assessment (BDA) of our strike. He reported several dozen secondary explosions and the destruction of a regiment-size force. Advised of our arrival, the wing commander met us at the aircraft after landing. The surprise of the day occurred when the wing commander and I recognized each other as I stepped down from the aircraft. He was Colonel Stillman V. Taylor, my former Squadron Commander from Hahn Air Base, Germany.

The world had just gotten smaller, and fate chuckled at this special moment. Apparently Colonel Taylor received an initial report of our mission. He called for additional cars to transport us to the Officer's Club for lunch. We spent about two hours at Ben Hoa receiving a Red Carpet treatment. Colonel Taylor proudly told everyone within earshot I was one of "His Boys" from Hahn Air Base. Whatever he thought of me back at Hahn was now overshadowed by my success in combat. I dismissed my negative thoughts and was thankful for being able to prove myself where it counted the most.

We took off for Korat while a group of well-wishers led by Colonel Taylor waved good-bye. Earlier that day, I was disappointed with being tasked for what was thought to be a 'milk run" mission. What took place was greater than anything I could have orchestrated. It was a true lesson in humility.

A few days later, the wing received an official BDA for our flight to South Vietnam. In addition to saving scores of friendly troops, the BDA confirmed we had destroyed a regiment headquarters including hundreds of enemy soldiers. This was one of the few times I actually received the results of my bombing in terms of body counts. I told myself this was war; nevertheless, I felt strangely responsible for taking another life. The flight was commended by both the U.S. and Vietnamese Headquarters and recommended for the Distinguished Flying Cross.

After the third week of combat, I was elevated to flight leader for all the missions assigned to the wing and began leading missions to the Hanoi and Hai Phong areas. When not flying combat, I spent time training newcomers or on the flight line interacting with the maintainers and weapon loaders. My favorite WSOs were Captains Ralph Reinhart and Francis "Frank" Sutscheck, a former student of mine at George AFB. My trusted wingmen included Captain Edward Raismus, First Lieutenant Gregory S. Martin, and First Lieutenant John Ashby Taylor. I was also assigned to provide combat checkouts for incoming squadron and wing leaders such as Colonel John T. Chain, Jr., the new DO, and Lieutenant Colonel Fredrick H. Green, a Squadron Commander in waiting.

The missions flown against targets in North Vietnam were having the desired effects thereby attaining the U.S. political objectives. However, Operation Linebacker was thwarted by several American dissidents visiting Hanoi and other target areas in North Vietnam. The North Vietnamese used international media coverage and posted these individuals at or near known military targets. Our Headquarters continued to schedule strikes to these areas, but dictated unrealistic approaches to the targets. Such was the case on Sunday morning, July 30, 1972.

A force of approximately one hundred aircraft was scheduled to attack the well-known Paul Doumer Bridge that spanned the Red River near Hanoi. This dual highway/railroad artery was a critical link for the movement of war materials from China and the Port of Hai Phong to Hanoi. This was to be the second attack since Linebacker One began. The F-4 bombers from Ubon RTAF were armed with laser guided bombs. I was flying with escort flights from Korat armed with air-to-air missiles and ECM pods. Once over the target area, our mission was to establish a barrier combat air patrol (Barrier CAP) to protect the bombers from MIGs during their departure from the target area.

The 7th Air Force headquarters-directed route into the target area was a straight, sixty-nautical miles leg at high altitude from the coast to Hanoi. This set the task force up as "sitting ducks!" The North Vietnamese took advantage and launched over a dozen SAMs above and below the ingress altitude of the task force. Some were radar guided while others were guided visually. The first missile struck one of the lead escorting F-4s as we approached the outskirts of Hanoi. Several aircraft were hit and seriously damaged over the target. My onboard Tactical Electronic Warning System (TEWS) indicated a missile site radar lock on my aircraft, and my WSO, Frank Sutscheck, visually sighted a SAM headed for us and called the break. As I maneuvered to defeat the first SAM, another radar lock sounded, and I picked up the second SAM fired against our aircraft. During the maneuvering, I sighted SAMs tracking other aircraft. In the midst of this chaos, Frank and I saw portions of the bridge topple into the river below. We defeated at least two more SAMs fired at us by diving as close to the ground as possible. At that altitude, I was dodging palm trees and power lines. The CAP plan was abandoned when everyone in the flight was forced to evade multiple SAMs. Several of us reached "Bingo Fuel" (the fuel remaining needed to reach the aerial tankers in the Gulf of Tonkin) prior to reaching the coastline. Others faced the possibility of running out of fuel before reaching the tankers.

I joined several F-105s at high speed to escape the MIGs that took off immediately following the SAM attack. To make matters worse, we were engaged by additional SAM sites as we neared the coastline. My last ditch, low altitude maneuvering caused me to reach "Minimum Fuel" (minimum required to get to the tanker under normal conditions) as I crossed the coast the line well beyond the range of the aerial tankers.

Upon reaching a safe distance from shore, I zoomed to 30,000 feet and turned toward the tanker track. Our situation became dire when my primary radio failed and the aircraft began to vibrate moderately. My G-meter registered twelve Gs, or three and one-half Gs above the maximum limit. This apparently had happened during the maneuvers to defeat the SAMs and was the likely cause of the aircraft vibrations. With less than fifteen minutes of fuel, only an emergency radio receiver, a vibrating jet, and over 200 miles from a safe airfield, we needed a miracle.

The aerial tanker force commander heard the bedlam over the radios and realized several damaged aircraft were in dire need of fuel. He correctly concluded some would not make it to the established refueling track. Despite the risk of MIGs and SAMs, he led the entire tanker fleet north to meet the emergency aircraft. By the grace of God, I detected a sun glint off the canopy of a tanker about twenty miles away and headed directly for it. I got a visual on the tankers at about ten miles while still ten thousand feet above their altitude.

I descended and passed abeam the lead tanker rocking my wings to signify loss of my radio. The boom operator signaled me to join for refueling and I maneuvered toward the pre-contact position. He successfully made contact with me before I reached the normal refueling position. We began taking on fuel with less than five minutes of fuel remaining, and I uttered a great sigh of relief. It was short-lived. While refueling, we heard the emergency beacons of three other F-4 aircrews that were forced to eject over water. We were one of the fortunate ones that day.

After refueling, I signaled to another Korat jet (JV tail code) to escort me home. We made it back safely, and I performed a precautionary landing pattern. Three hours and twenty minutes after takeoff, I shut the engines down, got out, and inspected the aircraft. Both engines were sagging against the floor of the engine bays. Further inspection by the maintenance troops confirmed two engine mounts were broken on one side and one on the other. It took all that to survive the mission, but I was thankful for the ruggedness of the F-4.

All of Korat's aircrew survived one of the most horrific missions of the war. The debriefings were long and cathartic. We had
dutifully followed orders and did the best job possible, but no one
wanted to repeat that day. We urged our bosses to petition the Headquarters against dictating mission tactics. Their directive for the attack on the Paul Doumer Bridge turned into a costly debacle. The
price we paid to avoid injury to a few American dissidents in North
Vietnam was unacceptable, and it angered us for many years to come.

That night in the quiet solitude of my room, I reflected on the
miracle that got me home to Korat unscathed. Those minutes over
Hanoi were the worst I encountered in over 220 combat missions
during both Vietnam tours. Deep down inside, I knew my skill and
cunning were not the source of my survival. God had mercifully intervened. I was still unwilling to express my gratitude openly; however, I did acknowledge and thank Him in a silent prayer. Later I
wrote to Peggy and thanked her for continuing to pray for me.

In August, the increased SAM and Triple A threats in North
Vietnam increased significantly. As part of the counter to this threat,
the 388th was directed to form Hunter-Killer Teams to search out and
destroy active sites. The team consisted of two F-105G Wild Weasels
with anti-radar missiles and a pair of F-4s equipped with high explosive ordnance. They were tasked to detect and destroy SAM or gun
sites prior to the arrival of the main task force. My recent encounters
with SAMs over Hanoi motivated me to volunteer. I was also motivated because I'd be flying with some of the most experienced pilots
and WSOs in the wing. In addition, I wanted to strike a blow for my
friend, Captain Joe Lee Burns and WSO First Lieutenant Mike Nel-
son. They were shot up near Hanoi and had to bail out over the Gulf
of Tonkin. Fortunately they were recovered by the Navy.

The flights were paired to develop coordinated tactics and
confidence in each other. My flight partners were Captain "Nordie"
Norwood and WSO First Lieutenant Dave Bland. My WSOs were al-

ternately Captains Ralph Reinhart and Frank Sutscheck. On most occasions, the F-105 flight was comprised of Major Tom Coady, Major
"Lucky" Eckman, and their backseat Electronic Weapons Officers or
EWOs. We reviewed SAM layouts in key target areas and developed
a map of priorities for our armed reconnaissance and strikes. Our orders gave us the latitude to conduct our flights so as to arouse, attack,
and destroy active SAM and AAA sites prior to the arrival of the task
force over the target.

The Hunter-Killer teams played a cat-and-mouse game with
SAM sites. The site operators demonstrated a high degree of coordination and experience. Often, two or more sites coordinated their
attack on us using radar and visual tracking. Our objective was to
counter their tactics and destroy the SAM site. If a site became active,
it was attacked by the F-105s or F-4s, depending upon who was best
positioned to destroy or neutralize it. The Hunter-Killer teams destroyed or suppressed SAM and gun activities to the point of enabling
other strike aircraft to be more effective. By early September, several
SAM and gun sites had been eliminated and a significant path cleared
for strikes against Hanoi.

On an armed reconnaissance patrol on September 14th, I noticed a large number of vehicle tracks that disappeared into a grove
of trees. My second pass over the area confirmed a new mobile SAM
site in an area we had previously cleared. I called my attack intentions and pulled high above the suspected area. While maneuvering for a dive bomb attack, my WSO and the TEWS alerted me to a
lock-on by another SAM site. In his typical calm, steady voice, Tom
Coady called the position of the in-bound SAM as I rolled in on the
target. The seven second flight before booster drop-off allowed me
to complete my attack then maneuver away from the path of the attacking SAM. That missile missed us and exploded harmlessly a few
seconds later. Tom and his wingman launched missiles at the active
SAM site while the area I struck erupted into more than two dozen
secondary explosions and fires. My wingman repositioned for a sec-

ond attack and finished off what was left of the first SAM site. Our team destroyed two SAM sites that day, and no losses were suffered by the strike force that followed. A post-strike reconnaissance flight confirmed the results of our efforts and the team was recommended for a Distinguished Flying Cross.

During the last week of September, Lieutenant Colonel Green invited me to move with him to the 432nd Tactical Reconnaissance Wing at Udorn Air Base in northern Thailand. The 432nd was being reconstituted as a wing with a mixed role of CAP, escorts, bombers, and reconnaissance. Colonel Green of the 469th at Korat was picked to be a squadron commander in the 432nd and wanted me to be his Squadron Weapons Officer. I had flown with him several times and had a lot of respect for his leadership. His 100 missions in the F-105 over North Vietnam during a previous tour were reflected in his airmanship and experience. I gladly accepted this offer and packed my bags as soon as we received orders.

And Kill MIGs

The 432nd Headquarters entry portal proudly displayed its slogan, "AND KILL MIGS!" Previously commanded by Colonel Charlie Gabriel, it was now led by Colonel Robert W. Clement. Several pilots and WSOs in the wing had scored aerial victories. Captain Richard Steven Ritchie, pilot, and WSOs Captain Charles B. "Chuck" DeBellevue and Jeffrey Feinstein later became the first Air Force aces of the Vietnam War. My friend, Captain John "Smash" Madden had bagged two MIGs. John had been assigned with me as an Instructor Pilot at George AFB. Two other former students from my flight at George AFB scored two aerial victories: Lieutenant Colonel Carl G. "Griff" Bailey and Captain Brian Tibbet. Griff's was a particular special case. While at George, he overcame a bout with cancer and resumed his career as a pilot. Brian was an exceptional young aviator who had great potential as a fighter pilot. It had been my privilege to instruct both of these MIG Killers.

The wing was in the midst of integrating aircrews from Da Nang AB, Republic of Vietnam and Tahkli AB, Thailand. Two outstanding African American aviators were in this group: Captain David H. Brooks, a pilot and former student at George AFB, and Captain Harold J. Brown, a WSO who preceded me at the Fighter Weapons School. David was assigned to the 421st TFS and Hal was assigned to the wing's weapons shop.

I flew my first sortie at Udorn on October 1, 1972. After a few bombing sorties, I was primarily assigned CAP missions. Since Steve Ritchie and Chuck DeBellevue had attained their ace status, others of us were scheduled for missions that were likely to encounter MIG threats. The luck of the draw resulted in being assigned one of the few F-4Ds equipped with the top secret electronic device, code-named Combat Tree. Combat Tree interpreted the transponders used by MIGs well beyond visual range and displayed identification and location information on a scope in the WSO's cockpit.

In mid-October, I was flying CAP north of Hanoi. "Red Crown", the US Navy GCI radar picket, ship alerted me to the possibility of a single MIG approaching my flight. I did not have the Combat Tree that day, so the rules of engagement required a visual identification (VID) before firing. My WSO detected and locked on to the unidentified bogey, and Red Crown directed a Navy flight into a pincer position.

The bogey suddenly reversed course and began to separate. I jettisoned my tanks and selected full afterburner in an attempt to gain closure enough to make a positive visual identification. I could see the bogey making a bee line for a cloud deck a few miles ahead. I was nearly one hundred percent certain and my fangs were down around my ankles. The target was just inside the missile envelope, and my finger was itching to squeeze the trigger. Yet the bogey did not turn and dove into the clouds. I came within a whisper of firing but somehow managed to demonstrate perhaps the greatest discipline in my entire Air Force career. The bogey got away. A few days later, the wing received confirmation that the target we chased was one of North Vietnam's top aces. This may have been the infamous Nguyen Van Coc, Nguyen Hong, or Pham Thanh Ngan. My missed opportunity knawed at my gut for a long time.

On October 22, I flew a roving CAP southwest of Hanoi with Lieutenant Colonel Griff Bailey. Both of us had F-4Ds equipped with the Combat Tree. Griff's history at George AFB, his two kills, and our friendship made this a pretty special day. Unfortunately, it proved to be special in another sad way. The wing executed a recall of all aircraft halfway through the flight. After ensuring all other flights were ahead of us, we returned to Udorn. Upon landing, we learned Linebacker One had been cancelled, and all combat sorties in North Vietnam above the 20th parallel were terminated. This restriction was to be effective on October 23, 1972. We were told this gesture of good-will was intended to help promote peace negotiations being held in Paris.

That night, near mutiny broke out at the Officer's Club as the disgust and frustration with the politics in Washington surged beyond the boundaries of self-control for many. The flow of alcohol, mixed with rage, resulted in some of the guys breaking tables, chairs, glasses, and doors. We fought our butts off for several months and believed the enemy had been considerably weakened. The aircrews felt betrayed, and the frustration was like bile stagnated in our throats.

We had no confidence that the North Vietnamese were ready to release our POWs and give a full account of our MIAs. Worst yet, more than 55,000 American lives had been lost in the Vietnam War with no end in sight. The cessation of bombing above the 20th parallel was a sorry repeat of the politics in Washington, DC during the 1960s. President Johnson allegedly boasted, "Those boys over there can't bomb an outhouse without my say." Most of us felt we were continually being jerked around. That night was a very low point for all of us at Udorn and I suspect all across Southeast Asia.

A Pact with God

The bombing restriction in North Vietnam was a personal dilemma for me. I was fiercely determined to make the North Vietnamese feel the pressure of every mission I flew. I took special pride in putting my bombs on target or supporting the force packages in every way possible. Consequently, I was angry and took the halt personally. My conscience cautioned me against my misplaced rage; however, these feelings could not be explained. I found myself standing in front of the base chapel but was reluctant to go in. Unlike my first tour, I didn't set foot in the chapel because I didn't want any confusion or distraction to my resolve. Peggy, my family, and friends prayed for me without ceasing, but my prayers were infrequent and superficial.

My early Christian teachings and the many blessings in my life contradicted my attitude and shamed me deeply. My moral and spiritual compass was misplaced, and I was not the same person who left home four months earlier. I wanted to talk to somebody, but could not bring myself to seek spiritual help. Perplexed about what to do, I decided to make a deal with God. I consciously vowed, "If you let me be, and allow me to survive this tour, I will come see you when I get home. Right now, this war is a mess, and I still have work to do. Please let me do that, okay?"

Looking back, it was the pure grace of God that allowed me to walk away without becoming a grease spot on the pavement! Amazingly, I had a measure of peace. I committed to obeying the orders of my superiors and hoped they knew what was best.

As Squadron Weapons Officer, my duties included training aircrews, mission planning, flight lead, and ensuring daily operations orders from headquarters were compatible with the assigned mission. Lieutenant Colonel Fred Green trusted me with considerable responsibility, and Lieutenant Colonel George E. Buchner, the Ops Officer,

scheduled me for highest priority missions. I was also allowed to select my wingmen and WSOs. Captain Dave Brooks was one of the
more experienced flight leaders whom I recruited to assist me with
my duties. Hal Brown was assigned to fly with the 421st as an instructor WSO, and I scheduled him in my flights whenever possible. It was
a unique experience to fly with Dave and Hal. Our lasting friendship
was based upon their skills, mutual trust, and professionalism.

On November 10, 1972 we began a two-week period of flying
night CAP for B-52s, F-4s, and other aircraft in the task force. The targets were located in Thanh Hoa, Vinh, Quang Lang, and other lucrative areas below the 20th parallel. Of my twenty-two missions flown
in November, twelve were flown in North Vietnam against targets
below the 20th parallel. Ten of those were at night. The darkness and
low overcast at that time of the year made it easier for us to defeat
SAMs. Conversely, Triple A wreaked havoc if attacks against targets
were made below the clouds. Given this, most of the night strikes
were flown at high altitude by the B-52s out of U-Tapao, Thailand.
The North Vietnamese launched dozens of SAMs against the forces
and often launched their MIGS to feign an attack across the 20th parallel. Red Crown, using onboard electronics and intelligence, did a
great job alerting the force to the threat of MIGs and SAMs, thus effectively mitigating these threats.

November 22nd proved to be one of the most significant missions of my combat experience. As the designated Mission Force
Commander (MFC), I had the responsibility for leading and directing
a force of about one hundred aircraft. The primary bombers used to
strike the assigned targets were B-52s out of the base U-Tapao. The
F-4s out of Ubon were tasked to establish a high altitude, chaff corrid-
er from just below the border to the target area and on the outbound
leg. The chaff was millions of aluminum strips dispensed from a
canister. These strips appeared as a cloud on the enemy's radar and
precluded detection of aircraft flying in it. The chaff consisted of
such minute particles that our friendly aircraft were not adversely

affected. To avoid radar detection, the B-52s were required to fly in a 10,000 foot block of chaff to target and out again.

I flew the main MIG CAP that night and situated myself between the ingress route to Vinh, the target, known SAM sites, and MIG airfields. Initially, I didn't have a Combat Tree aircraft, but relied on Red Crown, the seaborne warning ship, to identify the surface and airborne threats. Recent intelligence reports warned of a new SAM, the SA-4. It was thought to have a greater warhead and larger exhaust plume. Hal Brown was my WSO for the first time, and he did an outstanding job keeping me apprised of the progress and location of all the strike elements. However, the SA-2 SAMs kept us busy. We defeated at least three sets of two before getting the scare of our lives.

The sky suddenly lit up behind us, and I made a break toward a huge flame in the sky that we thought was the new SA-4. My initial maneuver did not get it to move perceptibly on my canopy. Hal and I became anxious and I maneuvered harder, changing my altitude, airspeed, and position. There was still no response from the fire in the sky. As our panic level increased, the fire in the sky suddenly broke into two pieces. Immediately we heard emergency beepers signifying personal ejections. In rapid succession, eight beepers were heard and we knew a B-52 had been lost to a SAM. This was the first B-52 lost to hostile fire in the Vietnam war.

Coordinating with the ABCCC, I called for the rescue response out of Nakom Phi Nom just across the border in Thailand. Red Crown confirmed the likelihood of a mobile SAM site near the vicinity of our CAP position. With the rescue effort underway, I called a Hunter-Killer team in on this suspected mobile SAM site. In the meantime, a couple of MIGs appeared headed for the strike force but turned before coming into our AIM-7 missile range.

I stayed on station until relieved by another MFC. Instead of aerial refueling, I requested permission to land and get the next available Combat Tree aircraft. Given the approval, we landed, switched aircraft, and returned to the CAP area. With the ability to identify MIGs, we were ready to repay the enemy in spades. Remarkably, the rescue of the downed B-52 aircrew was proceeding successfully, and we used aerial tankers to stay on station. The last aircrew member was rescued about 5:00 AM the following morning. We returned to base after logging over five hours of flight time.

During debriefing, we learned the very last B-52 had exited the chaff corridor to catch up with the rest of the flight. This exposed the aircraft to the enemy radar and the crew paid the price. Thankfully, all crew members were recovered safely. Hal and I went to breakfast about 7:00 AM, then to Happy Hour for a while. Exhausted, we walked to our quarters about 9:00 AM and flopped into our bunks for a bit of sleep. It had been a long day's night.

For the next five nights, I flew CAP sorties that averaged nearly three hours each. I ended the month with approximately fifty-five hours of combat, and the wing had not suffered a single loss. As a thirty-four year old captain, the month of November 1972 was the high point of my combat tour. My status in the squadron and wing was at an all time high, and I had a great sense of personal satisfaction in doing my part to end the war.

I switched back to the daytime schedule in December and continued flying CAP and bombing sorties into the southern part of North Vietnam. Bia Thoung Air Field had become a major threat, but it was not on the approved target list. The base was located ten nautical miles below the 20th parallel and about eighteen nautical miles west of Thanh Hoa. The North Vietnamese were thought to be secretly staging MIGs from the base to intercept our strike force then retreat back across the 20th parallel. In early December, the MIGs became more brazen, and we desperately wanted to take the base out. We got our wish on December 6, 1972.

On the evening of December 4th , Hal called to tell me a "biggie" was pending from headquarters. I flew on December 5th and was asked to remain at the wing headquarters afterwards to help plan a surprise attack on Bia Thoung Airfield. The 432nd was tasked to destroy or neutralize MIG and SAM threats in and around Thanh Hoa, including strikes across the 20th parallel. I was part of a task force of F-4s scheduled to strike the airfield at 10:00 AM that morning. The objective was to surprise the enemy and destroy the airfield and its support infrastructure.

Major Hal May, one of the Flight Commanders in the 421st, led a flight of four just ahead of me. We were sequenced in the middle of the wave and tasked to knock out the intersection of the runway and taxiway on the northern end of the airfield. My WSO, First Lieutenant Pat Farley, was doing a great job checking for SAM threats at our rear when we turned to the final attack heading. We were about to roll in on the target when the Triple A gunners woke up and began a withering barrage of fire at the first group of aircraft. I spotted an active gun pit at the far end of the airfield that had a bead on a flight just ahead of us. Forgoing my initial aim point, I pulled up in full afterburner and rolled toward the gun pit. From a steep dive, I could see the blazing barrels of the 37 MM guns. I released my full load and pulled hard toward the outbound heading. Pat let out a loud "Sierra Hotel" yell, and I caught a glimpse of the erupting earth and equipment in cockpit mirrors. Later, Pat and I were credited with scoring a direct hit on an imminent threat to several aircraft and aircrews. Post strike reconnaissance confirmed the major portions of the base were destroyed or heavily damaged. We were confident no MIGs would operate at Bia Thoung for quite some time. Our wing flew additional sorties over the next few days to eliminate numerous targets in the Thanh Hoa and coastal areas.

The unfathomable hand of fate played a strange part in my life later that month. After six intense months, I was allowed two weeks for rest and recuperation (R&R). There was no indication of any special actions over the Christmas holidays, so I was granted approval to spend my R&R with my family in the States. I departed about December 15th and arrived at George AFB, California the next day.

My family was excited over my being home for the holidays, but the joy was seriously dampened two days later. President Nixon ordered a full-scale resumption of bombing north of the 20th parallel, and December 18th marked the beginning of Operation Linebacker II. President Nixon finally untied the hands of the military, and the Air Force was allowed to employ its full force against North Vietnam. This resulted in the largest bombing raids in the ten-year history of the Vietnam War. It also provoked a fresh wave of anti-war demonstrations all across America. I tried to enjoy my visit home but felt an urgent need to be back at Udorn doing my part.

Operation Linebacker II was largely a night campaign. The strike forces shifted to include large numbers of B-52s from U-Tapao, Thailand and the island of Guam. This change was driven by the monsoon season of low ceilings and restricted daytime visibility over many of the targets. The B-52s were equipped with onboard radar bomb navigation systems and carried huge massive bomb loads. The tactical fighters once again laid chaff corridors and dropped bombs using the Long Range Aid to Navigation (LORAN) guided bombing systems. The strike force also included F-4s as fighter escorts, F-105 Wild Weasels, and EB-66 jamming aircraft. The U. S. Navy and the Marines supported the campaign with Task Force 77 in the Gulf of Tonkin.

Once again, the major targets in North Vietnam included the airfields of Kep, Phuc Yen, and Hoa Lac. Other targets in the vicinity of Hanoi were the Ai Mo warehouse complex, the Kinh No Railroad and storage area, Thai Nguyen thermal power plant, and Yen Vien complex. The nightly raids continued relentlessly for ten days. The North Vietnamese air defense system was inundated by the large number of aircraft it had to track in such a short time and by the dense chaff corridors spread by fighter-bombers. Still, they launched over 1,000 SAMS during Operation Linebacker II.

With action continuing in Vietnam, I curtailed my R&R and departed the U. S. on December 26th hoping to get back into the fray. That same day, a break-through occurred in the political negotiations between Washington and North Vietnam. I arrived back at Udorn on December 27th, but before I got sequenced in the flying schedule, President Nixon called a halt to aerial attacks on North Vietnam on December 29, 1972. Thus, Operation Linebacker II was terminated and I missed the whole thing! I pondered this missed adventure for many years. God only knows what I may have been spared.

The impact of Linebacker II apparently caused the North Vietnamese leaders to believe President Nixon truly meant to get a signed cease-fire agreement. Most of us were unaware of or did not care about the political objectives involved. The Hanoi leaders had jerked the American negotiators around since 1968, and the POWs had become political pawns. What meant most to us now was the immediate release of our POWs and a full accountings of MIAs. When the President halted the bombing, we hoped this would be announced immediately. In the meantime, we kept our powder dry, guns loaded, and airplanes ready to launch in a heartbeat. If the North Vietnamese did not get the message from the previous two weeks, every pilot in Southeast Asia was eager and poised to bomb the country into oblivion.

The long-awaited Paris Peace Accords between the United States, North Vietnam, and South Vietnam were signed on January 17, 1973. Ostensibly, this agreement intended to end the war and re-store peace in Vietnam. The most important issue for the American people was the return of captured military and foreign civilians. Not surprisingly, this was also important to the other side. This exchange was scheduled to be conducted simultaneously within weeks of sign-ing the Accords. The signatories agreed to help each other gather information about MIAs and the location of graves of the dead to facilitate exhumation and repatriation of remains.

Early reports on the Accords indicated the exchange of prisoners was scheduled for mid February 1973. There was a rousing celebration and relief the night this news reached Udorn. The unbridled joy was repeated at every base, station, and ship in Southeast Asia. It had been a long war. Many conditions of the agreement would later prove to be problematic for the U. S. Others were very complex and remained unresolved, but the hostilities in North and South Vietnam and Laos were finally over. We soon learned Cambodia was not included in the Paris Peace Accords, and U. S. combat missions resumed in support of the recognized government of Cambodia.

Operation Homecoming

The release of Vietnam POWs caused much anticipation and excitement back in the U. S. and overseas. This was especially true for those of us throughout Southeast Asia. The atmosphere at Udon and elsewhere in Thailand was euphoric. The North Vietnamese identified 591 Americans to be released; however, nearly 250 additional aircrew members were thought to be captives. Approximately 2000 others were listed as MIAs and were unaccounted for. The POWs were released according to their shoot down date and length of the time in captivity.

Navy Commander Everett Alvarez, Jr. was one of the first to be released on February 12, 1973. Alvarez, the grandson of Mexican immigrants, was a prisoner for eight and one-half years. He was shot down on August 5, 1964 during the Gulf of Tonkin Incident. Lieutenant Colonel Fred V. Cherry, an African American fighter pilot who flew combat in Korea, was also in that first group. Fred's F-105 jet was shot down on October 22, 1965 during a volunteer two-week extension of his tour. He was in captivity for seven years and four months.

The returnees were initially airlifted to Clark Air base for preliminary medical examination and health care. They were then flown home to America and the waiting arms of family, friends, neighbors and a host of others. Many of us had squadron buddies and close friends among the POWs. When possible, we were allowed to fly to Clark Air Base to greet them. On February 19, 1973, I took a two-ship to Clark to meet Herb Ringsdorf, Bob Biss, and Ken Cordier, my squadron mates from Cam Ranh Bay.

We were about an hour out of Clark when notified that the C-141 loaded with POWs was about to depart. I pleaded with the air traffic controller to delay the flight for a few minutes because of my buddies on board. We selected afterburner and flew supersonic the rest of the way. I spotted the C-141 on the ramp about twenty miles out and started my descent for landing. Upon contacting tower, I was advised the C-141 was about to start engines. After landing, I jumped into a Transient Alert truck and sped to the ramp. I waded through the crowd and rushed toward the last two pilots who were saluting the generals gathered to see them off. Incredibly, one of the POW's looked over and saw me and said, "Dick Toliver, is that you?"

I vaguely remembered the face from the past but could not put a name with it. The two grabbed me amid laughter and tears. They confirmed Herb Ringsdorf was on the aircraft, but Ken Cordier and Bob Bliss were scheduled for the next group out of North Vietnam. They literally dragged me up the ramp to meet the guys on board.

When I entered the cavernous jet, many in the group unbuckled their seat belts and surged toward me with more hugs, laughter, and tears. Their faces and bodies reflected years of unimaginable suffering. The next few minutes were an explosion of pent-up emotion and release. Herb emerged through the crowd, and the two of us embraced for a long time. We were simply brothers caught up in one of the most emotional moments of my life. One of the generals entered the aircraft and said, "Guys, this has been great, but there're some people waiting for you State-side. We need to be going."

I walked back down the ramp into a horde of news reporters and cameras. My initial greeting with the two guys on the ramp was captured for world-wide release. When questioned about my relationship with some of the ex-POWs, words stuck in my throat. Only my face and tears answered. When my flight members arrived, they were moved by what had happened. We went to the Officer's Club, and I spent a long time gathering myself together. We flew back to Udorn a day later and shared the experience at Clark Air Base. I have relived it many times, but have not been able to identify the POWs who dragged me onto the aircraft that day.

With the suspension of combat operations in North and South Vietnam and Laos, flying was greatly reduced, especially during the exchange of prisoners between the U. S. and North Vietnam. As with President Nixon, we did not want any misssteps to interrupt the release of POWs and delay the accounting of our MIAs.

Many aircrews completed their one-year tours and began to rotate February through April. To ensure the continuity of combat readiness, Colonel Clement, the Wing Commander, directed an intensive training program for the new guys. My friend and Wing Weapons Officer, Captain John Madden was placed in charge of the program, and he recruited the Squadron Weapons Officers to assist him. Each of us were tasked to check out incoming senior wing leaders and the squadron's flight commanders. Special emphasis was placed on flight management, situation awareness, tactical formations, combat tactics, evasive maneuvers, and systems knowledge. Hal Brown, as the Wing's Instructor WSO, also played a key part in training aircrews. Additionally, experienced flight leaders were used to enhance training. One of these was Captain Timothy O'Keefe, who arrived with the enhanced version of the F-4E in December. A graduate of the Air Force Academy, Tim was a class behind me in pilot training at Craig. He had previously completed a combat tour in F-105s, and was a graduate of the Fighter Weapons School at Nellis.

The 421st was very fortunate to get two highly experienced pilots as new Flight Commanders: Majors Ronald R. Fogleman and Ronald Soltis. Major Fogleman, an Air Force Academy graduate, had a previous Vietnam tour flying F-100s. He also had been promoted to Major in less than eight years and was already on track to be a top leader in the Air Force. Major Soltis had a solid fighter background, most recently in the F-104. Checking these two out as flight leaders was one of my easiest tasks at Udorn. The exchange of experience was clearly a two-way street. I also enjoyed the special privilege of having both Rons as my friends. Our career-long relationships were formed during our time together at Udorn.

Emotional Uncertainties

When the tempo of combat operations declined in the spring of 1973, many pilots, non-pilots, medical personnel, and others were left suspended on a "combat high." Many, including me, found it difficult to return to an emotional equilibrium or state of normalcy, whatever that may have been. This mental uncertainty caused complex and confusing inner feelings and turmoil. Most of us kept these thoughts to ourselves and we tried to disguise or set them aside at the bar of the Officer's Club.

The final accounting of the POWs, high number of MIAs unaccounted for, and the loss of 58,000 Americans during the Vietnam War were especially disturbing realities. Those who had been deeply involved over the years were left with a sense of futility and guilt for having survived. These feelings were casually shared with others, but they had a deep unnerving impact that was not voiced. Most of us suffered in silence and hoped these anxieties and frustrations would pass in time.

In 1973, Post Traumatic Stress Disorder (PTSD) as we know it today was not well-defined or understood. Today, we know it can be caused by circumstances or events associated with death, severe injury, or extreme trauma. It is most commonly related to military combat, but can be caused by events such as severe weather experiences, horrific incidents, or bereavement. In previous wars, military veterans who suffered emotional disorders were simply diagnosed as suffering from "combat fatigue" or so called "shell shock." Those with visible erratic or extreme behavior were simply treated at Veteran Centers and released.

Combat veterans in Southeast Asia likely suffered from PTSD but were unaware of the potential effects of this problem. Most of us were loathe to admitting the slightest emotional anomaly let alone talk to the flight surgeons or chaplains. For sure I would have taken the last place in such a line. Many continued to evade these uncertain emotions at the Officer's Club or by engaging in activities or behavior not easily explained. Since most of us responded to our environment in a similar manner, we considered ourselves "normal."

The false sense of security was shattered early one morning when one of my roommates, a major and flight commander, suffered a mental breakdown in flight. During an aerial refueling, he suddenly dropped off the tanker and dove for the ground. Fortunately, he had a huge WSO who was able to overpower him and recover the aircraft. The WSO declared an emergency and headed for Udorn. Several additional suicide attempts were made enroute to the base, but each time the WSO overcame the pilot or talked him back to a degree of rationality. The WSO's heroics saved the day, and he successfully landed the F-4 from the rear seat. The medics met my roommate at the aircraft and had to sedate him before extricating him from the cockpit. He was rushed to the hospital and kept isolated from visitors for several days.

This disturbing news reverberated throughout the base. Most of us felt we were coping with our hidden anxieties and gave no thought to a sudden disconnect like the one suffered by our fellow aviator. The resulting furor caused many of us to reassess our emotional state and openly discuss hidden feelings with peers, the flight surgeons, and chaplains. Medical teams arrived from the States to conduct interviews and counseling sessions. For the first time, individual problems were addressed and help was sought without negative consequences.

A significant finding from interviews and counseling was the positive contributions loved ones and family could have in resolving war-related emotional disorders. Consequently, R&Rs with wives and/or families were encouraged for those who wanted to get away for a few days. Many met their wives and families in Hawaii or brought their wives to Bangkok for a week or two. Taking advantage of this opportunity, I chose to bring Peggy to Bangkok.

The advice given to visiting wives and families was well intended, but it proved to be a blessing and a curse for some. The memories of those forever lost in combat were still too fresh in most of our minds. Furthermore, a visit to Hawaii or a few days in Bangkok could not separate us from the reality of an environment to which we must return. As for Peggy and me, the faces of those I knew would never return home filled the room where we slept and precluded the intimacy we desperately sought. This was particularly unexpected and frustrating, but we dealt with it as best we could. The most frightening part was the uncertainty of the duration of sexual impotency. At thirty-four years old, the thought of a permanent dysfunction was absolutely horrifying. As always, Peggy deserved a tremendous amount of credit for remaining calm, supportive, and understanding. More than me, she dealt with these uncertainties through her faith and maturity. To allay my fears, we spent time visiting the back country of Thailand and Burma, the people, and experiencing their cultures.

We were pleasantly surprised one morning at breakfast when someone walked up behind me and placed a hand on my shoulder. I looked up into the face of Brigadier General Charlie Gabriel. He had returned to Thailand on an assignment from the Pentagon and took the time to visit with Peggy and me. Soon it was time for Peggy to return home. She departed for home assured the Lord would work out the effects of Vietnam on my emotional state in due time.

The remainder of my tour at Udorn went by quickly as the wing experienced a heavy turnover in aircrews and other personnel. The majority of my flying was spent training newcomers and occasional combat sorties in Cambodia. In early May, the wing hosted a team of visitors from the Air Force Military Personnel Center (AFMPC) to brief changes in career progressions, particularly for aviators. I was pleased to learn I had been identified for special career monitoring and management. This was a welcome surprise. Later, I found out my good friend, Lieutenant Colonel Tim Boddie, was assigned at AFMPC and had a hand in this good fortune. A few weeks later, my orders arrived assigning me to Bitburg Air Base, Germany. At first blush, this was great news because my family and I loved Europe and wanted to be reassigned there again.

I flew my last combat sortie, the "Sawadee Flight," on June 20, 1973 in support of operations in Cambodia. Colonel George L. Schulstad, the Vice Wing Commander, specifically requested to fly with me. My additional wingmen, Captains Jim Clavena and Wayne Skora, were also flying their last sortie before leaving Udorn. The mission, an interdiction flight supported by a FAC in Cambodia, was completed without incident. We topped off on an aerial tanker before returning to home base. With prior permission, I led the flight of four on a high speed pass over the field with a sharp pull up at the end of the runway. Victory rolls were not authorized, but a cloud deck at 5,000 feet allowed me to make a sharp half roll into the clearing beyond it. Colonel Schulstad and the rest of the flight followed.

We landed shortly to a sizeable crowd of celebrants with the traditional pineapples filled with Thai-flavored rum. The Sawadee truck was waiting with signs depicting the number of missions flown during our one-year tour. Wayne Skora flew 106, Jim Clavena had 114, and I finished with 215. We drove to the squadron for the traditional but futile struggle to avoid a dunk in the tank filled with a foul smelling, bad tasting Green Grog. The Green Grog allegedly had been scooped from the small run-off canals around the base. The crowd awaiting us was larger than those at the end of the runway. We lost that battle!

The year at Korat and Udorn had been a full, high-paced combat tour. When added to my first tour, I had flown 446 missions over South Vietnam, North Vietnam, Laos, and Cambodia. My combat hours in the F-4C, D, and E totaled 828. During the year, I was recommended for a Silver Star, at least two Distinguished Flying Crosses, a Bronze Star, and over a dozen Air Medals. These were expected to be awarded at my next duty station. Reflecting upon these events, I knew it was the hand of God that got me safely through. I knew this intellectually, but failed to proclaim openly that the Lord was the source of my survival. Yet, He allowed my combat experience to come to a successful end.

I spent the next few days preparing to leave and requested the Intelligence Office to prepare and send my classified books and notes to Bitburg. I also spent time with Captain Tony Marshall, an African American former POW who returned to Udorn seeking closure for a number of things in his life. My departure date of June 27th finally arrived. Many in the wing and squadron joined me on the flight line to say goodbye. A few of my Thai friends came to drape leis around my neck.

The sweet aroma of Thai leis filled the air and mixed well with the bottle of champagne thrust into my hand. Dutifully, I took several swigs and prepared to board the airplane. The end had come

AN UNCAGED EAGLE

very suddenly. My emotions were a mixture of joy, remorse, sadness, and uncertainty. I tried to disguise these perplexing feelings with bravado and hoped those gathered would not discern my true inner emotions. I shook hands, embraced a few, and climbed aboard the jet for the long flight across the Pacific and home. I hoped my mind would settle down by the time I reached California. Finding my assigned seat, I sat down and buckled in. I closed my eyes to block the unexpected tears while whispering, "Sawadee Udorn and the sweet-spirit Thai people; Sawadee Vietnam; Sawadee my brothers in arms; and Sawadee to the thousands who will never join me again on the soil of America. Goodbye until we meet again on that final day!"

PILOT TRAINING - CRAIG AFB, AL

Class 65H
Dick is Top Row Center

General Robert Dixon

T-33 Jet at Craig
Ready to Fly

Pilot Wings
June 1965

559th TFS, D Flight, Tom-Tom Rowdies
(Front L-R) Mike Trent, Ken Holocombe, Tom Roberts, Joe Butler
(Rear L-R) Andy Anderson, Me, Dale Young

Returning From Combat

Receiving Air Medal
From Squadron Commander,
Chuck Wells

WARRIOR DEVELOPMENT
1967-1973

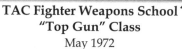

TAC Fighter Weapons School
"Top Gun" Class
May 1972

10th TFS,
Hahn Air Base, Germany

Returning From
Last Mission
Udorn, June 1973
It's Over!

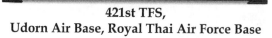

421st TFS,
Udorn Air Base, Royal Thai Air Force Base

CHAPTER TWELVE

HOME OF THE FIGHTER PILOT

The long trip home to California included stops in Tokyo, Japan and Anchorage, Alaska. The aircraft landed at Travis AFB, California the next evening at midnight. My emotional state did not improve during the flight home. I wanted to leave behind the person I became in order to perform effectively in combat. However, it was a struggle to mentally separate from him and resume the role of a loving husband and father. There were just too many faces of the missing and dead flooding my mind, and too many voices echoing from the jungles and rivers of Southeast Asia. The feelings of guilt and remorse for being allowed to come home to a wife and family were overwhelming. Adrift in a sea of confusion, I seemed to have lost my identity.

Instead of proceeding to the last stop at Norton AFB in San Bernardino, I checked into the Travis AFB BOQ for the night and continued the struggle to find myself. Sleep wouldn't come, so I found a Gideon's Bible in the desk and sought solace in the Scriptures. Those responsible for placing these Bibles in thousands of rooms in hotels, motels, and BOQs can never be thanked enough. I was one more grateful soul who found spiritual comfort in a desperate time of need. Several topics described my emotional state: anger, confusion, doubt, fear, frustration, and uncertainty. The authors clearly had me in mind when that book was written. As I read the suggested passages, a much needed calm slowly emerged. I finally dozed off for a few hours of sleep and awakened somewhat relieved.

The "Deal" I made with God back at Udorn came to mind. Part of me felt a deep need for redemption for my part in the war in Southeast Asia. The other part was reluctant to let go of the combat-seasoned, hot-shot fighter pilot. In the heat of combat, I promised to get reconciled with God if He let me survive. I failed reconciliation that night; ego and vanity won the battle. My promise to God was put on the back burner for later consideration, yet He allowed me to head home with some degree of peace.

I hopped another flight from Travis to Norton AFB the next morning where I met Peggy and two of our children, Gail and Michael. Their embraces and kisses were warm and comforting. The smile on Peggy's face and the light in her eyes reflected the relief of a tremendous burden.

The scenic drive to George AFB was great. The majestic mountains of the San Bernardino National Forest gave way to the expansive Mojave Desert, and both were welcomed sights. We were met by the rest of the family – Mom Elsie, Glenette, Renea, and a horde of neighbors and friends with their children. Although weary, the excitement of seeing everyone and the impromptu party were the salve I needed. My welcome was typical of those in Air Force communities at bases all across America. The families at George had embraced and supported my family while I was in Vietnam. Now they gathered to express their love and joy over my safe return. I began to feel good about being home, and verbally thanked God for those who faithfully prayed for me while I was away.

The internal demons subsided after a few days, and I spent the next few weeks visiting family and friends in southern California. The children had grown and matured considerably in just one year. Glenette was seventeen and going into the twelfth grade. Gail, Renea, and Mike were scheduled for the fifth, four, and third grade, respectively. Peggy and Grandma had been a great tag-team in teaching and nurturing our brood, and it showed in their positive attitude and behavior. Both of these ladies were "naturals" and I realized how fortunate the children and I were to have them in our lives. Even our dog, Pixie, seemed pleased with my return.

Our vacation was interrupted by a court appearance I had to make in Los Angeles for the benefit of two sons of my late sister, Arneater. Their father reneged on his agreement allowing other family members to be guardians and sought to regain control of the boys for Social Security benefits. Mrs. Dorothy K. Davis, the lawyer who had assisted me four years earlier, came to my rescue again. Family members who had been taking care of the boys lost guardianship, but we were allowed frequent visiting rights. Mrs. Davis continued her generosity of pro bono service. Her kindness mitigated my anger and most likely kept me from doing bodily harm to my brother-in-law.

We soon prepared for my assignment to Bitburg Air Base, Germany. The size of my family and age of our children required we delay their travel until I arrived and secured adequate housing. We completed the pre-travel arrangements, and I made my final calls to friends the Saturday before my Monday departure. My last call was to my friend and mentor, Lieutenant Colonel Tim Boddie at AFMPC in Texas. Tim was very upset when I told him of my impending departure. He said I was supposed to have been assigned to Nellis AFB. With the help of his friend, Lieutenant Colonel C. H. "Ted" Rees, Chief of Fighter/Recce Manning at AFMPC, he was able to get my orders changed. On Sunday morning, I received a telegram with instructions to report to Colonel Bernard J. "Bo" Bogoslofsky, Director of Operations, 57th Fighter Weapons Wing at Nellis.

I traveled to Nellis AFB on Monday morning and found the base unusually quiet. It was closed down for a memorial service for Lieutenant Colonel Guy Pulliam, a Squadron Commander who had been recently killed in an aircraft accident. I met my Weapons School classmate, Captain Ed Mangis, leaving the Officer's Club. Ed knew Guy as a member of the Officer's Christian Fellowship and was at Nellis to pay his respects. He asked me to go with him to the base chapel. Reluctantly, I accompanied Ed to Guy's service. Upon arrival, I was shocked by the crowd that filled the main sanctuary of the chapel, the balcony, hallways, and overflowed to the steps outside. We wedged our way in and found a small space in the balcony. What happened next helped change my life.

Guy Pulliam's memorial service was a celebration! I had never witnessed such powerful testimonies to a man's life. He was an outstanding husband, father, friend, and a deeply committed Christian. He was a great fighter pilot, officer, and Squadron Commander whom everybody loved. My soul was deeply stirred as I stood listening. I had spent so much energy trying to become the world's greatest fighter pilot, but this man had a greater and more meaningful ambition. How strange it was that he witnessed to me through his death! I silently wished my life would one day be a testimony like Guy Pulliam's. But I didn't know how to make such a commitment and was not yet ready. I left the chapel suppressing tears, more for me than for Guy. He had earned his freedom and was soaring as *An Uncaged Eagle!*

Top of the Mountain

I was assigned to the 422nd Operational Test and Evaluation (OT&E) Squadron. OT&E are ground and air tests conducted to verify the operational effectiveness and maintainability of a weapon system. The test environment is made as realistic as possible to anticipated combat conditions. The squadron was equipped with the A-7, F-4, and F-111 fighters. Major Dave Jacobsen, my old acquaintance from Cam Ranh Bay, was the director of the F-4 section and my immediate supervisor.

Being assigned to Nellis, the "Home of the Fighter Pilot," was tantamount to reaching the top of the mountain. The history of the base and its multiple missions were legend. It was the home of the world-famed USAF Aerial Demonstration Team, the Thunderbirds. The Air Force Fighter Weapons "Top Gun" School resided there along with the charter Aggressor Squadron that introduced Russian tactics to tactical fighter pilots for the first time. In addition, the extensive Nevada Test Ranges permitted an astounding environment for testing and training. This was a great place for me at just the right time in my career. I thanked Tim Boddie and Ted Rees for intervening as they did.

The assignment to Nellis brought me together again with my best friends, Captains Hal Brown and Gene Jackson. Hal was assigned as an Instructor WSO in the 414th Fighter Weapons School and Gene was a charter member in the new 64th Aggressor Squadron. This assignment was one of the most enjoyable personal and professional experiences in my career. Hal, Gene, and I were three proud men from the Deep South who overcame race and a myriad of other hurdles to achieve an enviable and highly respected record in the Air Force. Hal grew up in New Orleans, Louisiana; Gene hailed from Lufkin, Texas; and my hometown was Shreveport, Louisiana. We broke the shackles of racial oppression and pursued our dreams of becoming aviators. The three of us amassed a total of 1,391 missions in Southeast Asia and 2,678 combat hours in the F-4. During two tours each, we earned seven Distinguished Flying Crosses, eighty-one Air Medals, and a dozen other awards. What we appreciated most was the deep friendships formed between our wives and children. Rita, Hal's wife; Nelda, Gene's wife; and my wife, Peggy were cut from the same "character cloth" and were outstanding wives, mothers, and assets to the Air Force community.

Another pleasant surprise at Nellis was the discovery of a large number of relatives in Las Vegas. The matriarch, Atha Toliver, was a descendant of my great grandfather, Wesley Toliver and first cousin to my father. Other Toliver descendents included cousins and relatives by marriage. We held frequent mini-family reunions, the first at Christmas, and at other times during the year.

Major Dave Jaquish, my Christian friend from George AFB, and his family were also assigned to Nellis. He and his wife, Jane, invited us to the base chapel where we met Chaplain (Major) Bobby Black and his family. These two families reached out to us and helped our children embrace an early Christian commitment. Dave continued to demonstrate his Christian faith without being overbearing or straining our friendship. Peggy also attended a weekly Bible study at the home of another Christian couple, Major Ross and Jean Truesdale; however, I was not ready to go that far. We did attend chapel services regularly because I knew it was the right thing to do. Later, Chaplain Black encouraged me to participate in the Martin Luther King, Jr. Memorial Service, an event that began a lifetime of public speaking engagements. Despite my persistent foot-dragging in making a serious commitment, God was still gracious and allowed me to prosper. I didn't know it then, but Bobby and Marybel had been providentially placed in our lives. In addition to being true friends, Bob became my spiritual mentor and personal "pastor" for the rest of my life. His role as *An Uncaged Eagle* in all of the Tolivers' lives was played out in the years that followed.

In September 1973, Lloyd W. "Fig" Newton traveled from Clark Air Base to Nellis for his first interviews with the Thunderbirds. Those who knew him were ecstatic over his progress in the selection process and cheered him along. We had Fig over for dinner, and my family had the opportunity to see him up close and personal. We were very proud of Fig, and he passed muster in the Toliver household with flying colors. We also learned Gene Jackson had applied for the Thunderbirds and was in the final consideration. Both of these African Americans were tremendous aviators, but it was unlikely that both would become Thunderbirds. Nor was it time for women fighter pilots to be considered. Time would eventually change all that.

Operational Test and Evaluation (OT&E)

I transitioned to the latest F-4E, the leading-edge slat version and was selected as a Unit Project Officer. Using lessons learned from Vietnam, our test teams evaluated numerous retrofits for the F-4, A-7 and F-111. Most of the missions required simulated combat maneuvers and parameters that sometimes pressed the operational envelopes. After Vietnam, flying was just plain fun and we laughed a lot those days.

The test experience gained in the 422nd opened doors to other interesting opportunities with aerospace companies, the Air Force Flight Dynamics Laboratory (AFFDL), and the National Aeronautical Space Administration (NASA). In September, the AFFDL conducted a research project at McDonnell Aircraft Company (MCAIR) in St. Louis, Missouri. The program was initiated to investigate the application of new and emerging technologies for future tactical fighter concepts. I was one of four pilots selected from Nellis to participate in this program. The team consisted of Majors Ross Truesdale and Glen E. Frick from the Tactical Fighter Weapons Center (TFWC), Captain George "Tim" Mikita from the 64th Aggressor Squadron, and me from the 422nd Test Squadron.

To support the program, MCAIR developed two dome simulators to replicate visual flight. These platforms allowed various aircraft models to be programmed and flown against existing models or an optimum performing model, or "Iron Pilot." We spent two weeks flying against each other or against the dreaded Iron Pilot. Our efforts played a major role in determining the validity of a new design concept called the Vector Lift Fighter (VLF). The VLF incorporated several advanced features designed to enhance the air-to-air effectiveness of future aircraft. We applied our knowledge and skills while extending ourselves to explore the full potential of innovative maneuvering techniques.

The 422nd received a high-level opportunity in mid-October 1973. Earlier on October 6, Egypt and Syria led a coalition of Arab states in a surprise attack against Israel on Yom Kippur, the Jewish Day of Atonement. The Israelis suffered major loses during the first few days of the war, and the Soviet Union threatened to provide arms and other assistance on behalf of Egypt. President Nixon countered with "Operation Nickel Grass," a plan to replace all of Israel's material losses, including over fifty aircraft.

On orders from the Pentagon, HQ TAC alerted its units to identify fighter aircraft that rapidly could be deployed to Israel to replace their losses. The 422nd identified several F-4Es for the pool, and I was selected to lead a flight of four to Israel. We prepared ourselves and the aircraft for deployment and stood by for launch orders. An alert status was maintained for three days before the mission was cancelled. We later learned F-4s were launched from the bases in the eastern U. S. Once again, I suited up and prepared to go to Israel. As in the 1967 Six Day War, the opportunity was cancelled. I vowed to get to Israel one day, one way or another.

October 1973 was great for another reason. Hal Brown and I, along with dozens of our peers, were selected for major. We were anxious about this promotion because it was a tough year group that included many of the POW returnees. These men deserved every consideration and we wanted the best for them. Yet we hoped our recent tours in Southeast Asia would put us over the top for consideration. Making the list was a significant milestone in our careers that moved us from junior officer to field grade status. The Air Force emphasized education for career progression, so a few weeks later I enrolled in an on-base graduate program in Public Administration with the University of Northern Colorado. I also enrolled in Air Command and Staff College by correspondence with Air University at Maxwell AFB, Alabama.

In February 1974, I received another exciting opportunity from Colonel Fred Green, my former commander at Udorn. He had been promoted and recently assigned to the Tactical Fighter Weapons Center (TFWC). Colonel Green invited me to accompany him on a special TDY to the NASA Langley Research Center in Hampton, Virginia. We participated in a month long Differential Maneuvering Simulator (DMS) Parametric Program. The DMS was used to investigate the effects of changes in aerodynamic parameters on the maneuverability and performance of various American and foreign fighter aircraft.

Like MCAIR, NASA used dual dome simulators for the evaluation. The rigorous test scenarios paired Colonel Green and me against two Navy Top Gun aviators. The fidelity of the simulators enabled us to use realistic maneuvers and tactics. A side benefit of these simulators was realized later. Our air-to-air proficiency was noticeably improved by the experience gained in the simulators.

Two major events took place while I was at NASA Langley. First, I was visited by Major General Gordon Blood, TFWC Commander. He told me I was on the list of Nellis pilots he was recommending for the F-15 OT&E Program. The other pilots on the list included recently promoted Lieutenant Colonel Dave Jacobsen, Major Jim Beatty, and Captain Jeff Cliver. General Blood was scheduled to meet with General Creech that afternoon and wanted to be sure I had no problems with moving after just a year at Nellis. I don't know who smiled more at that question, General Blood or God. Remarkably, he inquired about the impact the move would have upon my family, especially my mother-in-law. Confident of their support, I assured him my family would be fine with the move.

Apparently, I had made a good impression on General Blood when I had flown as his instructor in the F-4 a few times. I could only wonder about his impression of me in a totally different setting. My family frequently encountered General and Mrs. Blood while attending chapel services. Mrs. Blood was especially cordial toward my seventy-four year old mother-in-law, and they never failed to exchange pleasantries. Afterwards, my mother-in-law turned to the rest of us and stated, "She's such a nice lady. I really like her a lot!"

The rumors back at Nellis about the pending F-15 OT&E had been hot and heavy, but the selection was closely held. In 1974, there were approximately 5,000 fighter pilots in the Air Force. Each would have given anything to fly the F-15. I was one of those but had no idea where my name was in the pecking order. My performance record had to stand up against the toughest competition at Nellis as well as throughout the Air Force. Fortunately, the 422nd OT&E experience proved to be a crucial factor in my selection.

My promotion to major was March 1, 1974, the day we finished at NASA Langley. I traveled home in my full dress uniform adorned with my new golden leaves. Peggy, the family, and neighbors welcomed me home with a new sign on the house that said, "Major Toliver." They heard about my selection to the F-15 OT&E program so we had another impromptu party. Peggy was worth her weight in gold. By the time I arrived home, she already had the family pumped up for the move. Life was indeed good!

Glenette's graduation from high school in May was a major achievement for the whole family. Peggy deserved a tremendous amount of credit for her years of encouragement, patience, and tutoring Glenette on almost a daily basis. We were very proud of Glenette for her academic performance that qualified her for college entrance.

In July 1974, it was time to pack up and head to Luke AFB. Peggy and I made several trips to Phoenix to look for a place to live, a college for Glenette, and a school for Gail, Renea, and Mike. During these visits, we were reacquainted with our friends, Art and Anne Peterson and their family whom we knew from Hahn Air Base, Germany. As usual, Peggy prepared the children for the move by casting Luke AFB and Phoenix as another exciting adventure. We were leaving friends and family in Las Vegas, but Phoenix was a short distance away. Follow-on visits were already planned.

The four years since our departure from Hahn Air Base underscored the validity of my decision in 1970. Instead of four years at the Air Force Academy, I had served as an instructor pilot, graduated from Fighter Weapons School, completed a second combat tour in Southeast Asia, gained OT&E experience and was selected for the F-15 OT& E at Luke AFB. I was grateful for those who helped me along the way as we left Nellis on our way to Luke.

CHAPTER THIRTEEN

F-15 EAGLE AIR SUPERIORITY FIGHTER

The Air Force senior leaders selected the 58th Tactical Training Wing, Luke AFB, Arizona, to be the first F-15 Eagle Air Superiority Wing in the United States. This was a real feather in the cap of the Wing Commander, Brigadier General Fred Haeffner. The South Dakota native was admired for his down-to-earth attitude. His affable and outgoing personality made him a great public relations champion throughout the Valley of the Sun. Colonel Jack O'Donnell, a seasoned F-105 fighter pilot, was the Director of Operations. The 555th "Triple Nickel" Tactical Training Squadron, (TTS) was selected as the training unit for pilots assigned to the F-15. The squadron gained its fame as "The Home of MIG Killers" during the Vietnam War.

The newly established Air Force Test and Evaluation Center (AFTEC) with Headquarters in Albuquerque, New Mexico was tasked to conduct the F-15 OT&E. The test team, drawn largely from TAC, was assigned to AFTEC and co-located with the 555th Tactical Fighter Squadron at Luke AFB. This maximized the use of resources, facilitated development of the F-15 training syllabus, and consolidated the collection of data needed for the OT&E.

The first cadre of F-15 pilots assigned to Luke included Lieutenant Colonel Ted Laudice, the 555th commander, and Majors Jim Thornton and Joe Merrick, formerly of Hahn AB, Germany. The OT&E Team was led by Lieutenant Colonel Art Bergman, recently transferred from Edwards AFB. The pilots from Nellis were Lieutenant Colonel Dave Jacobsen, Major Jim Beatty, Captain Jeff Cliver, and me. Major John Jaquish came from TAC headquarters, and Major Tim O'Keefe from Eglin AFB. All of us were graduates of the Fighter Weapons School, had at least two combat tours in Southeast Asia, and averaged 2,500 hours of fighter time. The team was later joined by Majors Jim Posgate of Air Force Systems Command and Omar Wiseman from Air Defense Command. Our maintenance personnel included Captains Vince Pigford and William "Billy" Barber and a top cadre of Non-Commissioned Officers. In addition, Major Augustus Letto and Captain Albert Albauch were assigned from HQ AFTEC as test team analysts.

Base housing at Luke was very limited, so we spent three weeks searching for homes in the Phoenix area. The majority of the team found accommodations in nearby Litchfield Park, but my family of seven required me to look elsewhere. Captain Fig Newton had recently been reassigned to Luke and graciously helped me locate a home near him in Glendale. Fig served as an F-4 instructor at Luke until his selection to the Thunderbirds in November of that year.

Among great blessings during our Air Force career were meeting new friends, beginning new relationships, and getting reacquainted with those we had met before. We were pleased to add the Johnsons and the Bells to our list of treasures. Dr. (Colonel) Leonard Johnson and his wife Evelyn were stationed at Luke when we arrived. Leonard was a Flight Surgeon and Commander of the hospital at Luke. He was assigned to fly with the 555th TTS and became a key contributor for assessing high G stress on pilots.

Lowell Bell and I met while shopping at the base commissary shortly after we arrived at Luke. At six feet four, I noticed Lowell above the shelves. He was a Lieutenant Colonel with Command Pilot wings. We greeted each other and went through "Where have we met before?" Lowell had an extensive aviation background in fighters and other aircraft. He spent most of his time in the Air Defense Command so we had not crossed paths during our careers. The conversation continued with where we grew up, finished high school, and attended college. Bingo! Lowell and I had met in 1953 at my high school in an Industrial Arts class. He was a student teacher from Tuskegee Institute. Lowell graduated from Tuskegee in 1955 and was commissioned a Second Lieutenant in the Air Force. He served in Europe, Vietnam, and numerous northern bases before being assigned to Luke. We traded addresses and discovered our homes were located on back-to-back cul-de-sacs in Glendale. Lowell was a master woodcraftsman, and their home was filled with collections of exquisite carvings, furniture items, and whatnots. Imagine the fun and excitement that followed when our wives, Pat, Peggy, and our children met.

Our new home was situated near Glendale Community College where Peggy got Glenette enrolled for basic college courses. The neighborhood school for our younger three and two of the Bell's three children were located about a ten minute walk from our homes. The Bell's older daughter attended high school less than a mile away. Given the similar ages of our children and the common interests, the Bells and the Tolivers became like one. Our families enjoyed many evenings around the pools in our backyards or climbing over the fence for food and fellowship.

F-15 OT&E

The development flight test program for the F-15 began in 1972 and continued for two years. The first F-15 arrived at Luke in November

1974 for the initial check-out of pilots in the 555th and OT&E team. AFTEC's OT&E was scheduled to be conducted between March 1975 and July 1976. The purpose was to verify the operational effectiveness and suitability of the production F-15 as a total weapon system. The OT&E was to determine if the jet could perform and be maintained in the combat environment for which it was intended. The test plan specified approximately 1,100 sorties to be flown to assess the aircraft in four primary areas: (1) air-to-air; (2) air-to-ground; (3) routine flight; and (4) logistics maintainability and reliability. Other assessments were to be made regarding mission success probability, manpower requirements, and cost of ownership.

The OT&E team gathered to review the test plan and to assign managers for specific areas of the program. Jim Beatty had bagged a MIG during his combat tour in Southeast Asia in 1972 and had a great reputation as an air-to-air pilot at Nellis. I was confident of my air-to-air ability and looked forward to working with Jim in the air-to-air phase of the OT&E. Art Bergman and Dave Jacobsen met earlier and decided otherwise. John Jaquish was assigned to lead the air-to-air phase with Tim O'Keefe, Jim Beatty, and Jeff Cliver assisting. I was designated the primary Air-to-Ground Test Manager. This was a great disappointment because Dave and I had flown together, and he was well aware of my air-to-air ability. I considered being assigned to oversee the air-to-ground role a slap in the face, and it cast a pall over my relationship with the team at the outset.

We spent the remainder of the summer studying the test plan, preparing test scenarios, and arranging range and deployment schedules. The entire test team was involved in this process and we developed a close working relationship with our maintenance people. I got to know Vince Pigford and relied upon his unique administrative talent as well as his ordnance expertise. Gus Letto and Al Aulbach were a great help in designing the test data sheets needed for flight testing. The professional experience and outstanding attitudes of all our people contributed to a great beginning, and we could hardly wait to get our hands on the jets. Beginning in October, the OT&E pilots made several trips to MCAIR to train using dual-dome simulators configured with the F-15 cockpit. The intense and thorough training enabled us to solo very early in our training program.

The introduction of the F-15 into the Air Force announced to the world that America had reclaimed superiority in fighter development and production. The Eagle was the most technologically advanced aircraft in the world. President Ford visited Luke AFB November 14, 1974 to present the first F-15 to TAC and the American public. The OT&E team finished up at MCAIR that morning and rushed to the airport for our flight to Phoenix but it was delayed. We tried desperately to reschedule a flight to get us there but failed. We eventually arrived at the Phoenix airport about the same time President Ford arrived in Air Force One. Lieutenant Colonels Ted Laudice and Art Bergman pre-positioned the F-15 at Williams AFB. The air traffic controllers directed commercial traffic to a designated holding pattern to allow sequencing the arriving F-15 behind President Ford. By the time we arrived at Luke, the ceremonies were concluded, the President had departed, and the crowd had dispersed. F-15 73-108, designated TAC 1, was a regal sight on the ramp, but only our families waited for us. Fate must have chuckled again as the proud, newly dubbed "Eagle Drivers" faced an empty ramp.

The OT&E team continued through December with pre-test planning and check-outs in the F-15. I maintained my instructor status in the F-4 and flew other team members to numerous agencies and units with which we anticipated interaction during active testing. My check-out was scheduled for January. The ecstatic mood of every pilot waiting in line was pervasive everywhere – in the building, on the flight line, and in the support areas. The excitement of having F-15s at Luke was felt throughout the base. Everybody on the training and test team smiled a lot and did little complaining. We were the envy of just about every fighter pilot and maintainer in the Air Force. We tried our best to be humble, but I doubt others saw us that way. Being an "Eagle Driver" was just too much to contain.

My first front seat flight in the F-15 occurred on January 29, 1975 with Lieutenant Colonel Ted Laudice as my "instructor." The one-hour flight was one of pure joy! The time spent at McDonnell Douglas (MCAIR) in St. Louis paid off in great dividends. Every moment in flight was spent verifying what I had learned in the class-room and simulator. The exchange between Ted and me was de-lightful and mutually beneficial. The approach and landing were completed with considerable ease. To this day, it's difficult to find words to express the tremendous pleasure I experienced during my first check-out flight in the Eagle.

The pilots, maintenance troops, and visitors gathered on the flight line to greet me after landing. Peggy, her mother, and several friends were among the greeters. Jeff Cliver was the first to douse me with the fire hose, and Dave Jacobsen handed me the traditional bottle of champagne. I was getting used to impromptu parties and was adept at taking a long swig on the refreshments offered. That day was one of the greatest in my life.

I flew again the next two days with Joe Merrick, and was cleared for solo after three flights. My first solo flight on February 5, 1975 was part of the first F-15 four-ship flight in its history. The flight was led by the 58th TTW DO, Colonel Jack O'Donnell. I flew as Number Two on the left wing, Jeff Cliver was Number Three on the right wing, and Jim Beatty was Number Four. Over the next month, I flew two dozen sorties in the F-4 and F-15 in support of check-outs for the test team and preliminary test flights. We spent April getting into the groove of testing. By then, everyone felt comfortable in the F-15. The cockpit layout and handling qualities of the Eagle were superb. Compared to the F-4, the reduction in pilot workload could be measured in quantum proportions.

The first major hiccup for the F-15 was encountered in April of 1975. The Pratt & Whitney F-100-PW-100 engine was developed and tested concurrently with the F-15. The demands on the engines during aggressive maneuvering in testing and training had an unexpected impact. The external fairings on the afterburner section of the engine began to melt during sustained use in flight. In addition, the rapid, repetitive movement of the throttles during close-in engagements resulted in stagnation of the large compressor fan in the forward section of the engines. The occurrences were loud and startling during flight and forced termination of the event and/or the flight. These events were even more spectacular at night. The aft section of the engine after stagnation in flight was a very ugly sight. The engine fairings that were designed to reduce drag and for a sleek appearance were twisted pieces of molten metal.

Reluctantly, HQ TAC grounded the fleet of F-15s at Luke until Air Force Systems Command and Pratt & Whitney could devise a fix for the problem. This essentially shut down both the testing and training programs. One night at home I came up with a work-around for the OT&E team. Given the power of the F-15 engines, the use of afterburners was not necessary during air-to-ground maneuvering and routine flying. Moving the air-to-ground phase up on the schedule would permit early completion of that phase and allow continued flying. The availability of the nearby Gila Bend gunnery ranges precluded a deployment elsewhere. I presented the idea next day to Art and Dave. They agreed with the idea and immediately presented it to HQ AFTEC and HQ TAC. We received approval within a few days, and the OT&E resumed.

Early on, I had been down in the mouth over being designated the air-to-ground Test Manager. My attitude quickly changed when this phase was moved to front and center of F-15 flying at Luke. The

test plan called for 200 sorties in this phase. However, we soon realized sufficient test data could be obtained to address specific test
objectives with considerably less sorties. We continued the air-to-
ground phase until the restriction was lifted on the F-15 afterburners,
then resumed the air-to air phase.

The air-to-ground and routine phases of the OT&E plan were
executed through early summer. The latter included aerial refueling, instruments, and night flights. By then, interim fixes had been
developed for the engines and the remaining restrictions were lifted. During the summer, we hosted the first of several fighter units
from other bases to begin air-to-air testing against dissimilar aircraft.
These units included Air Defense Command F-106s, Nellis F-4Es,
Navy F-8s, and Marine F-4Bs. I had the special pleasure of reunit-
ing with Lieutenant Colonel Jack Gagan, the Squadron Commander
of the Marine F-4s from El Toro Marine Air Station, California. Jack
was the Marine exchange pilot in my squadron at Cam Ranh Bay,
Vietnam in 1966 with whom I flew the crippled F-4 across the Pacific.
It is a small world after all.

We conducted our first deployment with the F-15 to Nellis in
late summer 1975. Art Berman and Omar Wiseman led the flight
over in TF 73-108, TAC 1. The three remaining members of the four-
ship included John Jaquish and Jeff Cliver on the right wing with me
on the left wing. Dave Jacobsen and Jim Posgate flew photo chase
in the F-4. On the way over, we conducted several pre-authorized
photo passes near Mt. Humphrey in Flagstaff, Arizona, in the Grand
Canyon, and over Hoover Dam in Nevada. Our arrival at Nellis was
met by a large crowd on the ramp. To impress the "Home of Fighter
Pilots," Art briefed an impromptu tactical pitch-up on arrival. However, the 57th TFW Wing Commander didn't think much of it. Later,
he reminded Art the tactical pitch-up maneuver at Nellis was strictly
reserved for the Thunderbirds. Duly admonished, the impressive act
was deemed, "No harm, no foul."

We spent three weeks flying air-to-air with Type-1, Type-2, and T-38 Aggressor aircraft. The "Type" designations were used for foreign-made aircraft acquired by the U.S. for training. We also flew the F-15 for the first time in the Red Flag Exercise at Nellis. One day I flew a single F-15 against a Type-1 and Type-2 aircraft on the Nellis range. At that time, it was the longest sustained high-g flight during the OT&E. At its termination, an unexpected data point was documented. I experienced a mild momentary paralysis that affected my ability to steer the aircraft. This phenomenon was later determined to be a classic case of stagnant hypoxia associated with sustained high-g forces on the body. Fortunately, the episode occurred at high altitude and I recovered within seconds.

While at Nellis, we took the opportunity on weekends to present the F-15 to family, friends, and the public in the Las Vegas area. One night I met what appeared to be two elderly civilians at the O'Club. They noticed the distinctive "Eagle Driver" patch on my flight suit and wanted to hear about the newest jet in TAC. Eager to be a good public relations representative for the Air Force, I cordially explained the outstanding features of the F-15. They asked if I could show them the jet up close, so I invited them to visit me the next day at the 422nd, our host squadron. About 9:00 AM the next morning, a call over the intercom stated I had visitors at the front desk. To my shock, the "older gentlemen" from the night before were Lieutenant General James V. Hartinger, Commander of ADC and Colonel Frederick C. Kyler, Commander of the 36th TFW at Bitburg, Germany! Their winks confirmed the surprised "gotcha" on my face. Thankfully, I made a "Good First Impression" with these gentlemen!

The test team returned to Luke after a successful trip to Nellis. It was great to be part of the prestigious group of F-15 pilots, and it was a measure of pride to be the only fully qualified African American F-15 pilot in the world. This distinction resulted in numerous speaking engagements in the local area of Luke AFB. One such exposure in the Phoenix area led to meeting another young African American captain who wanted to join the Thunderbirds. Captain Pete Peterson was stationed at Williams AFB in Chandler and wanted to transfer to TAC to get the requisite fighter experience. Like Fig Newton who preceded him, Pete had the charisma, dedication, and pilot skills to succeed. The next day, I called my friend, Captain Gene Jackson, at HQ TAC Rated Officer Assignments. With my recommendation, Pete was transferred to TAC and assigned to an F-4 unit. The rest is history. Pete eventually became the second African American pilot selected to join the Thunderbirds.

Like many people, I suffered from the lack of attention to smaller things while major events in my life were going great. I departed the squadron one night and headed straight home rather than making my routine stop at the O'Club. Less than two miles from the base, an apparent drunk driver barreled though an intersection and caused me to swerve out of control to avoid a collision. I went airborne in my Volkswagen and landed upside down across the intersection. The driver of the other car stopped briefly but drove off while I was trapped in the wreckage. After struggling to get free of the wreckage, I staggered down the road confused and disoriented. An angel of mercy came along the deserted road and took me back to the Luke hospital. Peggy was notified of the accident and rushed to the hospital. On the way, she passed the wrecked Volkswagen and was horrified by its totaled condition. I was terribly shaken but miraculously walked away without serious injury.

The accident was a wake-up call that made me realize I needed to make a few changes in my life. All of this happened in late November 1975, so I took a few days of vacation and drove my family to Shreveport for Thanksgiving. Wilbert and his family drove down from Detroit to join us. It was great to be together again. David was stationed at Barksdale, and we gathered at his house for dinner. We were particularly grateful for the progress of our late sister

Arneater's children. Glenette had grown into a beautiful young lady and was in her second year of college. Teenagers Daryl and Tharpsky had moved back with their father, and were coping with life in Los Angeles. James, Jr. was still with Earl and Nancy and doing very well in high school. Shirlevia was a healthy ten-year old living with Zella and AW. We were joined by my brother Ray, his wife, Dorothy and three children. Wendell, his wife Linda, and two small children were also part of our reunion. The years brought a lot of changes to the Toliver clan, and the gathering with my family was just what I needed to regain my focus. Still, I shied away from committing to a more permanent change in my life. God was merciful and forbearing beyond what I deserved.

F-15 73-107

The OT&E program began with four aircraft and finished with seven F-15s by the end of test. Each test team member had the privilege of picking up a jet at MCAIR and logging the first operational hours enroute to Luke AFB. MCAIR made a big event of presenting the F-15 to each of us with our names painted on the canopy rail. I picked up tail number AF 73-107 on December 15, 1975. The customary lettering on the jet was stenciled in white, but I arrived to find the lettering on my jet stenciled in black. I accepted the gesture as an act of special recognition and thanked everyone for their thoughtfulness. After all, this was an historical event for them, the Air Force, and me.

It was a cold, overcast day as I taxied for takeoff from Lambert Field in St. Louis. The tower held the commercial jets and cleared me for an unrestricted climb to 30,000 feet. Moving into position, I passed airliners and saw the faces of the pilots and passengers pressing to see the newest jet in the Air Force. Pure vanity got the best of me, and I raised my canopy to let the people see my face. That bit of egotism caused me to take a few more minutes to defog the canopy when I lowered it for takeoff.

I selected the afterburners and roared down the runway. Lifting off within seconds, I retracted the gear and flaps and reached approximately 400 knots at the end of the runway. My sixty degree pull-up was spectacular to those on the ground and exhilarating to me in the cockpit. I entered the cloud deck and started to reduce my climb angle but punched through within seconds. I reached the 30,000 feet initial level off altitude after slightly less than one minute and requested a hand-off to the regional air traffic controller. The coordinates for Luke AFB were preset in my onboard Inertial Navigation System, so I turned toward Luke and requested a cruise altitude of 45,000 feet. The air traffic controller paused a few moments and then asked what type of aircraft I was flying. I couldn't resist the temptation and stated, "I am flying the world's greatest aircraft, the F-15 Eagle Air Superiority Fighter!" The controller's replied, "Roger that sir, cleared direct to Luke. All the traffic is below you; have a pleasant flight."

With that, I relaxed and enjoyed the view of the Midwest that was largely covered with snow. The landscape soon changed hues and topography, and the distant Rockies emerged on the horizon as I approached Arizona. Turning south at Flagstaff, the Grand Canyon passed off to my right side. Phoenix came into view a few minutes later, and I landed at Luke after the three-hour flight and handed Air Force 73-107 over to our maintenance troops. My personal love affair and odyssey with that particular aircraft had only just begun.

Final Test Phase

The last six months of the OT&E were intense and challenging. We began the last of scheduled deployments to Nellis, Eglin, and Edwards for specialized testing. The air-to-ground phase was completed while at Nellis in February 1976 with only 160 of the allotted 200 sorties needed. I was resting on the steps of the BOQ one

morning after my usual jog when Major General Charlie Gabriel
came along. He was now the TAC DO, and it was a pleasure to see
him again. When asked about the F-15 OT&E, particularly the air-to-
ground phase, I gave him a quick overview. He had a pending trip to
Luke AFB and asked if I would be available to brief him on the results
while he was there. Upon our return to Luke, I prepared a briefing
for General Gabriel's visit. He arrived three weeks later, and I gave
an in-depth report on the air-to-ground test results. General Gabriel
was very pleased and said, "Dick, keep these results handy. We are
going to revisit this capability a few years down the road."

We deployed to Eglin from April to June to conduct live firings of the AIM-7 Medium Range Missile against drones launched
from nearby Tyndall AFB. These profiles tested the F-15's capability
against high altitude threats like the Russian Foxbat. The launch of
drones was timed to allow it to reach supersonic cruise above 80,000
feet outbound. Simultaneously, the previously airborne F-15 began a
supersonic maneuver to intercept the drone over the Gulf of Mexico
at an altitude above 40,000 feet. As the drone came into range, the
Aim-7 was launched from a final snap-up maneuver. These sorties
were packed with test objectives and were some of the most exciting
of the OT&E.

On one mission, the weather over the range caused the mission
to be flown 10,000 feet higher than the practiced profile. This reduced
the launch altitude to about 5,000 feet before reaching the ceiling of
50,000 for the pressurized F-15 cockpit. I was back-up shooter that day
for Omar Wiseman. He successfully acquired the drone on his radar,
but suffered a radar drop-off with about twenty seconds left in the test
profile. Within seconds, I locked on to the drone and the ground stations switched the telemetry tracking to my aircraft. I received clearance to fire at the minimum range and had to make a late snap-up.
At 1.4 mach, I inadvertently zoomed to 73,000 feet to keep the target
illuminated until intercept. My exposure to the extreme danger above

50,000 feet without a pressure suit caused several anxious minutes in my cockpit as well as in the ground tracking stations. I was greatly relieved upon safely descending below 50,000 feet, and there was pure jubilation on the ground. The mission was successful, and we saved a $300,000 test sortie. Omar paid a large bar bill that night.

While at Eglin, I received an emergency call from home telling me Peggy was scheduled for surgery in four days! She had gone to the base hospital to have a small lump in her breast checked. The doctor suspected the worst and scheduled her for surgery at the earliest possible date. I received this news early Friday night, May 21 and advised Art Bergman and Dave Jacobsen immediately. They fully supported my departure the next morning in the F-4 assigned from Luke. Tim O'Keefe flew home with me and took a commercial flight back to Eglin.

I arrived home to find Peggy under control emotionally, but her mother, the children, and I were very concerned. Nothing like this had ever happened, and it shook the foundation of our family. The Bells, the Petersons, the Johnsons, and many others joined us in praying for Peggy during this frightening turn of events in our lives. On May 25, the day of surgery, the doctor required us to sign approval for a radical mastectomy in case that was necessary during the procedure. I did so with fear and trepidation. Peggy simply said if that was needed to safeguard her health, so be it. The doctor estimated a four hour procedure, including diagnostics during the surgery.

I sat in the waiting room choking on guilt and remorse for not being more observant of Peggy. My focus on the job and thrill of flying the F-15 precluded my attention to matters in my home. Peggy was not an alarmist, so she wouldn't have spoken to me about a lump in her breast until the doctor became concerned. Even if she had, I may not have heard her.

My "Deal with God" resounded like a loud clap of thunder. I wanted to pray for leniency, but the words stuck in my throat. Surely, the Lord was not interested in my long overdue plea. Fear and guilt made me physically ill. After about four hours, the doctor came out to tell me the cyst was benign! I nearly collapsed with relief. Peggy was going to be all right, but no thanks to me. The Lord blessed her faithfulness and showed compassion for her mom and the children. I was certain her life and health had been spared for them.

In addition to Peggy's episode, my thirty-eight year old next door neighbor, Jim Oliver, suffered a major heart attack while I was at Eglin. He was still recovering, but would be medically retired from his job. The future prospects for his wife and four children were pretty dim. These events were very unsettling for me, and I desperately needed to get my life in order. My outward appearance as a model husband and father was a sham. I loved my family, but my priorities were woefully out of balance. Worse yet, I had neglected the most important people in my life. Suddenly, flying the F-15 was not that important anymore. I was ready to give it all up for Peggy and my family. I called Art and Dave to let them know I needed a few weeks off. They both agreed and told me not to bother with returning for the remaining three weeks at Eglin.

As soon as Peggy felt up to it, I drove the family to San Diego and the surrounding area for a vacation. I encouraged the children and my mother-in-law to select the places they wanted to visit and explore. I stayed close to Peggy and fussed over her as much as she would let me. I spent a lot of time meditating on how to get back on the right path. The evidence of the Lord's patience and longsuffering with me was overwhelming. His grace and mercy were abundantly clear. Still I wondered if it was possible for me to have a personal relationship where I reciprocated His love for me. This was really foreign territory for me. What sacrifices would I have to make? Did I dare face that question squarely? Did I have the courage to seek the answer? In the end, I really felt contrite and committed to doing better by my wife and family. I hoped that would be enough to pay the "Debt" owed to the Lord. We returned to Phoenix feeling a lot closer and more at ease. I reported to work when the rest of the team returned from Eglin and began preparing for the final weeks of the OT&E.

In mid-June, we conducted the final flight testing at Edwards AFB and China Lake Naval Test Range. The test objectives included firing the AIM-9 Infrared Short Range missile and live intercepts against the SR-71 high altitude reconnaissance aircraft. This was a fitting conclusion to the most comprehensive and rigorous testing of a fighter jet in the history of the Air Force. Thank God, we did it without a serious incident or accident. The return flight to Luke with the seven F-15s on June 25, 1976 was bittersweet. Art Bergman led the formation. One last time we lined up for a photo shoot over the desert of Arizona. Number Two through Six were Dave Jacobsen, Jeff Cliver, John Jaquish, Tim O'Keeffe, and me. Jim Posgate and Omar Wiseman took pictures from the two-seater. The seven-ship formation final approach to the airfield was another first for the F-15s and Luke AFB. It was a fitting and exhilarating conclusion to the flying portion of the F-15 OT&E.

Our families, friends, and base personnel gathered to greet and welcome us home. We gathered in the squadron for refreshments and remarks about the successful flight testing of the F-15. Peggy was especially beautiful that day as I looked at her across the room. She seemed to have felt my eyes, turned, and smiled at me. At that moment, I realized how much I missed her and how much she and the children meant to me. Later that evening, we gathered around the pool at home and reflected upon our two great years spent in the Phoenix area. It had been a wonderful experience all around.

Test Report and Briefings

The OT&E results proved conclusively the F-15 was operationally effective and suitable to be deployed as an air superiority fighter in the Air Force. The data to substantiate this conclusion was collected and evaluated from more than 1,100 sorties and the firings of thirty-four AIM-7F Sparrow and fourteen AIM-9J Sidewinder missiles. In addition, over 59,000 rounds of 20mm ammunition, 1,000 practice bombs, and one hundred MK-84 inert 1,000 bombs were expended. We flew the F-15 against sixteen different types of aircraft and four types of drones. The final challenge in the OT&E was to write an equally compelling story of the F-15's extraordinary performance.

We gathered at HQ AFTEC for several weeks to write the final test report that consisted of nine annexes. Everyone had a specific task in completing this enormous effort - the pilots, maintenance technicians, and administrative personnel. The support from HQ AFTEC was led by Test Director, Colonel Albert Pruden. I began writing the Air-to-Ground Annex during deployments. It was accepted by the AFTEC Review Board early, so I looked forward to helping with the Air-to-Air Annex. Instead, I was tasked to write the Systems Description Annex. This was another decision that irked me as it required me to work alone apart from the team.

The final task of the OT&E was to conduct approximately three weeks of briefings to the major air commands and HQ USAF. The briefing team was led by Art Bergman with Tim O'Keefe as the primary briefer for air-to-air. The "last straw" came when Art Bergman told me Jeff Cliver would brief the air-to-ground portion of the OT&E. As the Air-to-Ground Test Manager and author of its test report, I was outraged. I refused to accept that decision and sought advice and help from my friend Colonel Tim Boddie, now assigned at the Pentagon. He called Bergman and advised him to reconsider the decision to replace me on the briefing team. Art reversed his decision, and I briefed along side the rest of the team. However, the remaining time between the team and me was very strained.

The test team returned to Luke and prepared for reassignments. Art Bergman and Dave Jacobsen wrote the performance reports for members of the test team and recommended follow-on assignments. Those of us who came from Nellis were expected to return after the OT&E. I received a call from my friend, Captain Gene Jackson, at HQ TAC who told me I was not on the list for reassignment back to Nellis. The list included Dave Jacobsen, Tim O'Keefe, and Jeff Cliver. Dave Jacobsen was tapped to head up the first F-15 Fighter Weapons School. Tim O'Keefe and Jeff Cliver were scheduled to be part of the Air Intercept Missile Evaluation/Air Combat Evaluation (AIMVAL-ACEVAL). Everyone else on the team received the assignment of choice. John Jaquish was tapped to be a squadron commander in the 1st TFW at Langley AFB, Virginia. Jim Posgate returned to HQ AFSC, Omar Wiseman returned to ADC, and Vince Pigford was selected to attend the Air Force Institute of Technology.

My exclusion from a career advancement opportunity was very disappointing. What hurt most was Dave's apparent acquiescence in the matter. We had known each other for over ten years. He was my supervisor at Nellis, and we enjoyed a warm and professional relationship. The crowning blow came later when I received my performance report. Contrary to my previous reports, I received a rating below the block that likely would have assured my early promotion to Lieutenant Colonel.

I remained at Luke AFB and searched for an assignment on my own. What started out two years earlier as the greatest assignment a fighter pilot could hope for ended sadly. My refusal to accept real or imagined slights caused some Whites to accuse me of having a chip on my shoulder. I accept part of the blame because my tolerance for the slightest hint of racism was zero, and my response was swift and caustic. This was reflected in my performance report, and it really stuck in my throat.

One night at the O'Club bar, the 58th Commander, Brigadier General Haeffner, came up and placed a hand on my shoulder. He frequently visited the OT&E team and was surprised to hear I was looking for a job. He offered me a job in the Wing Weapons Office and tasked me to investigate the recent developing cracks in the F-15 wing. General Haeffner also asked me to participate in assessing the Singer Company Dual Dome Simulator in Binghamton, New York. Lastly, he asked me to assist the 555th in training five Israeli pilots selected to be the first F-15 pilots outside of the U. S. General Haeffner was a God-send, and I gratefully accepted his kind offer.

Training the Israeli

The reputation of the Israeli Air Force (IAF) was firmly established in the annals of aviation during the 1967 Six Day War with its Arab adversaries. The IAF pilots were respected by fighter pilots worldwide, friend and foe alike. Five highly experienced pilots arrived at Luke AFB in September 1976 to receive initial training in the F-15 Eagle. They were Lieutenant Colonel Eitan Ben Eliehu, Major Moshe Melnik, Major Joel Feldschuh, Major Benjamin Zin, and Captain Saul Simon.

The pilots arrived shortly after the completion of the F-15 OT&E, and I was the only team member left at Luke. The Air Force cleared the OT&E results for dissemination to the IAF pilots, so I taught them directly from the test reports. We spent a large amount of time on the F-15 capabilities in air-to-air, air-to-ground, and avionic systems. The Israelis had an insatiable appetite for knowledge, and the academic training sessions often extended into the night. Each pilot was assigned to return home as an expert in a particular F-15 system. Later, I flew against Captain Simon, the youngest of the group. Despite his limited time in the F-15, he proved to be a fearsome competitor. Peggy and I were invited to the going away party for the IAF pilots before they departed. My time with them had been very special, and I hoped to visit them one day in Israel.

False Hope

A few weeks later, Brigadier General Fred Kyler, the "elderly gentleman" I met earlier at Nellis, arrived at Luke AFB to check out in the F-15. The 36th TFW was scheduled to be the first F-15 Wing in USAFE, so I visited him right away seeking a job. General Kyler readily offered me a job at Bitburg with a reporting date in early January 1977. My family and I were excited about this good fortune and looked forward to returning to Germany and Europe.

Our happiness was shattered a few weeks later when I met Colonel Norman Campbell, the 36th TFW DO. I greeted him warmly and stated how pleased I was to meet him. His next words were a sharp dagger through my heart: "Well, you won't be so pleased when I tell you about the change in your assignment to Bitburg."

I knew immediately this was going to be bad news. He gave me a "song and dance" story about the critical need for F-15 experience at Headquarters United States Air Force, Europe (HQ USAFE) at Ramstein Air Base. Colonel Campbell had persuaded General Kyler to defer his offer of my assignment until after the bed-down of the F-15s at Bitburg. He prevailed in getting HQ USAFE Personnel to change my assignment to Ramstein.

Once again, I was filled with anger. Many questions filled my mind. Had the 36th TFW received bad press about me? How could a wing converting to F-15s pass up the opportunity to get a highly experienced combat veteran with over 3,000 hours of fighter time? Why would Campbell pass on a pilot who had recently logged over

250 hours during the F-15 OT&E? It was extremely difficult to discount the possibility that his decision was based upon race. His words sent me deeper into a dark cage of despair. I left the 555th greatly discouraged by another unexpected hurdle to overcome. It was a very difficult and low point in my life, and the nightly consumption of alcohol did little to relieve the bitterness and despondency.

My struggle to excel and become one of the best officers in the Air Force exceeded thirteen years. Ten of those were spent doing everything possible to be counted among the top fighter pilots in the operational commands. I had fought against racist attitudes, misperceptions, and ingrained stereotypical views of African Americans. I bristled at the notion of some that my presence in the highly competitive arena of fighter pilots was a "token" to prevent adverse publicity. My reaction was hostile and swift to those who believed I should be more gracious and humble for their acceptance of me. Campbell's roadblock in my assignment to Bitburg nearly broke my resolve to continue the fight. The resulting depression was so great it adversely affected my relationship with Peggy, Mom, and the children. I desperately needed help but was still too proud to seek it.

Damascus Road at 20,000 Feet

The last of the so-called "Dog Days" in the Valley of the Sun were ushered out by unusual thundershowers each night. The sky cleared by early morning, and the weather was perfect for flying. Such was the early morning on September 10, 1976 when I went out to fly the F-15 Eagle. After an hour of pure exhilaration, I began my descent from 20,000 feet for landing. A few clouds still hovered over the surrounding mountains below, but I could see Luke Air Force Base about twenty-five miles away. Suddenly, my aircraft was struck by a horrendous flash of light and a deafening explosion that rocked the aircraft and blinded me temporarily. I was totally disoriented for several seconds. My mind flashed back to North Vietnam three years earlier, and I thought I had been hit by a dreaded, unseen surface-to-air missile! After losing several thousand feet of altitude, my head cleared and I recovered the aircraft. My mind sped through every megabit of information. Nothing in my twelve years of aviation experience matched this event that occurred in clear air void of any visible weather.

Eventually, I landed the F-15 safely amidst a horde of emergency vehicles, safety experts, maintenance personnel, the wing commander, and others. After much discussion, it was postulated I had encountered a freak lightning strike and was lucky to be alive. Later, while recovering in the squadron, I was overcome by a powerful spiritual presence that seemed to demand a long-evaded accounting for my attitude and behavior. Here it was at last, the payday for my "Deal with God" back at Udorn. A voice seemed to speak to me quietly, yet it appeared loud enough to be heard throughout the universe.

"How long are you going to keep up this charade?
How long are you going to refuse to settle your debt with me?"

I was frightened by the events that morning, but they were vividly clear. There was no escaping this time. The consequence of trying to wiggle out was to suffer the wrath of God. My "credit card" was woefully overdrawn! With fear and trembling, I headed home. To this day, I do not know how I got there. I can't recall the route I traveled, or if I stopped for traffic lights or signs. There simply is a blackout in my ability to recall details of the trip home. Peggy met me at the door and was startled by my inability to speak. She assisted me to the bedroom, took off my boots, and I fell across the bed. I heard her mother praising the Lord about something but was confused by her exuberance. At the urging of her mother, Peggy left me alone in the room and closed the door.

In the deep recesses of my brain, I remembered the Biblical story about Apostle Paul, the fire-breathing zealot who traveled throughout Israel persecuting Christian Jews. On the road to Damascus to arrest Jews, he was struck by a blinding light. Paul heard the voice of Jesus, and it was a day of reckoning that changed his life forever. I experienced a "Damascus Road" event that day at 20,000 feet and it had a similar affect on my life.

For the next several hours, a dramatic phenomenon took place. I was put on trial for the way my life had been lived in recent years. My actions, attitude, behavior, and thinking were in stark contrast to the many blessings God had showered upon me. In my zealous pursuit to become a super fighter pilot, I had strayed far from the path of righteousness. My conscience was obscured by open rebellion and unbridled vanity. Excelling in my job had become my idolatry and obsession. My speech had become callous and profane, and I frequently hurt those closest to me. Too often, I allowed the frustrations of the job to come home with me; and my daily retreat to the booze closet approached alcohol abuse. To outsiders, the relationship with my wife and family appeared normal; but behind closed doors there was serious trouble in my home. My relationship with the children was especially strained. Even the pet dog avoided me.

The evidence against me went back farther than I wanted to admit. I cringed in shame, but the "Prosecutor" illuminated my sins with glee. The trial continued for hours, and I lost awareness of my physical surroundings. However, my consciousness of the transgressions was real. I was guilty as charged, convicted, and about to be sentenced to death when a "Presence" entered the room. I looked up through the tears of a distraught soul. The Presence stood in my defense. Incredibly, a message that was burned into my memory when I was a youth emerged. It came from a picture on the wall at 2907 Anna Street that my mother had purchased from a White salesman twenty-five years earlier! I remembered arguing with her about the needless spending of hard-earned dollars on a picture of Jesus standing at a door. At that moment, His inscribed words boomed in my mind:

> *"Behold I stand at the door and knock.*
> *If any man hears my voice and opens the door,*
> *I will come to him and eat with him, and he with me."*
> NIV Rev. 3:20

There were no audible words nor could I "see" Jesus, but every part of me sensed His presence. He was real and I cried out, "Jesus, please help me!" Satan, the Prosecutor, yelled louder, "He's guilty! Let me have him!" Jesus seemed to say, "I will wash away his guilt and give him a new life." When I heard those words, I begged harder, "Please God. Give me another chance; I want a new life!"

I don't know when the trial ended but the hand of Jesus reached down and grasped my outstretched hands. I was delivered from the door of hell and placed on the solid ground of redemption. With the Lord's help, I wanted to change my attitude, behavior, and my life. I was saved from death and vowed to do everything possible to walk the way of a Christian. Through God's grace and mercy, I was determined to become a new man. It was about 7:00 PM, and the room was dark when I got up to go to the bathroom. The face that stared back at me had been missing for over ten years! The Dick Toliver that stared back had just experienced a spiritual rebirth.

I heard someone in the hall and opened the bedroom door and saw Gail. She looked surprised at the sight of me but came and gave me a big hug. I couldn't recall the last time one of my children showed such spontaneous affection. Gail and I joined the rest of the family gathered in the kitchen. When I walked in, the other children rushed to give me hugs. Peggy's face and the light in her eyes spoke volumes. Her mother was on her feet shouting again: "Praise the

Lord! Praise the Lord! Thank you, Jesus! Thank you, Jesus!" Her rejoicing was no longer confusing. She knew I had been touched by God, and her celebration was appreciated. We sat around the table speaking in subdued but happy voices. I tried to explain what had happened and that more changes were going to take place in my life. Most of all, I wanted my family to know my absence was finally over. We said goodnight with more hugs and kisses and retired to bed. The day was not over.

About midnight, Gail rushed to our bedroom to tell us emergency vehicles were in front of our house. I went outside and encountered paramedics and policemen responding to a situation at the Carmacks, our neighbors to the left of us. Soon the entire cul-de-sac was aroused and families gathered around the officer posted outside. After about an hour, the body of Ed Carmack was brought out and taken away. His wife, Vickie, and a close friend, Ruth emerged shortly afterward and left. We later learned Ed suffered from severe depression and committed suicide on his 41st birthday, the same day I was reborn! I lay awake until the early morning hours of the next day pondering my own narrow escape from a deep pit of depression.

A New Walk

The flurry of activity the next three months involved several events. We spent considerable time helping the family of Ed Carmack cope with his death. The remainder of my tour at Luke was spent assisting with the training of the Israeli pilots and participating in the first exercise deployment of F-15s from Langley AFB, Virginia. I shared the news of my spiritual conversion with my close friends, the Johnsons and Bells, and drew great moral support from them. Both Leonard and Lowell provided encouragement and wise counsel at a crucial time in my life and career. I also continued with the graduate program at the University of Northern Colorado that I had started back at Nellis and Air Command and Staff College by correspondence.

My family received tremendous support from Pastor Clyde O. Speas and the Glendale First Baptist Church (GFBC). I was committed to a new walk with the Lord and prayed He would give me time to make amends for so much lost time. A year earlier while attending a revival at the church, all four of our children went forward and accepted Jesus as their personal Savior. This great event was accentuated by the fact our family was only one of three other African American families that attended the church. Also, our children were the first African Americans baptized at GFBC and by Pastor Speas. These events underscored the Lord moving in our lives as well as in others regardless of our comfort levels. For several weeks, I joined the men of the church for a 6:00 AM Saturday morning breakfast and Bible Study. This was a true test of my commitment to change. Two others included the cessation of profanity and reliance upon alcohol.

In the interim, we prepared for the move to Ramstein. This was our fourth full move as a family so everyone had a part in the process. Of course, the children were reluctant to leave their friends, but as usual, Peggy made the move another adventure for them. We put the house up for sale, identified the household goods that would be stored during our time overseas, and pre-packed our winter clothing and other items for the overseas shipment. I completed the paperwork required to make my mother-in-law an official dependent and prescheduled the packers and movers pending a firm date of departure for the family. In mid December, I drove our station wagon to San Franciso, CA for its shipment to Germany. We completed the immunizations required for everyone and got new passports. On-base housing was limited at Ramstein, so time was needed for me to locate housing for the family once I arrived. In 1976, we spent our last Christmas together in Phoenix as I prepared to leave for Germany.

My reporting date to HQ USAFE was in early January 1977. In December, I volunteered to fly one of three F-15s designated for maintenance training from Langley AFB, VA to Bitburg, Germany. My Grandpa Bob passed away just before Christmas, and I diverted through Shreveport, Louisiana enroute to Langley. I met my older brother, Wilbert, who had been an alcoholic for many years. He was deeply moved by my testimony of spiritual rebirth and promised to get help for his problem when he returned home to Detroit, Michigan.

I arrived at Langley and spent the last three days of the year preparing for the trip across the Atlantic. The aircraft were flown on functional check flights and declared ready for the deployment. Captain Dave Rickert from the 1st TFW led the flight of three that took off for Bitburg AB, Germany at 0100 AM local time January 5, 1977. The first aerial refueling took place about thirty minutes after takeoff to check out the F-15s refueling capability. Shortly after I hooked up to the tanker, the boom operator advised me of large amounts of fuel venting from one of the wings of my aircraft. I aborted and headed back to Langley. It was fortuitous the refueling procedure detected the problem, but a disappointing end to my attempt to be part of the first F-15s to cross the Atlantic and land at Bitburg. My effort at being part of that history making flight was not to be. After landing, I declined an offer to fly over at a later date and arranged to take a military flight to Ramstein.

CHAPTER FOURTEEN

GROWING SPIRITUAL WINGS

I arrived at Ramstein Air Base, Germany on January 7, 1977. The buildings and sights around the base were familiar. Little seemed changed after seven years. My former squadron mate from Hahn Air Base, Major George "Lippe" Lippemirer, was my sponsor. He met me later and we drove to a nearby village to visit friends and watch a football game on the Air Forces Network. The snow-covered countryside of Germany was just as beautiful as I remembered. Apart from the absence of my family, it felt good to be back in a country we loved.

I was assigned to the Directorate of Operations and Intelligence (HQ USAFE/DO&I) commanded by Major General Lloyd R. Leavitt, Jr. My boss was Colonel Chris Wright, Director of Operational Training, and my immediate supervisor was a former acquaintance, Lieutenant Colonel Jerry Shilt. Jerry and I crash landed an F-4 just before my departure from Cam Ranh Bay, Vietnam in 1966. Major Mike Trent, also formerly of Cam Ranh Bay, worked in the office. The circle of fighter pilots continued to be small.

Lee Pritchard was the Executive Secretary to Major General Leavitt. She was an attractive and stylish redhead who caused heads to turn when she walked by. Lee welcomed me to the staff, and I soon discovered a worth far beyond her outward appearance. She had worked at HQ USAFE for several years and supported scores of U. S. and Allied officers, enlisted, and civilians. She was a coach, mentor, and teacher with vast experience. Lee proved invaluable in my development as staff action officer for all F-15 matters.

I soon learned Lee was one of the greatest contributors to the mission of the U. S. military throughout Europe. She was fluent in several languages and facilitated interaction between US and NATO personnel at every level. Scores of general officers owed their success to her outstanding tutelage earlier in their careers. Lee's tireless commitment and dedication to the US and NATO forces made her one of the greatest patriots I have ever known. She gave unstintingly of herself in helping others, many times unheralded. Above all, Lee became a treasured friend to Peggy and me.

Lippe preceded me as staff officer for the F-15 and was due to rotate to Luke AFB within a few weeks. He did a great job in getting me up to speed on matters of the pending bed-down of the F-15 at Bitburg and Soesterberg in the Netherlands. Colonel Wright and General Leavitt welcomed me and expressed their pleasure at having an experienced F-15 pilot on the staff. My assigned priority was to get involved with the recently established Site Activation Task Force, (SATAF) responsible for the bed down of F-15s at Bitburg.

The F-15 SATAF was a highly organized team that included all the disciplines needed to get the 36th TFW operationally ready as soon as possible. The team welcomed my hands-on experience with the F-15. Lippe and I traveled to Bitburg for a couple of SATAF meetings and my orientation with the base. By the time he left for his assignment, I felt comfortable in my new job and developed an effective working relationship with HQ USAFE and the 36th TFW.

Meeting Colonel Norm Campbell again stirred my negative emotions. Nevertheless, our professional relationship evolved because of his quick grasp of every detail needed to get the wing combat ready in the F-15. I admitted to myself that Norm Campbell was one of the smartest human beings I ever met. I respected that very much because it made my job much easier.

God's Provision

My spiritual wings were just starting to develop when I arrived at Ramstein, and God already had a support group to come along beside me. Dave Jaquish, my first Christian fighter pilot role model, was stationed at USAFE headquarters. Dave, his wife, Jane, and their three children had me over for dinner shortly after I arrived. They introduced me to the local OCF Bible study group, and I began attending weekly. Dave also introduced me to Colonel Clifford "Bud" Henning and his wife, Marie. Bud was a Director on the USAFE staff. He held a weekly bible study in the headquarters during lunch and taught adult Sunday school at the base chapel. Bud invited me to attend both, and I agreed to do so. I also met OCF members Major Charles "Bucky" Dunn and his wife, Dale. This incredible group of Christians welcomed me with opened arms and treated me like family. Their commitment, dedication, and service to God helped me begin a slow but determined daily spiritual walk. I was amazed and humbled by the Lord's provision of this support for me.

Our house in Glendale sold in February about the same time I found a house in Germany. With a prearranged power of attorney, Peggy completed the sale, withdrew the children from school, and got the family ready for the trip, including our dog, Pixie. Glenette was almost twenty-one years old and decided to strike out on her own. Despite my pleadings for her to continue in college, she took a job in Glendale as a nanny. We were disappointed but respected her decision as she seemed happy with her independence.

Our new home was located in the small, picturesque farming village of Kottweiler, about twenty-five minutes from Ramstein. Our landlord was Herr Oscar Kneller, the village butcher. His wife and two daughters were excited about their first African American tenants adjacent to their home. The Knellers and my other new German friends helped me prepare the house for Peggy and the family who arrived the last day of February. They were quickly settled and Gail, Renea, and Michael were enrolled in the eighth, seventh and sixth grades respectively. Our German neighbors especially loved Peggy's mom, and at seventy-eight years old, she loved them and their beautiful country.

I introduced the family to my Christian friends, and they were immediately accepted as I had been. Getting settled into the Ramstein Chapel family was a blessing and delight for everyone. Peggy's mom received a new name during this time. One Sunday morning on the way to worship service, a small child ran up to her excitedly and wrapped his arms around her. He said, "You look like a grandma. Will you be my grandma?" Of course, Mom was delighted and gave the child a hug while promising to be his grandma. From that moment on, she was known lovingly as "Grandma."

My spiritual growth continued, and I spent a lot of time meditating on how the Lord wanted to use me as a Christian. About that time, Peggy and I were given another opportunity to rely completely on the Lord. We received news Glenette had gotten married without any word or discussion with us. She had returned to Shreveport to visit her paternal grandmother. There she met a man twenty years her senior who apparently convinced her he was her knight in shining armor. Although the man was known to her grandmother, none of my family back home had a clue who this guy was. We had very serious misgivings about this sudden change in Glenette's life, and prayed for the Lord's protection for her life.

My job was going well, but I missed flying the F-15. I tried to accept the non-flying job and serve faithfully in this capacity in the Air Force. I shared my thoughts with my Christian friends, and they encouraged me to let the Lord lead me. I knew a few pilots who gave up the cockpit to become chaplains. The fact that I even considered such a possibility was a watershed change in my life. The Lord soon provided me an answer.

I met a group of USAFE chaplains early one morning at breakfast in the O'Club. Although strangers to me, I approached them anyway. I briefly shared my recent recommitment and asked what steps one might take to trade his wings for a cross. They greeted me very cordially and listened respectfully. All asked me to continue praying for God's guidance, and one promised to get back to me soon with some information. I received a letter from one of the chaplains a few weeks later and opened it with anticipation. His letter set me back a bit. In part, it read:

"Dear Dick,

All of us were touched by your recent experience and resultant commitment to serve God. We discussed your situation and believe the Lord can use you among your fellow fighter pilots. For now, the Air Force has enough chaplains, but we do not have nearly enough pilots who are willing to be a witness among their peers."

Disappointed, I discussed this response with Peggy. She thought for a while and finally said, "Dick, I know you were serious and didn't want to discourage you. Honey, I agree with the chaplains. You have the aptitude, but you don't have the attitude. You still have a fighter pilot's temperament, and the Lord needs to work with you on that for a while." I pondered the words of the chaplains and my precious wife. They were right. My attitude needed lots of adjustment, so I resigned myself to let the Lord have his way with me.

F-15s at Bitburg

The Bitburg SATAF progressed on scheduled. In the meantime, NATO commanders had a keen interest in how the F-15 would be integrated within the force structure for Europe. General Ellis, the USAFE Commander-in-Chief, hosted a conference at Ramstein where the presentation on the F-15 was a key event. American and NATO generals from all the branches of the services - Air, Navy, and Army - were invited to attend. Major General Leavitt, the DO&I Director, was tasked to prepare and present the briefings, and I was called upon to perform these tasks. The practice briefings sailed through early reviews by Colonel Wright, General Leavitt, and the other two-star Directorates at the headquarters. The dress rehearsal before General Ellis also went well. The day of the conference arrived and I presented the F-15 capabilities briefing to the senior commanders of NATO. The visiting commanders were very pleased with my presentation. Thereafter, I was General Ellis' "go to" person anytime a request came regarding the F-15.

The official arrival of the F-15s at Bitburg was April 27, 1977. It was a huge media occasion for all of NATO, the base, the city of Bitburg, and surrounding communities. The NATO commanders jockeyed for places on the reviewing stand, but Lee Pritchard did a sterling job in establishing the proper protocol. Brigadier General Fred Kyler led the flight of twenty-three arriving F-15s across the Atlantic and to Bitburg. It was a cold sunny day, and the excitement on the ramp was at a fever pitch. At precisely the appointed minute, General Kyler turned onto the initial approach to the airfield approximately five miles out. The sight and sound of the F-15 were simply awesome. The demonstration of America's preeminent air superiority was not lost on anyone present. We were told the Soviet press was somewhere in the crowds gathered along the many roads leading to Bitburg. Our collective thoughts were, let the enemy beware! Over the next six months, the aircraft for the 22nd TFS and 53rd TFS arrived. By December 1977, the 36th TFW received its full complement of seventy-nine F-15s.

I met General Leavitt early one morning in the hallway. He stopped me and said, "Dick, how do you like flying a desk these days?" I didn't lie. "Sir, it's the pits, but I am here to do the best job possible." His reply was, "Well, you've done an exceptional job. You need to be flying the F-15 again. I am going to call Fred Kyler and tell him to get you back into the cockpit." I was astonished. The smile on General Leavitt's face confirmed I had just placed him a few notches below God. He walked away still smiling and said, "Go fly the F-15!"

I called Peggy immediately to tell her the great news. She is not an emotional person, but immediately praised the Lord for this incredible blessing. The news of my return to the cockpit spread throughout USAFE staff. Many well wishers stopped by my desk to congratulate me. I was surprised by the staff's appreciation of my service and considered it confirmation of my improved attitude, demeanor, and spiritual growth.

Unlike the response at HQUSAFE, my reception at Bitburg was noticeably cool. General Kyler welcomed me warmly enough, but Colonel Campbell's attitude was quite ambivalent. He had a list for future squadron commanders at Bitburg, and it was clear I didn't fit in his plans. Most of the pilots knew very little about me, yet Colonel Campbell's attitude was pervasive among them. I shrugged this off as the normal attitude toward the "pukes from Headquarters" that came to the wings to scrounge flying time. I made frequent trips to the Netherlands for the Soesterberg SATAF during the summer of

1977 but still managed to get in a few flights each month at Bitburg.

Lieutenant Colonel Ron Fogleman, my former squadron mate and friend, was Chief of Standardization and Evaluation (Stan Eval) at Bitburg. He called one day to remind me I needed an Instrument Check. He proposed I lead him on a flight to and from Torrejon Air Base, Spain for the check as this would allow us to get ample instrument flying accomplished. Ron told me we would be participating in the first Open House in recent history at Torrejon. The base, the Headquarters for 16th Air Force, was commanded by a two-star general. As host for the two-day affair, he invited high-ranking Spanish civilian and military dignitaries. Ron said the weekend would be fun, especially since he was the designated demonstration pilot for the visit. I was asked to explain the capability of the F-15 to the anticipated thousands expected to attend the event.

The traditional routes across France and Spain were still in place and in my head. We flew to Torrejon on October 1, 1977 and were greeted by the senior officers on the base. We were briefed on the activities and Ron conducted a practice flight. As expected the next day, the base was flooded with a horde of American and Spanish military and civilian visitors. Ron put on a brilliant show, and I spoke at length about the F-15 Eagle. It was an enjoyable visit and we departed for Bitburg later that evening. Thanks to Ron Fogleman, I had one of the most enjoyable check flights in my career. Driving home that night, I was deeply grateful to the Lord for placing Ron in my life.

Our three teenage children were involved in numerous activities at school that required Peggy to transport them to and from the base daily. During this time, we lost of one of our German neighbors in an automobile accident on black ice. These factors influenced our decision to move on base in early 1978 to ensure my family's safety. The move also enabled us to get more involved in the base chapel activities and bible Studies. Gail, Renea, and Michael joined the chapel's ecumenical youth choir that traveled and performed throughout Europe. Peggy and I joined Bucky and Dale Dunn for the weekly study in their home. Before long, Bud Henning encouraged me to be the facilitator of the adult Sunday school class. Under his great spiritual guidance and leadership, I began another important phase of my life.

Loss of An Uncaged Eagle

In the early morning hours of February 26, 1978, I drove to Bitburg to fly for a few days. While standing at the Ops Counter, the duty officer passed me a copy of The Stars and Stripes. The bold headlines were stunning:

"Air Force General Daniel James, Jr. Dies"

For the second time, the headlines of The Stars and Stripes brought tears to my eyes while I was stationed overseas. Ten years earlier, it was news of the death of Dr. Martin Luther King, Jr. This day, it was General "Chappie" James. I was blessed to meet both of these men and considered them two of America's greatest patriots. They had a tremendous positive impact in my life and were a source of great inspiration. General James, a legendary aviator and an original Tuskegee Airman, was the first African American four star general in the United States Air Force. He was a shining example to officers and enlisted airmen of all races. General James served as the Commander-in-Chief of North American Defense/Air Defense Command before becoming a special assistant to the Air Force Chief of Staff from December 1977 to February 1, 1978. He died February 25, just twenty-five days after retirement.

The poor weather in Germany that morning precluded flying, so I drove back to Ramstein grieving the loss of General Chappie James. My heart was very heavy and the tears flowed freely. I thanked God for allowing this man to make a difference in my life. His spirit is still with me today. General James was one of America's greatest sons, an outstanding Air Force leader, and a perfect example of *An Uncaged Eagle*!

Officer's Christian Fellowship (OCF)

Later that spring, the OCF held a European conference at Ramstein AB, Germany. The National Executive Director, Paul Pettijon, led a powerful group including retired Lieutenant Colonel Ward Graham, a former U-2 pilot, and Dr. C. N. Takloglu, a five feet, two inch spiritual giant. The participants varied in rank from general officer to lieutenant, and they came from throughout Europe. The teaching and fellowship was the greatest I had ever experienced. I was particularly moved by the commitment and dedication of these Christian officers and their wives who were not afraid to demonstrate their faith. It was especially encouraging to me that they represented a wide range of disciplines from aviation to base support. Most importantly, these were top performers in their jobs who achieved rank in their career fields. I left the conference remembering the late Guy Pulliam at Nellis. Being a top fighter pilot and a Christian was indeed possible, and I was grateful for the great examples I met that weekend.

Air Superiority in Europe

With the Soesterberg SATAF in full swing, Colonel Albert Pruden from HQ AFTEC was named the first F-15 commander for the 32nd TFS. The pending arrival of the F-15s at Soesterberg encountered a special problem. The Dutch military and royalty were very supportive of having the F-15s in the Netherlands, but a certain element of the public generated considerable opposition. Contrary to fact, this group alleged the F-15 would generate more noise than its predecessor, the F-4E. The clamor grew until the Netherlands' Ministry of Defense (MODN) was obliged to develop a response. The technical and military representatives of the MODN met at Ramstein with the DO&I staff where I served as chairman. We answered questions, presented factual data, and helped prepare an appropriate response to the public in the Netherlands. A factual and positive report was developed, and the MODN team departed relieved and satisfied. The report was presented to the media throughout the Netherlands and around Soesterberg. A few weeks later, our team received notice from MODN confirming the case was closed. The first aircraft arrived at Soesterberg September 13, 1978. The unit was fully equipped within the next few months and attained operational readiness status within six months.

With two bases and four squadrons of operationally ready F-15s, HQ USAFE and NATO were confident in owning the skies of Europe. This capability was complemented by the F-5 Aggressor Squadron at Alconbury AB, England and the pending Air Combat Maneuvering Range (ACMR) at Deccimomanu, Italy. My workload increased accordingly with the development of a NATO-wide Dissimilar Air Combat Training Program, a revised command training manual, frequent visits by NATO dignitaries, and numerous briefings.

My interaction with the staff during the two SATAFs opened opportunities to recommend individuals to HQ USAFE personnel. Major Gene Jackson was due to leave HQ TAC and wanted to be reassigned to Bitburg. Gene would be an outstanding addition at Bitburg, and I recommended him for the assignment. Major Eldridge Burns, a Tuskegee Alum and associate in HQ USAFE Personnel, traded a slot with HQ TAC to get Gene transferred to Bitburg.

Gene soon arrived with his wife, Nelda, and their two young sons. He completed transition training at Bitburg and became the first African American combat ready F-15 pilot in Europe. Gene quickly made a name for himself throughout NATO and USAFE. When I flew with him, it was like performing a symphony. Our mutual capabilities, sense of tactics, situational awareness, and even radio transmissions were harmonious and in synch. Deploying with

Gene for dissimilar training with NATO and USAFE pilots was particularly gratifying. His tactical call sign was "Tornado" and I was known as "Preacher." Flying at Bitburg was fun, especially when I was scheduled to fly with Gene.

Eagles in Saudi Arabia

With the exception of Israel, the Middle East was not on the radar scope of many staff officers at HQ USAFE. We were aware of the deteriorating political situation in Iran from Americans transiting Ramstein Air Base on their way back to the States. That limited scope dramatically changed early one morning in January 1979. My telephone rang at 5:00 AM. The voice on the other end said, "Major Toliver, please report to Brigadier General Browning at USAFE/DO&I as soon as possible. Please bring your passport and dress warmly. It's snowing outside." Somewhat bewildered, I said, "What? Is this a joke? What is this about at this hour in the morning?" The tone and urgency of the messenger appeared official when he said, "Sir, I can't tell you over the phone. You'll find out when you get here."

I quickly showered, shaved, got dressed, and reported to the headquarters about forty-five minutes later. General Browning apparently had been called much earlier and came as he was. His staff was alert and had already arranged travel orders for me. General Browning got right to the point, "Dick, you have been tasked to take a small F-15 SATAF team to Saudi Arabia right away. The relationship between Iran and America has failed, and the leadership in Washington decided to deploy a contingent of F-15s to Saudi as a show of force. You will have to travel to the American Embassy in Frankfurt to get your passport stamped then to continue on to the Saudi Arabian Embassy in Cologne-Bonn to get an entry visa. The staff has train tickets for you from Kasierslautern to Frankfurt and to Cologne Bonn. Transportation will be arranged to get you back to Ramstein. One more thing, you are scheduled to leave Ramstein late this evening."

I stood looking at General Browning in disbelief as he spoke. A dozen of questions came to mind, but I was too stunned to speak. Finally, I stammered, "Sir, what are the specific objectives of my mission? Are the other team members prepared to travel with me?

He answered a bit more considerately, "The planners and logisticians received a heads-up and prepared for a possible trip a few days ago. Four other individuals will be traveling with you. You are tasked to brief the U.S. Training Mission in Riyadh (USMTM) and the Royal Saudi Air Force (RSAF) on the requirements to temporarily host F-15s. The aircraft are scheduled to arrive from the States in about two weeks. Also, you are expected to visit each base identified to host the F-15s and ensure preparations are completed to do so. Since we don't have a contingency plan for Saudi Arabia, your team will gather pertinent information and brief the appropriate people upon your return."

Concerned about my family, I asked, "Sir, will I have time to go home when I get back?" General Browning said, "We'll have someone to take care of that. Dick, I know this has been a fire hose treatment, but you are our F-15 expert at HQ USAFE, and General Pauly selected you to lead the team. Now we need to get you to the train station in Kasierslautern. A driver is waiting for you downstairs."

I gathered a few things from my office and with my head spinning nearly tumbled down the stairs. Of the many deployments or TDYs in my career, nothing compared to this. I had to trust my military discipline and training. Fortunately, discipline took over on the way to the train station and my mind and body went on autopilot. We drove through falling snow and reached the station for an 8:00 AM departure. My German was fluent enough to find my way without any problems. I boarded the train and settled into my seat for the ride to Frankfurt. It was a very confusing beginning that day, but the beautiful countryside covered with fresh snow presented a storybook picture of Germany. I dozed off for awhile and woke up when the train pulled into Frankfurt. I took a taxi to the American Embassy and was pleased to find the staff ready to stamp my passport and get me on the way to Cologne. So far, so good.

The train ride to Cologne-Bonn presented different, but equally beautiful views along the great Rhine River. I arrived to find the Saudi Embassy closed, but an agent was waiting to process a visa for me. Everything went like clockwork, and I was provided transportation to the Cologne-Bonn airport. CINCUSAFE's small jet transport was waiting to fly me back to Ramstein. The steward knew it had been a long day, so he prepared dinner for me on the way home.

I was taken directly to General Pauly's office to join the other members of the team and to get a specific briefing on our mission. Major David Poli, from USAFE Plans was my co-team chief. I recognized the other officers in logistics and maintenance from previous SATAFs. The CINC's staff laid out various maps of Saudi Arabia and identified the key air bases of Dhahran, Riyadh, Tiaf, Jeddah, and Kuhmis Mushat. In addition, they pointed out other areas of interest and strategic sites. The Saudis approved the visit and we were told to expect full cooperation. General Pauly expressed his confidence in our team and wished us well. A communication link was scheduled to be set up once we were established in Saudi.

Peggy was called earlier and told to pack my summer uniforms, and bring them to Base Operations. We had only a few minutes to talk by telephone before I departed. A six-passenger T-39 jet was waiting to fly us to Athens, Greece via a refueling stop in Naples, Italy. We took off about 7:00 PM with a caution that adverse weather could be expected upon arrival in Italy. We arrived about midnight amid a horrendous thunderstorm that tested the pilot's ability to land safely. We quickly exited the aircraft and waited for the storm to pass before resuming the next leg of the trip.

We arrived in Athens about 2:00 AM. Our team was scheduled for a rendezvous with a planeload of communications technicians from the States. The jet from the States had not arrived so we were whisked to the BOQ for a few hours of sleep. Having been up almost twenty hours, I crashed the moment we arrived. It seemed only a few minutes when we were awakened and returned to Base Operations. The communications team from the States was delayed due to entry clearance problems. Our new instructions were to board a C-130 turboprop and continue on to Saudi.

We took off at daybreak and crossed the Mediterranean Sea toward Egypt. The route took us over Cairo and south along the Nile River that appeared as a dark snake across the stark desert 18,000 feet below. Our route crossed the Red Sea and continued to Jeddah, Saudi Arabia. By the time we passed Mecca it was night again. Our aircraft landed at Dhahran about midnight and the team transferred to an RSAF C-130 flown by American civilian pilots with an armed Saudi guard on board. We finally reached Riyadh, our destination, about 3:00 AM. Brigadier General Donald Kauffman, Commander of the U.S. Training Mission in Riyadh (USMTM), was waiting to provide us an initial briefing and in-country instructions.

General Kauffman confirmed the date of the F-15's arrival twelve days later. Lieutenant Colonel John L. Borling was selected to lead twelve Langley F-15s to Riyadh then disperse to Tiaf and Khamis Mushayt air bases. The F-15s were scheduled to rotate around the bases previously identified. Our team was provided a C-12 aircraft flown by U.S. Army pilots to visit each base to coordinate bed-down preparations. The pilots were also directed to fly over other areas and sites of interest for future contingencies.

Temporary offices were set up for us in the USMTM compound. Our team was assigned billeting in the nearby Corps of Engineers compound. RSAF contacts were identified and a first meeting was scheduled for the next day. Several USMTM liaison officers were assigned to travel with us to facilitate any support needed from the Saudis. The USMTM staff completed the initial briefings on what to expect at the bases and on how best to deal with the Saudis. After thirty-six hours, we gathered our bags and were driven to our quarters to get some much needed sleep.

We were awakened in the afternoon for our next briefing at USMTM. I faced a small problem when I unpacked my bags. Peggy did a great job despite the chaotic day back at Ramstein, but she forgot to pack my trousers! I borrowed a pair of khaki pants from our host Corps of Engineers and made the scheduled meeting. The afternoon briefings enlightened us on the changes to traditional Saudi culture and politics brought on by recent wealth. The late King Abdul Aziz Al Saud founded modern Saudi Arabia in 1932. In 1979, King Kalid bin Abdul Aziz Al-Saud, one of the late king's seven favorite sons, led the country. The country's wealth, foreign affairs, and stability were controlled by the ruling Al-Saud Royal Family, and the leadership was vested in a select group of princes. Prince Fahd bin Abdul Aziz Al-Saud, the heir apparent, was currently Crown Prince and Deputy Prime Minister of the Kingdom.

It was crucial for our team to understand the intricate network of power and influence in the Kingdom and to recognize that religion was the foundation of the country's politics. In addition, Saudi culture was being infused by modern technology. As we drove through the streets, evidence of this was apparent in the Saudi's booming economy, construction projects, a labor force of foreign nationals, and a penchant for highly decorated American cars. Foreign nationals from the Far East, Southwest Asia, and other parts of the world made up the work force. They included workers in construction, public works, service industry, and sanitation. Only a few Saudis were involved in manual labor of any sort.

The city skyline was dotted with construction cranes in every direction. New buildings rose dozens of floors above the ground next to camps of nomadic herdsmen with their flock of sheep that resembled goats. Hundreds of American automobiles – Buicks, Oldsmobile's, Cadillacs, and others - were parked in rows in open, dusty fields. Many of the autos driving through streets were adorned with ornaments right out of western movies. Wreckages of others appeared to have been left at the scenes of accidents.

Our next day began at the RSAF Headquarters. The officers graciously invited us into their headquarters and offered assistance in every way possible. Since the F-15s were scheduled to arrive at Riyadh, The RSAF staff gave us a tour of the base, ramp, and support facilities. Our team was allowed to visit the munitions storage areas, including the air-to-air missiles used on the primary Saudi fighter, the F-5.

Riyadh was used primarily for Saudi C-130 transports and a fleet of commercial jets for the Royal Family. The quality of the ramps, hangars, maintenance, and munitions areas was well below our Air Force standards and required significant improvement before the F-15s arrived. We explained the critical nature of these factors in terms of operational safety for the F-15, particularly the risk of foreign object damage to the engines. Our team was careful to make "suggestions" rather than demands. The RSAF took the suggestions in stride and promised to begin immediate improvements. We continued our assessment of the communications capability on the base and in the control tower. After the tour, the team had a pretty good idea of what to look for at the other bases. The RSAF were ahead of us and immediately notified the other bases of the results at Riyadh.

My team arrived at Base Ops for our flight the next day to a flurry of activity across the base and on the ramp. Foreign workers under Saudi supervision were everywhere repairing the ramps, painting buildings, and repairing or replacing equipment on the flight line. It was an amazing and impressive sight. Everything happened overnight. We felt good about the prospects of our pending visits to the other RSAF bases.

We took off in the Army C-12 for a circuitous flight to Tiaf, our first stop. The preplanned route flew over areas of interest and strategic sites dispersed throughout the desert. The Saudi's gave approval for us to plan routes as necessary except in the Tabuk area near the border with Israel. Our reception at each base was a repeat of the one at Riyadh. It was clear that the RSAF civilians and military had orders to do everything possible to make the F-15 visit a success. USMTM had an Air Force lieutenant colonel assigned as an advisor at each base. This made our job easier, and we soon developed a cordial and respectful relationship with our hosts at each location.

The planned communication team finally arrived and established a link back to HQ USAFE via the U. S. It also enabled me to get word to Peggy, and my trousers arrived on a transport from Ramstein a few days later. In the meantime, we made repeated trips across Saudi Arabia and along the Persian Gulf. As the arrival date approached, we returned to Riyadh to assist with finalizing the reception activities.

The U. S. Ambassador to Saudi Arabia, John C. West, Major General Kaufman, and the RSAF staff left no stone unturned in Riyadh. Prince Fahd, the Crown Prince, was designated to represent the Royal Family for the occasion. The RSAF general officers, themselves related princes, made certain an appropriate setting was established in the city and on the air base. On the day of arrival, hundreds of poles mounted with bouquets of flowers and banners were placed about fifty yards apart for miles leading into the base. Armed Royal Guards were spaced about the same distance along the way. The ramp was decorated with a royal stage and a red carpet laid out for Lieutenant

Colonel John Borling in the lead F-15. The Royal entourage and local dignitaries arrived and remained in the nearby hangar to await the F-15s. The planning and preparation had been incredible, but no one checked with God about the weather.

About thirty minutes before the scheduled arrival of the F-15s, a sudden "Gibley" stirred to the west of the airfield. A Gibley was the local name for a strong dust storm that occurs without warning. With winds up to about fifty miles per hour, it diminishes visibility and can spoil the best laid plans for an event. We were in contact with Lieutenant Colonel Borling when he called about the weather phenomena that blocked the path of the inbound F-15s. Thanks to our flights in the C-12, I was able to offer assistance. I rushed to the control tower and provided vectors to visual check points that allowed the flight to navigate around the temporary storm. The flight had sufficient fuel to do this and all of the F-15s landed safely. Prince Fahd gave Lieutenant Colonel Borling and the F-15 pilots a Royal welcome, and then we all made a hasty retreat to a reception at USMTM Headquarters as the Gibley hit the base.

Later that evening, Prince Fahd hosted a traditional Saudi dinner in a huge convention-like facility in Riyadh. The banquet was a spectacular lay out with whole roasted sheep every few feet apart and every kind of native food imaginable. The "Banquet Table" was a deep carpet along the length of the room. A RSAF officer sat across the table from each of us. The local USMTM people called this a "Goat Grab," indicating the manner in which one reached the roasted sheep to get a choice morsel. I had been advised that our host officers would likely pluck the sheep's eye, a delicacy reserved for guests, and pass it across the table. Forewarned, I maneuvered away from the reach avoiding this special treat, but still remained a few places across from Prince Fahd. It was an honor to be greeted by and sit at the table of a Prince who would soon be king of Saudi Arabia.

The final days of our TDY were spent ensuring the F-15 contingent was settled, initially supported, and able to accomplish their mission. USMTM assumed the responsibility for their post arrival support, and we returned to Ramstein after nearly a month in Saudi Arabia. Our C-12 crew flew us to Dhahran where we thanked them for their outstanding support, boarded a C-5 transport, and began the non-stop flight to Ramstein. The C-12 flights and base visits provided significant data for the development of a contingency plan for future operations in Saudi Arabia. We completed a draft report by the time we landed at Ramstein about eight-hours later. The trip was not over. We gave General Pauly and the key directorates a verbal briefing shortly after landing. The next two days were spent sequestered with key USAFE staff members from operations, intelligence, planning, logistics, and from the Army Headquarters at Stuttgart, Germany. We were finally released to go home to be with our families. It was gratifying to hear our commanders and bosses tell us "Well done!" General Pauly's orders to take a few days off were even more appreciated. I wanted very much to identify the other two team members from HQ USAFE Logistics, but my research was fruitless. However, their contributions to the success of this special mission were invaluable.

Shortly after our return from Saudi Arabia, the development of an Air Force contingency plan for Saudi Arabia became a top priority in HQ USAFE. A key element was the deployment of USAF Airborne Warning and Control System (AWACS) in the Persian Gulf. A contingent of aircraft and aircrews were later stationed in Riyadh, and maintained around-the-clock surveillance of the Persian Gulf. The home base of the AWACS was Tinker AFB, Oklahoma and its initial commander was Brigadier General John L. "Pete" Piotrowski whom I had met fifteen years earlier at Eglin AFB. We met again during one of his visits to HQ USAFE. It was a pleasure to find him still friendly and gracious toward all who crossed his path. General

"Pete" was the first Caucasian I knew who beat me doing the "Soul Brother" handshake!

Sweet Sixteen

I missed a major event while in Saudi Arabia. Our first born, Gail, reached her sixteenth birthday. We had planned a special day for her before I left but had to delay it until my return. The special day began with notes and cards from the family telling Gail what a beautiful young lady she had become and how proud of her we all were. When she arrived from school, I had a bouquet of flowers and an invitation to dinner for just the two of us. Since Gail had reached "the dating age," I wanted to demonstrate how a young lady should be treated. Gail and I had a wonderful dinner and we finished it off with the rest of the family upon our return. Renea's sixteenth birthday was a year away, but she reminded me not to forget it. Gail and the family appreciated my gesture and the memories lasted a lifetime.

Report from Israel

Following their training at Luke, the five IAF pilots returned to Israel and established the first F-15 Squadron outside of the United States. It was assigned to Tel-Nof AFB, located in the middle of Israel near Beersheba and Jacob's Well. In late June 1979, the tensions between Israel and Syria boiled over the sky of Lebanon when the IAF bombed terrorist's bases that were launch sites for attacks against Israel. The Intelligence Office of HQ USAFE routinely reported on the state of affairs in the Middle East, including Israel. We received a breaking report one day regarding a major aerial battle between Israel and Syria. Using the F-15s for the first time in combat, the IAF swept the skies clean and scored the first F-15 aerial victories in combat. The score was five enemy aircraft to no losses for the IAF.

No names were given in the report, but I was certain who the IAF pilots were. I tipped my hat to them and could imagine the revelry that took place that night. Later, an intelligence report confirmed four of the first F-15 pilots trained at Luke scored victories, and Lieutenant Colonel Moshe Melnik scored the world's first kill in the F-15. The five pilots eventually scored twenty-three victories against their adversaries with no losses. Moshe Melnik became a double ace with ten victories.

CHAPTER FIFTEEN

MISREADING ROAD SIGNS

The winter months of 1978 to 1979 and my TDY to Saudi Arabia caused me to lose currency in the F-15. Consequently, I was required to complete ground school and simulator training before flying again. Due to my workload at the headquarters, it took several trips to Bitburg to complete this recertification. I was cleared to resume flying March 1, 1979. It was great to be back in the air.

A month later, I requested release from the HQ USAFE for reassignment to Bitburg. Major General Robert W. Clement, the new DO&I and my former Wing Commander at Udorn RTAF, approved the request. Colonel Campbell, now the Wing Commander at Bitburg, agreed to initiate the action with HQ USAFE. Two months went by with no word so I asked Colonel Campbell about the assignment. He stated that the "ball was in HQ USAFE's court." When I inquired at the headquarters, I was told Colonel Campbell needed to put the request in writing but had failed to so. After my reminder, he sent a letter request to the personnel office. The headquarters' subsequent response stated a lack of funds precluded my transfer to Bitburg until January 1980. This news was very disappointing because prospective replacements for squadron commanders were expected to be in place by late summer 1979. Furthermore, I knew if Colonel Campbell really wanted me at Bitburg, it only required his verbal say to get the ball rolling. As a major, I had done as much to get Gene Jackson released from HQ TAC and reassigned to Bitburg.

This classic "runaround" encountered while pursuing my career objective was very discouraging. For sixteen years, I had diligently pursued a path in the Air Force that normally led to making Colonel between twenty to twenty-two years. I sought advice from those who were successful and tried to carefully emulate them. Setbacks and stumbling blocks did not deter my perseverance. The last major hurdle in my plan was to get assigned to Bitburg and compete for a squadron. Even though I was angry and disappointed, it was time to reevaluate the validity of my goal and the chosen path to success.

Spiritual Breakthrough

When encountering adversities or setbacks in life, my first emotion was anger. This was especially true if racial prejudice was perceived to be the cause. I believed race was a factor in the hurdles placed before me in my attempts to get assigned to Bitburg. Thus, my anger over not being allowed to transfer to Bitburg was a serious challenge in my spiritual walk. It took a lot of prayers to overcome this emotion and to accept how my life was unfolding. I was committed to allowing the Lord to guide my path, but "self" kept getting in the way. The Lord chose this time to reveal a deep-seated problem rooted in my past that caused my predisposition to anger toward anyone who caused me hurt. In searching my soul, I discovered unresolved anger toward two men in my life whom I had never forgiven - my father and brother-in-law. Years before, I mentally accused, convicted, and sentenced these two men for the untimely deaths of my mother and sister. Mother had been dead over eighteen years, and Arneater passed away eight years later. In my mind, both men failed their wives and families miserably. I held them accountable and refused to forgive them. Yet God had forgiven me for my many transgressions. This failure loomed before me like a resounding clash against the Lord's mercy. Scriptures from a recent Bible study emerged through my foggy mind,

> *"Do not judge, and you will not be judged. Do not condemn, and you will not be condemned. Forgive, and you will be forgiven."*
> NIV Luke 6:37-38

Unable to sleep, I got up about 4:00 AM and continued praying. The Holy Spirit helped me realize that no one could be held accountable for the lives of those whom the Lord had created or taken. Thus, my father and brother-in-law had no power over life and death. Equally important, mortal man did not have power over my life and my future, but God did. My anger and my hatred clouded my vision about a lot of things in my life. I needed to get refocused. I needed to seek the forgiveness from my father and brother-in-law for wrongfully hating them all those years. I needed to find the strength and a way to do this. The answer came in a whispered prayer: "Lord, if you let me complete my tour in Europe and get back safely to the States, I will find these men and ask for their forgiveness."

One "Deal with God" should have been enough, but there were still vestiges of an arrogant fighter pilot in me that died hard. However, the Lord knew I sincerely meant to keep that promise. I rose at daybreak spiritually relieved and uplifted as never before. The cage of bitterness, despair, and hatred had held me prisoner much too long. The Lord created me to be *An Uncaged Eagle*, but I kept myself imprisoned. The handle that could open the door to freedom was inside the cage, and I reached for it! Another scripture came to mind,

> *"Whatever you do, work at it with all your heart, as working for the Lord, not men..."* NIV Colossians 3:23.

I was truly humbled and committed to working harder for God instead of for my career. For the first time, I completely placed my future in His hands.

An opportunity to reinforce my commitment came a few weeks later. Our base chaplain preached a sermon about allowing Jesus Christ to be the perfect model for our children. He made it painfully clear that parents, at best, were only flawed, earthly examples. Our children needed the perfect model to emulate. Later that day, I confessed to our children my shortcomings as their dad. I encouraged them to take the chaplain's message to heart and allow Jesus Christ to be their example from that day on. I promised to do my best, but exhorted them to keep their focus on Jesus. Mike was the first to embrace me and said, "Dad, we know you are doing your best, and we love you. Jesus is already our example, but we want to keep you as our dad." Gail and Renea echoed Mike's words while Peggy and Grandma looked on approvingly. I believe my stature as a man improved significantly that day, and a tremendous burden was lifted from my shoulders. I realized the quiet work of Peggy and Grandma in steering our children in the right direction was what kept our family together. These two ladies deserved far more credit than I had given them. It was a great comfort to know all of them loved me in spite of my human frailties.

I requested two weeks of vacation to give me the much needed time to be with my family. We planned a trip to a Christian Retreat in Switzerland. Gail, Renea, and Michael were now teenagers, and I was about to miss a critical part of their lives. It was a very special time, and we thoroughly enjoyed being together. With God's help, I planned to be a better husband and father.

By the end of the summer, many of our friends rotated and new relationships were made. We opened our home for a weekly Bible study and hosted several Christian couples.

One of these was a young Army couple, Captain David and Yoshi Brown from the Army post in Kasierslautern. We met the Browns earlier in the year and invited them to visit us at the Ramstein Chapel. Later they told us our Christian witness impressed them and they wanted to know how an Air Force major could be so bold in his witness. David and Yoshi became our friends for years to come.

I received the news of my promotion to lieutenant colonel in October 1979. Despite my misgivings, the Lord was faithful. My job performance and the persistent efforts to further my military and civilian education paid off. More than my efforts, it was the prayers and support of Peggy, Grandma, our children, and many others who played a great part in this promotion. In late November, my family met early one morning in the office of Major General Clement for the promotion ceremony at which time he reiterated his recommendation to the personnel office for my assignment to Bitburg. We received orders for Bitburg in December and sincerely thanked the Lord for the years at Ramstein. In retrospect, He knew I needed a lot of spiritual growth that may not have been possible at Bitburg in 1976. The time at Ramstein was used to mold and shape me into a more useable vessel, and I was thankful for the experience.

We celebrated Renea's sixteenth birthday on January 2, 1980. Following the example I established with Gail, Renea received flowers and special date with me. Our time was equally exciting, and I saw a strong reflection of myself across the table from me. Renea's drive and determination were said to be a carbon copy of a younger Dick Toliver. Everybody in our home and others who knew us were amazed at our similarities. Both of us were quietly proud of this close resemblance but recognized early the need to leave a little bit of space between us. About this same time, Renea announced she wanted to attend the Air Force Academy. My initial opposition to this choice was eliminated by Renea's mature and sensible responses to my questioning. She had given much thought to the commitment and responsibility that came with the opportunity to attend the Air Force Academy. Above all, we thanked God for the bold and independent spirit of the second young woman emerging in our home.

High Cost of Command

On January 7, our young friend, David Brown, used his truck to drive me to Bitburg with our house plants while Peggy and Yoshi followed us in our car. We made this preliminary trip to secure base housing for the family. We met Lieutenant Colonel Daryl Olsen and his wife in the BOQ the day we arrived and had dinner with them that night in the O'Club. Daryl and I had met earlier in our careers. We both arrived with the expectation of becoming squadron commanders in one of the two squadrons coming open. Daryl had been out of fighters for a few years and was apprehensive about getting checked out in time for a command. Another competitor for a squadron had been recently reassigned from Bitburg to HQ USAFE due to an incident involving alcohol. Given that situation, I believed Daryl and I had a chance at least for one of the squadrons.

We moved our family a week later and spent another week getting settled and enrolling the children in school. They were pleased about the location of the school that was about two hundred yards behind our assigned quarters. We all were happy to be reunited with Major Gene and Nelda Jackson and their two boys, Cory and Craig, who lived in a nearby village.

Normally, the wing commander meets the lieutenant colonel who reports to base expecting to become a commander in his unit. Also, the officer and his wife are invited to dinner at the Commander's or the DO's home for informal discussions and social amenities. Peggy and I were not invited to either, but we shrugged off the slight. I was directed to report to Colonel Marcus Anderson, the DO, to discuss my assignment. We previously met at HQ USAFE during the development of the European Joint Jet Pilot Training Program to train NATO pilots in the United States. I was very disappointed when told of being assigned as the Wing Weapons Officer in the headquarters. This required moving a major out of his job and transferring him to one of the squadrons. The major was understandably upset because, like me, this was a huge step backward. I asked Colonel Anderson about plans for me to become squadron commander. He stated Colonel Campbell would discuss this matter with me when we met later. My first official day at Bitburg proved to be very unsettling.

The meeting with Colonel Campbell left me baffled and disturbed. During our conversations six months earlier, he indicated I initially would be assigned as a Squadron Operations Officer and later as Commander when the position opened up. Now, he told me the line-up of the squadrons had changed, and he was reconsidering where to assign everyone. He also said there was no need for me to attend the usual Squadron Commander's School "since I was about as smart as most who were selected to attend." This did little for my confidence. With the exception of Daryl Olsen and the two commanders scheduled to rotate, I was senior to the other lieutenant colonel pilots in the wing. Colonel Campbell apparently had a plan, but I was uncertain where I stood in line to become a squadron commander. Nevertheless, I trusted the Lord to work it all out.

Flying the F-15 was one of the great things about being stationed at Bitburg. Getting my family settled and having a few friends on the base was another. Besides Gene and Nelda, Colonel Bobby Black, our former chaplain at Nellis, was the senior chaplain at Bitburg. His wife, Marybelle, and their three children, Larry, Lori, and Brian were also with him. Bob continued to be a spiritual mentor and true friend. In addition, several people whom we met previously through the Protestant Chapel Men and Women groups were stationed at the base. Also, my friend, Lieutenant Colonel Hal Brown, recently had been assigned to Spangdahlem Air Base, a few miles from Bitburg.

Gene and Hal were head coaches of their base football teams, a huge popular program throughout USAFE. The competition for the championship had already begun. Often, I had to referee the friendly sparring between these two that took place in my living room.

With the family settled and my job responsibilities in hand, I continued my activities in OCF and the chapel. We attended weekly services, participated in the PMOC and PWOC, and conducted a weekly OCF Bible study in our home. I also enrolled in a couple of courses toward a Master's Degree in Public Administration at the Troy State University Overseas extension. My assigned squadron was the 22nd TFS where Gene Jackson was an instructor. Ten years earlier, I was the instructor and he was the student. At Bitburg, the role was reversed but we both enjoyed flying together. Fate smiled again!

In March, Lieutenant Colonel Philip Hanby, the 22nd Commander rotated. I still had not received any word from Colonel Campbell about moving up to that position. One day Gene called to tell me a rumor was circulating that I was scheduled to be the new commander of the 22nd. He told me my name was already stenciled on the commander's locker and flight equipment peg. Later that day, Peggy called to tell me the base communications personnel were at our home to install the red phone for the squadron commander's emergency use. These were encouraging events, but when I went to see Colonel Campbell, he had traveled to HQ USAFE the night before. Colonel Anderson could not shed any light on the happenings. The game plan became painfully clear the next day.

Colonel Campbell made a late night trip to HQ USAFE to plead the case for reassignment of the lieutenant colonel who was transferred earlier because of the alcohol incident. Until then, I didn't know this person was a classmate of Colonel Campbell at the Air Force Academy. That person returned to Bitburg and was named the new commander of the 22nd. My name was removed from the locker and peg in the squadron, and a communication technician returned to my home to disconnect the Red phone. These bizarre incidents left me very upset and distrustful of Colonel Campbell. Worse yet, he acted as if nothing unusual had happened. Again, Peggy and I were obliged to leave the matter in the Lord's hands. To do otherwise would have caused more anger and frustration, and I tried to avoid going down that road again. I flew my final training flight, a Flight Lead Evaluation, with the new 22nd Squadron Commander on April 14, 1980. It was an awkward event for both of us, but I was successful and certified combat ready. However, I was still assigned as the Wing Weapons Officer.

I was tasked to expand the dissimilar air combat training (DACT) between the 36th TFW and NATO fighter units. DACT was crucial training that allowed pilots to fly against different aircraft to perfect their skills. This required flying to air bases in Belgium, England, Denmark, France, and the Netherlands. It was great to fly the F-15 into these bases and brief our allies on the world's greatest fighter aircraft. All were eager to interact with Bitburg as well as Soesterberg. I coordinated the latter with Colonel Al Pruden, the new 32nd Commander; recently promoted Colonel Ron Fogelman, the Ops Officer; and Major Jeff Cliver, the Assistant Ops Officer.

A few weeks later, I met Daryl Olsen at Wing Headquarters. He was assigned to the 53rd Squadron whose commander was due to leave in June. Daryl was rushing to complete several written tests before his check flight. Three days later, the base was shocked and saddened by the tragic loss of Daryl Olsen in an F-15 accident. Apparently, he had a rudder problem in flight, never recovered the aircraft, and crashed. This news was especially difficult for me because I knew how hard Daryl tried to become a squadron commander. With just one squadron commander's slot remaining to be filled, he and I were competing for the job. I was already checked out and confident my experience, combat record, and overall qualifications matched or exceeded Daryl's. As a result, he was working very hard to prove himself competitive for the job. I was tempted to blame Colonel Campbell and others who pushed Daryl so hard, but was spiritually reminded no mortal man held the power of life and death over him. Peggy and I prayed fervently for Daryl's family and offered our heart-felt condolences.

Colonel Campbell called me in after Daryl's memorial service to tell me I would be the new commander of the 53rd TFS. My bereavement over Daryl's death made this news bitter-sweet. I was deeply saddened it took Daryl's death for me to reach this point in my career. The ultimate cost was far too high. The change-of-command between Lieutenant Colonel Paul T. Goldman, Jr. and me took place on July 1, 1980. That night, our family gathered to ask God's blessing as this career-long goal was finally reached. Early the next morning, Peggy and I drove to a hillside that overlooked Bitburg. We were humbled beyond words and recommitted our lives to giving the best in the service of our nation. Although uncertain about the future, we were confident the Lord was with us.

After the change-of-command, I expected the customary meeting with Colonel Campbell to get his direction, philosophy, and vision for the wing. That didn't happen. When I suggested we have a chat, Colonel Campbell told me to just do my job and everything would be fine. This left me to chart a course for myself and to sink or swim. Later, Lieutenant General Walter D. Druen, 17th Air Force Commander and chain-of-command for the 36th, called me in during his last visit to Bitburg. In a roundabout way, he told me to show my face more with my officers during Happy Hours at the O'Club. He also inferred my personal image of a "Bible Toting" Preacher was not too good with some of the pilots. My call-sign, "Preacher," reflected my deliverance from drinking, smoking, and the din of Happy Hours at the O'Club. For three years, I had made a practice of spending Friday nights relaxing with my family. I resented General Druen's subtle admonition. Unfortunately, I failed to hear what he didn't say.

Later in July, Major General William E. Brown became the new 17th Air Force Commander. We were stationed together at George AFB, California in the 1970s. General Brown was also the first and only African American Squadron Commander of the 53rd TFS twelve years before me. Shortly after taking command, General Brown hosted a visit at Bitburg for the U.S. Ambassador to Russia, Thomas J. Watson. Ambassador Watson was the eldest of three sons of Thomas J. Watson, the first president of IBM. He was an avid award-winning sailor and pilot who flew every type of aircraft from helicopters and jets to stunt planes. It was a great honor to have him and General Brown fly out of the 53rd TFS. We followed up the flights with a reception in the squadron. Mrs. Gloria Brown, who accompanied her husband, presented Peggy a hand-made tablecloth that had been used during squadron functions when General Brown was the 53rd commander. The visit was a great success, and we looked forward to additional visits with General and Mrs. Brown.

Six Seconds to Eternity

It was Friday, July 25th, the day after General Brown's visit, and the end of a great week for the squadron. I flew the last flight of the day with Captain Brian C. Dugle, my Squadron Weapons Officer, who had just returned from the Fighter Weapons School. The sortie was a one-on-one basic fighter maneuvering event to check out Captain Dugle before tasking him to train others in the squadron. We took off and proceeded to the training area without incident and began the set-ups. The first two engagements were flown mildly aggressively and terminated without a conclusive "winner." The third event was flown much more aggressively. Like hundreds of times before,

I used a rudder reversal to maneuver into a position of advantage. Without warning, the aircraft rapidly reversed direction and was non responsive to my control inputs. The incident occurred at 10,000 feet, the floor of the training area, but I continued below it in an attempt to recover the aircraft. An eternity passed while I tried to assess and correct the unprecedented condition.

I had flown the F-15 in the most aggressive scenarios possible for over five years, but had never experienced a loss of control. I believed the aircraft could be recovered, but in an immeasurable instant of time, I realized my experience, knowledge, and training could not save me. Well below the safe ejection altitude for my situation, I pulled the ejection handle and was miraculously spared from the jaws of death. Within two seconds, the canopy blew, the rocket seat ejected me, the automatic man-seat separator fired, and I was suspended in the parachute. By the pure grace of God, I ejected approximately six seconds before the aircraft impacted the ground. The entire near fatal sequence from start to finish took just seventeen seconds!

I was rapidly descending in the parachute and had to act fast. The years of training kicked in. I maneuvered the parachute toward a clearing in the forest a few thousand feet away. Fortunately, the aircraft missed a small village later identified as Reetz. Approaching the clearing, I tucked my legs up to miss the last row of trees before reaching the ground. My parachute caught the edge of the trees and broke my fall into a small stream. At that same moment, a strange looking helicopter landed in the only clearing within miles of the crash site. This was unbelievable, and my mind played tricks on me. It reverted back to Vietnam, and I rushed to extricate my parachute to escape the would-be captors. Amazingly, a crew member left the chopper and came toward me speaking English. I racked my brain to no avail for recognition of the helicopter. My mind played tricks again. The training area was only a few minutes from East Germany, and I worried we may have inadvertently strayed across the border.

By then, the crewmember reached me and helped me out of the knee-deep stream. He led me safely to the helicopter and provided first aid to my bleeding chin and bruised neck. In a moment, we were flying back to the crew's base camp. Enroute I learned this was a British Submarine Hunter from the west coast of England. The crew was on an exercise with the German army when the sound and sight of my ejection caught their attention. They immediately took off, followed my parachute, and landed to pick me up. This was the second miracle that day.

The events from the ejection to arriving in the British camp took about twenty minutes. I had difficulty keeping it together and asked for a note pad. I jotted down the timeline of events and sketched the engagement prior to incident. At that point, my memory faded and I could barely recall my name. The crew recognized my mild state of shock and gave me a few more sips of tea and time to recover. My head cleared again and I finished the notes. My rescuers drove me to the nearest village to find a telephone. The people were still buzzing over the nearby crash and explosion of the jet. Imagine the look on their faces when an African American fighter pilot and British aviators showed up asking to use the telephone.

Captain Dugle, my wingman, was equally shaken. Things happened so fast in my cockpit that I didn't have time to make a transmission. It took every bit of my mental capacity to deal with the situation, and I ejected without giving my wingman warning. He lost sight of me momentarily as I maneuvered toward his rear. What he saw next was an explosion on the ground. A few seconds later, he saw a parachute touch down and a helicopter pick up someone he thought was me. Although he reported the facts, the Command Post at Bitburg had trouble digesting the details of the mishap.

I reached the Command Post to confirm my status and what Captain Dugle had relayed. I explained what caused me to eject and told them the British had agreed to fly me back to Bitburg. Peggy was notified of my accident and told I was safe and would soon be home. Our family was immediately surrounded by friends including the Jacksons, Hal Brown, and Chaplain Bob Black and his family. Lori, his daughter, brought along cookies she had baked as an expression of concern. I didn't get a chance to eat the cookies; but Lori's compassion was never forgotten.

My Operations Officer, Lieutenant Colonel Edward Joiner and members of the squadron met me at Base Operations. After expressions of gratitude, we said good-bye to the helicopter crew who were truly angels sent by God. An official letter of thanks would follow later. I was immediately taken to the hospital for an examination. My body began to recover from shock and the adrenalin subsided. About that time, it seemed liked rigor mortis set in. I suffered severe body spasms. The opening forces of the parachute under the condition of my ejection caused severe stress on my back and neck. With injected medication, my body relaxed and a thorough physical examination was completed. Fortunately, the injuries were limited to severe body contusions and sprains. I was able to get through the night reasonably well, but it took several days for me to recover. The aftermath of the event lasted much longer.

Bitter Consequences

The responsible major air command convenes a Safety Investigation Board (SIB) to investigate aircraft accidents, identify the cause, and recommend preventive measures. This usually occurs within twenty-four hours, and the SIB is led by a Colonel with a bevy of experts and technicians. HQ USAFE established a team to investigate my accident. The command was especially concerned because Lieutenant Colonel Daryl Olsen's accident was related to a flight control problem. Also, my aircraft loss was the third one of the year at Bitburg Air Base. Prior to Daryl's accident, a young pilot was killed in a weather-related accident. Furthermore, the 36th TFW encountered eight F-15 uncommanded control inputs in the preceding eight months prior to my accident. These uncommanded inputs involved the rudder and ailerons, the primary maneuvering surfaces.

Following standard procedures, the SIB immediately collected personal records of the mishap pilots and aircraft. When possible, interviews are conducted with the pilot or pilots involved and anyone that may provide relevant information. Within days, Captain Dugle and I, maintenance personnel, radar controllers, and others gave testimonies to facilitate the investigation. The preliminary investigation cleared Captain Dugle and me as possible factors that caused the accident. Accordingly, our flight status was not affected.

On August 12, I was declared physically fit and resumed flying eighteen days after my ejection. To ensure my confidence was intact, I flew a mission similar to the one in which the accident occurred. It went without incident, and I felt good to be flying again. By the end of August, the SIB's final report listed the cause of the accident as "Undetermined." This was personally disappointing because a number of factors had been identified as possible causes. The SIB's conclusion opened the door for a lot of conjecture and second-guessing about my actions during the accident. Nevertheless, I continued to fly locally, in exercises, and on deployments through October. However, the relationship between Colonel Campbell, other wing leaders, and some of the officers in my squadron went downhill. The one exception was Colonel Howard F. Bronson, III. He had recently moved up as the 36th TFW DO and Colonel Anderson became the Vice Commander. Howard and his wife, Judy, had been stationed with us during our tour at Hahn AB. They continued to treat us with respect and as friends.

My tenure as squadron commander came to an abrupt end one morning after a wing staff meeting. Colonel Campbell told me I needed to visit General Brown at 17th Air Force Headquarters at Sembach, Germany. He refused to tell me the reason, but the message was clear. Throughout this book, I have sought to be accurate and truthful in telling my story. But sometimes truth can be very painful. Such was the case here. That week in mid-November 1980 ushered in the most difficult period of my professional career. It was also a very disruptive, traumatic time for our family, especially the children.

Peggy, Grandma, and I prayed before I left, yet the three-hour drive to Sembach was filled with foreboding. I arrived to find Major General Brown in a troubled mood, and he minced no words in telling me I was relieved of my command. He stated Colonel Campbell and my officers had lost confidence in me and the "air just needed to be cleared" in the squadron. Clearly, this was a difficult task for him. I managed to maintain my composure until he said, "Why couldn't you have just been a little less aggressive during that flight?" I lost it then, and my reply came from the old Dick Toliver: "General, how in the hell do you suggest we train a bunch of inexperienced pilots to fight the Russians? The enemy is an aggressive and highly trained adversary, and you can bet they train that way!" The General left the room for a few minutes while I struggled to get myself under control. He returned and said he was sorry for the way things turned out for me at Bitburg. I said likewise, and with that, I was dismissed.

I needed to vent before getting back on the road, so I called my friend Lieutenant Colonel Calvin Jeffries, also stationed at Sembach. Cal had a similar experience and offered me some much needed consolation. We had lunch while Cal tried his best to console me before I departed for the long trip home. On the way, I sincerely apologized to the Lord for the outburst of my anger and frustration. Thankfully, He knew I was still very much a work in progress. That work is still in progress twenty-nine years later.

While writing this book, I finally admitted that General Brown was right in one respect. The painful truth was I pushed too hard during that fateful day of my accident in 1980. A mechanical problem may have occurred anyway, but the impressions that led to my firing might have been avoided. The real tragedy was my efforts were meant to satisfy man rather than please God. I was so intent on being successful in the Air Force that it became my idolatry. That was my greater sin.

The effective date for relinquishing command of the squadron was on or about November 15, 1980. My replacement was assigned from HQ USAFE. I also had a friend at HQ USAFE. Earlier that summer, General Charlie Gabriel was assigned as the new CINC at HQ USAFE. I was later told he didn't like the findings of the SIB or the outcome that it caused. In early November, he made a surprise visit to Bitburg. It caused quite a stir because normally a wing is given weeks to prepare for a CINC visit. Colonel Campbell called to tell me General Gabriel wanted to see me during his visit. This came as another surprise because no one in the wing knew of my long-standing relationship with General Gabriel. He arrived at the squadron with Colonel Campbell in tow. The squadron was called to attention and we met at the Ops Desk. General Gabriel was resplendent in his dress uniform and displayed his usual warm smile. He spoke with the officers for a few minutes then said, "Dick, let's go back to your office for a chat."

Everyone was surprised as we made our way to what would soon be my former office. General Gabriel and I faced each other for a few inexpressible moments. We stood as two professionals in a manner that defied protocol and transcended rank. His eyes were filled with compassion and respect. Finally he said, "Dick, I am sorry the well has been poisoned for you at Bitburg, but I am going to see to it that you have a chance to continue your career. I called my friend, Wayne Whitlatch, the Commander at AFTEC, and asked him to give you a job. You know the test business, and I know you'll continue to do a great job for the Air Force. Wayne said he would be pleased to have you." My lips uttered words of gratitude while my face and eyes showed the great love I had for this man. The mist in his eyes told me the feeling was mutual. Struggling to find my voice, I managed to say, "Sir, I greatly appreciate your consideration and efforts. I will do my best." He said, "I know you will, Dick. Good luck to you."

I followed him to the door as Colonel Campbell looked on stunned. General Gabriel's party left and I returned to my office and began packing my belongings. Colonel Campbell called me later and asked if I had met Gabriel before. I told him yes but didn't elaborate. He told me he was going to announce the changeover in the 53rd TFS that night at the O'Club and suggested I not attend. The old Dick Toliver almost spoke again; instead, I told him not to worry.

As Christians, we sometimes fail to hear God speaking or see the "road signs" when we are on the wrong path. We may stop to pray about what we intend to do, rather than take time to seek His guidance. Such was the case in my circumstances. I was determined and focused on the goal of getting to Bitburg to become an F-15 Squadron Commander. Obstacles were used as stepping stones in my pursuit. In retrospect, my ambition blinded me, and my focus was misplaced. Even so, the Lord allowed me to get to Bitburg and to become a squadron commander. The consequences were a bitter disappointment, sadness, and shame. The assignment was one of the worst in my career, and it almost cost me both a career and my life.

The two weeks that followed were very painful as we prepared to leave Bitburg the day after Thanksgiving, November 28th. Our children suffered much because of the abrupt uprooting from their many activities. Gail was the Senior Class President, held a key position on the yearbook team, and was on the junior varsity volleyball team. Renea was a junior and on the varsity basketball, track, and volleyball teams. Mike, a sophomore, was on the varsity football and track teams. Each of them had to leave those with whom they had established lasting relationships. I expressed to each of them my deep regret for causing so much chaos in their lives at such a crucial point. Regardless of what happened beyond Bitburg, I vowed to not accept another assignment until after they graduated from high school. Our children demonstrated great maturity in support of me, and they confirmed their continued love and respect during my greatest career challenge.

Our friends came to see us and offered prayers and words of encouragement. Gene and Hal were there for me as brothers and comforters. On our last Sunday, our dear friend, Chaplain Black, honored our entire family, especially Grandma. Bob had been a tremendous supporter and encourager since our days at Nellis. He was especially so after my accident. On the day of our departure, Gene Jackson and our neighbor, Walter Lacy, drove us to the airport in Frankfurt. We departed later that day fighting desperately to hold onto our faith. My good friend Bud Henning once shared the following verse with me:

> *"And we know that in all things God works for the good of those who love him, who have been called according to his purpose."*
> NIV Romans 8:28

My family took this promise to heart as we flew across the Atlantic to an uncertain future, but clinging to the faithfulness of God and His word.

THE TOLIVER FAMILY 1974-1975

New Major
Leaves

Chapel Sweethearts

Glenette

Gail, Peggy, Michael, Mom,
Glenette, and Renea

Mom

Gail

Renea

Michael

Uncaged Eagles in My Life

General Daniel
"Chappie" James

Captain Lloyd "Fig" Newton

Captain Harold J. Brown

Colonel
Charles E. McGee

Colonel James T. and Mrs. Mattye Boddie

Flying the F-15, Luke AFB, AZ 1975-1976

Debriefing Test Mission

First Check-out Sortie in F-15
Jan1975, Mom and Peggy

First Israeli F-15 Pilots, Sept 1976
(L-R) Capt. Simon, Maj. Zin,
Maj. Melnik, Maj. Feldschu and
Lt. Col. Ben Eliehu

Successful Mission

**Major General
Gordon F. Blood**

Last F-15 OT&E Sortie, July 1976
I'm Number 4

53rd TFS, Bitburg, Germany
Change of Command

F-15 Pilot Major Gene Jackson

Discussing Ejection From F-15

Squadron Exchange with Belgium Air Force

**General
Charles A. Gabriel**

Promotion to Lieutenant Colonel, 1979

CHAPTER SIXTEEN

THE DOOR TO FREEDOM

Starting Over

We stopped in Baltimore, Maryland to visit Peggy's family and friends and to get Grandma settled there for a few months. Our departure was delayed a few days due to my severe back and neck spasms. I obtained medical help from a Public Health Center that allowed me to continue traveling after a few days. We reached Kirtland AFB in Albuquerque, New Mexico on a late night the first week in December 1980. I checked into the hospital the next day for additional treatment and reported to work a week later.

Major General Wayne E. Whitlatch, HQ AFTEC Commander, was a kind, sympathetic man who welcomed me very warmly. He assigned me to Joint Test under Director Colonel John Reeves. I spent two weeks becoming familiar with my new job while Peggy got the children registered and settled into a nearby school. Due to limited housing on base, we stayed in temporary quarters several weeks. In the meantime, we purchased a new car and planned a trip to Shreveport, Louisiana to spend the holidays with my sister, Zella, brothers Ray and Wendell, and their and families.

During the first weeks back in the States, we discovered two very serious family concerns that required our involvement. One was the failing marriage of our daughter, Glenette. The other was my brother Wilbert's battle with cancer. On the way to Shreveport, we stopped in Grand Prairie, Texas to visit Glenette and her two young children, Anna and Quinton. Her marriage was in serious trouble, but all we could do was offer counseling and a commitment to ensure their well-being. I spoke to my brother Wilbert the day before Christmas and encouraged him to join the family in Shreveport. He found a flight out of Detroit and arrived Christmas Day for our gathering in the home of Zella and AW.

Prior to Christmas dinner, the family gathered in a prayer circle for Wilbert and prayed for God's intervention in his illness. Later, Wilbert asked me how he could find the faith in God I demonstrated. This was a tremendous moment. I gathered the men together in the living room and we prayed fervently for the renewal of Wilbert's faith. I had an OCF distributed booklet, the Four Spiritual Laws, that was published by the Campus Crusade for Christ. I encouraged Wilbert to invite Jesus into his life. His prayer was a genuine act of contrition, and the Lord's immediate response was overwhelming. The glow on Wilbert's face reflected the lifting of an awesome burden of doubt, fear, and uncertainty. During that hour together, He rediscovered the faith to trust God no matter what lay ahead.

We spent the next few days visiting other family and our Grandpa Bob in East Texas. During this time, Wilbert and I had many discussions, and I had the opportunity to reinforce the "Good News" – God loves us and gave His son for our sins; His shed blood saves us from eternal death. For the first time in our lives, Wilbert and I were more than brothers by birth. We were sons of the King.

As the New Year began, the whole family had grown closer.

All of us departed from the family gathering spiritually uplifted and confident of the promises in the Lord's word:

> *"Never will I leave you; never will I forsake you."*
> NIV Hebrews 13:5.

Peggy, our three children, and I headed back to Albuquerque realizing the Lord had work for us to do in the States. If it took the loss of my squadron at Bitburg to get me home and involved in the needs of my family, so be it.

The year got off to a great start. My prior test experience and association with AFTEC paid off in the interactions with other major commands and Air Force Headquarters at the Pentagon. We moved into base housing in late January and began worshiping at the base chapel. The Christian group at Kirtland was a great encouragement to me, and my spiritual growth continued. I was asked to be the personal chaperon for Retired Army Lieutenant General William Harrison, the guest speaker for a special program. He was an eighty-five year old dynamo and spiritual giant. General Harrison had led the negotiations for the cease fire between the United States and North Korea in 1953. His booklet, "Can a Christian Be a Soldier" was an inspiration to me. General Harrison was imminently successful as a military leader, yet his witness as a Christian was even more powerful. He was an outstanding role model, and spending time with him was the blessing of a lifetime. My good fortune was soon interrupted.

On January 22, 1981, Colonel Charles Hausenfleck, AFTEC Vice-Commander, notified me of a letter from the Inspector General, HQ USAFE. I was advised that during the review by Safety Office, my "action or inaction" was identified as a possible cause of the accident at Bitburg. This finding, six months after the accident, upset me to no end. I exercised my option to make a rebuttal and gathered historical and test data needed to do so. The Safety Investigation Board's (SIB) earlier finding of "Undetermined" ultimately resulted in the loss of my job as a squadron commander. I accepted that consequence and was trying to move on with my career and life. This latest slap in the face was an egregious insult to injury, and I prepared to write the strongest possible rebuttal.

The SIB failed in many ways to conduct a thorough investigation. It ignored hard evidence collected during the investigation and from F-15 historical data. For example, a large charred screwdriver found in the wing area of the crash site was ruled not to be a factor. This conclusion was reached even though the name etched in the tool was traced back to its owner at MCAIR. Also, data on F-15 un-commanded flight control anomalies in the archives at MCAIR, HQ AFFTC, HQ AFTEC, and the 36th TFW were repeatedly ignored. Most distressing was the disregard of my testimony as a highly experienced fighter pilot. I was the only survivor of several recent F-15 accidents, yet the SIB gave little credence to my input as a live witness to what happened. Instead, the board used conjecture to reach its "Non-Conclusive" finding.

The initial attempt to write the rebuttal failed until my anger was overcome through meditation and prayer. I subsequently addressed the deficiencies of the SIB's investigation and the subjective evaluation of the USAFE Safety staff. Three crucial conditions were identified that could have caused my accident. These were: (1) asymmetrical wing fuel imbalance, (2) foreign object damage (FOD), and (3) un-commanded flight control inputs. In addition, I identified other significant factors that would continue to adversely affect mishap investigations, safe ejections, and overall accident prevention in the Air Force. These included delayed and confusing command staff reports, inconsistent command action following an incident/accident, and the lack of credibility given to a surviving pilot or aircrew member.

On February 14, 1981, my rebuttal was forwarded to the Inspector General of the Air Force and former Commander of AFTEC,
Lieutenant General Howard Leaf; CINCUSAFE, General Charlie Gabriel; and Commander HQ TAC, General Wilbur Creech. My cover
letter cautioned more lives would be lost in the F-15 if known flight
control problems were not fixed. Very tragically, a young Air Force
captain died that same day in a crash where a flight control problem
was suspected!

Within the same week, Chaplain Bob Black at Bitburg wrote a
letter on my behalf to his personal friend, General Robert C. Mathis,
Vice Chief of Staff of the Air Force. Bob's letter stated my firing was
a great disservice to the Air Force and requested an investigation be
made of all those who were responsible. A few weeks later, several major changes took place in USAFE. Colonel Norm Campbell
was relieved as Wing Commander at Bitburg; the president of the
SIB for my accident lost his job; and changes were made on USAFE's
Safety Staff. Also, HQ Air Force Inspection Safety Center, Norton
AFB, California called me to discuss my report and asked if I wanted
to change anything. My rebuttal stood as written. Although I was
finally vindicated, there was no delight in what happened in Germany. Instead, I felt sad that members of the SIB allowed bias, breaches
in their integrity, and misguided aspirations to cloud their judgment.
The consequences I suffered now seemed small compared to theirs.
More importantly, I had the comfort of the Lord in my life.

Free at Last

In early March, we received news that our second car had arrived
from Germany. Ordinarily, the arrival port for Europe was Bayonne,
New Jersey; however, the car was shipped to a port in Los Angeles,
California. Until then, I thought little about my promise regarding
my father and brother-in-law made while still in Germany. Now, it
reemerged with an urgent demand for action. These men did not

need to be "found;" they lived in the Los Angeles area. The time had come for me to make good on my word. My walk with the Lord was stronger, but the thought of actually locating and embracing my father and brother-in-law weakened my resolve. But I was not about to tempt the Lord to use another "spiritual two-by-four." One lightning strike was enough. Peggy, the children, and I prayed for courage and strength before I left for California.

The flight to Los Angeles and the car pick up went like clock-work. I drove away less than two hours after arriving. My brother-in-law's address in Los Angeles was the same as when my sister died twelve years earlier. My father's last known address was in Pasadena, about one hour away. I drove first by the house in Los Angeles and learned from neighbors that my brother-in-law, James, and two of his sons still lived there. They were not expected home until later, so I drove to Pasadena. After several hours and numerous dead ends, I finally found my father.

It was very difficult to accept the visible results of a hard life that stood before me. My dad's sad demeanor was accentuated by his downcast eyes and drooping shoulders. He was beaten down by circumstances and his poor choices in life. Still, the sight tugged at my heart. Without delay, I briefly shared the changes in my life and the purpose of my visit. It was difficult, but I managed to say, "I've come to ask you to forgive me for the anger and hatred held against you for the death of Mother. I was terribly wrong. God chose to take Mother when He did, and you had no choice and power in the matter. I am still saddened by whatever caused the failure of your marriage, and sorry you couldn't put it back together. Now I hope you will find it in your heart to forgive me for my misguided accusations."

My father looked at me with tear-filled eyes that reflected years of deep sorrow, frustration, and an inability to articulate his hidden thoughts. His face spoke volumes when he uttered, "Ain't nothing to forgive." We then embraced for the first time since I was a boy in Oxnard, California thirty-six years earlier. For the first time in my recollection, my father and I prayed together. I asked God to let me soon bring my father home to Albuquerque and to allow me to introduce him to rest of the family.

I drove back to Los Angeles and found my nephews, at home. We waited outside for about an hour before James pulled up in his truck and proceeded to unload some things. He didn't realize I was standing with his sons until one spoke to him. Looking up, he recognized me and immediately recoiled in fear. Our last meeting was in a courtroom after I returned from Southeast Asia eight years earlier. Then I wanted to do him bodily harm, so his reaction was understandable. I repeated the message given to my father. Afterwards, James and I embraced for a long time. Finally, he spoke in an emotionally-charged voice, "I always hoped you wouldn't hold me responsible for Arneater's death. I loved her very much and hurt more than anybody when she died." I understood this now and told him so. For all four of us, that day was the beginning of healing for the loss of a dear wife, mother, and sister.

Later that night, I drove across the desert toward Albuquerque. It had been a short but eventful journey that brought a long overdue reconciliation to broken family relationships. A tremendous burden was lifted from my shoulders, and the bright light of hope began to shine. When I unwittingly closed the door of forgiveness to my father and brother-in-law, a door was opened to Satan, thus allowing the hurt to continue its destructive influence. It took me thirty-three difficult years to overcome the adversities in my life that held me captive. Thirteen of those years were consumed as I doggedly pursued my career in the Air Force. By the grace of God, I escaped the dark dungeon of bitterness caused by my reaction to poverty, pitfalls, setbacks, and the vestiges of racism and bigotry. Once I had forgiven and received forgiveness from my father and brother-in-law, the healing began for past hurts caused by racial prejudice, slights, disappointments and other emotional barriers. I had finally found my freedom. The cage of despair had to be opened from the inside, and the path to freedom was beyond the door of forgiveness! That night I could finally sing that old Negro spiritual that Dr. Martin Luther King, Jr. sang: "Free at last; free at last; thank God almighty, I am free at last!"

CHAPTER SEVENTEEN

MOVING ON

After just five months back in the states, Gail graduated from high school in May with honors. She earned a one-year scholarship to the University of New Mexico. The only person she felt close to in her graduating class was Debbie, daughter of our friends, Jim and Bonnie Thar. Gail overcame a tremendous upheaval in her young life to achieve this milestone, and we were very proud of her. Our families celebrated together on graduation night, while thanking the Lord for the success of our lovely daughters. Gail landed a summer job with New Mexico's Department of Transportation. Her outstanding work ethic soon earned high praise and a semi-permanent position. She was accepted in the School of Architecture at University of New Mexico and planned to enter in the fall.

In June, I was selected to serve on a special team to study the structure of AFTEC, develop alternatives, and recommend changes for its reorganization. With increased tasking, HQ AFTEC was poised to grow from approximately 200 people to about 600. In addition, the test detachments were set to expand from two to six. The team of seven had expertise in the disciplines of environmental, logistics, operations, and resource management. We met in a separate office and worked exhaustively for six months. Three proposals were presented to Major General Whitlatch and the AFTEC Directors. Each alternative provided a streamlined process for test review, reporting, and maximization of resources. General Whitlatch selected the alternative that featured a Chief-of-Staff and created a Resources Management Directorate. He and the senior staff were pleased with our efforts, and we were released to return to our respective offices.

Two days after our presentation, Colonel Joseph R. Gerrish, the new Chief-of- Staff, asked me to come to his office. He stated General Whitlatch and he were very impressed with my capability and performance, and he offered me the job of Assistant Chief of Staff. My primary duty would be to advise and assist him in the formulation of policy and procedures. Specific tasks included the implementation of the commander's directives, preparation of executive correspondence, and review of all staff correspondence prepared for the command section. In addition, the job required interfacing with top management personnel in industry and government, including all services. Lastly, the task included supervision of the command section administrative staff. I was delighted and honored for this opportunity and readily accepted. The start of a great relationship between Colonel Gerrish and me began immediately, and I moved into the Command Section in an office adjacent to General Whitlatch.

Over the next several months, the revised way of doing business at HQ AFTEC was implemented during an effective and smooth transition process. My summary reviews of test reports, participation in command briefings, and preparation of executive correspondence enabled on-going interaction with the entire Research and Development community. One particularly rewarding aspect of my job was working to get end users involved in the OT&E process as early as possible in the product development. This participation gave credence to the conduct and results of operational tests completed by AFTEC. After settling in the job, I registered at Webster University's on-base extension program to complete my master's degree. My experience in OT&E and R&D, plus related courses I had completed in Public Administration, matched up with the requirements for a degree in Procurement Management, a goal I worked toward.

Later, I had the privilege of representing HQ AFTEC at the 1981 Annual Tuskegee Airmen, Incorporated (TAI) National Convention in Denver, Colorado. This was my first opportunity to get involved with TAI since its incorporation in 1975. The host TAI chapter, the Hubert L. "Hooks" Jones Chapter, was named after the man who greatly influenced my life at Tuskegee Institute in the 1960s. The convention was very special in three other ways. After twenty years, I met and spoke again with Mrs. Jane Jones, widow of Colonel Jones. Secondly, for the first time in eleven years, I was reunited with retired Colonel Charles and Fran McGee, my mentor and role model from Hahn AB, Germany. Last, the convention allowed me to meet Captain Pete Peterson, the young man I assisted in becoming the second African American Thunderbird pilot. This was the one and only time I saw Pete as a Thunderbird pilot. The following January, he was tragically killed with three other Thunderbird pilots.

At the end of 1981, General Whitlatch's participation in the combined CMF/OCF/Chapel Christmas celebration was a very special event for the base and community. No one had ever made such a request of him, and he felt expressions of faith were largely a private matter. With careful persistence, I succeeded in getting him to agree to be the speaker. The outcome was a tremendous blessing for those present to hear General Whitlatch speak and to see his wife, Nona, participate in the Kirtland Chapel Bell Choir that night. The more than 140 people took part doubled the attendance of previous events. General Whitlatch's powerful testimony reflected the foundation of his deep faith and commitment to God, our nation, and the Air Force. It was an exciting end to a great year, and I thanked God daily for allowing my family to come to HQ AFTEC and the Kirtland community.

Storm Clouds

Most of us have experienced dark clouds and troubled waters in our lives. There are never opportune times for such events, tragedies, or death. Christians face the same challenges as non-believers. All are tested. The emotional well-being and spiritual growth of our family were sorely tested by two major tragedies in 1982.

The first tragedy struck in the home of our daughter, Glenette, in Grand Prairie, Texas. I received a telephone call early Friday morning, January 22nd. In a fit of jealous rage, her husband, Charles, made threats to kill the entire family. Glenette called me after he left for work. I urged her to find a friend to stay with and cease contact with Charles until I arrived. With Glenette safe, I called Charles through the night and into Saturday evening to no avail. By Sunday night, I was very concerned and sought assistance from the Grand Prairie Police Department. I explained the situation to them and expressed my concern for the safety of Glenette and the children. They agreed to check the house, but required Glenette to be present in their vehicle during a search of the house. Two officers, Glenette, and her pastor went to the house early Monday morning. Getting no response to their knocking, the officers used the key and cautiously entered the house. They discovered Charles' body facing the entrance to the hallway. Sometime during the weekend, he took his life with a shotgun.

The consequences of that tragedy are beyond words. It was the most horrific situation ever encountered in our lives. Peggy and I were joined by Zella, AW and other family members in the days that followed to help Glenette get through the events. Anna was only four and Quinton was barely two. Details of this tragedy were withheld from them until later in their lives when they were able to cope with such knowledge. January 1982 truly tested our faith and ability to deal with these tragedies. With the help of the Lord, we pressed on.

The second storm cloud appeared in March. Wilbert was hos-pitalized for several weeks for the recurrence of cancer. I traveled to Detroit to encourage him and offer spiritual support. My young Christian friends from Ramstein, Captain David and Yoshi Brown, had transferred to the U.S. Army Tank Automotive Command near Mt. Clemens, Michigan. Dave visited Wilbert often to attend his physical needs and became his prayer partner. The timely presence of David and Yoshi near Detroit was a powerful confirmation that there are no accidental meetings in the lives of believers. This was a god-send for my brother, and a comfort to me knowing Wilbert was in good hands.

Strike Eagle

In the late 1970s, the Air Force stated its need to replace the aging F-111 long range, air-to-ground fighter bomber. The service sought a dual-role fighter (DRF) that could excel in air-to-air combat and carry a substantial bomb load, day or night and in all weather conditions. In December 1980, McDonnell Douglas Corporation proposed a two-seat ground-attack version of the F-15, the Strike Eagle. The proposal consisted of a strengthened airframe, conformal fuel tanks, improved avionics, and a multiple weapons capability. About that same time, General Dynamics gained approval from the Air Force Aeronautical Systems Division (ASD) for cooperation and support in flight-testing its prototype F-16XL. USAF supplied two test aircraft to be modified, two turbofan engines, and funding for the flight-testing. The advan-tage enjoyed at that time by General Dynamics could be attributed to politics, within and outside the Air Force.

In March 1981, the Air Force formally announced the program to procure a replacement for the F-111. The aircraft was expected to be capable of deep interdiction missions without additional support of fighter escort or electronic jamming-equipped aircraft. General

Dynamics submitted a proposal for the F-16XL, while McDonnell Douglas submitted a variant of the F-15D. In January, Air Force Systems Command directed ASD to establish a derivative fighter comparison organization to evaluate the two. By spring 1982, research and development of DRF moved to center stage. The F-16XL was rolled out on July 2, 1982 and began flight testing at Edwards AFB, California. Funding for the F-15E Strike Eagle testing was approved the following fiscal year.

HQ AFTEC, in concert with HQ TAC, searched for an F-15E Test Director to head up a team at Edwards. I gave no thought to being considered for the job for two reasons. First, I knew the wolves that attacked me previously were still around, and I had no desire to enter the fracas again. Secondly, I promised my three teenagers we would stay put until they graduated from high school. During a staff meeting, one of the director's advised General Whitlatch of my prior F-15 OT&E experience as the Air-to Ground Test Manager. General Whitlatch called me in and asked why I had not applied for the position at Edwards. I explained my reasons and he said he understood my priorities for the children. However, he thought the concern about the wolves could be overcome. Nevertheless, he left the decision up to me.

About a week later General Whitlatch called me in again and asked if I would consider going to Edwards on a TDY basis that allowed me to get home as often as possible. Since I hadn't been grounded as a result of the accident at Bitburg, he felt certain the Air Force headquarters in the Pentagon would approve his recommendation. I had made a promise to my family that we would not move again until the children completed high school. We talked about the opportunity to return to the cockpit and the family was very supportive. Everyone agreed that I should accept General's Whitlatch considerate offer and I did so. He retired June 1, 1982 and was replaced by Major General Richard W. Phillips, Jr., a highly experienced fighter and test pilot. During the briefings and reviews of on-going OT&E programs, he agreed with the recommendation of General Whitlatch and forwarded my name to HQ USAF for the Strike Eagle Test Director. The new Air Force Chief-of-Staff was General Charlie Gabriel, the former CINCUSAFE. The approval for my selection was received a few days later.

In the interim, I received a call from Major Gene Jackson who had finished Air Command and Staff College at Maxwell AFB, Alabama. Gene's credentials made him an easy selection for AFTEC. He was assigned to the Fighter Directorate and selected to be staff F-15E Test Manager. Major Raymond C. Willcox from AFTEC, Detachment 2 at Eglin AFB was selected as my Deputy Test Director. Ray, a former WSO in the F-111, had extensive air-to-ground experience. I spent the next two months working with Gene, Ray, and the AFTEC staff developing the test plan for the F-15E. The start date for the OT&E was six months later than the start of the F-16XL test program; however, both test programs were required to be completed not later than July 1983. The relationship between Gene, Ray, and me got off to a great start, and we accepted the challenge. Ray drove ahead to Edwards to find an operating site for the test team. I was scheduled for a refresher check-out in the F-15 at Luke before proceeding to Edwards.

The challenges on the job were successfully resolved, but several family concerns still required attention. In early June, I traveled to Detroit where Wilbert had major surgery in an attempt to save his life. Our daughter Gail completed a year at the University of New Mexico and was accepted at Louisiana State University School of Interior Design for the fall semester. After attending four high schools, Renea graduated. Her academics performance and athleticism resulted in recruitment by Army, Navy, and Air Force Academies. She eventually chose the Air Force Academy. Michael, a junior, had an outstanding year in football and track. Our children's success in school was largely due to Peggy. Despite numerous moves and interruptions, she was an outstanding constant in their lives. Her persistent oversight, teaching, and tutoring paid great dividends in their educational success

We traveled to Colorado Springs, Colorado in June to deliver Renea to the Academy. Lowell Bell and his wife, Pat moved there after retiring from the Air Force and became the home away from home for Renea. David, Yoshi, and their young daughter, Dana, drove out to New Mexico to visit us in early August. They later drove Gail to Baton Rouge on the way to visit their families in Alabama.

Wilbert recovered enough to fly to Albuquerque in late August for the first meeting with our dad in over thirty-five years. Dad came by bus from Pasadena, California to Albuquerque. It was an emotional and momentous reunion. All of us were impressed by Dad's humble attitude and words seasoned by time. One day I listened as father and son sat on the back porch, reminiscing and laughing about things in their younger years together. The healing had finally begun for them. Later, I reintroduced Dad to Zella, David, and Ray over the telephone and sent them a portrait made during his visit. My father and brother had a wonderful reunion and were very happy about their reconciliation. We all were thankful to the Lord for graciously allowing us to come together again. It was long overdue for us, but God's timing was perfect.

Wilbert's condition deteriorated rapidly after he returned to Detroit. He was readmitted to the hospital the third week in September and lapsed into a coma a few days later. Before departing for Luke AFB, I called his hospital room Saturday morning, September 25th, expecting to speak to his wife, Dorothy. Miraculously, Wilbert was conscious and answered the phone. Though in critical condition and extremely weak, he expressed faith in his favorite scriptures found in Psalms 23 and especially in NIV John 24:25-26: *"I am the resurrection and the life. He who believes in me will live, even though he dies;*

and whoever lives and believes in me will never die..." As he whispered these words, I encouraged him to cling to those scriptures. I promised to visit after completing my first week of training at Luke.

I departed Albuquerque for Luke AFB Sunday morning, September 26 and decided to take the scenic roads across the mountains instead of the freeway. I needed time to contemplate getting back into the cockpit and meditate over the things happening in the lives of my family. As I drove along the highway, beautiful cloud formations skipped over the distant mesas and mountains. A surreal, smiling image of Wilbert appeared in my mind, and I was overcome with a powerful feeling that I had spoken to him for the last time. My heart was extremely heavy, but I knew Wilbert wanted to be free from his suffering. Thankfully, he was at peace with God and ready to be in His presence.

I arrived safely at Luke AFB and checked into the BOQ. The training office was expecting me and I began the three-week refresher course the next day with academics and simulator training. A flight simulator check was completed on Friday morning and I flew my first flight five days later. Early on the morning of September 29th, I received word Wilbert passed away. The presence of other family members allowed me to continue that week as scheduled, and I arranged a flight for Detroit on Saturday morning. It was very difficult, but I managed to stay focused until the day ended Friday. Then, my grief erupted like a torrential storm.

I was struggling to accept the reality of Wilbert's death when someone knocked on my door. Incredibly, my friend Lieutenant Colonel David Brooks was standing there. He was on a cross country flight in an F-16 from MacDill AFB, Florida and heard I was at Luke checking out in the F-15. Dave's unexpected but timely visit was truly a God-send. In one of my darkest hours, the Lord sent a dear friend to console me. Dave was also a man of deep faith and his presence confirmed the matchless grace of God. He stayed with me through the night and drove me to the airport the next morning. Dave felt as I did; the Lord sent him to Luke on a special mission that was far superior to those we flew together in Vietnam in the early 1970s.

Family and friends gathered in Detroit for Wilbert's funeral on Tuesday, October 5th. He was a teacher in the Detroit school system for over twenty-five years and involved in many civic and community affairs. The testimonies reflected the love and respect everyone had for him. He had been small in stature, but a giant in overcoming adversity. Now Wilbert soared as *An Uncaged Eagle.*

I resumed flying at Luke and finished two weeks later. The last sortie was a one-versus-one basic fighter maneuvering check ride. By my own assessment, the performance on previous sorties was somewhat benign. I made a conscious effort to tone down my former style of aggressive flying to preclude any negative repercussions. However, I was surprised when we stepped to the aircraft. An evaluator from 12th Air Force Headquarters was brought in to observe my progress from the back seat of the instructor flying against me. This seemed a bit like a set-up, but it was just the kick in the seat I needed. If the wing wanted the Headquarters to participate in evaluating my ability to fly the F-15 again, so be it.

We proceeded to the training area and began the planned maneuvers. The first two engagements resulted in stalemates. The final event began from a head-on pass where the maneuvering began when passing abeam each other. For the first time in over two years, I felt the adrenalin of the former Dick Toliver. Using the maximum allowable parameters, I broke into the other aircraft and maneuvered into a position of advantage within the first minute. It took another thirty seconds to get in the lethal envelope for a simulated short range missile shot. A few seconds later, I put my piper on the "adversary."

With sheer delight, I transmitted over the radio, "Tracking, tracking, tracking! Disengage, disengage!"

My training was over. The Luke instructor and visitor from 12th Air Force could decide the outcome, but the thrill was not over. When we landed, the visitor rushing over to my aircraft looked vaguely familiar. He shouted, "Colonel Toliver that was great! Sierra Hotel! You did a great job!" He continued, "Sir, I am Major Figueroa. I flew in your backseat during the F-15 OT&E at Luke in 1975." Then, the major was a young captain who flew with me on a dissimilar air-to-air test sortie. What may have been a set-up turned golden in more than one way. Besides winning the engagement, I rediscovered my comfort zone in the F-15. I departed Luke with a great sense of humility. The Lord allowed me to return to the F-15 where it all began for me. My success was not so much due to my airmanship but His grace and mercy. I looked forward to Edwards and flying the Strike Eagle.

I joined Ray Willcox at Edwards on October 22, 1982. We were blessed to have an outstanding cadre of professionals on temporary duty from TAC. These included pilot Major Richard T "Lips" Banholzer; WSO, Major Larry H. "Scoop" Cooper; Analyst, Captain Robert "Bob" Barham, and twelve maintenance technicians. Our team was co-located with the DT&E team led by Lieutenant Colonel John Hoffman.

MCAIR also had an outstanding management team at Edwards to support both the developmental and operational test programs. The team was led by the legendary triple ace of WW II, Clarence E. "Bud" Anderson. Bud flew two combat tours during WW II with another legend, Chuck Yeager. He was credited with over sixteen aerial victories in his P-51, Old Crow. Bud became a test pilot after the war and retired as a colonel with more than thirty years of service. This extraordinary aviator was a soft-spoken gentleman when I met him in 1982. Anyone speaking with Bud as I did occasionally you would never hear about his greatness from him. Without knowing it, he taught me another great lesson in humility.

We were organized and ready to operate by the first week in November. The test aircraft included an F-15C equipped with conformal fuel tanks, an F-15D two-seater, and the primary Strike Eagle prototype, F-15B, 71-291. The prototype was equipped with improved avionics, advanced display systems, a new wide field-of-vision head-up display, and multiple-use screens. These modifications were on the cutting edge of technology and were a quantum jump in capability over the existing fighter bombers. I flew the first test sortie with Ray on December 10, 1982. We didn't stop smiling from that day on.

The OT&E program was on track as the holidays approached, so the team was released to spend Christmas and New Year's Day with their families. I arranged to have my father take a bus to nearby Lancaster, California so we could drive together to Albuquerque.

The drive took fourteen hours. We spent the time catching up on the years missed between us and dealing with some tough issues that needed to be resolved. After a while, no more questions were asked. All that needed to be said had been spoken. The Lord finally brought us together and the past was forgiven. However, I did discover a startling truth. My father still loved my mother and I remembered she loved him until her death. The break-up of their marriage was due in part to circumstances they could not control. Sadly, neither of them was able to cross the threshold of forgiveness that would lead to reconciliation and a restored relationship beyond their break up. I prayed my father would finally step into the light of freedom during his time with us over the Christmas holidays.

Peggy, Grandma, Gail, Renea and Michael had waited a long time and they embraced my dad very warmly. To all of us, he was a gentle, soft-spoken man who was very easy to please. Dad enjoyed getting to know everyone better and humbly accepted the attention we gave him. Even Pixie, our pet, took kindly to him. He was particularly taken by Gail who he said reminded him so much of my mother.

An unexpected event took place as more time was spent with Dad. I tried not to get too close but began to feel a love for him that hadn't existed since our days together in California thirty-six years earlier. This feeling grew with each passing day, and I was certain we both experienced it. All those years of anger, despair, loneliness, and every other negative emotion slowly faded away. Just as the Bible says, "Love overcomes a multitude of evil," this transformation was truly a manifestation of God's amazing grace. He answered my prayers for Dad and in the process blessed me beyond my expectations.

The two weeks passed quickly, and it was time for us to get back to our jobs, school, and routines. The return trip to California with Dad was much more enjoyable as we were now father and son as well as friends. We talked and laughed more, and I relished his subtle wisdom about many things I didn't think he knew. Christmas 1982 was a blessing we all appreciated for years to come.

Show Stopper

Everyone returned safely after the holidays, and we began 1983 refreshed, excited, and optimistic about the months ahead. Just when things were going great, a monkey wrench got thrown into the works. In the case of the F-15E OT&E, it was an electrical fire on aircraft 71-291, the prototype. MCAIR technicians were performing maintenance in the early morning hours of January 31st when a huge wire bundle caught fire along the length of the jet. I was notified a couple of hours later and advised the aircraft would be down for thirty to forty-five days. Our team met with the CTF and MCAIR teams to discuss the impact of a delay on the F-15E flight testing already six months behind the F16-XL testing. Ray Willcox and the ops guys quickly developed a revised schedule that would still allow us to complete testing by the end of July. However, the aircraft needed to be ready to fly in thirty days. A decision for such an enormous effort required approval from MCAIR's corporate office in St. Louis. In the meantime, we briefed our respective commanders, Major General Peter W. Odgers, HQ AFFTC and Major General Phillips, HQ AFTEC. The Air Force was prepared to do everything possible to make the schedule, but the ball was in MCAIR's court.

With a potential multi-billon dollar contract for F-15Es, MCAIR committed to a twenty-four hour workday to repair the aircraft. However, the corporate leadership wanted assurance the Air Force had the best qualified OT&E team at Edwards to do the job. To allay their concerns, I was directed to travel to MCAIR and join Lieutenant General Howard Leaf, Inspector General of the Air Force to brief the revised OT&E schedule. General Leaf was the former AFTEC Commander and fully understood the ramifications of the challenge. He was also familiar with my qualifications. I briefed a select group of MCAIR personnel and made a twenty minute separate presentation to a senior MCAIR executive. He turned to General Leaf and said, "General Leaf, it sounds good to me. I am confident you have the right team in place. Will you please join me for lunch?" Chalk one up for how the "cow really eats the cabbage" in a high stakes game.

Recovery

The MCAIR team at Edwards performed magnificently and returned 71-291 to flight status in just twenty-three days! Ray and I resumed flying test sorties on February 24, 1983. We picked up the pace with both test aircraft through the end of April including a deployment to Nellis AFB. Numerous firsts were logged with regards to maximum weapon loads, take-off gross weight, and maintainability and sustainability. All of the test objectives were met and the results proved the F-15E Strike Eagle would provide the Air Force with an outstanding air-to-ground capability. Our test team was confident of the Strike Eagle's advantage over current and projected competitors in range, payload, high thrust, and survivability. The survivability was enhanced by the powerful, dual high performance engines. The F-15E also demonstrated a high maintainability and reliability. Although the conformal fuel tanks reduced its close-in maneuverability, the aircraft retained a very credible air-to-air lethality.

As the flight test neared completion, I approached my counterpart, P. C. Burnett, with an offer to trade flights in F-15E and F-16XL. This was not in the test plan, but I thought it would provide a bit of data for potential questions regarding a subjective comparison and evaluation. When the CTF directors balked at the idea, I suggested we use our "Test Director's" prerogative. On May 6, 1983, P.C. and I became the first two Air Force pilots to fly both the F-15E and F-16XL. The CTF directors decided to follow suit, and John and Marty were the third and fourth pilots to fly both aircraft. All in all, this was a historical and exciting feat. The CTF directors received mild rebuke when they briefed their boss, Major General Odgers, and were told not to report the event. When P. C. and I told Major General Phillips about the four flights, he wanted to know the results. He chuckled and suggested we keep the information in our "hip pockets."

An Empty Nest

Our son Mike completed a fantastic two years at Eldorado High School in Albuquerque and graduated in May 1983. During his senior year, Mike initiated a Fellowship of Christian Athletes chapter at his school. He was ranked All-City in football with over 1,500 rushing yards, in the top ten percent of over 400 students, and elected King of his senior class. Mike was recruited by several colleges and universities including the Air Force Academy, Stanford, and the University of New Mexico. Like his sister, Renea, he eventually chose to attend the Air Force Academy.

Too soon our children were gone, and Peggy and I were left with the proverbial empty nest. Like most parents, the years had come and gone all too soon. Yet we were truly thankful for their achievements. I especially thanked God for Peggy and Grandma who had such a profound impact in the lives of all four of our children - Glenette, Gail, Renea, and Mike. With the Lord first in their lives, we were confident of their continued success.

Test Results

Major Gene Jackson, AFTEC F-15E OT&E Test Manager, arrived in April with a preliminary template for the test reports. AFTEC also acquired the services of BDM Corporation to assist with the reduction and analysis of the data obtained at Edwards. Retired Major Al Aulbach, formerly with the original F-15 test team at Luke, was the lead analyst for BDM. I respected Al's ability and was very glad to have him on our team. We started work on the test report and briefings while flight testing continued until June. Both AFTEC teams, the F-15E and F-16XL, met several times to ensure commonality in the test reports and briefings. Concurrently the AFFTC teams were at work on their reports. The relationships between our teams resulted in the preparation of the most accurate and objective report possible for our Air Force leaders.

The CTF test directors, John Hoffman and Marty Bushnell, were tasked to brief Major General Odgers. Major General Phillips asked P.C. and me to give a courtesy briefing to Major General Odgers prior to leaving Edwards AFB. The four test directors made a joint presentation to General Odgers with Brigadier General Ronald W. Yates from ASD attending. The briefings focused on the factual results of the test, and the F-15E emerged an early winner for the critical requirements of range, payload, thrust, and survivability. General Yates, however, appeared to be predisposed in favor of the F-16XL.

My observation was confirmed later that day when I received a call from John Hoffman. Brigadier Yates was selected by HQ AF-FTC to brief the CTF test results. He planned to ask Major General Phillips to allow him to include the AFTEC test results. Ostensibly a single briefer was intended to present a smoother, more coherent presentation for the high-level decision makers. The CTF directors were disappointed with the politics of this decision. P. C. and I were chagrined by such presumption, but were confident our boss would not agree with the request. We arrived the next day at HQ AFTEC and wasted no time telling General Phillips about the pending proposal from Brigadier General Yates. He summarily dismissed it and stated P. C. and I would brief our results as planned. Brigadier General Yates arrived with John Hoffman and Marty Bushnell for a joint briefing to General Phillips and the AFTEC key directors. General Yates briefed the DT&E test results, and P. C. and I briefed the OT&E test results. Again the F-15E emerged as the "winner" and General Phillips gave his approval to proceed with briefings as scheduled.

The presenters on the briefing team were General Yates, P. C., and me. John Hoffman, Marty Bushnell, and a small team of reliability/maintainability experts accompanied us as we made presentations at the headquarters of ASD, AFLC, Air Force Systems Command, and USAF. The briefings were well received at each location, and the exchanges were lively depending upon who favored which aircraft. Our earlier commitment to reporting accurately and objectively mitigated the emotion and gave decision makers at each stop a clear choice.

The final briefing was scheduled in late July 1983 for General Charlie Gabriel, Air Force Chief-of-Staff, and the Air Council of General Officers at the Pentagon. General Gabriel was called to Capitol Hill on the afternoon of the briefing so General Jerome F. O'Malley, Vice Chief of Staff, chaired the Council. Major Generals Phillips and Odgers flew to Washington, DC for the final presentations. There was a considerable buzz in the room as we waited for General O'Malley. By then, news of the test results had reached the Council. I had the pleasure to speak to Lieutenant General Jack Chain, Lieutenant General Howard Leaf, Major General Larry Welch, and others I knew on the Council. General O'Malley arrived, and we made our presentations. At the conclusion, he said, "Did you guys do any comparison flying during the test?"

In the expanse of a second, I looked at P. C. then over at Major Generals Phillips and Odgers. General Phillips gave a faint smile and shrugged his shoulders. General Odgers looked as if he wanted to leave the room. I looked quickly back at P. C. and spoke, "Well sir, we flew four sorties at the end of the test that permitted us to make a subjective comparison of the cockpit and handling qualities of the aircraft." He spoke very animatedly and said, "Tell me about it. What did you find out?"

At this, every general in the room was interested and sat up in his chair. Finally, John Hoffman and Marty Bushnell had a chance to participate in the briefing with P.C. and me. The four of us spent almost as much time answering questions as we did for the entire formal briefing. During this exchange, I glanced over at Generals Phillips and Odgers. Both were smiling broadly! Afterwards, General O'Malley spoke directly to P. C. and asked, "P. C., if you had to spend your money on one of these fighters, which one would you buy?" P. C. did not hesitate, "Sir, I would buy the F-15E!" General O'Malley stood up and smiled very warmly and said, "You made a good choice, and I agree with you. You guys did a great job at Edwards and we appreciate your efforts. I believe we'll be able to justify our proposed buy to Congress."

For the next few minutes, our briefing team received congratulations from the Council and other Air Staff members in the room. Generals Phillips, Odgers, and Yates gave us four test directors a special slap on the back. Within one second that day, we went from potential cannon fodder to being pretty savvy. Flying those four sorties in the F-15E and F-16XL was not due to great insight on my part but to the hand of Providence. Every member of both test teams gave their all in the service to Air Force and to our nation. Knowing that, gave me a lasting sense of fulfillment and pride.

Silver Eagles

I received an outstanding performance report at the conclusion of the F-15E OT&E, and Major General Phillips recommended my immediate promotion to full Colonel. Lieutenant General Chain, Deputy Chief-of-Staff, Plans and Operations at the Pentagon gave a similar indorsement. The timing of the report was crucial because the USAF Promotion Board for Colonel convened August 15, 1983. In the meantime, I was tasked to review and revise several AFTEC test programs in the Tactical Fighter Division. Two of these programs, the Low Altitude Navigation and Targeting Infrared for Night and Forward-Looking InfraRed were programmed for the F-15E. As a result, I continued to work with the headquarters recently visited during the briefings of the F-15E OT&E results.

On the night of October 5, 1983, General Phillips called to tell me I had been selected for colonel. The official release was the next day. This news was truly the greatest in my military career. This major milestone reflected the years of dedication and hard work, but it was also a testimony to many others who made it possible. The list would be much too long, and I don't want to risk missing anyone. Most importantly, my promotion was clear evidence of the Lord's indescribable grace and mercy. Truly, He deserves all the credit.

At the time of my promotion, only eight percent of all officers in the Air Force reached the rank of Colonel. The current list included twenty-one African Americans, six women, four Hispanics, and four other minority classifications. It was a pleasure to find that I knew and had served with many on the list. These included my dear friend Hal Brown; fellow Tuskegeans Carl Franklin, Tyree Parker, and Frank Todd; and also Joe Lee Burns, Jeff Cliver, Dick Myers, Nordie Norwood, Tad Oelstrom, and Omar Wiseman. It was great to know that many of my peers were promoted, and I looked forward to crossing paths with some of them again. My pin-on date was scheduled for February 1, 1984.

I received a multitude of congratulatory telephone calls, cards, and messages over the next few weeks. They came from officers, enlisted, and civilians nationwide, and it was great to be so well-remembered. Conversely, I was disappointed when word reached me that Colonel Norm Campbell, the former Bitburg commander, continued telling people I "failed as a leader." The Lord had delivered me from the bitterness of Bitburg and my conscience was clear. Yet, I was sorry to hear this rumor because I still admired Norm Campbell for his intellect, ability, and passion for the Air Force. As I prayed and meditated about a possible response, the following scripture came to me:

"If you are offering your gift at the altar and ...remember...your brother has something against you, leave your gift... First go and be reconciled...then come offer your gift." NIV Matthew 5:23-24

Even though Norm Campbell was not a "Christian Brother," I felt the need to reconcile the differences between us. I sent him a card wishing him well and asked forgiveness for whatever caused him to think negatively of me.   A few weeks later, I received a long letter from Norm that set my heart at ease. The key points of his letter are shared here:

> "First of all, congratulations on your promotion.
> It was deserved, and I'm sure will be an opening to bigger
> and better things for you both personally and professionally.
> Second, let me thank you for your thoughtful card. I know
> that it took a good deal of courage to send it, and am especially
> grateful to you for the kind thoughts you expressed.
>
> My first inclination in answering you was to say that I've
> held no hard feelings over the events in the 53 (Squadron). As
> I thought through that, I realized that such an answer would
> at best be dissembling, and at worst evading my real feelings.
> Since your assignment to AFTEC, I've told some people that I be-
> lieved you were an excellent staff officer, but that in my opinion
> you had failed in a leadership position. That may have been
> true, but the point is, it's immaterial now. ...even your detrac-
> tors have been forced to say that you've done well.....Finally,
> and perhaps most important, because I am not the judge...Each
> of us has to look in the mirror every day and come to grips with
> our strongest critic...ourselves. If we can honestly say that we're
> doing the best we can, then nobody should ask more...Nuff said
> about that, case closed..."

I appreciated Norm's words very much and was thankful for letting the Scriptures guide my actions. Whatever rumors came to me from that point on didn't matter. My conscience was clear, and there was peace in my heart. Praise the Lord, this eagle was still "Uncaged"! Norm Campbell finally resumed an upward path in his career. He was promoted to Brigadier General in late 1984 and even- tually retired as a Major General in July 1993. I never saw or spoke to him again, but believed there were no longer any hard feelings between us.

Christmas 1983 was a joyful time in many ways. Our family drove to Shreveport, Louisiana to spend the holidays with our extended family. My brother, David, flew down with his son, David, Jr. who was interested in attending the Air Force Academy. We gathered for a traditional Christmas dinner at the home of my younger brother, Wendell and family. God continued to bless us, and it was great to get together and celebrate His goodness. Renea and Michael spent a lot of time with David, Jr. When it was time to leave, he was convinced that the Academy was for him. All of us were pleased with David Jr's decision and looked forward to having three Toliver youngsters follow in the Air Force like their fathers.

Having successfully completed the job as F-15E Test Director, I was optimistic about my next assignment. We wanted to stay stateside because of eighty-five year old Grandma and our three children in college, plus I had served ten of my twenty years overseas. Unfortunately, my wishes were not favorably considered. The Colonel Assignment Office at Air Force Military Personnel Center offered me a position as the Deputy Base Commander at Misawa Air Base, Japan, an F-16 wing. This was a disappointment for two major reasons. First, the assignment was completely out of my career field as a pilot. Secondly, the assignment officer could not give me any visibility into my future beyond the offer. Given these circumstances and aforementioned reasons, I respectfully declined the offer. The assignment officer appeared to take offense and hinted I had made a mistake.

Several weeks passed without another word from the personnel center. It appeared they simply left me to find an assignment on my own. Without a sponsor, competitive jobs for new Colonels were hard to come by. Those who were fortunate to have a champion were already earmarked for key positions, especially in flying units. Nevertheless, I began my search in early December by writing personal letters to several general officers that I knew or had worked for during my career. For the time being, I still had a job in AFTEC.

My pin-on day of February 1, 1984 arrived, and Peggy and I gathered with General Phillips and others in AFTEC for the occasion. Twenty-one years earlier, I stood before a group of cadets at Tuskegee for the pin-on of my Second Lieutenant bars. The journey to getting my Eagles pinned on had been an eventful one, and I was truly grateful to God and the many people who helped me along the way. General Phillips pinned on one shoulder and Peggy the other. As he did so, he said quietly, "Congratulations, Dick. I had a hard time keeping you at Edwards after the fire. But you earned these Eagles. Good luck!"

General Phillips confirmed what I had suspected. The aircraft fire pushed the Strike Eagle further behind. Those who questioned my continued involvement had high stakes in the outcome of the F-15E tests results. They wanted to make sure the Air Force had the best possible team in place at Edwards for the recovery program. I tried my best to discount any concern they may have had because of my race. At any rate, I hoped the road behind me would be easier for those possibly constrained by stereotypical attitudes or racially biased predispositions.

In February 1984, the Air Force chose the F-15E over the F-16XL as the new dual-role fighter. The procurement plan called for 393 modified aircraft at a cost of $1.5 billion. The expected delivery of the first F-15E was in 1988. With those decisions, my hopes were raised again for an assignment somewhere in the operational or acquisition commands responsible for this enormous program. Apart from writing the personal letters, Peggy and I prayed and trusted the Lord for an answer. We were committed to allowing Him to direct our paths whatever the assignment.

I received a job offer in late February from then Lieutenant General John L. Piotrowski, Commander of Ninth Air Force, Shaw AFB, South Carolina. The offer was considered a "career broadening" opportunity as Assistant Deputy Commander for Maintenance at the 56th TFW, MacDill AFB, Florida. The wing commander was my good friend Colonel Ron Fogleman. I was offered the chance to be the understudy to Colonel Jim Yocum, a highly respected and well-known career maintenance officer in the Air Force. Although this was not a flying job, Peggy and I considered it a blessing and accepted the offer. It was a training base for F-16 pilots, and I hoped to checkout and become a flying maintenance officer.

On April 4, 1983, AFTEC was re-designated the Air Force Operational Test and Evaluation Center (AFOTEC) to clearly delineate its role as the Air Force's operational test agency. The same week, Major Gene Jackson hosted our going-away party. Many of our military and civilian friends came to say goodbye and wish us well. Gene, Nelda, Peggy, and I had been together through a number of rough spots over the years, and it was sad to leave them behind. The most difficult part of the event was saying goodbye to all of our Christian brothers and sisters. Our lives had been richly blessed by so many, and we knew the Lord would watch over these loved ones until we met again.

Being assigned again to AFOTEC turned out to be a tremendous blessing. As we departed, my thoughts returned to General Charlie Gabriel, the man who made it possible. He had been a great friend and influence in my life since I was a captain. The Lord used him to intervene at Bitburg to save my career. I appreciated General Gabriel's faith in me, and hoped to see him again to express my gratitude. For the time being, I asked the Lord to bless him wherever he was.

CHAPTER EIGHTEEN

ON EAGLE'S WINGS

In mid-April 1984, Peggy, Grandma, and I traveled leisurely from Albuquerque, New Mexico to Tampa, Florida. Along the way we visited family and friends in Texas, Louisiana, and Alabama. These included our daughter Glenette and her two children; sister Zella and brothers, Ray and Wendell and their families; and Tuskegee Airman, Doug Jones and his wife, Wihelmenia. Many positive changes had taken place in America since the 1960s, and the natural beauty of the South in the spring of the year was still enjoyable. Our stop at Tuskegee University brought back precious memories of Grandma's trip with Peggy when she first came to Alabama. Of course, Peggy and I began our lives together there. We strolled around a few sites on campus and thought back over the many blessings and experiences that filled our lives over the past twenty-one years.

We arrived at MacDill AFB the evening of April 20, 1984, nineteen years since my brief assignment there December 1965. Colonel Ron Fogleman welcomed the three of us with a warm note, excellent temporary quarters, and a basket of fruit in each of the two suites. His red carpet treatment on our arrival let us know this was the place for us. A house was available for us just down the street from the Foglemans and across the street from Colonel and Mrs. Jimmy L. Cash,

56th TTW Director of Operations. We were stationed earlier with the Cashes at George AFB as young instructor pilots. Colonel Jim Yocum invited Peggy and me to attend a maintenance function at the O'Club the night we arrived. We met him, his wife, Karol, and other leaders in the Maintenance Directorate.

I reported in the following week, received initial briefings, and attended my first daily staff briefing with Colonel Fogleman and the senior wing staff. The warm reception by everyone continued to make me feel at home. It was great to be back in Tactical Air Command (TAC). For the next few days, Jim Yocum introduced me to rank and file maintenance personnel as we toured all the units and facilities. The DCM organization consisted of 1,600 people, ninety F-16 fighter aircraft, and sixty-seven separate buildings. The wing operations and maintenance budget that year was $7.5 million. The size and complexity of the maintenance operation was impressive and challenging and I looked forward to getting involved. Jim Yocum proved to be one of the best DCMs in TAC. After orientation, I headed to Maxwell AFB, Alabama for a two-week course designed to familiarize senior officers with wing-level maintenance operations.

Maxwell AFB had changed considerably, yet many historical buildings and sites were still present. Coming to Maxwell as a new Colonel in May 1984 brought about a lot of memories. It seemed I was retracing my steps in time. While an Air Force ROTC cadet at Tuskegee Institute, I made numerous trips to Maxwell. Here I received my first flight in a Beechcraft C-45 in September 1957. In May 1958, I earned my first jet flight in a T-33 trainer. In 1965, our son Mike was born here while we were stationed at Craig AFB in nearby Selma. An amazing fact was the difference that life, wisdom, and a changed heart made in how I now viewed Maxwell and the south in general. Because the Holy Spirit now lived in me, the adversities of the past paled in the light of God's blessings. The freedom I now enjoyed made me feel good about being there.

Color Me Maintenance

The premonition of good tidings was confirmed upon registering for the Deputy Commander for Maintenance Course at the Leadership and Management Development Center at the Air University. Several other aviators were part of a class of twenty-seven new colonels, including my classmate, Frank Todd, from Tuskegee. We were introduced to the major changes that had been underway within TAC since 1978. General Wilbur L. Creech, TAC Commander, had instituted a revolutionary change in the leadership and management of tactical operations and maintenance. His focus addressed the steady decline in aircraft sortie productivity over the years in TAC and other MAJCOMS in the Air Force. The corresponding result of this deficiency was a decrease in aircrew combat proficiency and readiness. All of us in the class readily appreciated this and had witnessed the consequences first hand.

General Creech's thrust was to halt practices of excessive centralization and consolidation of operations touted by management theorists of the 1960's and 1970's that had not worked well for combat units in the military. Furthermore, explicit evidence proved these theories fostered a "dehumanized" and over-specialized organization. As a result, TAC's combat units had drifted away from identifiable goals, standards, and objectives. To overcome this malady, General Creech began the process of rebuilding an output, productivity oriented organization throughout TAC. The emphasis of the new direction for TAC was upon people, purpose (mission), pride, professionalism, and ultimately the product. His premise was people are fundamentally different than things; and in organizations the right leaders motivate and inspire people. He stated that a leader is...

> "A person who by force of example, talents, or qualities of
> leadership, plays a directing role, wields command influence,
> or has a following in any sphere of activity or thought..."

The entire class was excited by General Creech's leadership and vision and readily embraced his philosophy. I left Maxwell enlightened and pumped up about my opportunity to play a part in the ongoing transformation in TAC. My new job was maintenance, but the principles learned at Maxwell had universal application in every discipline in the Air Force as well as in the private sector. I looked forward to getting back to MacDill, rolling my sleeves up, and going to work. What followed was a total immersion into every phase of maintenance operations. It also included a Senior Manager's Maintenance Course at HQ TAC and visits to other TAC wings to observe and glean best practices to apply at MacDill.

After three intensive months, Colonel Yocum decided I would be ready for a DCM job within six months instead of the usual twelve to eighteen months. I took that as an opportunity to suggest getting a local check out in the F-16 to complement my emerging maintenance expertise. That was a mistake. Jim viewed my suggestion as a veiled attempt to get back into the cockpit at the expense of learning more about maintenance. He was strongly opposed to a check-out and stated he would tell Colonel Fogleman the same. Although disappointed, I didn't want to create dissension in the wing, so I let the issue drop and continued to get as smart as possible on the job.

By mid-summer, Jim tasked me to spearhead the large-scale modernization of the numerous maintenance facilities. These were wide-ranging projects that involved significant self-help efforts, a keystone to General Creech's vision. I made several trips to HQ TAC to brief our plans and petition for funding. As a result, MacDill obtained funds to resurface the runway, build an engine test facility, replace three hangar roofs, and renovate the living quarters for our enlisted personnel. The self-help initiative paid great dividends in improving the quality of life for our maintenance personnel as well as improving their pride and professionalism in areas where they lived and worked. It also spurred unit competition as each unit tried to outdo the other on the job and in their living areas. Utilizing their many skills and talents, the people built display boards to post monthly achievements, established unit recreational facilities, and renovated buildings and work places. These actions demonstrated their "stake in the action" and instilled an unprecedented sense of pride.

In August 1984, Colonel Ron Fogleman was assigned as the commander of 836th Air Division, Davis-Monthan AFB, Arizona. I had known Ron since our days at Udorn in 1973. His character and leadership were well known and respected by all who worked with him. He had a very special quality that was well above and beyond his peers. Ron Fogleman was another *Uncaged Eagle* providentially placed in my life to make a difference. As we shook hands and said good-bye, I said, "You are going to be the Chief-of-Staff of the Air Force one day!" He smiled and humbly downplayed the comment, but that was so typical of his greatness. Time proved me right.

Colonel Jimmy Cash was elevated to the 56th Wing Commander. Success of the wing continued because of the outstanding quality and performance of its leaders and people. Although the door to flying was currently closed, I was content with the job and tasks assigned to me. My future was in God's hands, and my focus was on the success of others rather than my own. I derived satisfaction from working closely with people and helping them achieve their personal and professional goals. I also was able to keep involved in chapel activities and a weekly Bible study in our home. Participation in the chapel provided Peggy and me several opportunities to counsel and witness to both officers and enlisted men and women. Two of these experiences were especially gratifying and blessed us immensely. The first involved an older, retired chief master sergeant in the Air Force who was hopelessly hooked on alcohol. My experience in helping my brother, Wilbert, enabled me to help this individual get on the path to recovery. We became brothers and our families became lifelong friends.

The second case involved Colonel Dawson Randle "Randy" O'Neil, 9th Air Force Director of Operations. Randy was one of my instructors at the USAF Fighter Weapons School at Nellis in 1972. Randy went on to be very successful in TAC and had commanded an F-16 wing in Utah. During one of his visits to MacDill, I met him on the flight line. We had not seen each other since our days at Nellis. Now, we were two colonels who had overcome a few stumbling blocks and were extremely delighted to meet again. As we talked, our changed attitudes and demeanor were readily apparent to each other. Randy asked first about the obvious change in that cocky young fighter pilot he had met years ago. I briefly told him about my "Damascus Road" experience and how it changed my life. Impressed by my story, he said he wanted to hear more about it. I invited him to our home that night to tell him the rest of the story.

Peggy and Grandma welcomed Randy to our home that night. Both were experts at preparing for a dinner guest on a moment's notice. Afterwards, Randy and I shared some of the experiences in our careers and lives that turned out differently than we planned. There was clear mutual confirmation the Lord had been very gracious and patient with us, and that He had blessed us beyond that which we deserved. Randy was impressed most by my faith and willingness to completely let God have rule over my life. In addition, he sensed the inner peace that now filled my heart and soul. Apparently, he still struggled a bit with total submission to the Lord. When the evening concluded, Randy and I prayed together for the first time in our lives. To this day, I thank God for answering our prayers. A few days later, Randy called to say he was turning his life over to Jesus Christ completely. He asked me to be his accountability and prayer partner during his more deliberate walk with the Lord. What a praise and privilege that was! Peggy and I eventually met Randy's beautiful Christian wife, Helen, and one of Randy's sons and grandson. We shared much as brothers in the Lord until a tragic motorcycle accident ended Randy's life twenty years later. He flew on ahead as *An Uncaged Eagle*, but I rejoice in knowing we shall meet again on that final day.

The Lord gave me another opportunity to serve His people. He brought Second Lieutenant Herrie Reed into my life as a new young chaplain in the Air Force. Herrie was an accomplished, powerful, oratorical Baptist minister, but he had trouble adjusting to basic military customs, courtesies, and professional standards of attitude, dress, and bearing. One day Herrie came to me and asked for help in getting off on the right foot. His outstanding ability and humility made it an easy task to mentor Herrie while Peggy counseled his wife, Gwen. One of the great delights in our lives was to be involved with this couple as they grew and served the Air Force and its families for many years.

The winter of 1984 was a very good time for us as our youngsters were doing exceptionally well at LSU and the Air Force Academy. Gail was a senior and made the dean's list each year at LSU. Renea was a track star at the Air Force Academy and established a couple of records in low hurdles. Mike completed his first year on the varsity football team that won the Commander-in-Chief's Trophy and the Independence Bowl Game in Shreveport, Louisiana. That year, the Academy won its third game against Notre Dame. David, Jr. entered the Academy and took to it life like a duck in water. He actually enjoyed "Beast," the five-week Basic Cadet Training, and was the only cadet known to have actually gained weight. David, Jr. also qualified as an aviation candidate. Gail, Renea, and Mike came home to MacDill for Christmas while David, Jr. went home to Aurora, Colorado to be with his mother and two brothers. Peggy and I were pleased at the growth and maturity in our children and their persistent faith and walk with the Lord. As was our custom, we gathered to pray in the New Year, 1985. We continued to be faithful and sincerely wanted to stay in His perfect will. Life was good.

January 1985 began with an emergency call from Colonel Jim Thar in Turkey. We met the Thars three years earlier at Kirtland AFB, and they were having trouble with one of their four children, seventeen year-old Daniel. He was a biracial, African American-Hispanic child the Thar's adopted when he was about fifteen months old. Daniel had been rebellious for about three years and did poorly in school. He was in trouble with the local Turkish authorities and the Thars had to get him out of the country as soon as possible. As a last resort, Jim asked if Peggy and I could take Daniel until their tour was completed in about a year. We knew countries such as Turkey could be extremely harsh on any foreigner who committed an infraction of their laws, dependent children notwithstanding.

Jim's request was enormous, but I told him to go ahead and bring Daniel to us. I then called Peggy and asked if she was up to taking in a teenager for a while. She was surprised but knew immediately there was more to the question. I explained the phone call from Jim Thar and asked for her thoughts. Peggy thought for a few minutes, then her response confirmed just how blessed we all were to have her in our lives. She simply said, "Dick, if that's the situation, as Christians we need to help the Thars. When are Jim and Daniel coming?" I told her in two days. When I arrived home that evening, Peggy was already preparing our spare bedroom for Dan.

Jim and Dan arrived Sunday night, January 20th, and I met them at the Tampa International Airport. My first impression when I saw Dan was he appeared small for seventeen and couldn't possibly be as tough as Jim had described. I hadn't seen him since he was thirteen, but at only a little over five feet tall, I didn't believe he would be too difficult to handle. He did, however, have a sullen attitude, and was not at all happy with having to leave his friends in Turkey. We arrived home where Peggy and Grandma embraced Jim and Dan warmly. After dinner, we had a family meeting to discuss our roles and responsibilities as full guardians for Dan. The Thars provided financial assistance but the control of it resided with Peggy and me. We next outlined the rules of the house that were used with our children when they were Dan's age. Jim agreed with our approach, and we spent the next few days getting Dan registered on base and enrolled in the local school.

Jim returned to Turkey after spending a week with us. The next few weeks were spent getting to know Dan and helping him adjust to school and the neighborhood. We soon learned he was remarkably articulate, intelligent, and wanted to please. Conversely, he resisted authority and lacked the academic aptitude for tenth grade. Peggy tutored him every night without appreciable results. The school classified Dan as a student with a learning disability, but that contradicted the intelligence and cognitive ability we observed at home. After considerable research and effort, we got the school to reclassify Dan as a student with a "learning deficiency" rather than a "disability." The doctors had prescribed for Dan daily doses of Ritalin to treat his attention deficit hyperactivity disorder since he was a toddler. We discovered this drug actually impeded Dan's comprehension in class. As a result, he only achieved approximately a sixth grade level performance in math, spelling, English composition, and other basic courses. Once Dan's problem was defined, Peggy began to tutor him at that level. It was a long, tedious undertaking for all of us, but we continued the investment of time. Dan's adjustment as a member of our family attending church, social activities, and other events went very smoothly. Peggy became "Mom," Grandma continued as "Grandma," I was "Dad."

Earlier in my career, I learned the benefit of letting my footprints be found everywhere in an organization. This was not difficult because I had a great appreciation for the young men and women who worked long and hard to keep the jets flying. To get a sense for how things really were in an organization, one must be willing to find out at odd hours. Motivated to do this, I spent several late nights visiting the flight line, back shops, and other places not often reached during normal duty hours. My visits were educational, enjoyable, and appreciated by the people involved. One night a picture formed in my mind, and I scribbled a note to Jim Yocum. It read,

"Dear Jim,

Most of my life I have known beauty to be in the eye of
the beholder and mostly of natural things – a tree, a sunset,
a new baby, a beautiful human being. Tonight, after three
months, several nights, and a lot of learning, I have discovered a new thing of beauty – an F-16 flight line at 0030 hours
in the glare of floodlights, fuel trucks, opened canopies,
engines on dollies, and a virtual beehive of activity.
Such a scene too often is not understood nor appreciated.
I have much yet to learn, but tonight, or better yet,
this morning, COLOR ME MAINTENANCE! Here's a
heart-felt Kudo to all our ...men and women..."

Jim was so moved by my note he still had it ten years later.

In early March, TAC suffered two back-to-back F-15 engine fires that resulted in the loss of one aircraft and the recovery of the other. The MAJCOM commander normally selects a recently promot-ed colonel to preside over a Safety Investigation Board (SIB). I was selected as president of this SIB because General O'Malley, the new TAC Commander, knew of my F-15 operational and test experience. Peggy and I had recently met General and Mrs. O'Malley during a social function at MacDill. I reported to the Safety Office at HQ TAC, where both aircraft had been assigned to the 1st TFW, Langley AFB. The wing was commanded by Brigadier General Henry "Butch" Viccellio whom I met while testing the F-15 at Eglin in 1976. The pilot of the recovered F-15 had made an emergency landing on the nearest base, U.S. Coast Guard Air Rescue Station, Elizabeth City, North Carolina. After initial briefings and a review of the aircraft and pilot records, I convened the SIB at the base in Elizabeth City.

As usual, the SIB consisted of experts and technicians from Air Force Material Command (AFMC), Air Force Logistics Command (AFLC), the using command (HQ TAC), and unit involved (1st TFW). We had thirty days in which to conduct the investigation, identify the cause(s) of the accident, and propose recommendations to prevent future recurrences. The attitudes, expertise, and dedication of the individuals involved in this accident, as in others, reflect great credit upon the professionalism that resides in the Air Force. I was very fortunate to lead such a group, and we organized into an effective team at Elizabeth City within twenty-four hours of our arrival.

The spectacular performance of the F-15 is made possible by two Pratt & Whitney F100-PW-100 afterburning turbofans. The engine is comprised of five segments that include a three-stage fan, a ten stage axial compressor, separate two-stage turbines, and a five stage afterburner. Approximately 16,000 pounds of thrust are produced in military power and 23,800 pounds in afterburner. Our strategy for the investigation of the engine fires began with identifying the origin of the fire. Next, we assessed the maintenance and repair history on the engine, both at the operational unit and the depot. Then, we evaluated maintenance practices and procedures; and lastly, the manufacturing process at the plant that produced the engine.

The mishap engine was removed from the aircraft for the initial inspection. Our fire experts explained how to read the fire pattern that identified the "finger" that pointed to the origin of the fire in the engine. I requested a fully operational engine to facilitate our investigation. The finger in this accident pointed to the third segment of the engine, the diffuser housing that surrounded the combustion chamber. The functional engine was disassembled for further investigation. After several days, the SIB's preliminary findings confirmed a ruptured diffuser.

A thorough investigation ruled out potential causal factors at Langley AFB, so we proceeded to San Antonio and continued at the Air Logistics Center (ALC). We reviewed and evaluated all the depot maintenance and overhaul procedures for the PW-F-100 engines. Several areas of interest were identified; however, the ALC was ruled out as a contributing cause of the diffuser failure. After eliminating the home base and logistics center, the final "finger" pointed to the manufacturer of the engine, Pratt & Whitney in Hartford, Connecticut.

The corporate officials at Pratt & Whitney allowed the SIB to continue our investigation there. We were given a series of detailed briefings and a tour of the facilities. The diffuser was manufactured using a process called "chemical milling." Exact chemical solutions were used in the process, but the actual production lacked adequate quality control. The results were "chemical undercutting" that resulted in inconsistent thickness of the diffuser that ultimately failed in flight. The engineers at P&W were obliged to agree with our in findings; consequently, the SIB was confident when we prepared the briefing for the commander of 9th Air Force and HQ TAC.

The results of the investigation were first presented to Lieutenant General Piotrowski. He cleared the SIB to proceed to HQ TAC to brief General O'Malley. Afterwards, he said, "Dick, your team did an outstanding job. We appreciate your efforts in identifying this critical problem. Please standby for a few minutes."

General O'Malley invited Generals Piotrowski and Viccellio to join him in his office while the team continued discussions with the TAC staff. A few minutes later, the executive officer came out and asked me to join Generals O'Malley, Piotrowski, and Viccellio in the office. All three reiterated their pleasure with the efforts of the SIB. General O'Malley said, "Dick, you did a great job, but how did you get Pratt & Whitney to open their doors for you?" I related that the facts that led us to their door, and it was in their best interest to let the SIB find the cause. He then asked about our findings at the ALC. I stated that the ALC needed a more aggressive and effective process for the depot maintenance of the PW-F-100 engine. He agreed and looked over at General Vecellio and said, "I agree with the findings. Butch has agreed to go to San Antonio as the vice commander to help make that happen." The expression on General Vecellio's face said, "Thanks a lot, Dick!"

General O'Malley continued, "Dick, General Piotrowski and I have decided to pull you out of MacDill. We need your talents elsewhere. The TAC Air Control Wing at Shaw is in deep trouble and needs help. I have just hired a wing commander, but I need you to go help him out as Director of Logistics. You should make vice commander in about a year and we'll get you a wing after that. What do you say?"

This was the first time in my career a future path was laid out in such a manner. I hadn't expected to leave MacDill after less than a year, let alone be promised an opportunity to command a wing. I was overwhelmed by this good fortune and graciously accepted General O'Malley's offer. General Piotrowski invited me to fly back to Shaw with him in his T-39 jet. We reflected on the times our paths crossed since the days at Eglin AFB in 1963. What a journey it had been for both of us. America had changed in many positive ways; however, General Piotrowski advised me that the racial climate in Sumter, South Carolina was still a work in progress. He assured me there would be no toleration of any mistreatment of my family and me during our tour at Shaw AFB. He then told me about Colonel Richard "Dick" Rhyne, the new wing commander in the 507th TAC Air Control Wing. Dick and Joan Rhyne received high praise from

General Piotrowski, and he was certain we would make a great team. By the time we landed at Shaw, I had dates and plans to move to Shaw within three weeks.

I checked into the BOQ for the night then called Peggy to share the remarkable news and to tell her about our impending move to Sumter, SC. It seemed we had a lot for which to thank God lately. We thanked Him for controlling the events in our lives and for allowing these two outstanding general officers to direct my path. They were tremendous leaders and warm human beings. From their actions, it was easy for me to conclude that the Lord placed both of them in my life in perfect timing. Each displayed the heart and spirit of *An Uncaged Eagle*.

I spent the next two weeks preparing to leave MacDill. Peggy, Grandma, and Daniel stayed on to allow Daniel to complete the tenth grade. He was familiar with military moves and was not too upset at leaving his friends of only a few months. Jim Yocum and the entire maintenance team scheduled going-away parties for the officers and enlisted personnel. Many wonderful relationships were established with the people at MacDill and the local community, and they were added to our list of cherished memories.

Tragic Losses

On April 20, 1985, the Air Force suffered a horrendous tragedy. General Jerome F. O'Malley, his wife, Diane, Lieutenant Colonel Lester Newton, and two other crew members died in the crash of a T-39 jet while landing at Wilkes-Bare Scranton International Airport, Pennsylvania. This was just ten days after I had briefed General O'Malley and met Lieutenant Colonel Newton at Langley Base Operations. It was a terrible personal loss for Peggy and me. General and Mrs. O'Malley were two beautiful people who were admired and loved by everyone who knew them. When General O'Malley met Peggy, he made a point to talk lovingly about his own daughter named Peggy. The Lord allowed these two very special people to enter our lives ever so briefly. Now they were suddenly gone, but their impact upon us was immeasurable. As we mourned the loss of the O'Malleys, our grief was compounded by the other losses in the accident. We later discovered Lieutenant Colonel Lester Newton was one of three younger brothers of Colonel "Fig" Newton. Such losses as these are so difficult to accept and are never understood. When Christians experience tragedies of this magnitude, there is only one reasonable response. God is still on His throne. Out of the ashes of the tragedy He gives new life and a renewed purpose. Though very painful to accept, Peggy and I, along with countless others faced the future with this hope. We prayed frequently for the families of the O'Malleys, Newtons, and others lost in the accident.

TAC Air Control Wing

The Tactical Air Control Wing (TACW) has the responsibility to plan, direct, and control tactical air operations and to coordinate these operations with other Services. It is comprised of control agencies and communications-electronics facilities that provide the means for centralized control and decentralized execution of missions.

I reported to Colonel Richard G. "Dick" Rhyne the last of April 1985 for initial briefings and orientation for the 507 TAC Air Control Wing, Headquarters, Shaw AFB. Dick and I hit it off immediately. He was a fine, southern-bred, southern-spoken gentleman from North Carolina who displayed outstanding character, humor, intellect, and appreciation for people. After our initial discussions, Dick stated, "Dick, with your outstanding record, you should have been given a wing to command, but I sure am glad you are here! This is going to be a tough job, but with your help, we can make it happen, make it better, and make it last." Dick and I accepted the enormous challenge of turning around the worst wing in TAC. His words of

"Make it Happen, Make it Better, Make it Last" became our slogan throughout the transformation.

As the Deputy Commander for Logistics, I was responsible for maintenance and logistics support for 2,600 personnel at twenty-two units in thirteen states and one Caribbean site. Our units included three tactical aircraft squadrons with sixty-eight aircraft and nine communications-electronics/radar detachments. The assigned aircraft were the Vietnam-vintage O-2, OV-10 aircraft used by the airborne forward air controllers (FACs). The wing was also equipped with the CH-3 helicopter for troop support and downed aircrew extraction. Initial review of the wing revealed most of the aircraft, equipment, and facilities were long neglected and in need of a major overhaul. The majority of the officers and enlisted personnel had been passed over for promotions and were considered castaways. Most had "homesteaded" in the units and were waiting to retire. Pride and professionalism were in short supply.

Given this grim picture, Dick and I devised a recovery plan that focused on former TAC Commander Wilbur Creech's five P's: People, Purpose, Pride, Professionalism, and Product. Both of us had firmly embraced the precepts of General Creech. We selected the most airworthy O-2 on the flight line at Shaw and began a circuitous visit of each unit in the wing. As the new leaders, we sought to demonstrate our personal enthusiasm about the importance of the wing's mission, confidence in its people, and our commitment to make their lives better. It took several days, but the visits paid off immediately. Word quickly circulated that Dick and I meant business.

When the people found out Dick and I were fighter pilots, they wanted to know how we accepted flying the O-2 or OV-10. My response was, "Dick and I were still fighter pilots disguised as TAC Air Controllers. The rest of the Air Force would soon see our true character and colors. Dick is 'pepper' and I am 'salt'!" The later comment resonated with the people and they believed our words. Now it was time to deliver.

Gathering input from throughout the wing, we built a list of requirements needed to jump-start a revival in the 507th. These needs were carefully justified, prioritized, and developed into a briefing to be presented to Brigadier General "Butch" Viccellio at the ALC in San Antonio and General Robert D. Russ, the new Commander at HQ TAC. Dick tasked me to travel to these bases and make the cases for immediate depot support and funding, respectively. Thanks to Brigadier General Viccellio, the wing began to receive long overdue parts and equipment. Our OV-10s were scheduled into the depot for corrosion remediation. General Russ provided an infusion of funds that enabled the wing to renovate and improve many maintenance facilities and living quarters for our people. The implementation of numerous self-help projects energized our people and stimulated competition between the units throughout the wing.

While I focused on maintenance and logistics, Dick Rhyne focused on improving the leadership in all twenty-two units. He brought the commanders to the headquarters to re-indoctrinate, motivate, train, and ensure their stake in what we were trying to accomplish. The social events of golf and other activities were used to solidify these efforts. I completed a check-out in the O-2 and began follow-up visits to the units. Also, we carefully reviewed the records of our personnel to identify those who deserved a second look on promotion boards. We worked especially hard to ensure the selected individuals had completed all possible requirements to make them competitive. Dick then did everything possible to get general officer indorsements for the next promotion cycle.

Peggy and I were blessed in May with our first college graduate when Gail finished at LSU with a degree in Interior Design. Gail worked very hard for three years and finished with honors. My youngest brother, Wendell, his wife, Linda, and my aunt, Rosie, from Shreveport, Louisiana joined us in the celebration. Peggy and I presented Gail with her first car as a graduation gift. We also had a contact for her first job. Earlier in the year, I met one of my classmates, Tarlee Brown, a successful architect in Atlanta, Georgia. He interviewed Gail in late May and referred her to a design firm in the same building. Gail was hired immediately by Carlsten Associates, a design firm, and began work in June. Later she helped Peggy, Grandma, and Daniel move to Shaw AFB and get settled in a house on base.

Missing in Central America

In early June, Dick and I took a trip to Honduras in Central America to visit our remote unit that supported a State Department program in that country. We had a contingent of people deployed to Tegucigalpa, the capital. Our team was assigned to help the Honduran Air Force build and operate a radar site high in the mountains that overlooked the neighboring countries. For political purposes, we were required to use civilian passports and dress in civilian clothes during our trip. It proved to be an interesting journey.

We departed the U. S. from Miami International Airport on a scheduled non-stop flight to Tegucigalpa. Our people were scheduled to meet us at the airport and transport us to their operations facility and living quarters. Upon landing, we disembarked the aircraft to pick up our bags and meet our hosts. The signs in the small airport were in Spanish and poorly displayed, so we followed the passengers to the baggage section. After waiting for thirty minutes, we approached an airport agent to inquire about our luggage. The person spoke only Spanish, looked at us suspiciously, and ushered us into a room with a window that opened to the arrival section of the airport. In the meantime, we were perplexed by the absence of our people to pick us up.

Two more aircraft arrived but we didn't see our bags in those offloaded. We became concerned after about two hours and left the room to ask for assistance in using the local telephone. We had no idea why our people had not arrived, and the airport agent was joined by security persons who motioned toward us as they spoke. Three hours passed, and no one was there to pick us up. By then, we were two concerned Air Force Colonels traveling in civilian clothes and apparently stranded. The lack of assistance from the airport people made us even more nervous. Finally, another aircraft arrived. A flight attendant who appeared to be an American entered the arrival area. I hurried from the room to explain our situation and asked for help. Thank God, she was an American and spoke Spanish. She told us we had gotten off at the wrong airport! Our flight made an unscheduled stop in Costa Rica. The flight attendant explained the political climate in Central America caused the airport agents to become suspicious of Dick and me, and that she would try to get us on her flight that was also headed to Tegucigalpa. Halleluiah!

We waited anxiously as the flight attendant spoke to the airport agent and security people, then to the pilot of the aircraft. The pilot allowed us to board without tickets, but there was standing room only on the crowded flight. We rushed on board and followed our "Angel of Mercy" back to the galley where she shared her seat with us for takeoff. We passed passengers holding loads of personal belongings, crates with chickens, and bundles of fruit and vegetables. It was a virtual flying village of Central Americans. The flight attendant told us this was usual on flights in the area and that "direct" flights often made unscheduled stops in these nations. Dick and I were blessed to depart Costa Rica without being arrested.

We finally arrived at our original destination to find terribly worried people who had been waiting for us nearly five hours. They had contacted our wing at Shaw AFB, the Miami airport, and the airlines. We were just a few minutes from being declared missing in

Central America.

Dick and I had a very eventful visit and instituted changes on the spot to enhance the safety and well-being of our personnel at the detachment. We departed a few days earlier than planned because I suffered the worst case of dysentery in my life. We stopped over at Anderson Air Base, Panama so that I could recover enough to fly on to the States. We finally arrived back at Shaw on the eve of Father's Day. The unstable political climate in Honduras was underscored just two weeks after our visit when two Americans were killed by grenades at the restaurant where we had dinner!

In the Potter's Hands

Dick Rhyne and I had just returned from the TDY to Honduras, and I was sick in bed the evening of Father's Day, June 15, 1985. Peggy brought me the phone to call my dad in Pasadena. He had traveled to Merced for his favorite pastime - fishing in one of California's many lakes. My dad told me he had not felt well for about two days, so I encouraged him to go to an emergency health center. He promised to do so the next morning if he was not feeling any better. At that point, Dad started to cough violently and dropped the phone. Someone picked up the phone while frantically calling my dad's name. Twenty minutes later, Dad's friend called to tell me he had a massive heart attack and died before the paramedics arrived.

The sudden loss of my father deeply saddened me, but the Lord was gracious enough to allow me to speak with him one last time. As with my brother, Wilbert, I was the last person to speak with my dad. We had a little over four years since our reconciliation, and made the most of it. At age seventy-three, I believe Dad died a happy man and was at peace with God. My sister, Zella, her daughter, Deborah, and my brother, David joined me in Pasadena for our father's service. His friends and many of our relatives in California came to pay their respects. Though a sad occasion, we were blessed to reunite with some in attendance whom we had not seen in many years. The sting of my father's death was softened by the forgiveness, love, and reconciliation we had shared.

It was Friday night, August 10, 1985, the twenty-third wedding anniversary for Peggy and me. We cancelled a trip because she was not feeling well and went to dinner in Sumter. Halfway through the meal, Peggy suffered severe abdominal cramps and we left for home. We treated the ailment as a temporary disorder, but Peggy's condition worsened through the night. About 4:00 AM the next morning, I took her to the hospital emergency room. After initial treatment to relieve the pain, further examination revealed Peggy was critically ill. The preliminary diagnosis was a severe blockage of her colon, most likely caused by cancer. Peggy had seen the doctors in April back at MacDill, but they failed to identify this pending crisis. The hospital at Shaw AFB was not equipped to make a definitive diagnosis, so an evaluation was scheduled early Monday at the local hospital in town. The results confirmed Peggy suffered from stage four colon cancer.

This staggering news hit us like a nuclear bomb. I notified Dick Rhyne, our family, and close friends of Peggy's condition. Gail returned home from Atlanta to be with Grandma and Daniel who was enrolled in a local high school in Sumter. The next morning, an Air Force emergency air evacuation transport flew us to Wilford Hall Medical Center, San Antonio, Texas. Peggy's condition had worsened by the time we took off, but the medical personnel did a masterful job keeping her sedated during the flight. She underwent surgery shortly after our arrival. The surgeons attached a colostomy and left the incision open to preclude septic infection. The next few days were agonizing as I helplessly watched Peggy suffer.

This crisis came without warning, and it shook the foundation of our family. However, we were consoled and strengthened by scores of people who prayed for us. The Officer's Christian Fellowship mobilized its worldwide prayer chain for the Tolivers, and encouraging words came from around the globe. In addition, more than a dozen Air Force families we knew from previous assignments lived in San Antonio and provided on-scene support. Our friend, Colonel Leonard Johnson, was now stationed in San Antonio and was my daily prayer partner. We also heard from Coach Fisher Deberry at the Air Force Academy. He wanted us to know the entire football team was praying for us and that Michael was in good hands. Retired Major Chet and Marla Rose provided me daily transportation and a local convalescent home for Peggy after her release.

Six weeks later, the doctors performed surgery to reverse Peggy's colostomy and removed additional cancerous tissue. Peggy's carcinoembryonic antigen (CEA), a blood test used to detect cancer, indicated widespread cancer cells in her body without discernable tumors. Physicians often use CEA results to determine the stage and extent of disease. It is also used to assess the outlook in patients with cancer, especially gastrointestinal and colorectal cancer. As a result of Peggy's CEA, chemotherapy and radiation treatment were withheld. Her CEA remained high, but she was allowed to return to Shaw for her weekly monitoring and tests. While everyone continued to pray for her improvement, I resumed my duties in the 507th.

I completed a check out in the O-2 aircraft in December 1985 and continued my visits to the twenty-two units in the 507th. The entire wing was energized by improvement projects in every unit. Pride, professionalism, and productivity were at an all time high. In early 1986, a number of our personnel were promoted on their second evaluation, including a colonel and senior master sergeant. Our side of the base was frequently visited by members of the 363rd TFW, the F-16s, to see what all the activities were about. Amazingly, the 507th TAC Air Control Wing began to receive requests for assignment to the unit.

By March 1986, the 507th was solidly on the path to becoming a top wing in TAC. Dick Rhyne and I made a great team and had become very close friends. On March 12th, Lieutenant General Kirk, 9th Air Force Commander, moved me up to Vice Commander. My immediate goal was to retire the O-2 from the Air Force. Unfortunately, it took a fatal accident and other hurdles before we were able to convince General Russ to support this initiative. We developed a replacement plan that required the acquisition and refurbishment of excess T-37 training aircraft. Brigadier General Viccellio, now at the San Antonio ALC, provided support in identifying and acquiring suitable T-37s from the Air Training Command. ALC did an outstanding job stripping the T-37 of years of paint, removing outdated communication systems, and repairing airframes. The modified jets were equipped with the latest communication and navigation systems and painted in camouflage to reflect the new tactical role as the OT-37 for the airborne FACs.

The arrival date of the first O-37 was attended by U. S. Congressman John Spratt, Mayor W. A. "Bubba' McElveen of Sumter, General Russ, Lieutenant General Kirk, Brigadier General Viccellio, and a host of other Air Force and local dignitaries. The 21st Tactical Air Support Squadron (TASS) and the 4507th Consolidated Maintenance Aircraft Maintenance Squadron (CAMS), commanded by Lieutenant Colonels Trent Pauly and Charles Gray, respectively, had a major role in retiring the O-2s. With their help, we completed the O-37 conversion program in eight months, well ahead of the allotted eighteen months.

Dick and I kept our word to our people. The men and women of the 507th Wing were back on the map and duly received proper recognition for the contribution to the mission of the Air Force and to our nation. For the first time in its eleven-year history, the 4507th CAMS received the Air Force Maintenance Effectiveness Award in the small aircraft unit category. Our Tactical Air Control Squadron was selected as the best large communications-electronics maintenance activity in TAC. In addition, the wing set new records for combat readiness in both radar and tactical air control elements. The culmination of our efforts was highlighted when the 507th Wing received the Air Force Outstanding Unit Award.

In April 1986, Peggy's CEA and x-rays identified a suspicious area in her liver that required monitoring. In September, tests at Wilford Hall confirmed a cancerous tumor in the upper lobe that needed to be removed. Peggy was scheduled for the third surgical procedure the following week and the prognosis was very uncertain. We were told the lower lobe of the liver could sustain life, but the doctors could not ascertain its condition until the surgery. If both lobes were cancerous, Peggy's probability of survival was minimal. As usual, Peggy took this news like a Trojan. She simply replied, "If the Lord is ready for me, I am ready to go home. I have had a great life, and I know God will take care of Dick, the children, and my mom. Though, the Lord slay me, yet will I still trust Him!" Despite Peggy's unshakeable faith, this was my lowest level of despair. Every part of me screamed against the possibility of losing Peggy. I stayed with her until late that night then went to my room and wept bitterly. I didn't have the heart to call the children or anyone else to give them the latest news.

That night was a torture unlike any I ever experienced. I arose at daybreak and walked along the back road of the Lackland AFB golf course. Falling to my knees, I cried out to God for a reprieve on Peggy's life. I was willing to exchange my own life for hers. Prostrate on the ground, I repeatedly pounded the earth as if beating on the very doors of Heaven. Just when I was on the brink of complete hopelessness, the still quiet voice of God seemed to say, "Look, don't you know I love Peggy more than you. I created her for my purpose; she is mine! She's been your wife for twenty-four years, yet you still don't know how much she means to me. If I take her now, that is my business. Where is your faith in me? Bring her to the alter and leave her in my hands!"

I lay on the ground that was wet from my tears. It was another moment of truth and this was a test of my faith and commitment to God. It meant total surrender of the most precious person in my life. I had to be willing to trust Him as Peggy did. As I regained consciousness of the scene around me, the sounds of nature filled the air. The birds were singing their sweet songs. The squirrels and rabbits skirted about on dew-covered grass beneath the trees. And the sun rose slowly over the horizon. God spoke through the simplicity of his creation to assuage my pain. The other "sound" was the quietness of a new day He made. I needed to rejoice in whatever time He was going to allow Peggy and me to be together. I got up, went to my room, cleaned up, and returned to Peggy's bedside. This time, I encouraged and told her we would always be together, in this world and the next. Whatever the Lord wanted to do, I would be at her side to the end. I promised to take care of her mother and our children with all that was in me. Holding hands, I walked beside her to the operating room.

The initial surgery lasted over five hours. A visiting minister in the waiting room came over and asked if he could pray with me. God showed His compassion through a stranger who comforted me in our hour of great need. The doctor finally came to tell me the lower lobe of Peggy's liver appeared healthy and they were going to leave it in. Time would tell if the remaining section could sustain her life. This was a tremendous message of hope, and I whispered a long prayer of thanksgiving.

The surgery was finally completed, but Peggy remained in critical condition in the intensive care unit for several days. The news of her condition was now known by an army of prayer warriors. The Lord *"carried us on eagle's wings and brought us to Himself"*

NIV Exodus 19:4. The doctors prescribed several weeks of hospital care for Peggy, and I stayed until she showed signs of recovery. I returned to Shaw to prepare for her eventual homecoming and to catch up on work. After a month at Wilford Hall, Peggy flew back to Shaw on the medical evacuation aircraft. A crowd of friends and neighbors waited to greet her as she gingerly stepped off the aircraft. Though very frail and weak, all of us were thrilled to have her home.

Peggy required daily assistance during her long period of convalescence, but family, friends, and neighbors responded beautifully. Yoshi Brown, David's wife, came from Fort Bragg and stayed several weeks. Thretha Thomas, an adopted sister, came from Baltimore for an extended stay. Our friends from Sumter were outstanding and went out of their way to support us. Cliff Goodwin, a wealthy patriarch of the community, became a dear friend and stopped by to visit Peggy and Grandma on several occasions. Others brought so much food and gifts that we graciously had to call a halt to their efforts. Peggy steadily improved over the next few months, but her CEA remained high. We held steadfast in our faith and prayed for her healing.

Our greatest challenge in 1986 was Peggy's health, yet we had a lot for which to be thankful as Christmas approached. Despite Peggy's illness, the prayers of the righteous enabled us to get through challenges of the job and school. With constant encouragement, tutoring, and summer school, Daniel earned his high school diploma and met the qualifications to join the Marine Corps. Our daughter, Renea, graduated from the Air Force Academy in June, and I had the privilege to administer the Air Force oath at her commissioning. While at the Academy, Renea received numerous top awards in high jump and hurdles. She earned All-American honors four times for the NCAA Division II Women's Track and Field. In September, she completed Maintenance Officer School at Chanute Training Center, Illinois and stopped at Shaw enroute to Spangdahlem Air Base, Germany.

While Renea was home, she met First Lieutenant Ginger Cook and brought her home for us to adopt. Ginger and her brother were orphaned very early by their biological parents and grew up with their maternal grandmother. Ginger was a scrappy, determined little fighter who fought her way through life and college. She was commissioned through the AFROTC at Mississippi State University. Ginger was a welcome addition into our family and fit right in. She was easy to love, and being parents to a young adult was just an extension of who we were.

In early 1987, Peggy suffered internal hemorrhaging and had to be returned to Wilford Hall. Given the trauma of her previous operations, she asked me to support her in refusing any further surgery. It tore my heart out, but I agreed. Thankfully, doctors found a way to treat her with oral medication and therapy. She returned to Shaw after two weeks to continue convalescing.

I received my first consideration for general officer in the spring of 1987. Peggy and I were invited to Maxwell AFB, Alabama where we were joined by more than a dozen other colonels and their wives. The week of screening and briefings were used by the Air Force to help decide who would be promoted to the most senior leadership positions. The men were briefed by general officers while our wives were entertained by their wives. Those attending came from various disciplines and represented the top colonels from their respective areas. Of note, two other African Americans - Colonel Leroy Gross and Lieutenant Colonel Irene Trowell Harris- were there. Colonel Gross was the commander of the hospital at HQ TAC, Langley AFB. He was a former TAC fighter pilot, a carrier qualified Navy exchange pilot, and flight surgeon. Lieutenant Colonel Trowell was a career Air National Guard (ANG) flight nurse and the first nurse in the ANG to command a medical clinic. All of the officers had sterling records, and Peggy and I were grateful to have been considered among them. We returned to Shaw and left the outcome in the hands of the Lord.

Sudden tragedies are always overwhelming. Such was the news I received the morning of March 9, 1987. My friend, Colonel Joe Lee Burns, Vice Commander of the 49th TFW, called me from Holloman AFB, New Mexico. His tone let me know the news was not good. Joe said, "Dick, I have some very bad news. Gene Jackson was killed this morning during takeoff in an F-15. I am sorry to break this news to you, but I know how close you and Gene were." Joe told me Gene was conducting a functional check flight of an F-15 he was scheduled to ferry to the Hawaiian Air National Guard the next day. The aircraft was configured with its three external tanks and fully loaded with fuel. Gene experienced a flight control problem on take-off and crashed less than a mile from the end of the runway.

Stunned by this tragic news, I went to my office and tried to accept the reality of Joe's phone call. Gene was more than a broth-er to me, and my heart nearly burst with grief. The minutes that followed were almost unbearable. I thought of Nelda and the two boys. Gene was their very life, their joy, and pride. I shuddered at having to break the news to Peggy, Grandma, and the children. Our families had grown very close while stationed together at Nellis, Bitburg, and Kirtland Air Force Bases. This was one of the most dif-ficult experiences I ever faced. I finally called Peggy. Because of all the uncertainty of her future, the news of Gene's death was very hard to accept. Peggy rarely cried, but she wept over this tragic news. Un-able to concentrate, I called Dick Rhyne, who was out of town, and advised him that I was taking the rest of the day off.

Peggy, Grandma, and I consoled each other and prayed for Nelda, the boys, and Gene's family in Texas. I called Nelda to of-fer our condolences and help in whatever way possible. All I could do was pray and promised to be at her side as soon as possible. At Nelda's request, I agreed to be the official Air Force escort officer for Gene's interment planned for the Houston National Cemetery near his hometown. I departed immediately for his memorial services scheduled at Holloman AFB for Wednesday, March 11th.

I arrived near midnight at the El Paso, Texas airport and was picked up by Chaplain (Captain) Wilfred Bristol and driven to Holloman. We went to Gene's home where Nelda, the two boys, Corey and Craig, and members of Gene's family awaited me. All I could do was embrace Nelda and the boys and let them lean on me during their heart-wrenching grief. Prior to the memorial service the next day, my duty as escort officer required me to perform the most difficult task in my life, verify Gene's remains at the funeral home. Only by the grace of God was I able to complete this official task. The memorial service later that day was led by Gene's boss, Brigadier General James F. Record, Commander of the 833rd Air Division. Many testified to Gene's exemplary character as a husband, father, brother, son, friend and fighter pilot. It was a beautiful and fitting service that culminated with a four-ship, missing man F-15 formation. Afterwards, I met with Gene's family including his mother, father, two brothers, Nelda, and other family members to review plans for the burial in Houston.

The family departed the next day for Houston and I escorted Gene's body from the funeral home in Alamogordo to El Paso and onto the aircraft. The airline captain who watched the process invited me to sit in the first class section for the flight to Houston. Once airborne, the impact of Gene's death finally hit me. I reflected on our relationship. Gene was like a brother to me. We had shared so much during the seventeen years I knew him – our hopes and aspirations, our doubts, fears, joys, and sorrows. Whenever one needed upholding, the other would somehow be there, regardless of the distance between us. In the crisis of our lives, we sought and found a deeper relationship with God. We laughed, cried, played, worshiped, and prayed together. At times we fussed with each other but always loved each other. So unique was this man that while he could be personally engaged with one, he was equally involved with many.

Whether he was in or out of uniform, flying jets, or coaching football, Gene was an intimate friend to countless others. He was a sage counselor, confidant, a 'father figure,' and much more.

So soon this great soldier completed his mission upon the earthly battlefield. While here, he faithfully served his God, his people, and his country. He was a proud patriot who worked to better himself, his family, and his nation. Gene always took time to reach back to help those coming behind him. Often he stooped low to help the down-trodden, and in doing so, his height rose well beyond his physical stature. Gene refused to be deterred by class, color, or religion. When there was a need, he simply gave of himself, whatever the circumstances.

Gene had a keen sense of the importance of timing, and we shared thoughts on this subject many times. His thoughts can be found in his favorite scriptures, Ecclesiastes Chapter Three, "A Time for Everything." Now it was his time to be with the Lord and the heavenly host. Although this was a hurtful time for us, it was still God's chosen time; and His timing is always perfect. Gene's family and friends gathered for the graveside service. Colonel Hal Brown and many other military officers joined us for the final farewell. Later, I assisted in getting Nelda and the boys back to Holloman and then departed for Shaw. I thanked God for allowing Gene to be such an important part of our lives. With His help, I would be available for Nelda and the boys for the rest of my life, confident Gene, *An Uncaged Eagle* would be flying top cover.

Our future in the Air Force became apparent shortly after Dick Rhyne scheduled his retirement for May 1987. Dick and Joan planned to leave the Air Force after twenty-six years of an outstanding career. By all accounts, Dick and I had done a fantastic job in the 507th and received numerous plaudits from General Russ, TAC

Commander, and Lieutenant General Kirk, 9th Air Force Command-er. Thus, we thought I would be selected to command the wing upon Dick's retirement. Instead, Colonel Gene L. Juve and his wife, Penny, were selected to replace Dick and Joan. This was a great disappoint-ment because I had done everything possible to be competitive for the 507th or any other wing. I went to see General Kirk regarding the decision and he told me Dick's replacement was decided by General Russ. I then asked about the possibilities of a command for me in the future. General Kirk's response was evasive and vague, but he gave me a clear signal that I had gone as far as possible in the Air Force. I left his office fighting the temptation to believe race still played a part in such decisions.

When I was considered for general officer, there was intense "horse trading" between the commanding generals of TAC, PACAF, and USAFE. The ultimate selection of wing commanders and even-tual promotion to Brigadier General depended upon personalities and circumstances of those involved in the process. Most important-ly, a colonel needed a sponsor who advocated for his or her selection. Of my two sponsors, General O'Malley had been killed, and General Piotrowski had moved on to another major command. In the final decision, Peggy and I accepted the reality that God apparently had something else in store for us. As committed Christians, we were obliged to continue entrusting our future to the Lord. Accordingly, I requested an assignment change back to Kirtland AFB and planned to retire in a little over a year.

We had the bitter-sweet opportunity of conducting several days of farewell events for the Rhynes. The outpouring of apprecia-tion and love for them was expressed by members of the 507th, the 363rd TFW at Shaw, and scores of people from Sumter. Lieutenant General Charles A. Horner, the new 9th Air Force Commander offici-ated at Dick's retirement ceremony on the flight line.

A few weeks after Peggy's return from Wilford Hall, her CEA began to recede. Weekly checks confirmed a steady decline, and excitement began to build at Shaw and at Wilford Hall. After six weeks of an inexplicable reduction, the doctors requested she return to Wilford Hall for testing. The miraculous readings persisted, and I joined Peggy and her doctors for a consultation. When I arrived, the news of her improvement was known throughout the hospital and she had been visited by the hospital commander, a two-star general. All three doctors were waiting for me in her room. Dr. Eisenberg, the lead surgeon, simply shook his head and said, "Colonel Toliver, in my twenty years of surgery, I have never seen anything like this. Mrs. Toliver is cancer free, but we don't have a medical explanation. Whatever prayers were offered, we say keep on praying. Her recovery is nothing short of a miracle." Another doctor echoed Dr. Eisenberg's words and wiped away tears. Peggy smiled and said, "Praise the Lord! My faith and trust in Him is steadfast. His grace is sufficient. His mercy endures forever. It doesn't matter what happens now. I know my Jesus is real. I'm ready to go home!"

We were told of the close follow-up planned for Peggy at Wilford Hall during the remaining period of uncertainty. After hugs and handshakes, we said good-bye to the doctors and hospital staff. All of us had been on an extraordinary two year journey and trial by fire. Our gratitude abounded for the many health professionals at Shaw and at Wilford Hall. No words could ever express how much we appreciated every one, so we asked God to bless each one in the months and years to come. To this day, we pray for those who work in hospitals, clinics, and care facilities all across the land.

We arrived back at Shaw in time to prepare for Michael's graduation at the Air Force Academy. The entire family, including Ginger, flew to Colorado for the event. I had the pleasure of administering the Oath of Office to our second graduate from the Academy. Mike had an exciting four years at the Academy while playing defensive back for the Falcons. The team beat Notre Dame four years in a row, Virginia Tech in an Independence Bowl, and beat Texas in a Blue Bonnet Bowl. The Air Force Academy was the 1986 Co-Champions of the Western Athletic Conference with Brigham Young University and won the Commander-in-Chief's Trophy. Mike also qualified for a pilot slot and was scheduled to enter pilot training in September.

Daniel Thar, who came to us earlier in 1985, chose to continue with us as our "son" beyond high school. With his self-determination and many prayers by others, he successfully completed basic and advanced infantry training in the Marine Corps. This was truly an act of the Lord. Dan looked great in uniform when he came home for a visit, and he went to his former high school to encourage the students to stay in school. We were very proud of Dan's success and growing maturity. God's grace was an abundant blessing for all of us.

Crisis in the Persian Gulf

I am still amazed at how the Lord intervenes in our lives. We make specific plans but He often redirects our course. Peggy and I felt our decision to return to Albuquerque and retire was sound since we had a house there. Furthermore, my Air Force and OT&E experience were considered very marketable in the aerospace companies in New Mexico. My plan, however, would have precluded me from participating in one of the most important assignments of my career – the 1987 Persian Gulf Crisis.

On March 17, 1987, an Iraqi Mirage F-1 fighter misidentified the USS Stark frigate and launched two Exocet AM-39 air-to-surface missiles in a deadly attack. The first missile tore a ten-by-fifteen foot hole in the warship's steel hull on the port side before ripping through the crews' quarters. The second one plowed into the frigate's superstructure killing thirty-seven American seamen! Instead of being reassigned to Albuquerque, I was asked to do a base transfer to 9th Air

Force Headquarters as the senior Tactical Air Control Director.

The political and international fallout of the Stark incident was intense and complex. In a press conference, President Reagan vowed to keep the Persian Gulf's shipping lanes open to the world under the escort of American warships flying the American flag. He also stated the Royal Saudi Air Force (RSAF) would complement USAF's AWACS coverage to provide radar surveillance in the Gulf. There was just one big problem with President Reagan's statement to the world. The RSAF was not capable of manning an around-the-clock AWACS operation. Moreover, they had not agreed to do so. The fun had just begun!

To save face for President Reagan, Marine General George B. Christ, U. S. CENTCOM Commander, was tasked to get the Saudis into an AWACS orbit immediately. General Christ summoned Lieutenant General Horner to the headquarters at MacDill AFB, Florida to discuss the strategy for this delicate task. I was tasked to accompany him. My recent experience with command and control operations and equipment modernization provided the expertise needed to integrate the proposed RSAF AWACS with ours. My prior experience with the Saudis in 1979 also proved helpful.

General Christ tasked General Horner to head up a team to go to Riyadh and do whatever was necessary to get the RSAF into an air defense orbit. The RSAF had five E-3 AWACS aircraft and eight KC-135 aerial tankers on the ramp at Riyadh. However, they had only a fraction of the required trained aircrews to man the jets. General Horner had been the CENTAF commander for a little over two months, but he had a firm grasp of the challenge ahead. He also had a keen appreciation for Saudi people and their culture. The proposed start date for the escort of re-flagged vessels was just three weeks away, so time was critical.

The team assembled at HQ CENTCOM included general officers from the Navy, Army, and six key colonels from the CENTAF staff. We provided the collective expertise in logistics, operations, personnel, and other crucial disciplines. The next day, the team rendezvoused at Seymour-Johnson AFB, North Carolina. We boarded General Christ's four-engine jet for a seventeen hour, non-stop, aerial refueling flight to Riyadh. During the flight, the specific options and details of the proposal General Horner would offer the RSAF were planned and reviewed at length. When he was satisfied with the plan, we were allowed to get a few hours of rest.

We arrived in Riyadh the next evening and went directly to the RSAF Headquarters. General Horner met privately with Crown Prince Lieutenant General Ahmad Ibrahim Behari, Chief of the RSAF, while we awaited our instructions. After the meeting, he appointed me to be the chief negotiator for the USAF team to meet with the RSAF team and develop the required operational agreement. My counterpart was Colonel Jehani, a bearded, ultra religious commander of the RSAF AWACS squadron. Colonel Jack Gray was our Air Force AWACS detachment commander and an invaluable tutor on interactions with the officers in RSAF.

The negotiations commenced the following day in a conference room carefully arranged with tables across from each other. As a courtesy to the host, Jack Gray sat on the RSAF side. From the outset, Colonel Jehani was terrified of any agreement that he perceived could be a potential failure for the Saudis. Furthermore, he demanded assurances the Air Force would provide an assortment of spare parts, supplies, and aircrew personnel. For the next three weeks, our team met with the RSAF and painstakingly forged an agreement. The heart of the agreement was the command, control, communications, and intelligence (C3I) system that linked the AWACS and ground-based surveillance radar with fighters and ground air defense. Key elements required the modification of the RSAF Command and Control Center in Riyadh, upgrade of the Tactical Control unit at Dhahran, and a cadre of instructors to train the RSAF AWACS aircrews.

We met with the RSAF during the day and with General Horner during the evenings. Almost daily, Colonel Jehani came in with new demands or with requests to rewrite some minute detail of the agreement. Moreover, his fear pervaded the entire process and made the negotiations outright tortuous at times. General Horner met periodically with General Behari, but protocol precluded them from coming into the conference room. General Horner was very patient and understanding, but after two and one-half weeks with no agreement, he began to get anxious and exhorted us to work harder. Our team realized what was at stake and worked diligently to allay Colonel Jehani's concerns. Privately, I did a lot of praying for discernment, wisdom, and patience, the latter of which was stretched to the limit.

The morning General Horner was scheduled to depart to meet General Christ in Washington, DC came much too quickly. We were down to dotting "Is" and crossing "Ts." General Horner reiterated his exhortation to do whatever it took to get Colonel Jehani to concur with an agreement for General Behari's signature. Jack Gray took me aside and said, "Dick, General Horner is standing by to depart. Kiss Jehani on both cheeks, shake his hand, and thank him for the agreement. "

Jack's advice was well-meaning, but beyond my earthly ability. Instead, I excused myself and went down to the men's room to pray. Colonel Jehani followed me and overheard me whispering to God for help. Surprised he asked, "Are you praying? What do you ask God?" My response was spontaneous and unexpected even by me, "Colonel Jehani, I personally pledge my life to do everything possible to ensure your success. Please understand I have nothing left to offer." It was my turn to be surprised. He said, "My brother, my brother, you are a good man! Come, I trust you. I agree with the plan and will take it to General Behari." We hurried back to the room and Colonel Jehani took the signature page to General Behari. The engines were running on the ramp when we delivered the document to General Horner. He sent his thanks and gave instructions for most of the team to return to Shaw. My instructions were to proceed to Bahrain and coordinate the details of the agreement with the Navy operators in the Gulf.

I retired to a quiet place and thanked God for what General Horner and our team had accomplished. We were sorely challenged, but everyone worked hard to forge an unprecedented agreement to get the Saudis airborne. The mission was accomplished. President Reagan would be able to declare a joint Saudi/US agreement to protect the shipping lanes in the Persian Gulf. However, neither General Horner nor I could publicly state all that went on behind closed doors to get the Saudis to fly their AWACS in support of the operation.

I flew to Bahrain the next day and met onboard the USS La Salle, flagship of Rear Admiral Harold Bernsen, Commander U.S. Navy Middle East Task Force. I reviewed with him and his staff the command and control procedures and communication links for the planned escorts. The La Salle remained anchored in the Bahrain harbor during my three day visit, and I received my first tour of a U.S. Navy combat ship. While I was in Bahrain, the USS Stark, attacked earlier in the spring, was anchored in harbor. I saw the jagged, charred gaping holes made by the two Exocet missiles that caused it to be called a ship of death. Belatedly, I offered a prayer for the thirty-seven dead seamen and their families. I departed the next day on a commercial flight home by way of England. The month spent in the Gulf seemed much longer, and I was anxious to get home to see my family.

My immediate task upon returning was to coordinate the establishment of CENTCOM'S satellite ground communication site for the Persian Gulf at Shaw AFB. We constructed a large replica of the Gulf in our command and control center that provided electronic models of ships being tracked through the Straight of Hormuz to Kuwait. This provided a real-time status of escorted vessels in the Persian Gulf around-the-clock.

In late June, I received news of another tragic personal loss. My dear friend, Colonel Leonard Johnson, was killed in the crash of his private aircraft. At the time, he was the Command Surgeon of the Electronic Security Command in San Antonio, Texas. Leonard had just visited his daughter in Tennessee and was enroute to his hometown in Elkhart, Indiana to attend his high school reunion. He was alone in his Piper Comanche and apparently was struck by lightning on final approach. Leonard was a great friend and mentor to me and many others. His death was a tremendous loss for his family, friends, and the Air Force.

Leonard, a child prodigy, was born in St. Augustine, Florida and grew up in Elkhart, Indiana. He finished high school at fourteen years of age and earned his private pilot license at sixteen. He graduated from Howard University in Washington, DC at age eighteen, finished medical school there at age twenty-three, and earned a master's degree from Harvard at age twenty-seven. He later joined the Air Force and became a pioneer in Aerospace Medicine. His expertise and knowledge were sought internationally. He frequently traveled overseas to participate in medical seminars and conferences. Above all, Leonard was a very humble person with an outstanding personality that attracted people from all walks of life. His personality reflected a great sense of internal peace and a free spirit. Leonard was the epitome of *An Uncaged Eagle.*

As the U. S. Navy escort of re-flagged ships in the Persian Gulf progressed, the British, French, Belgian, Dutch and Italian warships joined the Americans and Soviets in patrolling the gulf. Notwithstanding this coordinated operation, Iran frequently initiated hostile acts or threats that prompted an authorized response by the U.S. Navy. A year of surprise Iranian attacks put nerves on edge in the Persian Gulf and resulted in a tragic incident. On July 3, 1988, a civilian Iranian airliner with 290 people failed to identify itself and was inadvertently shot down by the U. S. Navy. This horrific event, plus numerous setbacks in the land war with Iraq, finally persuaded Iranian leaders to seek improved relations with the West. The Ayatollah Khomeini and the Iranian Parliament finally sought a foreign policy that would defuse tensions in the Persian Gulf. President Reagan's firm stand in the Gulf during the 1987-88 crisis improved the standing of the U. S. with our allies, not only in the Middle East but worldwide.

I made several staff trips to Saudi Arabia to ensure RSAF concerns were continually satisfied to keep them flying in support of President Reagan's initiative. Trips were also made to the Pentagon to brief the Middle East Affairs staff officers. While there, I visited my friend, Colonel Fig Newton before he departed for an assignment to Vance AFB, Oklahoma. Fig was disappointed over his pending job as the Deputy Commander of the 71st Air Base Group. Remembering my similar experience with an assignment, I encouraged Fig to go to Vance and let the Lord decide his future. Years later, Fig told me he took my advice. After one year, he commanded the 71st. He went on to command a larger wing and an air division. The rest is history. Eleven years after our talk, Lloyd W. "Fig" Newton retired as a four-star general!

By early 1988, General Horner had solidly earned the respect and trust of the RSAF leaders and several of the Crown Princes in the Kingdom. Their respect for him resulted in an unprecedented trust in CENTCOM. On one occasion Crown Prince Turki of the Dhahran province hosted our visiting team for dinner at his palace. The progress made in the country since my first visit in 1979 was reflected in the palace. As Westerners, we were served dinner in a dining room with traditional table and chairs. Along the way, we observed dining rooms for Asians, Arabians, and other cultures. Other parts of the palace were elaborately furnished and equipped with modern technology and comforts. Dressed in a thobe, ghutra, and agal (the traditional Arab robe and head pieces) General Horner was the hit of the evening. Each of us was personally hosted by a Saudi prince or other royalty. My host was one of King Fahd's sons, also an F-15 pilot.

My final trip to the Kingdom took place in November 1988 to assess the progress of the Gulf operation and report back to General Horner and General Christ. During the visit, Colonel Jehani afforded me the exceptional honor of meeting his wife over the telephone and hosted a dinner for me at the RSAF Officer's Club. He was especially proud to introduce his teenage son to me at the dinner. I was very proud to accept the accolades the RSAF offered for our Air Force, our leaders, and the nation.

My report was optimistic. The Gulf operation was running smoothly, and the reputation of the U. S. government and the military was at an all time high. The men and women of all the services in the area were doing a fantastic job, often in the face of difficult circumstances. The tension in the Persian Gulf persisted, and our deployed forces maintained a perpetual state of readiness and vigilance. A major concern was Iraq. CENTAF had a continuous liaison team assigned with the Iraqi Air Force in Baghdad, but the true intentions of Saddam Hussein couldn't be determined. Our people on the ground were allowed only limited insight into the Iraqi operation. More often than not, they were advised of an operation after the fact. Given these circumstances, their ability to preclude another Stark incident was limited. Furthermore, some observers in the region thought it would be only a matter of time before Saddam Hussein flexed his muscles in the Gulf. To what extent and where could not be determined at the time.

After meeting with General Horner, I traveled to HQ CENT-COM to give my report. I met with General Christ and Lieutenant General Hansford T. Johnson, Vice Commander, CENTCOM. The report was well received, and I was commended for my work over the past eighteen months. General Johnson was kind in his remarks and wished me well in my pending retirement. Upon returning to Shaw, Peggy and I prepared to bring our twenty-six years in the Air Force to a close. General Horner kindly agreed to be my retirement official.

Retirement

Our retirement ceremony was held December 12, 1988 at the Shaw AFB Officer's Club. It was an exciting event for my entire family. The highlight of the event was the attendance of a large number of family and friends. Our children included Gail from Atlanta, Renea from Germany, Mike from Texas, Daniel on leave from the Marine Corps; and Ginger who was stationed at Shaw. My sister, Zella and her husband, AW, came from Shreveport, Louisiana. Our special guests included Brigadier General and Mrs. Tim Boddie (Mattye) and retired chaplain Bobby Black, his wife, Marybel, and son Brian. Tim had pinned on my Second Lieutenant bars in 1963. He and Mattye was a pair of special *Uncaged Eagles* who had flown top cover for me for over twenty-six years. The Blacks had been with us at Nellis, Bitburg, and the years afterwards. Others were Mayor Bubba McElveen and Cliff Goodwin, our friends from Sumter. We also had a tremendous turnout of men and women stationed at Shaw. By the time of the ceremony, it was standing room only.

General Horner did a fantastic job conducting the ceremony and highlighted our most recent challenge in the Persian Gulf. Peggy and I were given citations and gifts to commemorate our service to the Air Force and our nation. Finally, it was my time to make a few comments. As fate would have it, I inadvertently left my prepared speech at home, so I spoke from my heart. I decided to verbally "paint" faces on many people the Lord allowed to cross our paths during our Air Force career. They included faces of the unknown as well as the famous, the old and young, and people of several nations. When I came to my family, my sister Zella, and her husband, AW, stood out as two *Uncaged Eagles* who deserved immeasurable credit for my success throughout my life and career. Their presence was a very special blessing. Peggy, our children, and Grandma held the most precious place in my heart, and I could not say enough about them. Across the room, Peggy was attentive and beautiful. I told her how much she had been a part of my career and how much I loved her. She mouthed back, "I love you, too!"

Those public utterances across the room were some of the most intimate exchanges of our lives, and they instantly touched many in the room. The moment reflected the profound love between us and the sanctity of a God-centered relationship. I realized that my whole life and career were an expression of God's love and faithfulness to Peggy, Grandma, and our children. He graciously allowed me to be a vessel through which His blessings flowed to them. As my career ended, my greatest accomplishment had been the twenty-seven year marriage to Peggy, our children, and grandchildren. Their faith in God, success in life, and service to humanity were precious gifts to us. The appreciation, love, and respect we shared made me a very blessed and wealthy man.

Finally, it was the Lord to whom all credit was due. He deserved praise for His grace, love, patience, and persistent protection over me. He carried and guided me through peril, trials, tribulations, and war. He filled my life with immeasurable joy and success. Earlier, I asked my friend, Chaplain Ted Chumley, to pray at the end of the ceremony. He prayed that God would grant me desire, perseverance, and wisdom as Peggy and I prepared to take the next step in our lives. We all said, "Amen, and to God be the glory!"

Peggy and I spent the last days at Shaw clearing the base. We sent Grandma to Baltimore to be with the rest of her children and family during our transition. We said final good-byes to Ginger and our neighbors at Shaw. Leaving Ginger was particularly hard for her and for us. She had become so much a part of our family because love relationships trumped blood relationship. We thanked God for giving us another beautiful young woman to call our daughter.

We put Shaw AFB in our rearview mirror the morning of December 21, 1988 and headed west to Atlanta, Georgia. We picked up Gail and continued on to Shreveport where we spent Christmas with Zella and the rest of our family there. The reality of our retirement slowly emerged as we crossed each state line. The highway signs that said "You are leaving...." and "Welcome to...." were poignant parallels to our "leaving the Air Force" and "entering retirement." We continued toward New Mexico the day after Christmas and arrived December 31st. We checked into the guest quarters after a safe and pleasant journey to our new "home." Although it was just the two of us, Peggy and I continued our tradition of praying as 1988 ended and 1989 began. We felt God's presence and assurances for our life ahead.

Kirtland AFB, NM and Edwards Air Force Flight Test Center, CA 1980-1984

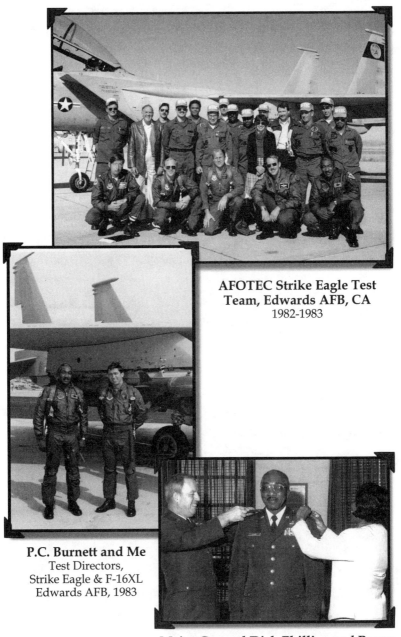

AFOTEC Strike Eagle Test Team, Edwards AFB, CA
1982-1983

P.C. Burnett and Me
Test Directors,
Strike Eagle & F-16XL
Edwards AFB, 1983

Major General Dick Phillips and Peggy
Pinning on Silver Eagles, Colonel
February 1, 1984

MacDill AFB, FL & Shaw AFB, SC

**Senior Maintenance
Commander's Course**
Maxwell AFB, AL 1984

**56th TFW Commander
Colonel Ron Fogleman**
Presenting Award,
MacDill AFB, 1984

**Deputy Commander
for Logistics**
Shaw AFB, SC 1985

TAC Commander
General Bob Russ and me

Zella and AW Presenting Family Plaque at Retirement

Lieutenant General Chuck Horner, Peggy, & Me
Retirement Ceremony, December 14, 1988

PART THREE

EXPERIENCING FREEDOM

Chapter Nineteen

New Horizons

We began the New Year by visiting dear friends, Chuck and Renee Knowlan who lived next door to our house in north Albuquerque. Sharing breakfast with them and their teenage daughter, Elizabeth, it was as if we never left. Later we checked on our house and confirmed what the Knowlans suspected, our tenants had recently moved without letting us know. Fortunately, the house was in reasonably good shape and only required minor maintenance and repairs before we could move in. Before leaving the block, we visited other friends who still resided in the neighborhood. It was good to be back in Albuquerque and gratifying to not have deadlines or schedules to meet. For the first time in many years, we were able to totally relax and just enjoy each other. In doing so, we realized the need to rest and recuperate from the rigors of twenty-six years in the Air Force.

While waiting for completion of repairs and painting, we contacted several families of our former chapel family at Kirtland AFB. Chaplain Bill Rhoades wrote to us prior to our departure from Shaw and invited us to visit the chapel before looking for a local church upon our return. We attended Sunday school and worship service the first Sunday back. Many with whom we formerly worshiped still attended the chapel, and it was an old-fashion reunion after the services. These friends included Bill and Gloria Johnson, Charlie and Carolyn Carson, Clausel and Clare McCorkle, Donn and Sylvia Byrnes, Sam and Joan Marks, Harry and Marge Toppins, and several others. We also discovered a classmate of mine from Tuskegee Institute who had recently been assigned to Kirtland. Rear Admiral Mack Gaston was the Commander of the Defense Nuclear Agency and the only Navy flag officer ever to have graduated from Tuskegee. His wife, Lillian, and daughter, Sonya, were a great addition to Kirtland AFB and the local community.

We moved into our house after three weeks, and I began the restoration of our lawn, shrubs, and garden. By early spring, we were comfortably settled, and Grandma returned to live with us. Gail also moved from Atlanta to Albuquerque and soon found a job with an interior design firm in Albuquerque. We decided to worship at the base chapel, and Chaplain Bill Rhoades wasted no time in getting Peggy and me involved in chapel activities. Peggy joined the choir and became a member of PWOC. I was recruited to teach an adult Sunday school class and joined the PMOC. After five months of retirement, Peggy grew tired of me telling her how to arrange closets and replace the toilet paper in the bathroom. She lovingly suggested I consider another avocation. To ensure the peace, my search for a "real" job in the Albuquerque area began.

Breaking New Ground

It was a pleasure to contact, visit, and leave resumes with several people I had served with at HQ AFOTEC or at times during my Air Force career. They were employed with companies such as BDM, SAIC, DynCorp, Honeywell, and Intel. I also left resumes with the city of Albuquerque and the state of New Mexico. John Brothers of SAIC, with whom I served at HQ AFOTEC, called me a few weeks later regarding a possible opportunity. ENTEK, Inc., a small business

company, had recently won a contract with AFOTEC and was looking for a project director/office manager.

ENTEK, Inc. was a small minority-owned company with headquarters in Arlington, Virginia. Dan Rodriguez, its founder and
CEO, was a former Air Force officer as was Warren Cook and Herb
Brasington. Warren was one of the vice presidents and Herb was the
Western Region Director. The company employed approximately
sixty-five people at the corporate office in Arlington, Virginia. The
contract with AFOTEC was ENTEK's first venture outside the Washington, DC area. It was a multi-year, modeling and simulation contract for the C-17, B-2, and other aerospace systems.

I contacted Herb and was scheduled for an interview in Albuquerque. After our meeting, Herb invited me to corporate headquarters for follow-on interviews with Dan Rodriguez, Warren Cook, and
other senior staff. The interviews went exceptionally well and the
interaction with everyone in the company made me feel at home. I
looked forward to hearing their decision.

An offer arrived from ENTEK a week later on the same day I
received an offer from the state of New Mexico for a job in Santa Fe.
Since my experience was more suited to ENTEK, I accepted their offer. My initial task was to locate and open an office in Albuquerque,
hire people, and establish a successful relationship with the client,
AFOTEC. Herb had previously hired a technical analyst and a secretary, Dr. Sharon Ellis and Trish Keane, respectively. I reviewed
resumes and hired three additional technical analysts.

I found space in a building near the airport and had it built
into an office to accommodate up to ten people. We opened ENTEK's
western office in mid-June 1989. Herb, who lived in Telluride, Colorado and owned a private airplane, flew down to help us celebrate
the official opening. Shortly afterwards, we hired John Von Loh, an

engineer out of California. By the end of the summer, we hired three additional analysts to handle the tasking from AFOTEC.

Sharon Ellis and John Von Loh were highly talented and made my job easy. Within the first year, the initial $49,000 task at AFOTEC increased to over one million dollars of new work. During this time, Herb and I conducted an intensive marketing campaign to grow the company in the West. We were blessed with remarkable success over the next two years.

By the end of our second year, we secured a $3,200,000 dollar contract with the Air Force Space Command in Colorado. In addition, our office was awarded a multi-year subcontract to support the Naval Air Weapons Center at China Lake, California. We were also selected as a subcontractor to work on a $25,000,000 dollar contract with the Air Force Phillips Laboratory at Kirtland, AFB. These rapid successes improved the competitive posture of ENTEK and increased its overall technical staff by twenty per cent.

After two years, Peggy and I decided to build our "dream" house in Albuquerque. The Lord blessed us to find William "Bill" Hooten, a Christian and very successful owner of a construction company. Bill and his wife, Phyllis, helped us design and build a beautiful home with exceptional features that accommodated Grandma, Peggy, and me with comfort and style. The friendship we established with the Hootens was long-lasting and rewarding.

Dan Rodriguez was elated with the progress of the Western office, and I was considered for promotion to vice president. This was great news; however, Herb and one of the company's vice presidents wanted me to continue in my present role. By then, I was confident of my ability to manage technical projects while marketing for new business. Rather than cause a conflict in the company, I resigned from ENTEK and started my own consulting business. I left with the bridges and friendships intact.

My decision to go it alone proved to be the right move at an optimum time. Within two weeks, I secured work with Teledyne Brown Engineering of Colorado Springs, Colorado and Proteus Corporation of Albuquerque. Both of these opportunities involved modeling and simulation, thus enabling me to make a seamless transition. In early 1993, my good friend, retired Colonel Donn Byrnes of DynCorp, introduced me to his boss, George Locke. The local office needed someone with my expertise, and George hired me to begin work three days later. I had become involved with a citizen's activist group, and the flexible working hours at DynCorp allowed me to stay involved in political affairs. My military leadership, discipline, and professionalism proved to be great attributes in resolving issues that impacted our community, city, and state. Consequently, I was drawn deeper into the affairs of New Mexico related to business, education, and government.

The 1993 New Mexico Legislative Session was the battleground for those who supported traditional education versus others who sought to greatly liberalize the curricula of all the schools in New Mexico. The schools already suffered a large drop-out rate, high teen pregnancy, and low test scores. Furthermore, teachers were overloaded, underpaid, and frustrated with the preponderance of social issues. I sided with those citizens who stressed the values as math, English, history, reading, and writing. However, our group was strenuously opposed by the Gay and Lesbian Coalition of New Mexico (GLCNM). I held no rancor toward the GLCNM but strongly opposed their agenda that sought precedence over teaching basic educational values.

Two key bills were the focus of a major battle that year. As a key spokesperson, I soon encountered verbal attacks, threats, and character assassination. Our group requested help from Neal Isbin, the leader of GLCNM, to keep the debates respectful and non-violent. Neal was a small, gentle man who under different circumstances could have been a friend. He respected our position and was responsible for reducing the tension between the two groups during the legislative debates. Using facts, common sense, kindness, and logic, we won the battle but the war was far from over. Searching for a middle ground, Neal and I agreed to meet at a later date to explore the possibilities of resolving our competing objectives. It was not to be. Neal died about a year later.

United We Stand America

Looking back, I clearly see God's hand guiding my every step. That was the case at DynCorp. While there, I worked with retired Lieutenant Colonel Michael Keenan and was completely unaware he paid attention to my political activism. He rang my doorbell one day to tell me about United We Stand America (UWSA) and Ross Perot. I was aware of Mr. Perot's support of the POWs during the Vietnam War and the rescue of his employees from Iran. I also recalled his campaign in 1992 for president, but had not followed his latest activities. Mike explained UWSA was a Perot-sponsored, grassroots organization that was being established in all fifty states to help make government and elected officials more accountable to their constituents. Earlier, Mike supported the Perot campaign and had been recently approached by a UWSA representative seeking to fill the role of the State Director of New Mexico. He said, "Dick, you were made for this job. If you apply and get it, I will work for you." I appreciated Mike's words but had no desire to get involved in politics beyond the local and state level. The work with DynCorp was completed, and I was preparing to take a two-week vacation. Mike called Libby Craft of Mr. Perot's office and told her about my background. Two days later she called and asked me to fax my resume. Libby called back a short time later and arranged an interview with a UWSA representative who was scheduled to pass through Albuquerque.

Things were moving a bit fast, but my inner sense cautioned me to comply with Libby's request. I discussed this with Peggy, and she agreed I should follow through with the interview. Meanwhile, I learned as much as possible about Mr. Perot and UWSA. Mr. Perot's commitment to our country, his family, employees, and humanity in general was astounding. His personal financing of UWSA to enable people across America to take part in their government was especially impressive. I was eager to learn more and looked forward to meeting the representative from Dallas.

I met Rusty Stricker at the airport two days later. He was particularly interested in how I organized my recent political activities to wage a successful campaign during the legislative session in Santa Fe. He also wanted to hear my opinions about government programs, spending, and the overall political process at the local, state, and national levels. After nearly four hours, Rusty suggested I come to Dallas to meet Mr. Perot.

The following Monday morning, Rusty called and asked if I could meet Mr. Perot on Wednesday. The plans for New Mexico had been moved up, and I was a candidate for the State Director's job. I agreed to go to Dallas and tried to mentally prepare to meet a man of Mr. Perot's stature. I called my friend, retired Lieutenant General Leo Marquez, to seek his advice. During lunch together, he said, "Dick, just be yourself. Perot is just a man like you and me. He puts his pants on one leg at a time. Don't sweat it. You'll do just fine." General Marquez's words were reassuring and I felt better about the pending interview.

I arrived the night before the interview and met the UWSA staff the following morning. The energy and excitement in the office were everywhere. Rusty Stricker introduced me to Darcy Anderson, the UWSA Director; Sharon Holman and April Cotton, Director and Assistant of Public Affairs; Bill Walker, Texas State Director; and other key staff members. Later, Darcy took me to meet Mr. Perot. I was told to expect about fifteen minutes with him because he was scheduled that night to be on Larry King Live TV show. I was still apprehensive about meeting this accomplished billionaire, an event unsurpassed by any other in my life. Nevertheless, I tried to heed General Marquez's advice as much as possible.

Mr. Perot's office was located on the seventeenth floor of a nearby beautiful office building. His suite housed an impressive array of historical artifacts, memorabilia, and art works. These included an original copy of the Magna Carta, a copy of the Declaration of Independence, portraits of famous American patriots, and souvenirs from around the world. I was greeted by his executive assistant, Sandra Dotson. Within minutes, Mr. Perot came in and greeted me like an old friend. He seemed genuinely pleased to see me and immediately allayed my fears by his infectious smile and down-to-earth persona. I was equally impressed when we entered his office. The desks and walls held numerous photographs of his beautiful wife and children at various times in their lives. I knew instantly this man loved his family as much as I loved Peggy and our children. This, plus his obvious love for our country, confirmed we had much in common.

Mr. Perot began by asking me if I knew the late General "Chappie" James and several other Air Force personalities. We spent the next fifteen minutes sharing stories about mutual acquaintances before he spoke about the mission of UWSA and his hopes for a better America. Forty-five minutes passed before Sandra politely reminded Mr. Perot of the next event on his calendar. He excused himself simply by saying he looked forward to having me on the UWSA team and instructed Darcy to work out the details of getting me on board.

Darcy and I returned to his office to make arrangements for me
to join UWSA. I was excited and ready to sign on until the matter of
compensation was discussed. The salary offered each state director
was based upon Mr. Perot's intent to hire those who truly wanted
to make a contribution to the country. The wind went out of my
sails when I learned the amount offered was approximately $30,000
per year less than I was currently earning. While appreciating Mr.
Perot's purpose, I was not ready to make such a personal sacrifice. I
needed some time to think about the opportunity and promised to
respond in a few days.

My return trip to Albuquerque was very unsettling. I was torn
between wanting to join UWSA and the sufficiency of the salary offered. Later, Peggy and I discussed the pros and cons of such a decision. As we meditated and prayed, the night of Dr. Martin Luther
King's death rushed back to my mind. Twenty-five years earlier, I
had begged God to show me what I could do to help my country. At
that time, I was just a captain in the Air Force. As a retired colonel,
and reasonably secure, the questions now were did I still have the
desire to serve in the spirit of Dr. King? Was I more concerned about
money and pride? Was I willing to make that kind of a personal sacrifice in order to serve my fellow Americans? Who would even care?

As a Christian, I was challenged to work for God rather than
for man. I had fought to protect America from all enemies, foreign
and domestic. But in the 1990s, our beloved nation faced an insidi-
ous threat from within. This enemy was characterized by a national
malaise of apathy, indifference, moral decadence, and vestiges of illiteracy and poverty. Moreover, many citizens no longer trusted our
national leaders and elected officials, thereby withdrawing from active participation in the political process. UWSA provided me an
opportunity to rededicate my life to helping preserve our country
for which so many had sacrificed. The critical question was could
democracy as we knew it be saved? The challenge for me was even

greater than serving twenty-six years in the Air Force. Ultimately, Peggy and I decided that my entire life had been a preparation for the task before us. We concluded the Lord's sufficiency and the salary Mr. Perot offered were reasons enough to take another leap of faith. Mr. Perot had reignited the fire and passion that propelled me forward throughout my life. There was a new horizon before me, and the Lord equipped me with wings to soar toward it without fear and trepidation. I called Darcy to let him know I was ready to roll up my sleeves and go to work.

Mr. Perot articulated his vision for our country in the books, United We Stand America, Not for Sale at Any Price, and Save Your Job, Save Our Country. The values he espoused about patriotism, service to the country, and family were those that had kept me committed in the Air Force for twenty-six years. As a taxpayer, I fully appreciated and understood the pressing need for economic, education, and government reform in our country. Consequently, embracing the mission of UWSA was an easy choice for me.

My priority was to interact with previous Perot supporters in New Mexico. In 1993, the population of the state was approximately 1.5 million people in three congressional districts and thirty-three counties. Over 9,000 New Mexicans voted for Mr. Perot in the 1992 election. Ed Campbell, the UWSA Western Region Director, and I scheduled a series of initial visits to the major cities in New Mexico. Our first rally was held in Albuquerque where 200 people attended still energized from the earlier Perot campaign. The solid core of leaders and volunteers were particularly encouraging. One of these was John Bishop of Santa Fe who led the petition drive to get Mr. Perot on the ballot in New Mexico. Another was Bill Turner of Albuquerque who coordinated the Perot campaign throughout the state. Bill also organized the visits to the state for Mr. Perot and Admiral Stockdale. Bill Hooten, a very successful home developer, provided a follow-on meeting facility; and Carol Rickert, a commercial realtor, facilitated acquiring a permanent UWSA office. Others offered temporary office space, secretarial support, legal assistance, and fundraising skills. In addition, an appreciable number were identified as "foot soldiers" ready and willing to go work for UWSA. One of these was Dyan Jojola, a member of the Isleta Pueblo. Dyan became the UWSA point person who facilitated my visits to the nineteen Native American Pueblos in New Mexico, three Apache tribes, and part of the Navajo Nation.

My visits confirmed significant dissatisfaction with the way our nation's affairs were conducted by the Clinton Administration as well as by members of the U.S. Congress. Many citizens no longer had confidence their interests were considered in decisions regarding federal programs, spending, and national priorities. In addition, they were increasingly savvy about the need for campaign and lobbying reform, health care, tax reform, and term limits. Clearly, there was a wide-spread hunger for change. Instead of dropping out, UWSA supporters were motivated by Mr. Perot to take action to help fix the broken political system in our country. They passionately wanted a better life for themselves, their children, and grandchildren. Thus, mobilizing the state into an effective voice looked very promising.

Thanks to Carol Rickert, I was able to open the primary UWSA office in a prominent location in Albuquerque. Carol also interceded in soliciting support from her associates in the realty business. One of the greatest volunteers in Albuquerque was Zoe Ciscon who became my able executive assistant, office manager, and secretary. Her prior office experience at Los Alamos Laboratory was invaluable to the entire operation in New Mexico. Zoe put in an incredible number of volunteer hours virtually seven days a week for over a year. She also recruited and directed teams of supporters for all the planned activities in the state. The outstanding collective support of dedicated workers resulted in New Mexico being organized into an effective political voice by mid October 1993.

While UWSA was being organized in the fifty states, President Clinton launched a major effort to implement the North American Free Trade Agreement (NAFTA). This program was backed by a huge group of lobbyists of the world's largest corporations and by many members of Congress. Proponents promised NAFTA would create hundreds of thousands of new, high-wage jobs in America. They also vowed better living standards in the United States, Mexico, and Canada; improved environmental conditions; and the transformation of Mexico from a poor developing country into a booming new market for U.S. exports.

The truth was, NAFTA obscured its real detriment to the working people in America. Instead of providing mutual benefits for the three countries involved, it granted foreign investors new rights and privileges that promoted relocation of factories and jobs abroad. It also facilitated the privatization and deregulation of essential services such as water, energy, and health care. In addition, NAFTA contained 900 pages of mandatory rules that required each nation to realign its domestic laws - regardless of previous policies enacted at the local, state, and national level.

Mr. Perot led a UWSA national movement to enlighten the American people and to persuade members of Congress to vote against NAFTA. A nationwide media and television campaign culminated with a large group of UWSA staff working Capitol Hill November 15-18, 1993. Teams were dispatched to specific Senate and House member offices to advocate a "NO" vote on the up or down vote on NAFTA. I focused on the Congressional Black Caucus (CBC). In 1993, all forty members of CBC were Democrats, and they represented the largest and most populated urban areas in the U.S. We found an ally in Congressman Kweisi Mfume, Chairman of the CBC. He was staunchly against NAFTA and welcomed the support provided by Mr. Perot. However, thirty of the forty members planned to support President Clinton on NAFTA. I arranged a visit between Mr.

Perot and Congressman Mfume to discuss efforts to win back some of the CBC members. Congressman Mfume provided me a list of CBC members who were uncommitted or who might be persuaded to change their planned vote.

The battle against NAFTA was also supported by Reverend Jesse Jackson, labor unions, environmentalists, and consumer and religious groups. They believed that poor people, African Americans, Hispanics, and other minority workers would be adversely affected by the wholesale loss of jobs caused by NAFTA. Had it not been for the support of Republicans in Congress, NAFTA would have failed. On the late evening of November 17, 1993, the bill passed 234 "AYES" to 200 "NAYS." Of these AYES, 132 were Republicans and 102 Democrats. The agreement was signed in December and became law January 1, 1994. The sad impact of this sellout by members of the U.S. Congress would come to light in the years that followed.

By February 1994, UWSA was organized in all fifty states with elected State Directors. To ensure cohesion, cooperation, and common purpose, the state directors were invited to Dallas for orientation briefings and training. A key outcome of this conference was the identification and consensus of critical issues that needed to be articulated by state organizations in the upcoming 1994 mid-term elections in the U. S. Congress. The efforts in New Mexico were facilitated by the enthusiastic support of volunteers. The meeting hall provided by Bill Hooten enabled UWSA to hold its meetings and to sponsor public debates by candidates for city, state, and national offices. Members from across the state hosted similar meetings and encouraged candidates to address the critical issues that faced our nation and their respective communities.

Dyan Jojola, one of our volunteers and activists, deserves special mention. She was one of the most prominent Native Americans involved in the UWSA movement. Dyan had a phenomenal drive and was totally committed to helping her people on the Isleta Reservation, in the state, and nationwide. At one hundred pounds, four feet and ten inches tall, she was a powerhouse of energy who lit up an entire room with her attitude and infectious smile. Dyan produced a weekly public television program to enlighten the citizens throughout Albuquerque. She graciously interviewed members of Congress, governors, candidates, educators, and others from around the state and nation. Dyan expended her energy, passion, and zeal to make sure America was truly "united" and inclusive. Her total humility in putting others first made her one of the greatest Americans I ever had the privilege of knowing.

In September 1994, I was selected as the Southwest Region Director for twelve states from Nevada to Mississippi. My new responsibility required extensive traveling and speaking engagements, television appearances, and radio broadcasts in dozens of venues across the twelve states. These trips put me in touch with citizens of every imaginable race, creed, culture, and circumstance. UWSA also provided me the platform from which to share my passion for a greater America.

Retired USAF Colonel Cres Baca was appointed by the UWSA National Headquarters as my replacement in New Mexico. Cres was a native New Mexican with family roots in the state dating back nearly 300 years. He graduated from Park College in Parkville, Missouri with a Bachelor of Arts degree in History and Sociology. He received a Master of Arts degree in Administration of Justice from Webster University, Missouri. Cres' military experience spanned over 35 years in worldwide assignments. He also had extensive experience in leadership and management of large, diverse organizations throughout New Mexico. I met Cres while we both served on active duty at Kirtland AFB and was extremely pleased to have him as a partner in UWSA.

UWSA had a significant impact on elections at the local, state, and national level in November 1994. The organization was credited with helping to elect New Mexico's Governor Gary E. Johnson and Lieutenant Governor Walter D. Bradley, Republicans; re-election of Republican Congressman Steve Schiff; and the election of numerous other local officials. By the end of the year, the members of UWSA had made significant contributions toward improving the political process in New Mexico and elsewhere in the nation.

In January 1995, UWSA celebrated its two-year anniversary, and Russ Verney was selected the new Executive Director. Russ was a decorated U. S. Army veteran, worked in the Civil Service, became a political consultant, and joined the Perot team in 1992. In addition to his strong leadership skills, Russ brought to UWSA a wide range of experience that included media relations, public and community relations, public policy analysis, and team building.

The National Board of Directors met and endorsed an aggressive program to expand UWSA membership in every neighborhood across the country. Local chapters were allowed considerable flexibility in organizing according to the circumstances and dynamics in each state. The objective was to empower members to use their creative talents to ensure a better country for our children and grandchildren. They were encouraged to organize as clubs, chapters, committees, or other entities and to get involved with recruiting, fundraising, or other self-sustaining activities.

UWSA became recognized as a force with which to be reckoned, and members were sought out for advice and/or support. In April 1995, I was called upon by Senator Pete Domenici, Chairman of the Senate Finance Committee, to testify before the Senate Budget Committee Hearings. My testimony regarding the need for education, government, and political reform helped justify several critical state and national issues for the Congressional Record. I was also asked to provide input on National Defense-related issues to the Congressional Black Caucus Alternative Budget for 1995.

Despite the rhetoric of both political parties and presidential candidates, by the middle of 1995, many citizens all across America felt the political system was still broken. They considered there was little real difference between the parties once candidates were elected. Mr. Perot took this feedback to heart and sponsored an historical event August 11-13, 1995. He hosted a UWSA Conference in Dallas, Texas entitled, Preparing Our Country for the 21st Century. Some of America's most prominent experts, politicians, and decision makers attended and spoke at this historic conference that addressed the critical issues that challenged our country well into the next century. The participants included twenty members of the U. S. Senate and House of Representatives and ten Republican presidential candidates. Others were the Reverend Jesse Jackson, Alan Keyes, former Congresswoman Barbara Jordan, and Thomas "Mack" McLarty, Counselor to President Clinton.

Approximately 4,000 concerned citizens from all across the country paid their own expenses to Dallas and participated in the three-day conference. They were dedicated to making America a better place by listening, learning, and participating in interactive workshops where they shared their ideas on problems our nation faced. The conference was also attended by over 1,000 representatives from television, radio, and the news media from the U. S. and twenty-four foreign countries. The gathering was an unequivocal success. Once again, Ross Perot lit the flame of determination and inspiration in the thousands who attended, listened in, or read about it. More than ever, they were unwilling to accept the stale rhetoric and false promises offered up by elected officials and candidates for office. They were committed to doing everything possible to ensure a better country for the generations that followed.

The Reform Party

As UWSA grew and carried its message across scores of cities, towns, and communities, there was a persistent message from the people. An alternative to the Democratic and Republican parties was desperately needed. By early summer, Mr. Perot directed Russ Verney to begin a low-key exploration of the feasibility, practicality, and viability of forming a third party. Russ identified ballot access as the major hurdle that had to be overcome if the party expected to participate in the 1996 election. Ballot access meant getting voters to register with the proposed new party. Compounding the problem, each state had a different set of rules and timetables. Of the fifty states, California posed the greatest challenge. After careful consideration of the difficulties, likelihood of success, and the determination of the UWSA members, Mr. Perot gave the go-ahead.

A team met at the headquarters in Dallas to select a name for the party and to develop a platform. As a result, the REFORM PARTY was established with a platform that included principles of the highest ethical standards for the White House and Congress, a balanced budget, campaign finance reform, term limits, and a new tax system. The platform also stressed carefully developed plans to deal with Medicare, Medicaid, Social Security, and restrictions on domestic and foreign lobbyists.

In September 1995, Russ Verney led the entire UWSA team to Los Angeles to conduct the voter registration drive. Mr. Perot kicked off the drive with a rally in nearby Orange County that was attended by several thousand excited citizens. We had the enormous task of getting 89,000 new registrants in about three weeks. Teams were dispatched to major metropolitan areas throughout the state. Our goal was to meet as many people as possible and get them to sign up with the Reform Party. We covered job fairs, sporting events, fairs and festivals, shopping malls, stores, bowling alleys, movie theaters, and unemployment offices. Tables and in some cases, ironing boards were set up on sidewalks in front of city halls, post offices, and other public places. Some of us solicited family and friends to help with the drive. Others successfully engaged local media, public television, and prominent, well-known personalities. An incredible result was achieved when approximately 120,000 California voters registered with the Reform Party in just three weeks!

Encouraged by the success in California, we continued registration drives in the remaining forty-nine states. Russ Verney led the effort while Mr. Perot crisscrossed the country holding rallies in key states and locations. People everywhere responded enthusiastically to the Reform Party. They believed it could make a real difference in their lives. Consequently, many eagerly enrolled and signed our petitions.

The Reform Party had a unique opportunity to attract thousands of conservative African-Americans and other minorities who also were seeking a new political home. The clarity and validity of the party's principles had universal appeal in every community. Our message was delivered with credibility, sensitivity, and sincerity. We demonstrated a consistent focus on economic and government reform and related how such changes could eventually result in a greater prosperity for all Americans.

We worked through the winter, braving frigid weather, austere conditions, and long hours. The challenges were daunting and sometimes seemed impossible. Russ Verney's leadership and the outstanding headquarters support of Sharon Holman, Renee Jordan, and others were invaluable to the teams in the field. Despite the hurdles, the indomitable spirit of the entire Perot organization got the job done. We secured ballot access in all fifty states in just eleven months! And "they" said it couldn't be done.

The next challenge for the Reform Party was to identify candidates for president and vice president. Although Mr. Perot spent a huge sum of his personal wealth sponsoring UWSA and the voter registration drive, he left the door open for others to step up. The former Governor of Colorado, Richard D. Lamm, was the only person to announce his candidacy for President on the Reform Party ticket. However, the Federal Election Commission indicated that only Mr. Perot was eligible to secure federal matching funds since he campaigned as an Independent in 1992. Consequently, Mr. Perot entered the race the summer of 1996.

The Reform Party kicked into high gear mid-summer 1996. The date and site of the inaugural national convention was set for August 11th in Long Beach, California. I received the surprise of my life when Russ Verney called me to ask if I would be willing to introduce Mr. Perot at the convention. There simply are no words to express the humility and privilege I felt. After telling Russ yes, Peggy and I sat down and prayed about his request. We believed it was a blessing from God, and once again, my mind flashed back to Dr. Martin Luther King, Jr. Somehow, this unprecedented opportunity seemed linked to my offer to the Lord the night Dr. King died. Regardless, we believed God would give me the guidance and wisdom needed to do the best job possible.

I arrived in Dallas a few days later to meet with Mr. Perot, Russ, the campaign team, and speech writers. True to form, Mr. Perot thanked me for agreeing to the task. To this day, the man's graciousness causes me to smile. We discussed the agenda, convention, and the outline of the message Mr. Perot planned to give. I was also provided a draft of a suggested speech to use. I returned to the UWSA office to review the materials and consider how best to make the introduction. The suggested speech was good, but I sensed more was needed. Many questions and comments regarding Mr. Perot had been made over the past three years, so I felt the public had a keen interest in knowing more about him. He was a very private man who rarely let anyone know about his huge heart for the poor and unfortunate. I decided to ask if he would allow me to insert a few examples of his great philanthropic activities. The answer was a resounding no. Nevertheless, I tried to make a case for it. His second no was a little less emphatic, but I decided to leave the matter alone.

I received another surprise when Mr. Perot called me directly and said, "Dick, I thought further about what you said, so I asked my sister, Bette, to put something together for you to look at. Do you have time to come over?" You know what my answer was, but use your imagination to envision the speed at which I went to Mr. Perot's office. When I arrived, his sister, Bette, and daughter Carolyn, welcomed me very warmly. They presented a list of charities, events, and awards dating back many years. I sat alone in an office and read about the phenomenal generosity of Mr. Perot. He rose from a humble beginning to his position of great wealth and prominence. He counted it a blessing to have been able to pursue and live the "American Dream" while possessing a deep compassion for those less fortunate. Throughout his life, Mr. Perot faithfully shared his blessings with countless individuals and organizations. He had a special interest in underprivileged children and gave over $100 million to a wide variety of charities. Many of these were directed specifically to minorities such as the NAACP.

My eyes clouded over, and I had to sit back to digest the truths of Mr. Perot's story that should be told. After selecting several examples, I went to get his approval to use them in my speech. He agreed, and I revised my speech accordingly. We completed our preparation in Dallas and prepared for the big night in Long Beach.

August 11, 1996 was a day to remember. It ranks as one of the most significant experiences of my life. My task that night was easy because I spoke from my heart, and I had come to know Mr. Perot up close and personal. I respected him for being a great American patriot and a God-sent humanitarian; but I loved him as a friend. Considering my total life's journey up to that point, it was a night for which we both were born. Only God could have directed our paths to such a historical intersection.

Immediately following the Long Beach presentations, I received numerous calls from across the country asking if I was Mr. Perot's running mate on the Reform Party's ticket. Some of these calls were received by Peggy at our home at all hours of the day and night. Although very flattering, we directed the callers to the party headquarters in Dallas. Within a few days, Mr. Perot announced Patrick "Pat" Choate as his running mate. In 1996, this fifty-five year old Texan was an economist who co-founded the Congressional Economic Leadership Institute in 1986. He served as its chair or co-chair for eighteen years. Pat has a B.A. from University of Texas at Arlington and a M.A. and Ph.D. from University of Oklahoma, all in economics.

In the interim, Mr. Perot asked me to help develop a studio lead-in for the thirty-minute speeches he planned to run during the campaign. We used the part where I compared Mr. Perot to Dr. Martin Luther King, Jr. This was another easy burden, and I was honored to be involved. The six-minute footage ran on three of the five presentations. In addition, I was selected to be the National Spokesperson and Coordinator for Minority Community Outreach for the Reform Party and tasked to take its message to the inner cities of the country. Approximately eighty-four percent of African Americans lived in the metropolitan areas from coast to coast. My itinerary included Los Angeles, Las Vegas, Denver, Kansas City, Dallas, Houston, Oklahoma City, New Orleans, Birmingham, Miami, Washington, DC, and New York City. With the help of state chairpersons, directors, and local activists, I visited scores of venues, conducted dozens of radio and TV interviews, and spoke in many churches. Getting minorities to break their allegiance to the Democratic Party was a hard sell, but the reaction to our message was encouraging. More than a few were ready to hear Mr. Perot debate incumbent President Bill Clinton and Republican candidate Senator Bob Dole. It was not to be.

After the 1992 campaign, the Commission on Presidential Debates (CPD) changed the rules about how candidates must qualify to participate in presidential debates. The CPD was a non-profit corporation headed by the past chairmen of both the Democratic and Republican parties. In 1996, it ruled that Mr. Perot did not qualify to participate due to certain vague criteria. The CPD's disqualification was based on a shortage of Perot's endorsement by "a substantial number of major new organizations." The problem was the CPD decided what "substantial" was on a case-by-case basis. Since Mr. Perot performed extremely well in the 1992 debates, this was a devastating blow to his current campaign.

Like many unexplained events in the political arena, the action by the CPD was a disservice to the American people. The ruling forced the Perot campaign to rely on the thirty-minute TV commercials which could not possibly reach the viewers during news coverage of the debates. Despite the valiant efforts of Mr. Perot, Mr. Choate, and the Reform Party members, the candidates received only nine percent of the vote. Following the 1996 election, the CPD certified the Reform Party as a national political party eligible for federal campaign matching funds. This historic first did little to erase their detrimental and biased decision that cheated the American people out of hearing Mr. Perot debate the real issues in the campaign.

In 1997, Mr. Perot relinquished control of the Reform Party to its nationally elected officers. In 1998, Jesse Ventura was elected governor of Minnesota on a Reform Party ticket. This was the highest office won by a national third party candidate in the twentieth century. The Reform Party also received more votes than all the other third parties combined, thus becoming America's largest third party.

The above accomplishments reflect the tremendous contributions of Mr. Perot to the political process in America. History will judge his dedication and strivings to make our country a better place in which to live. He spent over $100 million of his personal funds to wake up this country and inspired millions of citizens to get involved to take back their country. His persistent exhortations forced the national politicians and elected leaders to deal with the real issues that challenged our nation. All the while, Mr. Perot continued to be one of the most generous and humble philanthropists in the world. Today, the seeds of his contributions and labor are growing all across America and around the globe. I am very proud to say he gave greater purpose to my life and enabled me to answer a higher calling. In addition, he enabled me to leave a personal legacy of service for my children, grandchildren, and generations that follow. No words can adequately characterize this great American patriot. Thankfully, God is the ultimate judge of our work on this earth. When the "roll is called up yonder," I just want to be near enough to hear the Lord say, "Well done, Ross Perot, my true and faithful servant." Ross Perot is *a quintessential Uncaged Eagle*!

Grandma's Homegoing

In February 1997, my mother-in-law, Elsie Caulk Hairston, passed away after a brief illness. She lived in our household for nearly twenty-seven years and was just two weeks away from her ninety-eighth birthday. I sat quietly on her bed and reflected over our time together. Grandma, as she was called by all who knew her, was truly a God-send in our family. She was a model of faith, hope, and love; she was the calm in the midst of storms. Grandma was there for Peggy and the children when I left for my second combat tour in Vietnam. She was there when I came home a year later tired, disillusioned, bitter, and angry over the futility of that war. Her prayers sustained me through my struggles, and she never gave up when I strayed from my Christian teachings. When I failed as a husband and father, Grandma still covered me with her love and prayers. The Lord allowed her to witness His intervention in my wayward life, and I am certain her intercession with Him saved me from the wrath I deserved.

Grandma didn't just love my family and me, she loved everybody. I can't remember a single person she didn't love. She dearly loved her children, her sisters and brothers, good people and bad people, sinners and Christians alike. In thirty-five years, I never heard her say one disparaging word about anybody. She just loved people like Jesus called us to do. Grandma was my close personal friend, confidant, and tremendous prayer partner, but she did most of the praying. My success in the Air Force and in life was due largely to the ready access to God made possible through her direct line to Heaven. She was a virtuous woman.

> *"Many others have done exceedingly well, but she surpassed them all. Favor is deceitful, and beauty is vain: but a woman that feareth the Lord, she shall be praised."* NIV Prov 31:29-30.

Grandma was *An Uncaged Eagle*.

Ross Perot and the MLK Family

The remarkable grace of God is reflected in His perfect timing for events in our lives. Two other powerful truths are His faithfulness and answers to prayers. The Lord heard my deep groaning the night Dr. Martin Luther King, Jr. was killed. Thirty years later, He decided I was ready to help continue Dr. King's work in a very specific way. He chose Mr. Perot to create this amazing opportunity.

In late 1998, Martin Luther King, III was elected President of the Southern Christian Leadership Conference (SCLC) headquartered in Atlanta, Georgia. Forty years earlier, Dr. King, Reverend Ralph Abernathy, and others established SCLC to institutionalize nonviolent resistance as the guiding principle for the civil rights movement. After several years of struggle, the organization was challenged to remain relevant in a complex and dynamic environment. Martin III needed financial and professional help to chart a new course for the 21st Century. Several individuals in Dallas were members of the local SCLC chapter and knew of Mr. Perot's philanthropic outreach. They arranged a meeting with Mr. Perot, Martin III, and SCLC representatives. Mr. Perot invited me to attend the meeting and to offer comments. Subsequently, he hired me to provide on-site support in Atlanta. The five-month project was another extremely fulfilling effort in my life.

We assembled a team in Atlanta to develop the SCLC Transition Plan for the 21st Century. The goal was to prepare the organization for an orderly transition from a reactive, crisis-centered organization to a proactive agent for positive social change. I worked in the original headquarters of SCLC just down the street from the historic Ebenezer Baptist Church, the King Center and National Monument, and Dr. King's birthplace. Often, I spent time in the small conference room where Dr. King had held meetings with his associates. Sometimes I sat quietly, meditated, and prayed for guidance and wisdom. Just being in that building gave me the spiritual inspiration needed to complete the task at hand.

In addition to working daily with Martin III, I met with his brother, Dexter, and former Ambassador Andrew Young who was a close personal friend of the King family. Later, I had the honor of meeting with Mrs. Coretta Scott King to gather her views regarding the direction SCLC should take. One afternoon, we spent over three hours in the home purchased by Dr. King. This was an extraordinary experience as Mrs. King was a most beautiful and gracious lady. She spoke at length about the beginning of SCLC, its growth and decline, and the need to be a Christ-centered outreach organization again. She reiterated the unwavering faith of her late husband in God and his profound love for America and the world. This, she said, must be embraced by all who sought to make Dr. King's dream a reality. At the conclusion of our meeting, I was invited to attend worship service with her the next day. There I met Dr. King's only surviving sibling, Dr. Christine King Farris, a professor at Spellman College in Atlanta. Sitting in the pew between those two ladies that day was a very moving and memorable event.

By mid November, the team completed a five-year plan that was subsequently presented to the SCLC Board of Directors for approval. Key elements included a streamlined mission statement, redefined goal and objectives, specific programs, a revised organizational structure, and a realistic list of required resources. My task was completed in early 1999, and I flew to Dallas to give Mr. Perot a final report. His generous support provided SCLC the "jump start" it needed and a realistic plan for the 21st Century and beyond. SCLC now had a way forward, but its success would depend upon the leadership of Martin III and the visionary support of the Board of Directors.

True Freedom

After my work with SCLC, I returned to Albuquerque to resume work as a Consultant for Business and Economic Development. Fate continued to present many interesting opportunities in my life. I was hired by Century Aviation Corporation, a small start-up company, to build business jets in the city. My job was to help find interested investors and/or potential buyers. Roy Johnston, Vice President and General Manager, was my primary contact. He was a retired WW II Naval pilot with several photos and mementos in his office. One of these was a stick grip taken from a crash landing he survived while a student pilot. The discussion that followed rocked both of us back on our heels. Roy was the pilot in the crash I witnessed in Oxnard, California nearly fifty-five years earlier! We sat for a long time pondering the odds of such a coincidence and the reasons for it. The answer remains hidden somewhere in the fullness of God's time.

Roy and I continued the search for potential investors in Albuquerque and the state. I solicited the help of Dyan Jojola to target the growing wealth derived from the casinos of the Native Americans. We came close, but Century Aviation was surpassed by a competitor that established a plant to manufacture small business jets in Albuquerque.

After the incredible coincidence of meeting Roy Johnston, the allure of Oxnard, California tugged at my heart. I wanted to experience my boyhood fantasy of taking off from Oxnard Airfield that still existed. Earlier in the decade, my sister, Zella, Cousin Annie Felder, and I initiated the first Anderson-Davis-Toliver biennial family reunions. We successfully held gatherings in Shreveport, Louisiana; Dallas, Texas; Las Vegas, Nevada; and Anaheim, California. Since scores of Davis descendants resided in the Oxnard area, it was chosen as the site for the 1999 reunion. More than 200 family members gathered for an outstanding event, but I had a special thrill.

The small Oxnard Airport served as a base for small commuter airlines and private aviation. Its Cessna-172s were down for maintenance, so my son, Mike, and I rented one from nearby Camarillo Airport. We flew back to Oxnard, landed, and requested a few extra minutes on the runway. I held the brakes while revving the engine and tried to envision what the young WW II pilots felt just before takeoff. With my heart pumping and mind full of emotion, we roared down the runway and took off into memory lane. It was a sensational experience that had taken me fifty-five years to achieve. As my son and I turned out over the Pacific and headed back to Camarillo, I thanked God for allowing me to fly for a large part of my life. I still smile because of it today.

I continued my employment with ARES Corporation and EMT, Inc as a technical consultant/project director while accepting other opportunities to serve my community. These included appointments by Governor Gary Johnson of New Mexico, and consent of the Senate, to serve on the New Mexico Public Safety Advisory Commission and the Board of Regents, University of New Mexico (UNM). As a Commissioner of Public Safety, I shared the oversight of New Mexico State Police with seven others. The stark contrast between the responsibilities of this appointment and the tribulations in my early life was extraordinary.

As the first African American regent in the 113-year history of UNM, I had another unique opportunity to give back. The seven-member UNM Board of Regents is given authority to govern the University, including fiduciary responsibility for assets and programs, establishment of goals and policies, and oversight of the functioning of the University. Specific duties include appointment of a President; periodic reviews of the mission, goals, objectives of the University; development of a long-range campus master plan for the physical development of the University; and the creation of colleges, schools and branches. UNM is a Carnegie Research I University with a $1.2 billion budget and 32,000 students at five campuses. As New Mexico's state largest university, UNM is home to the state's only schools of law, medicine, pharmacy and architecture. During my six-year tenure, I had the privilege of serving as Chairman of Academic and Student Affairs Committee, a member of the UNM Hospital Committee, and as a key member on the Facility and Finance Committee. Serving as a regent was one of the most rewarding experiences of my post military career. Service to others continues to be a fulfilling and important part of my life today.

The twenty years since my retirement from the Air Force have been an incredible journey, and I can't thank the Lord enough for His abundant blessings. The greatest of these has been the growth in our extended family: daughters Stephany Snowden and Renata Mills; sons Elliott Tate and Avieon Morgan; Renea's husband Grover Lewis, III; and Michael's wife, Nicole and their three beautiful daughters, Maya, Marissa, and Alina. And the circle continues.

Looking back over my entire life, I am filled with awe and amazement. He carried me through trials, tribulation, strife, and the perils of war. The past ten years have been filled with opportunities for me as a writer and motivational speaker at home and abroad. I joined four original Tuskegee Airmen on a motivational tour to Germany, Iraq, Kuwait, and Spain. In 2007, I represented the Officer's Christian Fellowship for several days visiting members of the Air Force, Marines, and Navy in Hawaii. My latest opportunity to serve was in 2009 at the request of the 18th TFW, Kadena, Japan. During the Martin Luther King Memorial week, I had the privilege of speaking to nearly 1,000 people at several venues, including four church services. In all of this, the Lord deserves the glory and praise, for nothing I have achieved or done has been apart from Him. As I look to the future, there is much I want to write about and to use my lessons in life to encourage and motivate others. Above all else, my intention for all tomorrows is to live everyday in such a way that honors Jesus Christ, my Lord and Savior.

I sincerely appreciate the opportunity you have given me to share my story. Hopefully, this book has been inspiring and meaningful to you. I pray you've seen the omnipotent hand of God throughout my life as well as in those of whom I've written. It is my deepest hope that you believe there is nothing in your life that cannot be overcome. In God, all things are possible. In my opinion, as long as there is life, we should strive to reach beyond our human limitations. Only when we totally surrender our *finite* selves to God, can we appropriate His *infinite* strength to be all that we were created to be. As we strive to live our earthly lives to the fullest, there is still a higher realm to be reached. It is beyond where eagles fly. It is the place where true freedom is realized. True freedom allows us to transcend the constraints of anger, doubt, fear, and uncertainty. It enables us to act selflessly, forgive all injuries, love unconditionally, and humbly serve without expectation of rewards. It is the spiritual state that reaches the very presence of our Creator.

RETIREMENT YEARS

Renea, Gail, and Mike

Daniel

Ginger

Michael
Getting His Pilot Wings

The Tolivers at the Air Force Academy
(L-R) Renea, Ginger, David, Jr., Peggy, me, and Michael.

RETIREMENT YEARS

Family Reunion
Michael, Renea, and Gail
With Peggy and Me

Ginger, Husband York, Megan,
Nicholas, and Angela Thrope

Skiing in
New Mexico

Still Sweethearts

RETIREMENT YEARS

Grover and Renea Lewis

Nicole and Michael

Renata, Nicole, Michael, Renea, Grover, and Gail

Stephanie Snowden

Gail, Peggy, Maya, Marissa, Nicole, Me, and Mike

Grandson Quinton, Elizabeth and Sophie Jones

Family Reunion
(L-R) Wendell, David, Me, Zella, and Ray

Medal of Honor Recipient
Bernie Fisher, Peggy, Realla Fisher and Me

EPILOGUE

COMING FULL CIRCLE

Reunion in Israel

When gathering data to write this book, I searched for the F-15 aircraft I picked up at McDonnell Douglas Aircraft Company in December 1975. The exhaustive search led to retired Brigadier General Moshe Melnik and the Israeli Air Force Museum near Beersheba, Israel. Moshe was one of the five IAF pilots I helped train at Luke AFB in 1976. In May 2007 circumstances brought us together again after nearly 31 years. Peggy, our daughter Gail, and I fulfilled a long-held desire to visit the Holy Land. Moshe graciously hosted us for much of the trip.

One afternoon, Moshe, Aharon Berenson, another former Israeli Pilot, and I stood high on the wind-swept pinnacle called the "Finger of Israel." It is wedged tightly between the borders of Lebanon and Syria, a stone's throw from each. We stood on a strategic post that overlooks the entire Golan Heights. The area has been contested by the three nations for generations, but on that day it was quiet and peaceful.

In the hazy distance, Mt. Hermon rose majestically to over 9,000 feet above the lush green valley of the Jordan River. This vantage point provided a breath-taking panoramic view of Israel's modern agricultural area that feeds the nation of nearly seven million people. Further south, the ancient city of Tiberias and towns of Capernaum, Bethsaida, and Magdala surround the Sea of Galilee. There, according to Biblical history, Jesus of Nazareth recruited His first disciples, performed miracles, and established the foundation for the Christian faith that has continued for over 2000 years. Unconstrained by racial, religious, or denominational differences, we stood in solemn wonder gazing over the hallowed ground that the patriarch Abraham trod centuries ago. The aviation careers in our respective Air Forces provided a mutual bond of professionalism, but that day we could be called descendents of Abraham, two by ancestral birthright and one through Christian faith.

Peggy, Gail, and I visited Tiberias, Caesarea, Beersheba, Jerusalem, and Tel Aviv. Along the way, we stood in the Jordan River, waded in the Sea of Galilee, stood at Mary's Well in Nazareth, and entered the Church of the Nativity in Bethlehem. We walked through the Old City of Jerusalem, stood on the Mount of Olives, and meditated in the Garden of Gethsemane. We passed by the hill of Golgotha and entered the tomb thought to be the burial place of Jesus. These experiences brought to life the scriptures in a spiritual and life-changing way.

A highlight of the trip was the visit to the IAF Museum developed and still overseen by Brigadier General Yaakov Terner, a renowned IAF aviator. It was a spiritual moment when I stood beside what used to be USAF F-15 Number 73-107, the aircraft I picked up at McDonnell Douglas. The history of this aircraft, linked to the U. S. Air Force, Air National Guard, and the IAF, was now preserved as a permanent static display at the IAF Museum. I was honored with an impromptu flyby of a formation of four F-15 pilots returning from a training sortie.

Later, we were treated to an outstanding evening and dinner in the home of Moshe and his wife, Raya, a former IAF officer and current lawyer in Tel Aviv. Three others of the five retired initial IAF F-15 pilots were able to attend with their guest or wives: Major General Ben Eliehu, Brigadier General Joel Feldshu, and Major Saul Simon. This gathering of early F-15 "Eagle Drivers" was an historical occasion. The exchanges of stories and personal experiences over three decades will long be cherished and remembered. As surviving aviators for over 40 years, we have been blessed to enjoy the freedom to soar as *Uncaged Eagles*.

Moshe, Raya, and all those we met during the trip took generosity and hospitality to a new level. The Israeli people, particularly the aviators, have established standards of excellence the whole world can envy, friend and foe alike. In defending their nation, the IAF pilots' record is unequaled. The Israelis are also pace-setters in education, technology, agriculture, and many other disciplines. All Americans can be proud and thankful for such a proven ally and friend since Israel became an official nation over sixty years ago.

Bellevue Revisited

"There is a time for everything, and a season for every activity under heaven." NIV Ecclesiastes 3:1

During my work with the Perot campaign, I was speaking in East Texas and took the opportunity to visit my birthplace, Bellevue, Louisiana. That fateful diversion was the first step in the conclusion of a story that began in 1942. My cousin, Levandis Davis, another great grandson of Henry Davis, lived on Bellevue Road adjacent to the farm of John Vickers, son of Frank Vickers. Over fifty-four years had passed since my family fled Bellevue to avoid the dire consequences of my father's altercation with Frank Vickers. The dirt road had long since been paved, and small homes and farms dotted the landscape. The large Black Angus farm of John Vickers was directly across the road from the old Vickers' homestead. The remnants of the house were obscured and overgrown by shrubs, trees, and weeds. In contrast, the home of John Vickers sat neatly back from the road beneath a pecan grove surrounded by recently mowed acres of pasture.

As Levandis and I drove by, I noticed the gate was opened, and asked him to take me to meet John Vickers. By then, a cordial relationship existed between the Vickers and the Davis family, so my cousin readily agreed. We found John and a friend standing in the yard talking. John greeted us warmly, and Levandis introduced me as another great grandson of Henry Davis. During the conversation that followed, I shared my plans for a future book that would include stories about the history of Bellevue and some of its families, including the Vickers. John remembered hearing stories about my great grandfather when he was a boy and was very interested in providing information about his family. I didn't mention the altercation that took place between our fathers, so the visit ended quite amicably. I did state, however, that I would return someday to gather information for the book. John readily agreed and said he would invite his older brother, Billy, an Air Force veteran, to join us. With that, Levandis and I departed.

Nearly eleven years passed before I called Levandis and requested he arrange a visit with John Vickers again. To my shock, he told me John had accidentally drowned in the lake on his farm eighteen months earlier. I was deeply saddened by this tragic news and struggled to keep my emotions under control. When I asked about John's brother, Billy, Levandis told me he also had passed away a few years earlier and was buried in Arlington National Cemetery in

Virginia. At this news, I realized a meeting with the sons of Frank Vickers would never take place in this life. Although I met John only once, an inexplicable connection had been established between us. Now, fate precluded my plans for a meaningful dialogue between the sons of two bitter adversaries of long ago.

I sought to find any possible children of John and Billy. Levandis knew of an only child of John, Betty Sue Young, thought to live about twenty miles away in Bossier City. She frequently came to her dad's home to look after things since her mother recently moved to an assisted care facility. An internet search for Betty Sue Young throughout Bossier City, Shreveport, and the surrounding area proved fruitless. A similar search for William "Billy" Vickers ended with the same results. I finally decided to call John's number in the event his daughter might be visiting the home. Bingo, contact was finally made with a Frank Vickers' descendant, his one and only granddaughter. Betty Sue had arranged to have all calls to her parents' home forwarded to her home in Bossier City, Louisiana. For the next few days, an exciting dialogue ensued over the telephone and e-mails between Sue and me. My wife and I had planned to attend my 50th high school reunion in Shreveport during the summer, so Sue invited us to visit her home and her dad's farm.

Peggy and I drove to Betty's home on a warm summer July morning as my mind filled with memories of the 1940s. The Old Benton Highway, once a two-lane road through the forest, cotton fields, and sharecroppers' shanties was now lined with restaurants, car dealerships, service stations, and other businesses. My emotions, a mixture of anticipation and trepidation, were tied to the past. For years, I envisioned meeting the sons of Frank Vickers to bring closure to a bitter memory for the Toliver family. I slowly realized that it was Sue Young and I who were destined to meet under these circumstances at precisely this time in our lives. Pushing my fears aside, I quietly thanked God for His divine providence.

Sue lived in a quiet, gated community of townhouses neatly tucked away from the highway, well maintained, and quaintly decorated. Sue was a diminutive, energetic, and attractive sixty-two year old lady. She welcomed Peggy and me into her cozy home with open arms and heart, and the interaction between us was that of long-lost friends meeting after many years. Both of us loved her immediately.

The walls and furniture of Sue's home were decorated with family photos dating from the late 1800s to recent wedding pictures of her son and daughter. For the first time in my life, I saw a picture of Frank Vickers and his sons taken in front of the old homestead on Bellevue Road in the early 1940s. It was an emotional moment for me as I gazed upon the likeness of the small-frame man who left such a huge, indelible mark in the minds of my family for sixty-five years.

Sue shared documented history of the Vickers family that originated in Thomasville, GA. in the 1840s. One very impressive document was a beautifully hand-written diary of Frank Vickers' mother, Mary Ann Tabitha Dickey Vickers. Sue kept the original dairy and other precious keepsakes in a special box in her home. She freely shared many warm and intimate stories about her father and grandfather whom she dearly loved. As we listened, a subtle transformation began to take place deep in my heart. Bitter memories and enmity were dissolved by the kindness and warmth Sue so naturally displayed. Her sincere smile and twinkling eyes were like a gentle salve reaching back over time to heal the harm done by those she loved. As we departed for her dad's farm, I realized that the "rest of the story" between Frank Vickers and my father was vastly different than its beginning in 1942.

I drove down the highway to the land homesteaded by the Davis and Vickers families nearly 130 years earlier. Now, as then, the two families were still neighbors. Sue honked a prearranged signal when we drove by the home of Levandis. As we pulled into the yard of John Vickers' home, my emotions flared up again. Sue welcomed us into the home of her late father, and we waited for Levandis to join us. We settled into comfortable leather sofas in a beautiful, rustic family room with a huge fireplace. The bricks of the fireplace and hearth were taken from the old home where Tennessee, Levandis' mother, was born. Like Sue's home, family portraits adorned the furniture, mantle, and walls. The lingering presence of John Vickers was everywhere. His hats, boots, clothing, and other personal belongings were just as they had been the day he died. No one spoke for a while as the full impact of this emotional and historical moment engulfed us all. I sought in vain for meaningful words, but none could adequately capture that moment. We could only smile at each other and allow our eyes to express the profound appreciation that sprang forth from a deep well of reconciliation. We began to share a spiritual union that transcended the painful memories of the past.

Sue and Levandis finally spoke and told several enlightening stories about Frank and John. Both agreed Frank Vickers could become mean and cantankerous without warning, and anyone near would be subjected to his ire. Levandis remembered that his mother worked for Vickers and was the only one who could approach him and calm him down at such times. Two other stories were particularly tragic. Frank Vickers lost his only daughter when she was a baby in 1922. About the time he was giving my father trouble in 1942, Frank lost his son, Bobby, and his wife, Beulah, died six months later. The circumstances of Bobby's death while a student at Louisiana State University in Baton Rogue were never fully determined. He was only twenty-one years old. At forty-seven, Beulah suffered a cerebral hemorrhage and died at a hospital in Shreveport. Many in both White and Black communities mourned these devastating losses. Frank never fully recovered from them.

Sue was twenty-one years old when Frank died. She stated he was not a religious man and never attended church. He did, however, faithfully give money to a local church as far back as she could remember. Frank appeared to mellow in his later years and the hostility between him and my relatives in Bellevue diminished with the passing years. On the other hand, John Vickers was a faithful member and usher of his church until his death. Just one day before he died, Sue's son posted a marker on the long-established animal cemetery near the house. It read:

> "John Vickers
> Understood the Language of Animals
> And Therefore Knew
> The Voice of God"

My recollection of John and the love displayed for him by Sue made it easy to believe these words. Some of his ashes were buried among the graves of numerous horses, dogs, cats, and other animals. The rest were sprinkled around the land that he loved so much. As we toured the farm on ATVs, I had the sense John would have been very pleased with our visit. My last stop was the historic Bellevue Cemetery where Frank and his family are buried along with several members of Levandis' family. It is the official burial ground for at least two former judges, four Bossier Parish sheriffs, and twenty-one Confederate soldiers. Somehow, this all seemed fitting.

Later that night, I recounted that most eventful day and realized that one more stop had to be made. Peggy and I returned early the next morning and drove down several roads until I recalled the location of the graves visited by another cousin, Gerald Davis and me. The Hawkins Cemetery is situated at the end of a dirt road several miles off the Bellevue-Princeton Road. As we drove slowly along the tall grass and ruts, I could almost hear the sounds of mourners long ago as they must have trudged behind the coffins on mule-drawn wagons. The names and faces of those I remembered flashed before me and evoked a heart-felt sadness. This feeling gave way to a quiet peace after so many years. The entire trip to the land of my birth had been a serendipitous and spiritual journey. When I stood among the headstones of Grandpa Henry, his wives and children, an epiphany emerged. Finally, a bridge had been built across the deep chasm of bitterness and hatred. The past had been reconciled, the present celebrated, and the future filled with hope. Now the children and grandchildren of the Davis and Vickers could live in harmony and enjoy the land they shared by the grace of God. Sue, Levandis, Peggy, and I built a bridge of hope that all may walk across in either direction.

When Peggy and I left the cemetery, the billowing clouds overhead suddenly burst into a downpour as if to wash away the bitter past. The sun soon reappeared with a brilliance that seemed to proclaim an ancient prophetic message:

> *"The heavens declare the glory of God;*
> *the skies proclaim the work of his hands.*
> *Day after day they pour forth speech;*
> *night after night they display knowledge.*
> *There is no speech or language where their voice is not heard.*
> *Their voice goes out into all the earth,*
> *their words to the ends of the world."*
> NIV Psalm 19:1

RETIREMENT YEARS

Balad Air Base, Iraq 2005
(L-R) Msgt (Ret) James A. Sheppard, a Crew
Chief of the Original 332nd, Tsgt (Ret) George
Watson, Sr., a Supply Sergeany of the Same Unit;
Col (Ret) Richard Toliver, a Second Generation
Tuskegee Airman; Lt. Col (Ret) Lee A. Archer,
Jr., the Only Confirmed African American Ace
in the History of the Air Force; and Lt. Col (Ret)
Robert Ashby, One of the First African American
Airline Captains.

**Dedicating
Maintenance Library
Balad Air Base, Iraq 2005**

**"Eagle Drivers"
in Israel June 2007
(L-R) Simon, Feldschuh,
Ben Eliehu,
Toliver, Melnik**

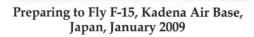

**Preparing to Fly F-15, Kadena Air Base,
Japan, January 2009**

INDEX

A Shau Valley, South Viet Nam 172, 173, 175
Abdul Aziz Al Saud 328
Abernathy, Ralph 49, 464
Aeronautical Systems Division (ASD) 371- 372, 383
AIMVAL-ACEVAL 302
Air Combat Maneuvering Range (ACMR) 323
Air Command and Staff College (ACSC) 281, 309, 373
Air Defense Command (ADC) 293, 302
Air Force Central Europe (AFCENT) 195, 206-208, 210-211
Air Force Flight Dynamics Laboratory (AFFDL) 279
Air Force Logistics Command (AFLC) 383, 401
Air Force Military Personnel Center(AFMPC) 190, 266, 275
Air Force Reserve Officers Training Corps (AFROTC) 45-47, 50, 53, 55-58, 71, 81, 129, 144, 417
Air Force Operational Test and Evaluation Center (AFOTEC) 390, 442
Air Force Systems Command (AFSC) 88, 286, 291, 372, 383
Air Force Tactical Fighter Weapon Instructor Course (Top Gun) 192, 229-230, 234, 242, 251, 263, 277, 283, 286, 302, 345, 396
Air Force Test and Evaluation Center (AFTEC) 285-286, 288, 291, 301, 322, 351, 359, 361-362, 367-369, 372-373, 380, 382-383, 385, 387-388, 390
Air Medal (AM) x, 170, 175, 183, 189, 267, 277
Air National Guard (ANG) 120, 417, 418, 474
Air Proving Grounds Center (APGC) 95, 99, 105-106, 108
Airborne Command and Control Center (ABCCC) 243-244, 255
Airborne Warning and Control System (AWACS) 332, 424-427
Air-To-Ground Operations School (AGOS) 196
Air University 281, 393
Aulbach, Albert 288, 393
Albuquerque, NM v, 285, 359, 361, 364- 365, 378, 381, 391, 423, 441-445, 447, 449-451, 454, 466, 467
Alexander, Halbert 229

Allen, James R. 166
Alvarez, Everett, Jr. 260
Anderson, Clarence E. "Bud" 377
Anderson, Darcy 447-450
Anderson, John V. "Poncho" 129
Anderson, Marcus 340
Anti Aircraft Artillery (Triple A) 170-171, 176, 184, 242, 248, 254, 257
Armstrong, Donald 229
Ault, Richard 121

Baca, Cres 454
Bailey, Carl G. "Griff" 250, 252
Banholzer, Richard T. "Lips" 377
Barber, William "Billy" 286
Barham, Robert 377
Barrier Combat Air Patrol (BAR CAP) 245, 251-252, 254-256
Bachelor Officer's Quarters (BOQ) 88, 91, 166, 192, 273, 296, 327, 340, 375, 404
Beatty, James 242, 282, 286, 288, 290
Behari, Ahmad Ibrahim 425-427
Bell, Lowell & Pat 287, 374
Bellevue, LA 1-7, 475-476, 478, 480
Ben Hoa Air Base, South Vietnam 243
Bergman, Arthur 286, 288-289, 298, 300-302
Bernsen, Harold 427
Birmingham, AL 93, 104, 141, 143, 145, 461
Bishop, John 450
Biss, Robert "Bob" 183-184, 261
Bitburg Air Base, Germany 206, 266-267, 275, 293, 304 -305, 314, 318-321, 324, 335-336, 339-345, 347-348, 350-352, 361, 363, 372, 386, 390, 418, 431
Black, Bobby vi, 278, 341, 431
Bland, David 248
Blood, Gordon 281
Boddie, James Timothy 73-75, 80, 82, 128, 152, 184, 266, 275, 277, 301, 431
Bogoslofsky, Bernard J. "Bo" 276
Bomb Damage Assessment (BDA) 244
Booker T. Washington High School 27-28, 56
Borling, John 331
Bossier City, LA 37, 477

Boyd, Willis A. vi, 187, 189, 191-192, 195-196, 199, 204-206, 210-211, 222, 225

Bradley, Walter D. 455

Brasington, Herb 443-444

Bronson, Howard 349

Brooks, David H. 254, 375

Brothers, John N. 442

Brown, David and Yoshi 339, 340, 371, 416

Brown, Earl & Nancy 203-204,

Brown, Harold J. 251, 254-255, 262, 280, 341, 386, 420

Brown, Noble E. 89, 107, 109

Brown, R. H. 27, 35-38, 50, 214

Brown, William E. 215, 345, 349, 350

Burnett, P.C. 381-384

Burns, Eldridge 323

Burns, Joe Lee 242, 248, 386, 418

Bushnell, Martin "Marty" 382-384

Butler, Joseph 167, 169, 170

Butt, Richard 184, 242

Byrnes, Donn and Sparks x, 445

Cam Rahn Bay Air Base, South Viet Nam 167-169, 174-175, 177-182, 184, 186, 189, 192, 216, 226, 229, 261, 277, 292, 313

Cambodia 169, 243, 260, 266-267

Campbell, Ed 450

Campbell, Norman "Scotchman" 304-305, 315, 319, 335-336, 341-344, 349-352, 363, 386-387

Campbell, William A. 45-46

Carcinoembryonic Antigen (CEA) 412, 414, 416, 422

Carver, George W. 34, 41, 43, 74

Cash, Jimmie L. 392, 395

Central Tactical Air Forces (CENTAF) 424-425, 430

Chain, John T., Jr. 245, 384-385

Chase, Levi 162, 176

Chatman, Rosie 24-25

Cherry, Fred 242-260

China Lake, CA 300, 444

Choate, Patrick 461

Cison, Zoe 451

Clark Air Base, Philippines 167, 172, 177-178, 239, 261-262, 278

Clinton, William "Bill" 452, 456, 462

Cliver, Jeffrey G. 282, 286, 288, 290, 292, 300-302, 343, 386

Combat Tree 251-252, 255-256

Commission on Presidential Debates (CPD) 462

Combined Test Force (CTF) 380-383

Commander-in-Chief, USAFE (CINCUSAFE) 326, 362, 373

Congressional Black Caucus (CBC) 452-453

Conner, Lorenza 242

Consolidated Maintenance Aircraft Maintenance Squadron (CAMS) 413

Cook, Warren 443

Cooper, Larry "Scoop" 377

Cordier, Kenneth 181, 183-184, 242, 261

Cotton, April 448

Craft, Libby 446

Craig Air Force Base, AL 112-113, 119-120, 133, 137, 159, 184, 191, 392

Creech, Wilber L. 282, 393-394, 406

Cribb, Vance 204-205, 207

Davis, Dorothy K. 203, 275

Davis, Harry 1

Davis, Levandis 475-481

Davis, Minnie 1

Davis, William Henry 1

DeBellevue, Charles "Chuck" 250-251

Deberry, Fisher 412

Deberry, TX 1

Department of Defense (DoD) 103, 105

Deputy Commander for Maintenance (DCM) 392, 394

Detachment 4, ASD 88-90, 94, 100, 103, 107, 109

Development Test &Evaluation (DT&E) 377, 383

Dhahran Air Base, Saudi Arabia 326-327, 332, 426, 429

Distinguished Flying Cross (DFC) 183, 189, 244, 250, 267, 277

Dixon, Robert J. 132, 133, 190, 191

Drain, Jane vi

Domenici, Pete 455

Druen, Walter D. 344

Dual Role Fighter (DRF) 371, 389

Dugle, Brian C. 345, 347, 349

Dunn, Charles "Bucky" & Dale 315, 321

Dwiggins, Mattye 57, 70, 80

Dyess Air Force Base, TX 149

DynCorp 442, 445-446

Ebenezer Baptist Church 465

Eckman, Lucky 249

Edmund Pettis Bridge 138-139, 142

Edwards Air Force Base, CA 87, 286, 296, 300, 359, 372-373, 377, 380, 382-383, 385, 389

Eglin Air Force Base, FL 84, 87-88, 91-93, 95-97, 103 104, 106-110, 112-113, 152, 286, 296-300, 332, 372-373, 377

Electronic-Countermeasures (ECM) 241, 245

Eliehu, Eitan Ben 303, 356, 475

Ellis, Richard 318

Ellis, Sharon 443-444

ENTEK 442-445

Euro-NATO Joint Jet Pilot Training Program (ENJJPTP) 340

F-15 73-107 295-296, 474

F-15 OT&E 281-283, 285, 287, 297, 300, 303, 305, 372, 377

Fahd bin Abdul Aziz 328

Fairburn, David R. 122, 124, 129

Fairchild Air Force Base, WA 234-235

Farley, Pat 257

Farris, Dr. Christine King 464

Felder, Annie 204, 215, 222

Feldschuh, Joel 303, 482

Finlay, John S. 186, 191

Fisher, Bernard 173, 199, 201- 202
Fogleman, Ronald R. 263, 320, 390-392, 394-395
Fort Walton Beach, FL 92, 96, 109
Forward Air Control (FAC) 171, 198, 406
Fourth Air Tactical Air Force (4ATAF) 195, 207

Gabriel, Charles A. 218, 250, 266, 297, 351-352, 362, 373, 384, 390
Gagen, Jack 170, 176-177
Gast, Phillip 196, 199-198, 200, 204
Gaston, Mack 442
Gerrish, Joseph Roger 368
GIB 152, 159, 162, 170-171, 181-182, 184, 188-191, 195, 205, 270
Gibbs, Thomas 232, 240
Godman Field, KY 229
Good, Don & Libby 136, 143, 159, 178
Goodwill Missionary Baptist Church 26, 66-67
Goodwin, Cliff 416, 431
Graham, Ward 322
Gray, Charles 413
Gray, Jack 425-426
Greene, E. L. 17, 34
Greene, Odile 34
Green, Frederick H. 245, 250, 253, 281
Gregory, Emma J. 95, 104-106
Gross, Leroy 417

Hadock Elementary School 8, 9, 11, 16
Hahn Air Base, Germany 183, 185-186, 192, 196, 200, 206-207, 216, 222, 228-229, 237, 242, 244, 271
Hai Phong Harbor, North Vietnam 179, 240, 245
Hairston, Elsie 80, 97, 101, 197, 274, 463
Hairston, Harvey 76, 97, 100-103, 111, 193
Hall, Louis 204, 222
Hanoi, North Viet Nam 179, 184, 240. 245-246, 248-249, 251-252, 258-259
Hardaway, Ben F. 90, 98, 99, 107, 109
Harrison, William 361
Hartinger, James V. 293
Harvell, John 95
Harvey, Francis 48-49, 80
Harvey, James, III 229
Hatch, Emmett 46-47, 51, 128
Hausenfleck, Charles 361
Hawkins Cemetery 480
Haeffner Fred 285, 303
Henning, Clifford "Bud" &Marie 315, 321, 353
Hickam Air Force Base, HI 165-166, 178
Hines, James M. 224, 226, 228
Ho Chi Minh Trail 169, 171-172
Hoffman, John M. 377, 382-384
Hofstead, Gene 174-175
Holcombe, Kenneth 170, 176
Holloman Air Force Base, NM 159, 418-420
Holman, Sharon vi, 448, 458
Holzapple, General Joseph R. 207
Honolulu, HI 166
Hooten, William "Bill" vi, 444, 450, 453

Horner, Charles A. vi, 421, 424-427, 429-431
Hulbert Field, FL 92-93
Hunter-Killer Team 248-249, 255
Hussein, Saddam 430

Isleta Pueblo 451, 454
Israeli Air Force (IAF) 192, 303-304, 333, 473-475

Jackson, Gene E. 220-221, 277, 279, 294, 302, 323, 336, 342, 347, 353, 373, 382, 390, 418
Jackson, Jesse 453, 456
Jacobsen, David 170, 229, 231, 277, 282, 286, 288, 290, 292, 298, 300, 302
James, Daniel "Chappie" 150-151, 153, 157-158, 162, 194, 206, 218, 321-322
Jaquish David F. 218, 223, 225, 278, 315
Jaquish, John E. 240-241, 286, 288, 292, 300, 302
Jeffries, Calvin 350
Jehani Colonel 425-427, 430
Jever Air Base, Germany 195
John A. Andrew Hospital 45, 48, 81
Johnson, Bill and Gloria 442
Johnson, Buford 229
Johnson, Hansford T. 431
Johnson, Leonard 286, 298, 309, 412, 428
Johnston, Roy 466-467
Joiner, Edward 348
Jojola, Dyan 451, 452, 467
Jones, Douglas 56, 64, 82, 391
Jones, Hubert L. 53-54, 57-58, 60-62, 70-73, 369,
Jordan, Renee vi, 458
Juve, Gene L. 421

Kalid bin Abdul Aziz Al-Saud 328
Kastellaun, Germany 187-189, 192
Kauffman, Donald 327
Keane, Trish 443
Keenan, Michael 446
Kennedy, John F. 110-111
Kep Air Field, North Vietnam 240, 258
Keys, Ronald 234
King Coretta Scott 463
King, Dexter 483
King, Martin Luther, Jr. xvii, 48-50, 80, 98, 139, 144, 193-194, 199, 278, 321, 366, 447, 457, 459, 482-484, 487
King, Martin Luther, III 462-464
Kirk, William 413, 423
Knowlan, Chuck and Renee 441
Knox, George 73
Korat Air Base, RTAFB 240, 244-245, 247-248, 250, 267
Kottweiler, Germany 316
Krautkremers, Phillip 188, 211
Kwajalein Island 167
Kyler, Frederick C. 293, 304, 318-319

Lane, Walter 176-177, 184
Langley Air Force Base, VA 281-182, 302, 309, 311, 327, 400, 402, 404, 417

Laos 169-171, 179, 183, 235, 260, 262, 267
Laudice, Theodore "Ted" 286, 289-290
Leaf, Howard 362, 380, 384
Leavitt, Lloyd R. Jr. 313-314, 318-319
Letto, Augustus 286, 288
Lincoln, Ruth S. 35, 37
Lippemeier, George "Lippe" 242, 313
Locke, George 445
Long, Delores 27, 81, 84
Long, Eliza 26, 66
Luke Air Force Base, AZ 283, 285-287, 289, 291, 293-298, 300, 302-305, 309, 314, 333-334, 373-377, 382, 473
Lyles, Robert 196-198

MacDill Air Force Base, FL 157, 161-164, 168-169, 375, 390-391, 394, 396-397, 400, 403-404, 411, 424
Madden, John "Smash" 219, 250, 262
Major Command (MAJCOM) 393, 400
Mangis, Edward 232, 276
Marks, Sam and Joan 442
Marquez, Leo 447-448
Marshall, Anthony "Tony" 267
Martin Luther King, Jr. Kinderheim 199
Mason, Robert 95, 109
Maxwell Air Force Base, AL 30, 47, 51, 73, 134, 137, 255, 281, 373, 392, 394, 417,
McCleary, Meredith 95
McCorkle, Clausell and Clara 442
McDonnell Aircraft Company (MCAIR) 279-281, 289-290, 295, 362, 377, 379-380
McElveen, W. A. "Bubba" 413, 431
McGee, Charles E. 199, 201, 207, 369
McGuire Air Force base, NJ 184
McHale, Edward M. 241
McIver, Charles 95
McKimmey, Joe 90-91, 94-95, 98
McMurray, William 226-228
ME-262 Jet 196
Melnik, Moshe 303, 334, 473, 475
Melnik, Raya 475
Memmingen Air Base, Germany 196-197
Merkling, Richard E. 240
Mfume, Kweisi 452-453
Mitchell, Frank 121, 136-137, 143
MK- 4 Gun Pod 95, 99, 103,
Montgomery Bus Boycott 49
Murphy, Jack vi, 205-210
Myers, Richard B. 242, 386

Nakom Phanom, RTAFB 255
National Aeronautical Space Administration (NASA) 279, 281-282
Nellis Air Force Base, NV 224, 229, 242, 275-276, 380
Newton, Lester 404-405
Newton, Lloyd W. "Fig" vi, 233, 240, 278, 286, 294, 404-405, 429

Ninth Air Force 389
Norris, Steve 3,4,5
North American Free Trade Agreement (NAFTA) 452-453
North Atlantic Treaty Organization (NATO) 187, 195, 198, 210, 314, 318, 323
Norton Air Force Base, CA 273-274, 363
Norwood, George "Nordie" 248, 386

O'Donnell, John 285, 290
O'Keeffe, Timothy 286, 288, 298, 301-302
O'Malley, Jerome F. 384, 400, 402-405, 421
O'Neil, Dawson R. "Randy" 232, 396-397
Odgers, Peter W. 380-385
Oelstrom, Tad 234, 386
Officer's Christian Fellowship (OCF) 223, 315, 322, 342, 360, 369
Officer's Club (O'Club) 88, 227, 232, 293-294, 303, 317, 341, 344, 352, 392
Olsen, Daryl 340-341, 343, 348
Operation Homecoming 260
Operation Linebacker I 240, 245, 252
Operation Linebacker II 258-259
Operational Test &Evaluation (OT&E) 276, 279
Oxnard, CA 6-10, 15-16, 33, 41, 55, 94, 147, 237-238, 364, 466-467

Pacific Air Force (PACAF) 234, 421
Paris Peace Accords 259-260
Parrish, Roger 232
Pasadena, CA 364, 374, 410
Paul Doumer Bridge 245, 248
Pauly, John W. 325-326, 332
Pauly, Trenton 413
Payne, Hazel 35
Perot, Bette 460
Perot, Ross vi, xii, xvi, xvii, 446-453, 455-466, 475
Persian Gulf Crisis 423-424, 427-431
Peterson, Arthur 199, 202, 283, 298
Peterson, Joseph "Pete" 294, 369
Philippines Islands 146, 167, 172, 177, 233, 239
Phillips, Richard vi, 372, 380-385, 389
Pigford, Vincent 286, 288, 302
Pinsett, Freddie 31, 32, 51, 53
Piotrowski, John L. vi, 92, 332, 369, 402-403, 421,
Poli, David 326
Porter, Rufus 145-146
Posgate, James 286, 292, 300, 302
Post Traumatic Stress Disorder (PTSD) 264
Preston, Maurice A. 196-197
Price, Clark 152, 218, 225
Pritchard, Lee vi, 314, 318
Pritchard, Robert 121, 130
Protestant Men of the Chapel (PMOC) 342, 442
Protestant Women of the Chapel (PWOC) 342, 442
Proteus Corporation 445
Pruden, Albert 301, 322, 343
Pulliam, Guy 276, 322

Ragland, Dayton 242

Ramstein Air Base, Germany 304, 313, 324
Record, Major General James F. 419
Red Crown 251, 254-255
Reddock, John H. 95
Redlands, CA 154
Reed, Herrie 397
Rees, C. H. "Ted" 275, 277
Reeves, John 359
Reform Party ix, xvi, 457-459, 461-462
Rest and Recuperation (R&R) 257-259
Reinhart, Ralph 245, 249
Rhoades, William "Bill" 441-442
Rhyne, Richard G. "Dick" 403, 405, 407, 410-411,
    413, 418, 420
Rickert, Carol 450 -451
Ringsdorf, Herbert 182-184, 242
Richie, Lionel 82
Ritchie, Stephen 250-251
Riyadh Air Base, Saudi Arabia 325-327, 329-332,
    424-426
Roberts, James E. 107-109
Roberts, George S. 51
Roberts, Lawrence E. "Larry" 54, 58, 61-62, 73,
    82, 128
Roberts, Lucimarian Tolliver vi
Roberts, Robin 82
Roberts, Russell C. 121, 124
Roberts, Thomas S. 170, 176
Robinson, Jackie 34, 48-49
Rodriguez, Daniel 443-444
Rose, Al & Becky 237, 241-242
Rose, Chet and Marla 412
Rousey, James 120-121, 124
Royal Saudi Air Force (RSAF) 325, 327, 329-331,
    424-426
Ruby, Jack 111
Russ, Robert D. 407, 413, 420-421

Safety Investigation Board (SIB) 348-351, 361-363,
    400-403
Saigon, South Viet Nam 169, 172
Sawadee 266-268
Schiff, Steve 455
Schulstad, George 266
Secretary of Defense (SECDEF) 105, 132,135
Selma, AL 112, 122, 131-136, 138-139, 141-142,
    145-147, 194, 392
Shaw Air Force Base, SC 389, 403, 405, 408-409,
    411, 428, 431, 433
Shenwar, Akram 121
Sherman, Cora 32
Shilt, Jerry 182, 313
Shreveport, LA xii, 4-6, 13, 16-19, 21, 27-28, 32, 34,
    36-39, 53, 56, 61, 82, 84, 97, 131, 140, 154, 174,
    214, 277, 294, 311, 316, 359-360, 388, 397, 408,
    431, 433, 467, 477, 479
Simon, Saul 303, 475
Simon, William 137
Site Activation Task Force (SATAF) 314, 318-319,
    322, 324

Six Day War 280, 303
Sixteen Street Baptist Church, Birmingham, AL 104
Smith, Federic H. III 241
Soltis, Ronald 263
Southern Christian Leadership Conference (SCLC)
    464-466
Spangdahlem Air Base, Germany 206-209, 341, 416
Speas, Clyde O. 310
Sprague, Roger L. 210
Spratt, John 413
Steinhoff, Johannes 195-196, 198
Stewart, Austin E. 36-38, 50-52, 74, 82, 84, 174, 214
Stewart, Harry 229
Stipe, Alfred C. 170, 218, 220-222, 227, 235
Strategic Air Command (SAC) 205
Stricker, Rusty 447
Strike Eagle (F-15E) 371-373, 377-378, 381, 389
Stroud, John P. 137-138, 140-143
Surface-To-Air Missile (SAM) 170, 243, 246, 248-
    250, 254-255, 257, 259
Sutscheck, Francis (Frank) 219, 221, 245-246, 249
SUU-16A Gun Pod 94-95, 99
SUU-23A Gun Pod 103

Trabucco, Jack 204-205
TAC Air Control Wing (TACW) 405
Tactical Electronic Warfare System (TEWS) 241,
    246, 249
Tactical Air Command (TAC) 146,
    151, 234-235, 285-286, 289, 291-294, 297, 302,
    323, 356, 362,372, 377, 392-394, 396, 400-403,
    405-407, 412-414, 417, 420-421
Tactical Air Support Squadron (TASS) 413
Tactical Fighter Wing (TFW)
    1st - 302, 311, 400-401
    12th - 169, 176, 179
    15th -168
    35th - 226
    36th - 293, 304, 314-315, 319, 343, 348-349, 362
    49th - 418
    50th - 185, 187, 192, 195, 202, 206
    56 th - 390
    57th - 292
    363rd - 412, 421
    388th - 240
    432nd - 218, 250
    479th - 215
Tactical Fighter Weapons Center (TFWC) 279, 281
Tahkli Air Base, RTAFB 251
Takloglu, C. N. 322
Taylor, Stillman V. 191, 196, 204-205, 244
Tegucigalpa, Honduras 408-409
Teledyne Brown Engineering 445
Tel-Nof Air Base, Israel 333
Temple, Alva 229
Temporary Duty (TDY) 108, 205, 216, 228, 236, 281,
    325, 333, 335, 372, 410,
Terner, Yaakov 474
Thai Nguyen Power Plant 240, 258
Thar, James and Bonnie 398

Thomas, Thretha 416
Thornton, James 170, 192, 199, 200, 228, 288
Tibbet, Calvin Brian 250
Todd, Frank 386, 393
Tonkin Gulf 153, 246, 248, 258, 260
Toppin, Harry and Marge 442
Torrejon Air Base, Spain 320
Traster, Kermit L. 218, 220-221, 224, 225
Travis Air Force Base, CA 165, 227, 237, 239, 273
Treyz, Fred A. 215, 226, 228
Trowell-Harris, Irene 417
Troyer, John 121
Tucson, AZ 147, 149, 156, 159
Turner, Bill 450
Tuskegee Airmen 44-46, 53-55, 89, 151, 194, 229, 369, 469
Tuskegee Airmen, Inc. 369
Tuskegee Institute, AL 27-28, 30-31, 35, 38, 40-43, 45, 47-48, 55-57, 76, 80-81, 84, 104, 144, 150-151, 225, 287, 369, 392, 442

U. S. Military Training Mission (USMTM) 325, 327-328, 330-332
U.S. Air Force Academy (USAFA) 130, 211, 234, 263, 283, 339, 342, 373, 382, 388, 397, 412, 416, 422, 423
U.S. Central Command (US CENTCOM) 424, 425, 427, 429, 431
Udorn, Air Base, RTAFB 218, 250-252, 258-260, 262-264, 266-268, 274, 281, 306, 335, 395
United States Air Force (USAF) 371, 373, 383, 385, 396, 424, 425
United States Air Force Europe (USAFE) 195-198, 207, 234, 304, 310, 313-315, 317-319, 323, 324-326, 330, 332-333, 335, 340-342, 348, 351, 361- 363, 373, 421
United We Stand America (UWSA) 446-457, 359
University of New Mexico Board of Regents 468
US Central Command (US CENTCOM) 424-425, 427, 429, 431
USAF Fighter Weapons Instructor's Course (School) 192, 229-230, 234, 242, 251, 263, 277, 283, 286, 302, 345, 396
USAFE Director of Operations & Intelligence (USAFE/DO&I) 313
USS Stark 423, 427

Varela, Jamie 121, 132
Ventura, Jesse 462
Verney, Russ vi, 455, 457-459
Viccellio, Henry "Butch" 401-403, 407, 413
Vickers, Francis "Frank" 1, 3-6, 476-479
Vickers, John 476, 479-480
Vickers, William "Billy" 477
Victorville, CA 216-216, 228
Vinh 240, 254-255
Visual Identification (VID) 251
Vojvodich, General Mele 240

Von Loh, John 443-444
Wade, Horace M. 240
Waikiki Beach, HI 166
Walker, Bill 448
Washington, A.C. 18, 84
Washington, Booker T. 1, 34, 41, 43, 74, 225
Watson, Thomas J. 345
Wells, Roger A. 199-200, 229, 233
West Shreveport Elementary School 16-17, 34
Wheelus Air Base, Libya 191, 200
Whitehurst, Jim 150, 152
Whitlatch, Wayne E. 351, 359, 368-369, 372-373
Whitley, Bebe 37, 83
Whitten, William 220-221, 225
Wilford Hall Medical Center, San Antonio, TX 411, 414, 416-417, 422
Wilkes-Barre Scranton International Airport, Pennsylvania 404
Wilson, William 229, 232
Wing Operations Center (WOC) 226-228
Wiseman, Omar 286, 292, 297, 300, 302, 386
Wright, Chris 313

Yates, Ronald 383, 385
Yen Bai Air Field, North Vietnam 184, 385
Yocum, James 390, 392, 394, 400, 404
Young, Betty Sue Vickers 477-481

Zin, Benjamin 303
Zuberbuhler, Rudolph "Rudy" 242

Colonel Richard "Dick" Toliver, USAF, Retired

Since retiring from the Air Force, Colonel Toliver pursued several business, economic development, and political ventures in New Mexico, Alabama, Georgia, and Texas. His public service includes several years in New Mexico on the Public Safety Advisory Commission; Board of Regents, University of New Mexico; and Board of Directors of the Kirtland Partnership Committee. Since moving to Arizona in 2003, he has served on the Board of Director's for the West Valley Hospital in Goodyear and held a key role in securing the Congressional Gold Medal for the Tuskegee Airmen. His extensive professional writing experience in the military and private sector has resulted in many articles for newspapers, magazines, and periodicals. Colonel Toliver continues to be in demand as a motivational speaker nationwide and overseas, including recent trips to Germany, Iraq, Kuwait, Spain, Hawaii, and Japan.

TRIBUTES

Colonel Dick Toliver's autobiography is an impressive work. He presents with remarkable recall people, events, and attributes that influenced the course of his life. His odyssey of "victory over adversity" embodies the drive to excel, the struggle of a people for civil rights, and a personal journey of Christian faith. It covers a dramatic period in aviation, military and American history. It is a perennial story of the perseverance of love and resilience of the human spirit.

Charlene E. McGee Smith, PhD
Author of TUSKEGEE AIRMAN,
The biography of Charles E. McGee,
Air Force Fighter Combat Record Holder

An Uncaged Eagle is a testimonial in faith--to risk all, to save a society, to build a family, to defend a nation. I am proud to call Dick Toliver my brother; you'll be proud as well after you read this book."

Bruce L. Fister
Lieutenant General, USAF, Retired

A wonderful expose' of the successful struggle of an African American USAF fighter pilot after the Armed Services were integrated by President Truman's Executive Order 9981 on July 26th 1948. Colonel Dick Toliver's experiences belie that myth that "everything was O.K." after the Services were integrated. Today the struggle continues, but not with the intense overt obstacles that existed during the 1950s and 1960s. A well-written tribute to all fighter pilots who do it better.

J. Timothy Boddie, Jr.
Brigadier General, USAF, Retired

Tributes

Dick Toliver has written a book that describes his struggles as a Black Southerner determined to achieve greatness in a White world. His avenue was through one of the most exciting career fields one can choose – that of a fighter pilot. As a fellow fighter pilot, Christian, and Southerner, I saw and understood the prejudice so vividly described by Dick. His description of the Vietnam War brought back many memories and portrays a keen insight into what we fighter pilots endured during those challenging years. "An Uncaged Eagle" highlights many patriotic and dedicated Americans, with one of the most patriotic being Colonel Dick Toliver.

Richard G. Rhyne
Colonel, USAF, Retired

This "Red Hot" extraordinary story of Colonel Richard "Dick" Toliver's unabashed expressions of crucial events in his life is a compelling and energizing read. Through disappointments and hardships, he never gave up and held onto his fierce determination to fly airplanes. He faced ugly racism and rejection, yet through an ultimate commitment to faith, he became more than a conqueror. His 446 comabt missions over Southeast Asia justified more than his "wings" in the Air Force. Today, Colonel Dick Toliver is the most dynamic motivating speaker, writer, and teacher I have ever known.

Chaplain Bobby C. Black
Colonel, USAF, Retired

Starting out dirt-poor in Louisiana, Dick Toliver clawed his way upward through life to become a decorated fighter pilot with two F-4 tours in Viet Nam. Along the way he gained a loving, very patient wife, acquired an engineering degree, raised a loyal family, reached out to others in need, stood face-to-face with his own personal demons, and prevailed. His inspiring story keeps you reading from the beginning to the end.

Donn A. Byrnes
Colonel USAF, Retired
Author of BLACKBIRD RISING - Birth of
an Aviation Legend and AIR SUPERIORITY
BLUE - The F-15 Story

This is a great book about a young cocky, self-assured fighter pilot who knew God but only wanted Him as a co-pilot. But Dick experienced God in a very special way and decided to let Him file the flight plan and be the pilot of his life.

Bill E. Hooten
Retired Businessman
Elder, Hoffmantown Church
Albuquerque, New Mexico

It is a privilege to know retired Colonel Dick Toliver today. It was a pleasure to read about his growth from a boy and man determined to direct his own destiny to one who placed his future in the hands of God. Along that journey are sobering accounts of racial barriers that he endured and overcame as well as fascinating insights into historical and political events of our lifetime. His candid reflections on his own emotional and spiritual struggles are a challenge to those who desire to put God first. Above all, one can see the grace of God at work as He used people and circumstances to teach a man to walk in true freedom.

Pastor James D. and Frances Porter
Apollo Baptist Church, Glendale, AZ

Over coming many obstacles, Dick Toliver's journey to become a crack US Air Force fighter pilot parallels a spiritual quest of self-knowledge and religious affirmation. This engrossing autobiography adds to the lore of unsung American heroes.

Calvin J. Jeffries
Lieutenant Colonel, USAF, Retired

Dick allows us to witness an incredible journey, first through the innocent eyes of a young dreamer, then as a young man navigating through daunting challenges and disappointments. We see him gain gaining knowledge and learning life's applications at Tuskegee, the hallowed grounds where legends were made. Dick's personal and professional accomplishments were many; above all, he found contentment, happiness, and peace. The life and times as recalled by Dick is a great work. I was reminded of much, but I learned much more!

David Toliver, Sr.
Brother, Retired Government Employee